Mary
Ingraham
Bunting

Mary Ingraham Bunting *Her Two Lives*

Elaine Yaffe

Frederic C. Beil
Savannah

Copyright © 2005 by Elaine Yaffe

Published by
Frederic C. Beil
609 Whitaker Street
Savannah, Georgia 31401
http://www.beil.com

LIBRARY OF CONGRESS CATALOGING-IN-PUBLICATION DATA
Yaffe, Elaine, 1937–
Mary Ingraham Bunting: her two lives / by Elaine Yaffe.—1st ed.
p. cm.
Includes bibliographical references and index.
ISBN 1-929490-26-7 (alk. paper)
1. Bunting-Smith, Mary Ingraham, 1910–1998.
2. Feminists–United States–Biography.
3. Scientists–United States–Biography.
4. Women scientists–United States–Biography.
5. Deans (Education)–New Jersey–Biography.
6. Women deans (Education)–New Jersey–Biography.
7. College presidents–Massachusetts–Biography.
8. Women college presidents–Massachusetts–Biography.
9. Douglass College–Faculty–Biography.
10. Radcliffe College–Presidents–Biography.
11. U.S. Atomic Energy Commission–
Officials and employees–Biography.
I. Title.

CT275.B785185Y34 2005
305.42'092—dc22
2005006128

First edition

All rights reserved

Without limiting the rights under copyright reserved above,
no part of this publication may be reproduced,
stored in or introduced into a retrieval system,
or transmitted, in any form or by any means
(electronic, mechanical, photocopying, recording, or otherwise),
without the prior written permission of both the copyright owner
and the above publisher of this book.

Printed in the United States of America

To

my husband of more than forty years

JAMES YAFFE

for all the usual reasons—and then some

Contents

Illustrations   ix
Preface   xi
Acknowledgments   xiii

Part I : Beginnings
   1. The World Is Such a Good Place   3
   2. A Funny Little Girl   14

Part II: The First Life
   3. The Life of a Grind   25
   4. All Things Seem Visible   36
   5. Niches as Well as Nests   52
   6. A Garden Not a Racetrack   63
   7. A Busy Life   75
   8. The Best Years of All   96
   9. Heaven on Earth   101

Part III: The Second Life
   10. A Sightseer in a New Land   111
   11. A Great Cultural Change   117
   12. A Neophyte at the Deaning Business   122
   13. Mother, Scientist, Educator   130
   14. The Tidal Wave   138
   15. The Awakening   146
   16. A Bit of Rebellion   158
   17. A Kind of Pedestal   164
   18. The Messy Experiment   171
   19. A Geneticist With Nest-Building Experience   187
   20. It's Hard to Say "No" to the President   198
   21. We Believe in Education for Women   208
   22. Radcliffe Sticks to Its Knitting   216
   23. The Fuzzy Relationship   247
   24. A Society Gets the Kind of Excellence It Values   264

Part IV: Endings
  25. Enough of Women   271
  26. I Don't Look Back Much   281
  27. An Interesting Life   303

Afterword   306

Appendix: Speeches
  The Modern Scientific Revolution   309
    Introductory Remarks at Alumnae College,
    Douglass College, June 3, 1959
  Women's Education for New Horizons   313
    The University Women's Forum,
    Philadelphia, February 4, 1961
  Radcliffe Inauguration Speech   320
    May 19, 1960
  The University's Responsibility in
      Educating Women For Leadership   327
    Southern Methodist University, January 28, 1966
  From Serratia to Women's Lib and a Bit Beyond   337
    New Brunswick Lecture,
    American Society for Microbiology,
    Minneapolis, May 5, 1971
  Women: Resource for a Changing World   348
    An Invitational Conference at the Radcliffe Institute,
    Radcliffe College, April 18, 1972

Endnotes   357

Bibliography   367

Index   371

Illustrations
(Between pages 176–177)

1. Polly with her brother Gardner
2. Astride Wedding Bells, the pony
3. At Vassar, competing in the long jump
4. Vassar Sophomore Party Committee in 1928
5. Vassar Junior Class Hockey Team in 1929
6. Polly's sister, mother, grandmother, and niece
7. Polly, 1933
8. Polly and Henry Bunting, 1937
9. Ingraham family, late 1930's
10. Polly and Henry, 1938
11. Polly and Henry with daughter Mary, 1940
12. Bunting basement
13. Polly and her four children
14. Polly at Douglass "Campus Night," 1955
15. At Douglass Friday night dinner
16. Breaking ground at Douglass, 1959
17. Polly's inauguration day, Radcliffe, 1960
18. Ingraham family at Polly's Radcliffe inauguration
19. Polly and her four children at Radcliffe
20. Polly with freshman seminar at Radcliffe
21. Polly with the bees at Radcliffe
22. Polly with Radcliffe students
23. In Cabinet Room of the White House, 1964
24. Polly on holiday with daughter Mary and granddaughter Laura, 1969
25. Polly with granddaughter Laura, 1970
26. Polly, 1972
27. After her retirement, 1980's
28. After her retirement from Princeton
29. Polly attending discussions at Bunting Institute
30. Polly with her second husband, Dr. Clement Smith

31. Polly's eightieth birthday at the Bunting Institute
32. Polly's last house in New Boston, New Hampshire
33. Polly with one of Bill's oxen

Preface

The name of Mary Ingraham Bunting does not appear in the galaxy of American feminists, but it should. Though her professional accomplishments were impressive—she was the dean of Douglass College, the president of Radcliffe College during the tempestuous sixties, a special assistant to the president of Princeton, the first woman on the Atomic Energy Commission, a member of many boards and presidential commissions—most important was her contribution to American feminism.

She was one of the first to perceive—and come up with remedies for—the ways in which American society was stifling the cultural, intellectual, and scientific aspirations of women, preventing them from making the most of their abilities, crippling them as surely as if it were binding their feet. To Polly Bunting it was a matter of common sense that this situation was as wasteful as it was unjust. A microbiologist with a Ph.D. from the University of Wisconsin, a meticulous observer of the natural world, she understood that there is room for all kinds of talents, and that it is foolish to squander any of them. It is a testimony to the truth and depth of her ideas that they are accepted now as commonplace. But they had to be fought for.

This book chronicles what she did and how she did it, the obstacles she overcame, the prejudices and obtuseness she confronted. It attempts to understand the traits in her character that led her to accomplish these feats, and how her background, her family, and the experiences of her life combined with her extraordinary gifts to make her achievements possible.

It also chronicles the extraordinary shape her life took. Until early middle age, she was not even thinking about women's struggles. She was leading a private, domestic life with a husband and four children, enjoying occupations that completely satisfied her. That was her first life, and she would have been content to go on living it all of her days.

But then circumstances—sudden and cataclysmic—compelled her

to reinvent herself. In her mid-forties she embarked on an entirely new career. This was her second life, the one that helped to change the lives of countless women who came after her, but easily might never have happened.

Acknowledgments

I am indebted to a great many people who helped me during the writing of this book.

I was extremely fortunate in having the support of the extended Ingraham and Bunting families, particularly Polly Bunting's four children: Mary Decher, Chuck, Bill, and John Bunting, and her sister and brother-in-law, Winifred and Harold Warner. They willingly delved into their memories, their filing cabinets, and their photograph albums, and offered not only trust and encouragement but also hospitality.

I was helped enormously by many at the educational institutions Polly Bunting attended or administered. At Douglass, Deans Mary Hartman and Barbara Shailor gave me access to the campus; Seymour Becker provided me with invaluable help in locating Douglass faculty; present and past administrators and many faculty members shared their insights and recollections; Tom Frusciano and Thelma Tate helped open archives. The book could not have been written without the help of many at Radcliffe, particularly Jane Knowles, Radcliffe's incomparable archivist and her able staff at the Schlesinger Library. I was helped, also, by many present and former Princeton faculty members and administrators, especially William Bowen.

The following people generously gave me their time and recollections. I interviewed many of them in person or on the telephone. Others wrote helpful letters, detailing conversations or encounters they had had with Polly Bunting or describing official occasions at which they had been present. Others helped by deciphering scientific material or putting me in touch with others who could. I am grateful for the assistance of each of them: Margaret Albrink, Diane Balter, Josephine Banfield, William Banfield, Deborah Batts, Katherine Beer, Nao Belser, William Belser, Derek Bok, Sue Bolman, Susan Vaill Bonner, William G. Bowen, Miriam Brush, Mary Bundy, Adam Bunting, Ann Bunting, Jennifer Bunting, Matthew Bunting, Meredith Bunting, Francis Burr,

Edward Cabot, Orton Camp, Loy Ann Carrington, Katherine Kaufer Christoffel, Michele Cortese, Flora Cowen, Calvert Crary, Mary Crary, Miner Crary, Elizabeth A. Daniels, Guy Darst, Kitty Darst, Eunice Davidson, Laura Decher, Meika Decher, Reiner Decher, Marie Lymberis DeCordoba, Emily DeHuff, Louise Donovan, Richard Donovan, Beth DuMauro, John Dunlop, Yvette Edmundson, Alvin Eisenman, Hope Eisenman, Linda Eisenmann, John Fine, John Fox, Barbara Gaffney, Carl Gerber, Sanford Gifford, Mary Goethals, Robert Goheen, Irene Goldfarb, Carol Greenhouse, Linda Greenhouse, Lucy Hackney, Sheldon Hackney, Elsie Hahnenfeld, Mary Hartman, Jan Harvey, Linda Hennessy, Ann Heuer, Stanley Hoffman, Kathryn Voelker Holmes, Matina Horner, Rose Ann Howarth, Elex Ingersoll, Barbara Ingraham, Laura Ingraham, Polly Ingraham, Rob Ingraham, Sandy Ingraham, David Jackson, Ethel Jackson, Diane Jacobs, Eliza Janeway, Toni Joseph, Eva Kashket, Phyllis Keller, Kathy Kraft, Pamela Lach, Anne Lacy, Florence Ladd, Hubert Lechevalier, Joshua Lederberg, Donna Lieberman, Judy Lieberman, Rachel Lieberman, Maryel Locke, Phyllis Logie, Jessie G. Lutz, Katheryne C. McCormick, Richard McCormick, Nancy Weiss Malkiel, Ellen Mappen, Betty Lou Marple, Jacquelyn Mattfeld, Elizabeth Mayer, Ellen Messer, Carlin Meyer, Edna Newby, Priscilla Norton, Nelson Ordway, Nathan Pusey, Will Reed, Suzy Eisenman Restino, Rachel Ritvo, Laurance Rockefeller, Roger Rosenblatt, Neil Rudenstine, Ursula Victor Santer, Barbara Shailor, Fadlou Shehadi, Marie Siewierski, Adele Simmons, Hillary Smith, Thelma Tate, Carol Thompson, Marjorie Trayes, Marjorie Angell Van Hoy, Sandra Walker, Alice Sizer Warner, Elga Wasserman, Harry Wasserman, Thomas Weber, Henry Winkler, William Winternitz, Evelyn Witkin, Gail Wittman, Peter Wood, Tom Wright, and Adelaide Zagoren.

Beth Greenfeld, Susan and Howard Kaminsky, Karen Nangle, Victoria Newhouse, and Kathy Perkins all helped me, in different ways, to publish the book.

Like all writers, I owe an enormous debt to my own family. My husband, James Yaffe, was an indefatigable editor. My older daughter Deborah, a fine journalist, was the first to see that I should turn my admiration for Polly Bunting into her biography. Her knowledge of the women's movement and her tireless editing were invaluable. My daughter Rebecca, an inexhaustibly talented artist, urged me on as much by her example of commitment as by her encouraging words. My son Gideon explained abstruse scientific concepts, and then patiently explained them yet again, and responded to my computer panics at all hours. I owe much, too, to my in-law children: Alastair Bellany, a superb historian, guided me to many sources I would otherwise have overlooked and served as my navigator in the byways of Douglass; my daughter-in-law Susan Chan showed me, through her feisty optimism and courage, what women's liberation is all about. And my two small grandchildren, David and Rachel, brought unmitigated joy to every single day.

But finally, my biggest debt is to Polly Bunting herself. In keeping with her deepest principles that women, particularly older women, should be given their chance to "shove into the stream of life," she gave me her unqualified encouragement for this project. She entrusted me with her letters, her diaries, her journals, her notes for speeches, her papers—willingly exposing to my scrutiny her half-finished sentences, fleeting insights, and developing ideas. These documents are the foundation of this book and inform not only its structure but also its substance and its heart. Direct quotations from them are on nearly every page, and the insights I gained from them animate my conclusions. I am only sorry that Polly Bunting did not live long enough to see this compilation of her achievements. I hope she would have recognized herself in the pages of this book. I hope she would have enjoyed it.

E.G.Y.
New York
May 2004

Part I
Beginnings

1

The World Is Such a Good Place

One evening in the spring of 1922 when there was a particularly beautiful sunset, twelve-year-old Polly Bunting climbed into her favorite apple tree in Seven Acre Field on her family's property in Northport, Long Island. She called it her "thinking tree" and she had a lot to think about. Some confusing things had been happening. A few days earlier, she had led her brothers and some of their friends on an expedition to pilfer cherries from a neighboring farmer's orchard; he had caught them, but then he had thrashed only the boys and not her. Why had he let her off so easily? And after a succession of small illnesses, her parents were letting her stay home from school for the rest of the year, something she knew they would never let her brothers get away with. At the same time, what her mother did get upset about was her staying out in the sun, warning her that too much sunlight could make her "all hairy," which wouldn't be very attractive when she got older. Her mother hadn't exactly said attractive to whom, but Polly understood what she meant. And there was all this talk at home about the new constitutional amendment that gave women the right to vote, something men had had for a long time. So what did it all mean—these differences between boys and girls? Was this something she ought to worry about?

She knew she was interested in getting married one day and having children, but she also liked to ride her pony, tend her beehives, and watch the birds. And sometimes she wrestled with the boys, or ran races against them, or climbed apple trees. She knew she hadn't been out in the world much, and didn't know much about what other girls enjoyed, but didn't it stand to reason that some of them enjoyed the same things she did? She knew there were many different kinds of boys in the world, so why shouldn't there be just as many different kinds of girls?

After a long time up in the apple tree, Polly finally came to a conclusion: there was no reason for her to stop being a tomboy. After all, how could she find out what kind of girl she was if she couldn't be herself?

And it would probably be good for the world to know that some girls would be a little different. So, she finally concluded, although there was no way to change being a girl, she could find out what kind of girl she was and decide what kind of woman she wanted to become.

She climbed down from her "thinking tree" quite satisfied. She felt she had worked it all out.

She did not know then, of course, that these questions would dominate her life. She had no idea how complicated it would all become, and how hard she would have to fight to win for herself and for other women the right she thought was self-evident: that each individual could decide for herself just what sort of person she was and what she would become.

The world Mary Ingraham Bunting was born into, on July 10, 1910, no longer exists. It was a world of order and civility, where there was reading aloud in the evenings, where servants stayed for twenty years and became part of the family, where the family ate dinner together every evening, and where unmarried daughters lived at home and looked after their mothers. It was a world of solid, comfortable well-being and extended families—not only of loving parents and grandparents, but also of aunts, uncles, and cousins—who gathered for Thanksgivings that everyone still remembers. And it was a family of strong women.

Mary Ingraham was born on a Sunday at 11 P.M., the first grandchild on either side of her family. She was the eldest of four children, and was followed by two brothers, Gardner and David, and a sister, Winifred. Her father insisted she be named Mary, his favorite girl's name. But it was also his wife's name; and when the baby was only about two weeks old, the presence of two Marys in the same household was becoming confusing. When her father's brother Edward pointed out that the English nickname for Mary was Polly, that seemed a perfect solution for a family whose ancestors were British. It was a nickname she retained all her life.

Although her father's law office was located across the Brooklyn Bridge in Manhattan, the Ingrahams and both sets of grandparents all lived in Brooklyn. When she was born, Polly's parents lived at 258A Brooklyn Avenue, but they moved while she was still a small child to a brownstone at 363 Adelphi Street. It was in the Fort Greene section of Brooklyn, a silk-stocking district named for the adjacent park where architect Stanford White had erected a Doric monument to the twelve thousand prisoners who died at the hands of the British during the Revolution.[1]

The house had windows on three sides letting plenty of light into the long, narrow rooms. Polly's parents added a dining room that ran the length of the house; it was painted white, which was unusual in those days, and had sconces on the wall and a small separate table for the children. On top of the dining room was a fenced porch where Polly, who always enjoyed solitude, slept on a cot, summer and winter, and studied the stars and how they moved.

The house had hardwood floors and Oriental rugs. A variety of prints were on the walls—birds, Japanese landscapes, a delicate, golden Mary Cassatt of an Asian woman holding a baby. The Ingrahams felt they couldn't afford to buy paintings, but in those days prints were readily available and affordable.

In the early days of the century Brooklyn had close to a million residents and very much its own character. It had mile after mile of brownstones like the one on Adelphi Street, wide streets, and wrought-iron fences that enclosed small yards. Trolley cars were the chief means of transportation,[2] and Polly used to lie in bed at night listening to them traveling along Greene Avenue, only a house away. Sometimes, just for the fun of it, she would take a nickel and ride a trolley car to the end of the line. Once in a while she even hitched a ride on a garbage truck.

All her grandparents lived nearby as did most of her aunts and uncles. The extended family was not only geographically but also emotionally close, and managed to see a great deal of one another. This sense of equilibrium and solidarity is reflected in one of the first entries in Polly's baby book, written by her mother from the baby's point of view, under the headline "Baby's First Christmas." "I had a great big Christmas tree that reached from the floor to the ceiling and it had many red and blue and white lights on it. My father and I lay down on the floor together and played and were happy because the world is such a good place."

Her mother's father, Henry Titus Shotwell, a rotund, bald man with a pudgy face and a bushy moustache, was sweet and kind, but never very successful financially. He moved from job to job throughout his life. At one time he managed an estate in Locust Valley, Long Island, which belonged to a prosperous New York lawyer. At another time he had a stable and rented out horses and carriages. Later he ran a dairy farm on Long Island. Because money was a problem for them, the Shotwells didn't have a home of their own throughout Polly's childhood. Instead, they lived during the winters on the third floor of their son Willets' Brooklyn house and in the summers in a Long Island house owned by Polly's parents.

Polly's maternal grandmother, Alice Gardner Shotwell, "Nana," was originally from Nantucket, one of three sisters referred to by Polly's father as "the three Nantucket beauties." A woman of great energy and vitality, Nana taught arithmetic in the public schools for a good many years when her family suffered financial reverses. And it was she who saw to it that Polly's mother, Mary Shotwell, went to college—to Vassar. "My grandmother thought that my mother should go," Polly said years later, "and made all sorts of sacrifices to see that she did."

Polly's paternal grandfather, Henry Charles Murphy Ingraham, was a Brooklyn lawyer. "Everybody called him 'the Judge,'" said Polly. A distinguished looking man with a snow-white beard, he so much valued peaceful time with his family that for many years he refused to have a telephone in the house. He died when Polly was an infant.

His wife, Winifred Andrews Ingraham, was called "Grandmother." Of all the grandparents, she had the most profound impact on Polly. She had inherited her intelligence from her father, a Methodist bishop, who had a volume of his sermons printed every year and sent to all the pastors in the church. (They were not required to use them, but if their own inspiration flagged, he gave them the freedom to take his ideas or even to use parts of his sermons verbatim.)

At age sixteen, Grandmother Winifred met her future husband at a Wesleyan graduation. At first her family objected to the romance because she was so young, but family lore has it that she "pined away" until they gave their consent. She was seventeen when she married.

Although she gave birth to nine children—seven of whom survived—and never went to college, she nonetheless managed to be a prodigious reader and was often considered the best educated person in the family. When her children were small, she always got up at six in the morning to get in a good hour of reading before the day started. She managed to read most of the serious books that were being widely discussed in intellectual circles. Her children remembered particularly her reading, with great interest, Darwin's *The Origin of Species*. An imposing-looking woman, she was, by today's standards, somewhat stout, with her hair parted in the middle and pulled back. She was not beautiful, but she had the rare quality of making strong, positive impressions on people. Once, when Polly and a friend shoveled her walk after a snowstorm, the friend assumed that Polly didn't know her grandmother well because Polly had been so polite to her. "Everyone," Polly remembered saying, "is polite to her."

In spite of her imposing manner, Grandmother Winifred had a kindly streak and a sensitivity to other people's feelings. When Polly's brother-in-law, Harold Warner, was brought around to meet Grandmother, he leaned back in a chair and broke it. Without missing a beat, the family matriarch turned to her son, Edward, and said, "I told you this morning to glue that chair."

But it was the formal side of her nature that characterized occasions in her home. One of the most memorable family rituals was the weekly Sunday midday meal at the family homestead at 444 Clinton Avenue. The long table was always set with a starched white tablecloth. Grandmother sat at one end, and she placed the minister of the church they attended at the other. Sometimes, in addition to the aunts and uncles who lived there, they would be joined by spinster relatives of Grandmother Winifred's, who lived alone. Dessert always featured an ice cream concoction with many pale colors—green, pink, and yellow—and, when it was cut, Grandmother made sure that everyone got some of all the colors.

The Ingraham children took turns attending these luncheons. The invited child sat at Grandmother's right and there was a present. Once, Polly received a copy of *Swiss Family Robinson*, a book Grandmother had enjoyed as a child. Polly kept it in her library all her life.

The formality of these Sunday dinners did not stifle the vigorous exchanges of views that fed the intellectual side of Grandmother's nature. There was a lot of friendly, but spirited, discussion at that table, arguments in which everyone took part. For strangers it could be disconcerting. Years later Polly's uncle, Mark Ingraham, described the reaction of one of their ministers: "Before meeting us he had believed there were two sides to every question, but after knowing the Ingrahams he realized there were seven."

After the Sunday meal an uncle or aunt would take the invited child out somewhere, to see one of New York City's museums or the Cloisters or the Statue of Liberty, or just to play a game in the parlor. These aunts and uncles, who had no children of their own, formed another important part of Polly's childhood.

Her father had six siblings, three of whom were among the most continuous presences in Polly's life. They never married and continued to live with their mother. Ruth became a doctor and eventually head of the X-ray department at Brooklyn Hospital. Grace, who was quite shy, was for many years treasurer of the YWCA. Perhaps because she was the youngest daughter, unmarried, without a profession, she accepted, apparently without question, the responsibility of taking care of her mother until the very end. "In those days," said Polly's sister, Winifred Warner, "that's what daughters did."

The sense of family solidarity and obligation that had motivated Grace also influenced the choices Edward made. His real loves were birding and the outdoors. He wanted to be a farmer and had planned to set up his life out on Long Island. But when his father died and his older brother, Polly's father, married, Edward didn't think it proper for his mother and sisters to be without a man in their house. So he went to law school and became a lawyer, never an enthusiastic one. He always kept his Sundays free to go hiking in the outdoors, and as she got older Polly would often go with him. They would take the train to New Jersey, get off at one station where he knew the trails by heart, hike down to another station, and take the train home. Edward died during one of his walks, sitting against a tree on a trail in the Adirondack Mountains.

Polly's father, Henry Andrews Ingraham, was the eldest of the Ingraham siblings. He was a successful lawyer, but also something of a Renaissance man. He was interested in art, not only as an observer, but also as a collector and practitioner. He collected rare books and prints and was an accomplished photographer and watercolorist. He was also an expert gardener, and the family house in Northport was always full of fresh flowers from his garden, which he would carry inside in big pails of water.

He was an avid fisherman and spent time fishing in the Adirondack Mountains. He had a scientific side to him too. He was interested in archaeology, geology, natural history, biology, and the history of science. In college, at Wesleyan, his main interest had been biology; he confessed to Polly that he would have preferred to go on in that field, but "I couldn't have supported your mother in the style she would wish to live if I had. She would not have been content being the wife of a professor." He died on September 18, 1962, at the age of eighty-four. A Unitarian minister, who had been a friend of his, read Gerard Manley Hopkins' poem, "Pied Beauty," at the funeral. "Glory be to God for dappled things." "It was so appropriate for him," said Polly's cousin, Mary Crary. "There was so much in there about fishing tackle."

He even wrote a book about trout fishing that was published in 1926 by the Angler's Club of New York, of which he was the president for two years, 1927 and 1928. Writing a book was one of several things he thought every person ought to do. He was an avid reader and kept the house full of books, which he was always talking about and leaving open where he thought they might catch the eye of some child. He had advanced textbooks, such as one of Thomas Hunt Morgan's on genetics, as well as popular works such as H. G. Wells's *The Outlines of Science*. He memorized much poetry—many of the English classics—and encouraged his children to do the same.

Polly's father had great physical as well as mental energy. Each morning he would walk his children about two miles in the direction of their school and then would walk across the Brooklyn Bridge to his law office, Gleason, McLanahan, Merritt, and Ingraham, on Wall Street. In the evenings he walked back across the bridge, about eight miles a day.

In spite of all of his interests and activities, he still found time to involve himself in the raising of his children. He loved children, and just as his father had resisted the inroads of technology, he also was slow to have a radio around because he didn't want distractions to interfere with the family's life together. "Any night my parents were home," Polly remembered, "my father would read out loud, Mother would sew, we would be around, doing homework or whatever." He remembered birthdays.

Even more significantly, he involved himself in his children's moral development. Once, Polly remembered, shortly after the end of the first World War, she heard people on the street using derogatory language in describing Germans. Her father brought the children into his office at the back of the house and told them firmly never to use such language in talking about anyone. "It was a solemn moment," Polly said.

He was a less rigid disciplinarian than his wife. If the children misbehaved, their mother might raise her voice and lecture. But if the transgression seemed to him to be trivial, he would take them upstairs and laugh. He had a lot of tolerance for mischief; what he had no tolerance for was cruelty. "He never raised his voice," said Winifred. "All he had to do was look at us." If the boys were teasing Polly and her sister, he would say, "That's enough," very quietly, and that would be the end of it. There was never any invective. The strongest language anyone ever heard from him was when the chicken house burned down. He looked out the window and said, "Oh, the dickens."

Henry Ingraham wrote well and all his children, grandchildren, and even great-grandchildren born after his death remember and treasure his stories and illustrations. When Polly was growing up, his bedtime stories were high points of the day. When he went on a brief trip to Washington, D.C., in 1915, he took time to write his children a letter telling them what he had seen at Mount Vernon and drawing a lively pen-and-ink sketch of George Washington's coach and four horses. He created imaginary characters—Pudge Mudgen and Dickle Pickle—and over the years they continued to have adventures in an imaginary world of his creation. After his death these stories were lovingly passed down from parents to children. .

In a birthday letter to him in 1944, his younger son David wrote:

"Not infrequently do I wonder at my good fortune in having for a father a man so wise in so many ways—so kind in all ways. Muddled though he may be in his political thinking, he has passed on to his four children a natural respect for the best which culture and learning have to offer. This could not have been easy in a world which had manufactured so many conflicting ideals and temptations."

Henry Ingraham met his future wife, Mary Shotwell, when she was a student in his Sunday school class in the Locust Valley, Long Island area, where his family had a summer house and her father was in charge of the Guthrie estate. He was ten years older than she and, according to Polly, "He waited a long time for her to finish college and had established himself in law before they were married."

Their marriage, which lasted fifty-four years, was by all accounts a happy one, and they always seemed to take pleasure in each other's company. On Saturday afternoons they made a point of going somewhere together, often into Manhattan to look in at art galleries. Occasionally they would buy a print they liked. They went to lectures and concerts at the Brooklyn Academy of Music in their neighborhood and once a month dressed up in evening clothes to attend a performance at the Metropolitan Opera.

Everyone seemed to speak of Henry Ingraham with great affection and of Mary Shotwell Ingraham, called "Gwy" by her grandchildren, with great admiration. Tall and imposing, she was a formidable woman; "a full rigged ship," remembered an acquaintance. "You didn't have any choice but to be influenced by her," said her grandson, Chuck Bunting.

Among the many things that set her apart was her manner of speech. She was a Quaker and addressed her family and children as "thee" and "thou." During their childhood they sometimes worried that she would embarrass them by using this form of speech in public, but she never did. She used it only with those close to her, and so it was a sign of acceptance.

In spite of the Quaker speech, Gwy went to the Presbyterian church in Brooklyn. Often Polly went with her, the only one of the family who did. It wasn't an every-Sunday requirement, but on some Sundays the request was made in the form of a question: "Would thee like to come to church this morning?" There was really only one answer.

Gwy was conscious of having married into a family with more money, more social connections, and more intellectual power than her own, so she tried to compensate as best she could. She ran a formal household and imposed that style on her family. No child could ever leave the table until asked, "Has thee had sufficient?" This insistence on formality, on things being done just so, continued into her old age. When Polly's daughter-in-law Ann wanted to send the family a photograph of Polly, dressed in baggy jeans and a funny hat, ready to embark on a walk in the woods with her grandson, Polly made Ann promise not to show the photograph to her mother. She made it clear that Gwy would not enjoy that picture.

Although she ran two homes—one in Brooklyn and one on Long Island—and had four children, and made many of their clothes herself, her domestic responsibilities did not keep her from what she saw as her larger civic and community commitments. She served on a large number of boards and committees all her adult life. She began doing this in 1908, right after her graduation from Vassar, when she started working with the Young Women's Christian Association in Brooklyn. She continued, uninterrupted, until she was well into her seventies, when her children urged her to drop at least some of her boards.

The YWCA consumed much of her energy for a good portion of her life. In 1922, when Polly was twelve, her mother became president of the Brooklyn YW, joined the national board in 1930, and in 1939 relinquished the presidency of the Brooklyn branch to become the national board's president. She was also a director of the New York Council for Adult Education; vice-chairman of the Brooklyn Council for Social Planning; a member of the board of directors of the National Conference of Christians and Jews; and during World War II, one of the founders, original directors, and then vice-president of the USO. For this President Harry Truman, in 1946, awarded her the Presidential Medal for Merit, the nation's highest civilian award. She was the first woman ever to receive it.

In 1938 Mayor Fiorello La Guardia appointed her to the Board of Higher Education of New York City. She stayed on that board for thirty years, into her seventies, and was closely involved with the planning of the City University. In 1952 Wesleyan, the alma mater of her husband and sons, awarded her an honorary doctorate of humanities for "a public career of great distinction." In 1961 Columbia awarded her an honorary degree for the significant part she had played in the creation of the City University. In the 1950's and 1960's, awards like this were not often given to women, especially not by men's colleges.

Her physical stamina was considerable. In her seventies she would drive from Brooklyn to Long Island after meetings, often late at night. She was a formidable driver: at a younger age she drove so fast in a convertible with the top down that younger relatives, following behind, had difficulty keeping up with her.

Mary Ingraham died at the age of ninety-four in 1981, in a nursing home, something no one, including herself, had ever anticipated. Her wry sense of humor stayed with her to the end. When Harold Warner, her balding son-in-law, visited her, he said, "I got a haircut today. And the barber said to me, 'Mr. Warner, on which side do you part your hair?'" That prompted her to speak the first words she had uttered in some time. "Thee should have told him it was de-parted."

Her Quaker funeral was at a meetinghouse on Long Island. Her by-lined obituary in the *New York Times* ran to ten paragraphs.

In a letter written after her death to her children, Henry Ingraham's younger brother Mark wrote: "She was a person of strong emotions both as to individuals and as to matters of social justice ... people knew when she liked them. I believe they also knew when they were disliked."

Though ahead of her time in many ways, Mary Ingraham was also a woman of her own day. She held to her generation's concept of noblesse oblige—for example, she looked after the family's maids until they got married. Her involvement in the civil rights struggle was also tinged, in Polly's opinion, by an old-fashioned paternalism. "She was talking all the time about the importance of integration and doing what you could to help black people, but it was all at arm's length," Polly said. "I was not comfortable with the fact that Mother could work so hard for the cause of integration and never invite any blacks into the house."

She also accepted much of the prevailing orthodoxy about a wife's obligations to her husband. In deference to Henry, she took up fly-fishing, and even managed to overcome her aversion to unhooking the fish. And she remarked to a younger cousin how grateful she was that Henry allowed her to continue her work even though it meant that she had to drive home alone late at night. "My father thought she had really important abilities," Polly said, "and she was using them to the best advantage for herself and society." Both of them "were into doing good."

Above all, they shared an abiding commitment to the family, which eventually included the great-grandchildren and generations of cousins. They all came together once a year for Thanksgiving, often as many as thirty-five people. "Thanksgivings in Brooklyn were memorable events," said Chuck Bunting. "There was a big table, which of course the children did not sit at, and then a series of smaller tables where one uncle or another was delegated to keep order. And after dinner, the children would go down on the esplanade over the docks and run up and down and just have fun. My grandfather had a large sack of lollipops in the closet and he would haul them out and each grandchild could reach in and take as many lollipops as he could hold in one fist. So it was a great scramble to see how many you could get."

This then was Polly's family, a stoic, Yankee family, not given to excesses. They did not indulge in extravagance or showiness. They spent their money carefully; they gave their intimacy sparingly. Eminently civilized, always gracious, like them she had an inner reserve, a center of calm. Polly's aversion to bragging, to self-aggrandizement, to self-pity or complaining, she learned from this family and she learned well.

Many years later, when she herself was in her eighties, Polly would harken back to these first significant figures in her life. She considered them touchstones, reference points. Whenever anyone praised her courage, her intrepidity in the face of daunting challenges, she pointed to the achievements of her parents and grandparents. "I think my mother or my father or my grandmothers would have acted in the same way as they went along. I've never been different from the older people in my family. We just faced different things."

2

A Funny Little Girl

"Thee is a funny little girl," her mother used to tell her. And in many ways, Polly must have appeared that way.

In childhood photographs she usually looks a little disheveled. No wonder, since her idea of fun was to play running games like ring-a-lievo, touch football, or hockey with the boys. According to everyone but herself, she was a formidable athlete, terrifying relatives by swimming underwater and disappearing for what seemed like extended periods of time. As a teenager she earned a medal for swimming two miles across Huntington Bay. "I just played harder than most other girls," she said.

She was an avid rider, and during her elementary school years her parents kept a horse for her at the Brooklyn Riding and Driving Club. She got to be accomplished enough to ride sidesaddle in the Madison Square Garden lady saddle-horse class and managed, she said, "something like a reasonable fifth." But she preferred riding bareback on her Shetland pony—wearing bloomers and wrinkled knee socks. She even had a polo pony and played what her son Bill described as "blue collar" rather than "blue blood polo."

At the family's country home on Long Island, she got into all sorts of unladylike mischief. In revenge against the farmer who had refused to thrash her, she organized her brothers and seven neighborhood boys into a gang called "The Terrible Ten." They opened the gate to the farmer's pasture, fed wild mustard to his cows to spoil the taste of their milk, and tied notes to the cows' tails that read "Beware the Terrible Ten is on your trail." The farmer became alarmed and came over one evening to have a serious talk with Polly's father. Polly waited nervously upstairs for her punishment, until, after the farmer left, she heard her father roaring with laughter.

The most ingenious trouble she got into involved her favorite pony, Wedding Bells. One rainy spring morning, when Polly was about nine and the entire family was away for the day, she found that the book she was reading had ceased to absorb her. Seeing Wedding Bells on the porch made Polly wonder if the pony might be interested in seeing what the inside of the house looked like. So she brought her in and when she found that Wedding Bells seemed to be quite interested in the downstairs, she wondered if the pony would also enjoy the upstairs. Wedding Bells went up like a flash, but nothing would induce her to come down. Polly finally went for help to the hired man who rounded up three other neighboring farmers. Each took one leg and carried the pony down the stairs and out the door. "They were big men; Wedding Bells was a small pony," Polly said. In thinking back on this escapade, Polly remembered that "There was that awful feeling when I got her up there—here I was in trouble again. I hadn't meant to get into trouble and I wasn't really naughty, but I just seemed to get into situations. I had a sense that I was always getting into situations."

The mischief she got into wasn't limited to the country. She often went to the Brooklyn Academy of Music, where on Saturday afternoons the stage was turned over to Burton Holmes or Frank Buck for travelogues. "The kids piled in there," said Polly, "and you tried to sit in the front row of the balcony so you could put a Necco wafer on your knee, and send it down on to the bald head of some man. If they were projecting something in front, you could make an arc through the light beam and nobody knew what it was. It added an extra zest."

She had serious interests too, and they stayed with her throughout her long life. From her Uncle Edward she learned about bird watching; from her father, about gardening and keeping bees, which she found to be "interesting creatures with interesting life histories." But what she loved more than nearly anything else was reading, and all her life she was a voracious reader.

Looking back on her childhood, Polly remembered her growing-up in terms of a succession of ideas that she confronted, grappled with, and researched. By the time she got to high school, she had been thinking deeply about a number of concepts that seemed to her extremely intriguing. She remembered, with great clarity, the introduction into her life of each of them.

In fourth grade, when she read in her geography book that "the inhabitants of Arabia are Mohammedans," she began puzzling over the nature of religion. So she rummaged around in second-hand bookstores and found the Koran and works of Confucius. She also read the Bible carefully, and for a long time she assumed she would be a minister when she grew up.

Her next big intellectual encounter occurred a few years later when she came upon a book of her father's, *The Origin of Birds* by Gerhard

Heilman, which contained the phrase, "Ontogeny recapitulates phylogeny." When she found out what this meant—that the embryo in its development goes through the same stages as the whole of evolution—she became fascinated by this idea. She wondered if individuals go through all the evolutionary stages of the whole human race as they grow up. In the Sunday *New York Times* she had seen photographs of drawings done by some primitive people she thought resembled the drawings of her younger brothers.

Ontogeny and phylogeny led her, by the time she was in the seventh grade, to two parallel studies—one of history and the other of herself. It was an interesting way to read history, she said, "because you didn't care about the wars too much but concentrated on what the people were thinking."

But even more important than her historical studies, she began what became a lifelong habit of self-examination and the practice of keeping detailed journals. "I thought, I'm fairly young. If I could figure out where I'm at intellectually, and then watch as I develop, would I sort of go the way history went? And I started writing things down that were important to me. That was one of my early projects—to try to keep track of what it was like to be myself. And then I decided if somebody found that book, I just couldn't stand it. So I destroyed it." She had already developed her penchant to protect her privacy at all costs.

One of the things this meant was that she usually preferred to be alone. The bees, birding, and gardening "offered a welcome opportunity to be by oneself," Polly said years later. "I didn't particularly like to do things in groups. I liked to do things by myself. Just going off alone was suspect. . . . It wasn't legitimate, made grown-ups ask questions. But if one went off with one's bird glasses or a butterfly net or even a basket and a trowel, they might question your tastes but they didn't worry about your psyche."[1]

Although Polly insisted all her life that she never suffered because she was a maverick and a loner, nevertheless, from an early age she was scrupulously careful about keeping her inner life—which for her meant her intellectual life, her preoccupation with ideas—to herself. She didn't let anyone know when she was reading or thinking something unusual. She could just imagine the kind of things the grown-ups would say. "Do you know what that little girl is reading now?" Sometimes they would let out "these tiny little laughs."

She remembered the few times she did try to share things with her relatives and how disappointing it was to have her mother say "yes, yes," but not really understand, or to dismiss her with "thee is a funny little girl," or "thee does have such ideas." "I didn't share my inner life with the family. Not with my brother. Not with anyone. If you don't want people in on something, you don't share it at all. You better not. You better keep it to yourself."

Polly denied that this protective privacy was to ward off pain. It was just, she said, that she never had any real childhood friends, any soulmates to share things with. "The extended family saw each other a lot. My parents had special friends, but most of my parents' friends' children didn't interest me much."

Perhaps one reason she had no close childhood friends was that she didn't attend school regularly. Until high school her attendance was erratic because she was continually sick. She missed most of the third, fifth, and sixth grades, and did not attend any of the seventh grade. Apparently her immune system didn't start operating efficiently until adolescence. "I would catch things and not get over them well. Those were the days before penicillin and if one got strep throats and other infections, they would last quite a while. I would start school in the fall and would go until the first time I caught the flu and then maybe get over that and start again. So it would be very spotty some years. Sometimes I would have started school and then be out so long that it didn't seem worthwhile going back that year. I didn't like school, so I would urge my parents not to bother for the rest of that year."[2] This lack of traditional schooling, Polly believed, showed her the satisfaction and excitement of investigating something that interested her for its own sake, "rather than working for grades or approval."[3]

Her parents thought that perhaps extra doses of fresh air might strengthen her, so they set up a makeshift shed on the balcony above the dining room and had her sleep on a cot outside. It was cold, but she loved it. She lay under layers of warm blankets and watched the stars.

Most of these illnesses were not dangerous, but when she was eight Spanish influenza swept the world and she became seriously sick. Without antibiotics to keep it under control, the epidemic kept gathering momentum until the death toll at home was greater than that among American troops fighting in Europe.

Since Polly was sick so often, at first she didn't pay much attention to this particular illness. But then she began to notice the doctor's air of gravity and his insistence on talking to her mother downstairs where she couldn't hear what they were saying. She knew something was really wrong; she was sure this meant she was going to die. She looked out her bedroom window. "It was a nice day and we had a vine by the window," Polly remembered years later. "A sparrow was on it and kids were playing in the street. I remember realizing that no matter what happened to me there would still be birds and there would still be kids playing." This experience, which she always thought of as religious, made her decide she "wasn't going to worry about death anymore."

She never suffered again from an illness as serious, but she still continued to be plagued by episodes of ill health. Sometimes, to help her recuperate, her parents put her in the care of the Shotwell grandparents out in Northport, Long Island. They thought that since Nana had taught in the public schools she could tutor Polly.

The Ingrahams divided their lives between Brooklyn and Northport, where they spent their summers and winter weekends. Northport was completely country in those days, without finished lawns or fences. They might see an occasional house when they took drives, but their property had more than enough attractions for the children. There was a clear woodland stream and a freshwater pond with snapping turtles. The pond also had quicksand where once a cow almost sank. The children were warned constantly not to go near it. There were woods and rumor had it that once there had been an Indian village. "We all thought that was wonderful," Polly said, "and every so often we would find an arrowhead—maybe." Once they held a big funeral ceremony in those woods to bury Winifred's foal.

Polly found plants in Northport she could not identify, and took them to the Brooklyn Botanic Gardens, whose head was the father of one of her classmates. He would check out her specimens in one of his books. Once, she brought a great big puff ball in a tobacco can, and when he couldn't figure out what it was, he sent it to an expert in Cincinnati. "And he got back word with pictures of it and just what it was," Polly said. "It was nice to be part of that."

The Ingrahams had two Northport houses. In the summers they lived on Asharoken Beach, right on Northport Bay with their twelve-foot sailboat, *Sonora*, tied outside their door. The beach was wonderful for many things, but not for the farming much loved by Polly's father. So when she was small he bought some property about a mile or two away, on either side of Locust Road. They eventually built a white wooden farmhouse there, which is still owned by a nephew of Polly's. It was this house which her parents made available to the Shotwell grandparents when the Ingraham family was living in the beach house.

When they were in Northport, the Ingrahams lived an authentic farm life. They grew their own hay and field corn and some of their wheat and rye as well as vegetables and fruits and stored some in the basement for the winter. They kept a cow, and the self-sufficiency that represented was always, for Polly, a symbol of what it meant to live in the country. They also had horses, geese, ducks, chickens, turkeys, and a corncrib with guinea hens. There were dogs who were part of the family, a collie called Laddie and a little mutt named Pete Smith. And on one side of a hill there was a cement slab for the pigs, to keep them from digging under the fence.

But while the Ingraham family all loved and respected animals, they were not sentimental about them. At the end of the season no one complained when the brood of piglets was slaughtered and taken to their butcher in the city.

Even in the country the Ingrahams retained their gracious way of living. Instead of the formal Sunday lunch, they had Sunday evening get-togethers either at their home or at the home of one of two other closely connected families: the Mudges or the Crarys. Although the gathering would rotate among the three houses, the menu was always the same: egg salad and onion sandwiches with the crusts cut off, ham rolls, and sarsaparilla or loganberry juice. There were no maids at these occasions, so the children did most of the cleaning-up in the kitchen while the grown-ups had high-planed discussions of civic affairs. They all had the same views about social issues in New York City. When the discussion turned to national matters, there was less unanimity. The Crarys were strong Republicans and Polly's mother, a staunch Democrat. But, as one of their descendants was to say many years later, "They were all gentlemen. They had intellectual differences, but they didn't let that come into their personal relations. And they all loved each other."

For Polly, Northport was an idyllic place that gripped her imagination and stayed in her memory. She described Northport, years later, in almost elegiac words. "There was the beauty of the country: night and day, fields and woods, swamps and marshes, the beaches, the bay, the Sound, our little woodland stream and the nearby fresh water cove. I loved them all."[4] Her experiences there cemented her relationship with the natural world, developed her respect for it and her comfort in it. Northport influenced her choices—of a career in biology and of the places she chose to live as an adult. "The outdoors is my church," she said.

At Northport, Nana tutored Polly for certain set hours each day in arithmetic, Latin, and English. She was supposed to keep Polly from falling too far behind, but it was also a way of giving a little more money to the Shotwells. Unfortunately, when Polly finally was enrolled in school full-time she discovered that her grandmother had not been a very good teacher. Polly's arithmetic was inadequate; she hadn't even learned her multiplication tables well enough to use them. And she had a tenuous grasp of English grammar. "I handed in a theme in English and the teacher said, 'It doesn't look as if you have ever gone to school.' I said, 'You're right. I didn't.'" Polly kept this disappointment to herself. "I never told the family," she said years later. "I thought, 'What's the use of hurting Nana's feelings? I've got a problem and it can't help a thing by telling people.' I just had a challenge."

Polly never did learn to spell, but then her Uncle Olin never had either, and she speculated that maybe it was something genetic. She never mastered contractions, and she never got to be very good at arithmetic although in college she managed calculus and in graduate school succeeded in courses in probability and statistics. Eventually she learned punctuation and grammar. Fortunately, during her first year back at school full-time she had an excellent English teacher who, Polly said, enjoyed challenges as much as Polly herself.

It wasn't until high school that Polly went to school on a regular daily basis, to Packer Collegiate Institute, a private all-girls Brooklyn school that both her mother and her Grandmother Winifred had attended. Her father was treasurer of the board of trustees, and her mother was a member of the advisory visiting committee of the alumnae.

The red brick structure on Joralemon Street looked a little like a Victorian castle with a black wrought-iron fence and an arched doorway, high ceilings, and wide corridors whose walls were lined with portraits in gilt frames. There was a beautiful Gothic-style chapel with Tiffany glass windows and carved mahogany pews where each morning began with a compulsory service. The school was well equipped, with forty classrooms, laboratories, art studios, and a library containing 10,500 books.[5] There was also a gymnasium, although some calisthenics classes were held on the roof where girls in white middy blouses with ties, bloomers, dark stockings, and ballet slippers exercised in unison.[6]

For students like Polly, who were preparing for college, the high school curriculum was rigorous: four years of English, four years of mathematics, two years each of French and German, one year of history, and two years of science (both physics and chemistry), and four years of physical education. In addition, students had their share of the arts. There was a ten-minute organ recital on Tuesdays and Thursdays, choral singing, sight-reading, and the singing of songs and anthems on Mondays and Wednesdays. In art class they drew from a live model, fully clothed in a tailored suit, hat, and gloves. In addition to all this, the school added a one-year course in civil government "as a means of instruction in political organization and administration and as a preparation for the responsibilities imposed upon women as voters."

Even elementary school students were expected to do two to three hours of homework each day. Polly was not one of the students who followed these instructions too conscientiously. "I always felt that for homework, if you had to write it you did it, otherwise you prepared for the first class of the day and did the preparing for the second class during the first class. I wasn't someone who was out for the As."

At one time, science at Packer had been practical and homey—testing milk, visiting bread factories, and eating through visits to candy factories. But fortunately for Polly, coinciding with her arrival, the science curriculum changed. The students were now required to do work in laboratories—thirty experiments in physics—as well as additional work in chemistry. "Our science teaching has been given wings," one teacher wrote.[7]

For Polly, the scientific work was a revelation. She described years later the moment she discovered the excitement of scientific principles and understood, viscerally, that this was the work she would commit her life to. It was the first day of school her junior year in high school, and she was on her way home on the trolley car. "I was supposed to walk home at the end of the school day, but this was a hot, sticky, horrible day, as first days of school in September were apt to be, and I was lazy and decided to spend a nickel and take the trolley home. I got in the back seat and opened this new chemistry book and in heavy print I read something called *Charles' Law* that said that at constant pressure the volume of a gas varied directly with the temperature. . . . I hadn't known that anyone knew anything like that about gases, or that that kind of precision was at all possible. And then right underneath was *Boyle's Law* that if the temperature was constant the volume varied *inversely* with the pressure. Wonder on wonder! And then Avogadro's magnificent proposition, that equal volumes of gas at the same temperature and pressure had the same number of molecules. That just blew me. I had to get up and get out of that car. I couldn't stand being cooped up in a moving box, surrounded by people, with all that turmoil and excitement inside me. That people could think that way, that they could measure such things. Nobody had told me. I had grown up to age fifteen and nobody had told me that anyone could count the molecules in air. . . . I certainly knew that much as I loved literature and history, it was science that I would want to pursue."[8]

Part II
The First Life

3

The Life of a Grind

In spite of her irregular schooling, or perhaps because of it, when the time came, Polly was more than ready for college. She had clearly defined intellectual interests, a voracious curiosity, and a habit of going to books for information, satisfaction, even for comfort. She chose her mother's alma mater, Vassar—one of the Seven Sisters—an all-female college relatively close to home.

In 1927, when Polly headed off to Vassar, the economic cataclysm that was to transform the next decade was still a few years off. It was an optimistic time, far better than the preceding decades for a young woman to begin college. Society's attitude toward higher education for women had changed radically. Barely fifty years earlier a retired Harvard medical school professor, Dr. Edward Clarke, had written a book which went through seventeen printings, in which he concluded that if women used up their "limited energy" on studying, they would endanger their "female apparatus." What was good for an individual girl, he maintained, was inconsequential, compared to the possible damage to the society if girls were to squander their power and have nothing left for their "essential childbearing function."[1]

But by 1920 almost as many women as men were enrolled. College students of both sexes, however, tended to be from families who could afford the tuition, since financial aid was not readily available and the idea of offering it to all qualified students had not yet taken hold. Vassar charged $800 for tuition, room, and board during Polly's years—a significant sum when $37 a week was considered a good wage.

The stock market crashed in Polly's sophomore year and Vassar, like other colleges, was soon feeling the impact of the Depression. More and more students were broke, and as things got worse they tried all sorts of ways to make money, working at jobs ranging from undertaker's assistant to dog-sitter to soda jerker.[2] "Typing papers for others, waking friends in the morning, for the first time became regular industries."[3] By January of 1931, Polly's senior year, Vassar had used up its entire year's food budget because students didn't have money to eat off campus. Fewer students left campus for vacations.

Polly was well aware that economic hard times were having a profound impact on many people. She felt sympathy and concern, but soon found out that the Depression was not going to affect her directly. After the stock market collapse, she asked her father if he regretted spending money on a trip the family had taken out West the previous summer. He told her he was glad the family had had a good time and they had adequate funds for everything they believed to be important.

She did economize, but this was more a matter of temperament and habit than necessity. She described her nature as "scotch," to explain why she always used both sides of a piece of stationery and diluted her ink with water to make it last longer, even if it made her letters faint and hard to read. When asking her parents to purchase a rare book for her, she explained that she would get a summer job to pay for it. She used her Aunt Edith's college graduation present to pay for her membership in a professional association. As she had been taught, she respected money for what it could accomplish; she never indulged herself in extravagances.

What really occupied her mind in these years was the unexpected joy of her college experience. Vassar proved to be a good choice for her. It was in the midst of beautiful rural surroundings—the sort of landscape she loved—just outside Poughkeepsie, in the middle of orchard country. Two crystal-clear lakes were close by. The unpaved back roads were perfect for bicycle rides or walks, often to the local hangout, the Cider Mill, where students ate doughnuts and drank cider made from Dutchess County apples. In the spring, asparagus from the college gardens was served so frequently, students wondered if it had been endowed by some benefactor.

Polly explored the countryside on long, usually solitary walks. Her letters to her parents had both rhapsodic descriptions and meticulous observations of all she saw: the changing seasons, the flowers, the trees, and always the birds. She had brought along her bird traps, little wire traps with a weighted door with bait inside, and had plenty of opportunities to use them. She described six cock pheasants on a half-dead cedar tree, "each red head glowing with reflected radiance," the cedar tree itself "a fantastic candleholder;" the clear marks in the snow made by pheasants' wings and tails; "about seventy-five meadowlarks playing tag over the frost-whitened hockey field. The spruce tree to the west was home, but no bird stayed there very long for it was a beautiful morning and all were ready for fun." Never squeamish, she wrote, "Another treat was the sight of a young northern shrike which killed an English sparrow within twenty feet of me, as I banded the third chickadee of the day."

She also often walked to the college's farm, which until 1954, when an efficiency expert called it impractical, was the source of a third of the food consumed by the campus community—milk, eggs, fowls, pork, and most vegetables. She would "snoop around the barns," talk to the farmers about what they were planting, "taking adventures as they came." She even wrote her parents about the content of the pigs' meals: "the husks of cauliflower from supper and orange skins from breakfast."

She often slept on the dorm roof and, as she had in Brooklyn, watched the night sky. "I certainly enjoy being able to look clean up to the stars whenever I open my eyes, and in the mornings to see the birds flying over almost due South," she wrote her parents. Sometimes, to clear her head while studying for an exam, she'd stand on her head for a different perspective on things and, as she put it, get the blood flowing in the right direction.

Even though she continued in some of her familiar habits, in many ways Polly reinvented herself at college, becoming less the solitary intellectual and more the gregarious participant. She joined the hockey team. She took part in all the silly college events and sentimental ceremonies. She urged her parents to come to the ice carnival. "It's one of the best customes we have. Everyone has such a thoroughly good time—food, bonfire, band, bright lights, bright clothes!" (Polly's spelling continued to be her own.)

She wrote them about the departing seniors serenading juniors in their dormitory, even about the most sentimental ritual of all: the Daisy Chain, Vassar's defining graduation ceremony in which a foot-wide chain of daisies was carried on the shoulders of students who had been specially chosen for this honor. Even though Polly knew she would never be one of the chosen few, and, in fact, thought it was a silly custom, she collected her share of daisies. "Institutions have all sorts of silly things they do," she said years later. "You save protests for the important stuff."

She took on a series of responsibilities that were far from her usual interests. She became the fire chief, in charge of organizing fire drills, junior class treasurer, business manager of the yearbook, one of the organizers of the junior prom and Founder's Day. She believed she got a great deal out "of the experience of directing fairly large groups of people when the work to be done was difficult and tedgious."

During her sophomore year she attended a country auction to get some props for a play and a curious incident occurred. Polly described the scene to her parents with distaste. "The humanity represented was of the lowest type," she wrote, "many of them maimed and crippled." It is one of the few examples, either in her writings or in her treatment of people, of her recoiling from those she perceived to be in unfortunate circumstances.

Most important, for the first time she found real friends. Freshman year she shared a mailbox with Mary Lee Hutchins, called Leal, a "golden girl" as Polly described her—a great beauty, an avid tennis player, appreciated and admired by everyone—who was also a serious intellectual and an excellent student. (She graduated Phi Beta Kappa.) Leal's family background was similar to Polly's. She had grown up in a Boston suburb and attended private school. Her father was a doctor and her mother, one of the first nursing students trained at Johns Hopkins. Polly even took Leal with her into the woods, sharing moments that, ordinarily, she much preferred to enjoy alone. In one of her journals she described the two of them watching a storm and some birds: "Leal & I standing, silent and gazing one to the west, one to the east, were lost in the wildness." At the end of freshman year Polly was "utterly amazed" when Leal suggested they room together. They were roommates throughout their Vassar years and friends for life.

Leal was Polly's passport to a whole group of intelligent, lively, socially adept young women. Without Leal's endorsement, Polly didn't think they would have noticed her. One of this group, Eliza Janeway, said many years later, "Polly wasn't the sort of person who made an impression on you immediately. It took Leal to figure out there was a lot there besides what met the eye."

Polly threw herself into her new friendships with the same energy and enthusiasm she brought to everything else, but Leal remained the center of her circle. When Leal was elected president of the class, Polly had a party for her. When Leal received a food parcel from home, Polly set up an elaborate treasure hunt, hiding things all over the dorm. When Leal was chosen for the Daisy Chain, Polly celebrated.

Among her new friends were some who were able to introduce her to a somewhat different standard of elegance from what she had been accustomed to. The day after her senior prom, the Harvard escort of one of her friends invited twenty-four of them to his family's Rhinebeck estate, where they had a complete Sunday dinner served by "I don't know how many people." On another occasion one of her roommates took a group to the family mansion in Greenwich where, although none of the family was at home, "everything was prepared to perfection for us, flowers artistically arranged, the swimming pool full," and the butler, Stanley, in attendance. In her letters to her parents Polly described these excursions with her customary precision, but without either envy or excitement. She just enjoyed the occasions, the easy camaraderie, the pleasure of friends' company.

Her enjoyment of the social side of life surprised her. She told her parents about junior prom in great detail, describing gowns—her own and other people's—and decorations and even the "beautiful light yellow roses in lavender violets" brought to her by her escort. "So with everything else patched and pressed, I hope you will realize that yours truly, while laughing up her sleeve, is doing a good job of prom. But everything has limits." Then she added—"(She refuses to wear gloves.)" Finally she expressed considerable surprise that she had so much fun.

But she never became totally caught up in the social scene. In her sophomore year she wrote a letter to her brother Gardner about the junior prom. "It is funny to watch all the professionally bored ones revive under the male influence."

And her reputation as a maverick prevailed. Toward the end of her senior year, she wrote her parents that the president of the college had mentioned at some gathering that "last year while sitting in the balcony and observing junior prom, he had asked a junior in overalls why she hadn't gone to the prom. She said, 'The marshes were the most beautiful things to be seen at that time of year.' At this, ten seniors burst out with, 'but Polly *was* at the junior prom.' So that's the kind of rut one gets pushed into just because one has an interest a little different than the majority."

Although she had the reputation of caring nothing about how she looked or dressed, her letters to her mother were filled with descriptions of clothes she bought, dresses she needed sent from home, shoes that had to be dyed, hats that matched coats. She may only have been reassuring her mother that she was looking presentable, or trying to discourage her from sending more clothes, which her mother did with regularity. Often they were much too big. Often Polly didn't like them. The subject of clothes was part of a continuing tug-of-war she had with her mother, who always wanted Polly to be more fashionable, more conventional.

Polly would never expend the time and energy on her appearance that other Vassar students did. They spent hours sunbathing (some even in the nude) suffering because they didn't want a line between the tan and the skin. Polly observed that late-spring ritual with detached amusement informing her parents, "this place has gone absolutely kuku. Ever since the sun came out to stay, everyones efforts and conversations have been relative to the color of their skins. Any poor soul who, like myself, has confined herself to the library, is a sickly object to be pitied."

In spite of her impatience with some of her fellow students, Polly recognized that Vassar was a good place for her. From its first year the college offered courses in astronomy, philosophy, physiology, physics, chemistry, botany, zoology, and mathematics. Henry Noble Mac-Cracken, Vassar's president from 1915 to 1946, concluded that "Few colleges for men could at the time offer an equal basis in science." In 1911 "major fields in bacteriology, anthropology, sociology, comparative literature and archaeology were begun."[4]

MacCracken was a visionary educator, a Chaucer and classics scholar, who once played Theseus in Greek for a college production of *Hippolytus*. He had progressive ideas, believing in the ability of people to make a better world. He wanted Vassar women to become better citizens and improve the quality of life in their communities. He and his wife founded Poughkeepsie's only settlement house in 1918 and kept it going throughout the Depression.

Unlike most of his contemporaries, MacCracken made students his main concern, maintaining that they "were not pieces of wood and metal, but people." "When I came to Vassar," he wrote to an alumna, "I found everywhere throughout the college an attitude towards students as though they were inmates of a corrective institution of some kind. . . . You could not imagine how difficult it was to remove the attitude from our staff."[5]

He was accessible. Without warning he would drop in for lunch with students, or would come over to the dorm in the evenings to have coffee and sing Kentucky ballads. He and his wife had at-homes, where he would often sit on the floor and talk to students. By her senior year Polly didn't wait for these formal gatherings to drop in on the man she called "Prexy." One afternoon, during one of these impromptu visits, she and Leal "had a fine discussion of all sorts of college problems," she wrote her parents, "comparing conditions here with those abroad, in the west, in 15th century Europe etc. etc. It is certainly a treat to talk with anyone who has so thoroughly domesticated their knowledge."

Polly enjoyed the MacCrackens and the president recognized her capabilities. He supported her interest in birds, giving her complete authority over a bird sanctuary she set up on college property. He encouraged her to work with a group of Poughkeepsie boys who had established their own birding club, and he sent her state reports on birds to prepare for their instruction. He allowed her to set up her bird traps outside his kitchen window. Sometimes she took Cady MacCracken, the president's seven-year-old son, with her on her bird walks. Cady, who was the same age as Polly's younger brother, David, shared her interest and she was lonesome for little kids.

Her bird-watching took on new, academic rigor. Her sophomore year she convinced a Vassar professor to work with her to set up a bird-banding station with feeders. She wanted to see if a flock would fly faster as it approached the station and documented that its habits did change.

As her college years progressed, her academic work assumed more and more importance. Ideas were what interested her; the more difficult, the more enthusiastically she embraced them. She discovered Einstein's theories her sophomore year and determined to spend the summer learning more, writing her parents that she intended "to get about ten good books on relativity for this summer and then read and reread them" until she grasped "the significance of his new conceptions. Why should they necessarily be 'above our heads'? . . . There is one thing about reading something you don't understand; it certainly is stimulating. It makes you concentrate, and above all it makes you want to know lots of other things (higher mathematics in my present case.)"

She saw the ways in which she differed from many other students in what she was looking for in her education. She wrote her parents in the second semester of her junior year that most of her contemporaries, excluding Leal and a few other close friends, "are after a certain skill, an array of facts which will help them do something later, not an attitude of life, or a philosophy. They want something to click when Kant is mentioned in the parlor." She determined that "If there is any conclusion to be drawn from this year of organized outside activities, it most certainly is that such executive jobs are for me, absolutely inadequate. I have gotten to the state where I steal away Saturday nights to the libe for recreation. By a process of elimination I resolve upon living the life of a grind, at least next year. (Maybe.)"

She structured her life carefully, writing out detailed schedules guaranteeing that she made use of every minute. She'd be up at 5 A.M. and going strong until 10:30 at night, with time carefully built in for sports and friends. She always had prodigious energy, writing her parents matter-of-factly that while her date for the junior prom slept away the morning she had checked her bird traps and completed her German homework before joining him for breakfast.

Most important, her studies led her to what she thought would be her life's work. She had come to Vassar knowing she wanted to focus on the sciences, but not knowing which one. She began by majoring in physics, because she considered it basic, but realized fairly quickly that it wasn't a congenial discipline for her. She began botany her sophomore year, but it wasn't until she hit on bacteriology her junior year that she became convinced that she had found her future. Years later she recalled some of her early exhilaration: "The more I learned about what was and wasn't known about microorganisms the surer I became that this field was at the right stage for me, that there were problems here that fascinated me, that I wanted to tackle. . . ."[6] "There were hundreds of species of microorganisms, each with extraordinary capabilities, each exhibiting distinctive behavior. How did they manage to make sugars and proteins and fats if they were merely globs of undifferentiated protoplasm? How did they multiply so fast? They were supposed to be just tiny little bits of gel, they weren't even supposed to have nuclei when I was in college, and yet there were hundreds, thousands of species each of which could reproduce itself. It didn't make sense unless they had quite complicated internal structures."[7]

Her discovery of bacteriology was one of the defining events of Polly's life. It was not just that she found it intriguing, but that it introduced her to the essential purpose of science: the challenge of formulating questions for which there are, as yet, no answers. Years later, she said, "The living cell presented an area of ignorance that seemed to me particularly annoying and intriguing. The notion that a tiny bagful of unorganized freely interacting materials could reproduce itself every half-hour, indefinitely, complete with untold carbohydrates, fats, proteins, purines, pyrimidines, enzymes, co-enzymes, and genetic mechanisms, seemed too incredible to let alone. Furthermore, there were obviously thousands and thousands of different kinds of microorganisms, each with its characteristic kind of behavior. Nothing seemed quite so necessary as trying to find out something more about how all of this was accomplished."[8]

These questions never stopped interesting her. But between junior and senior year she experienced a crisis, triggered, apparently, by some acute eye problems. She had been complaining of difficulties with her eyes since freshman year, but in her junior year the situation became serious. As she explained in a letter to her parents, it was caused by "an excess of ultra-violet light given off by the mercury arc used in calibrating and working with the spectroscopes in physics lab."

She revealed the extent of her pain only in her journal, written in the middle of her senior year. It is one of the longest and most introspective reveries anywhere in her many journals, laying out the depth of her misery, her struggles to redefine herself and her aspirations. The entry began, as she often did, with a description of the day and observations about the weather. "The rain has stopped but the sky is heavy with storm clouds which move off to the north like whales rolling off to a new feeding ground. The full notes of an unseen Thrasher shout the gladness of the spring & recall to mind the first Thrasher of two years ago, seen in the early morning of my first day in W. Virginia. . . .

"How much has passed since then. The restlessness of the spring and summer was covered over with the glacier park trip . . . but during the next fall & early winter it grew to a great discontent.

"Work was easy & not too successful. To be sure there was bacteriology & a certain almost unrealized joy suffused any room containing just me & Zinsser[9] but against this was the command: 'know that if you want to be happy, you must pick a job not demanding eye work.'"

After that discouraging diagnosis, she consulted another doctor who in direct contradiction said, "No amount of eye work will hurt her," but that reassurance was not enough to quiet her doubts about her future. She had never doubted that, whatever she eventually chose to do, it would be intellectually challenging. But now she wasn't so sure. "The important question now was—why go on. I felt that I only went from day to day learning a few facts but gaining no experience. Evidently college had nothing further to offer—moreover it was cramping my style. To have to attend classes was pure waste etc etc—was I the coward to stay just because it would take initiative to get out? No.

"But if not college then what—One thing was certain—only intellectual employment would satisfy in the long run. There were museum & exploration jobs, gardens, horses—" She questioned all her assumptions about herself—her innate abilities, her predispositions. But then she came to understand that her discouragement was only temporary, brought about by her impatience with her progress . . . "and then very slowly the mind staggered thru to this humiliating discovery—It was remarkable that one who had gotten all there was from college ie one who had attained complete independence should feel so limited by this very same college." As she had done so often and would continue to do again and again, Polly broke apart her conundrum into its components.

"Perhaps, then since B was an observed fact, A did not hold. The fault was with my own stage of ignorance—ah. . . . Perhaps after all I did not want an intellectual life?—This was the challenge that turned the scales." Confronting her dissatisfaction guided her to a new understanding of herself. "This brought courage & determination and purpose. The rest was easy. I was not yet ready for advanced work of an independent nature. As a test I would drop all nonacademics & take as difficult a course as possible and cram."

She then outlined what became her senior year schedule—and a demanding schedule it was. She eschewed zoology as too easy. She took embryology instead, and also took calculus, bacteriology, physics, and German. She still permitted herself one hour a day for her birds.

"And believe it or not it worked. All semester, I rose at 5:30 & retired at 10:30 (about)—never relenting cramming, tired but passionately proudly happy. Before in the summer I had often promised this sort of thing but never had had confidence in the promise. And now I had done it—I wasnt a failure—that the work didnt seem too good (marks) was inessential for I knew that I knew it. (15 hrs of A & one B were a pleasant surprise) And with this had come the knowledge sure & sweet as a summer rain on growing corn, that bacteriology was the field for me . . .

"Second semester has been pure bliss. . . . For the first time, I know that there is no hurry, that I am part of a movement from which I can not escape. Being helpless I have no further responsibility other than following my own mind. In this lies my joy & my justification & there is no use or need of explaining either of them to the world. I am only myself & can be no other."

Her spirits further improved when she came up with an idea for a research problem concerning fluorescence. It was a problem she could work on independently, the sort of focused, private work she enjoyed the most. Her mentor, Professor Anne Benton, agreed to be her sponsor for this project during the second semester of her senior year. Polly was ecstatic. She wrote her parents: "Right then and there a little compact was made which whether it results in anything of value to science as a whole or not will certainly not be without value to me." She felt an affinity with Benton, someone with whom she could really talk about whatever was on her mind: life on Mars, the domestic habits of rats, the scientist Michael Faraday, and theories of education.

Her letters to her parents in succeeding months are filled with her excitement over her work. "It is funny how fertile every page of reading I do along this line is compared with physics. The latter I study with pleasure and reproduce when called for but with bac. everything suggests a new experiment which ought to be tried." Between periods of wild enthusiasm, she repeatedly warned her parents and herself that "it may very well lead to a blind alley."

She often said, in her frequent letters home, that her grades weren't all that good, but that she didn't care about them and hoped her family wouldn't either. Nonetheless, contradicting her expressed indifference, she knew to the tenth of a percentage point exactly what her grade-point average was and what average was required to earn honors. In a junior year letter to her sister Winifred, Polly wrote: "Also, may I correct an idea which seems to have permeated you all, ei [Polly's version of ie]—my marks are still way below any possible honors. Even the good ones I got this time could only pull me from 3.33 to 3.46 while honors are about 3.7+ with all sorts of other fancy conditions.

So don't let that worry any of you—any more than it worries me."

When it was over, however, she had done extremely well, elected to Phi Beta Kappa in her junior year, graduating with honors, and earning the largest undergraduate fellowship Vassar offered for graduate studies. And it was not only in science that she was successful. In her senior year her English professor singled out her paper on Shelley, spending nearly an entire class period reading it to the class and telling them it contributed something to the knowledge of Shelley. "I can't wait to read it again myself," Polly commented wryly in a letter home.

As much as she had enjoyed Vassar, she didn't want to linger there for all the graduation ceremonies. She even told her father not to bother coming to graduation, because there wouldn't be anything for anyone of any sense to do and it would be horrendously hot.

4

All Things Seem Visible

Polly's intellectual interests propelled her naturally to graduate school. She wasn't even aware of making a decision. She just knew that's what she would be doing next. She chose the Agricultural College at the University of Wisconsin, in part because her Uncle Mark was a mathematics professor there, in part because she liked the idea of living in the Midwest and being in a state university. Even more important, Wisconsin dealt with bacteriology from the point of view that interested her. "The places I'd heard about in the East seemed to be more interested in what bacteria did than in what they were."[1] She decided to spend the summer at Cornell University to complete a six-week organic chemistry course she thought she needed for her graduate work. Cornell proved to be a happy interlude. She enjoyed what she described as her "loss of identity."

She described the students as "a very mixed lot: a great many foreign men, a great many Jews and some coloreds, greasy grinds, pre-medics ... and a few of the more interesting type of graduate students."

Her social life took off with a vengeance. "Evenings get gayer and gayer," she informed her parents. She was one of only a handful of women in the chemistry labs, and the male students, assuming that she needed their assistance, were eager to provide it. They were always hovering around, and she found their interference amusing if unwelcome. "They offer me all their notes. They invent elaborate plans whereby they can do half of the experiment for me while I do the other half etc. In fact there seems to be only one way to keep them out from under foot, and that is to keep ahead of them. . . . The funny part is that . . . they take each rebuff as a bid to supper. . . . The professor, who is no fool, is having the time of his life, and yesterday when it was my misfortune to break an essential glass tube and when I was offered four others but said I 'refused all substitutes' and went out to make another, the poor man almost died laughing."

On July 12th, after she had been at Cornell barely a week, she wrote her brother Gardner a letter lecturing him on the sensible treatment of women. "When you're going to ask a girl to do something, for heaven's sake, don't spend over 20 minutes beating around the bush. The poor guy I went out with last night made 7 full trips, 4 half trips and I don't know how many starts down the lab before he asked me 'whether I was busy tomorrow night.'" She had discovered she was not an ugly duckling—she definitely was a swan. Nonetheless, she informed her parents that a certain Grace Collins "has been very generous in including me in swimming parties and such like," as if she still did not take friendly invitations for granted.

But there was no slacking off with her academic work. As at Vassar, her schedule was unrelenting, beginning with "good hard study" from 6 to 7:30 A.M. ending at 10 P.M. with more study. She took the first semester of organic chemistry in the mornings and the second in the afternoons, and was to say later that she went too fast. Nonetheless, while she was at Cornell she still found time to conduct some of her own experiments.

It surprised her that, even though she was only a six-week summer student doing elementary work, the bacteriology department was willing to give her materials and space for her experiments. "In half an hour I was able to start an experiment which it would have taken a day or so to prepare for under Vassar lab conditions," she wrote her parents, "to which is added absolute privacy and independence."

At Cornell Polly became even more convinced of her affinity for scientific research. "I've gotten far enough on some of these fool theories so that I can't take anyone's authority, no matter who it is, even tho perfectly aware that they know 10X as much about it and that anyone who listened to me would be the biggest kind of a dumbell."

The opportunity to be in the laboratory, grappling with problems that intrigued her, was totally satisfying. "What fun is there in lying on the floor with a few notes, and a blank pad and just squirming externally and internally until somehow things slip into place. The machine is ready and off you fly to heights from which, for the moment, all things seem visible in their true proportions.... One's pleasure certainly does not arise from any confidence of present or future benefit to oneself or mankind for if there is any universal characteristic of the experience it is the feeling (no it isn't a feeling at all)—it *is* loss of all identity, complete oblivion of self and absorption in the object of contemplation."

In the fall of 1931 she set off for the University of Wisconsin's Agricultural School. The university was overcrowded. Her Uncle Mark's freshman class had increased from 472 the preceding year to over 700. There was a frantic search for instructors, "which is a very novel experience in my academic career," she wrote her parents. "Various federal committees are at work distributing jobs and doles to students, undergraduate and graduate." But Polly's own department was small and academic matters were handled informally.

The science graduate students were a congenial, capable, hardworking group, almost all of them men, many of whom went on to have distinguished careers and one of whom, Edward Tatum, later won a Nobel Prize for his discoveries of how genes control biochemical processes in the living cell. She enjoyed the camaraderie, the easy, friendly social life. The graduate students hung out together, going on picnics and roller-skating, playing mixed tennis doubles, baseball, even hockey, until, she said, the men complained they were too stiff. They played poker and bridge, and greatest fun of all, played games of "murder" after dark in the main building. She didn't think of any of them romantically. "The laboratory is being gradually filled with young men who may emerge, but who, at first glance, appear only too anemic." Eventually, however, she had a succession of attentive male admirers; particularly a musician named George, who showed up in the laboratory with some regularity.

The students at Wisconsin were different from those at Vassar. For the first time in her life Polly was getting to know people who didn't have much money. What they had was a strong commitment to their education. Polly described one of her friends' parents as being "financially down and out" but owning an unusual library of books and music, "which they know how to use."

Her Vassar fellowship was for only her first year of graduate study, but for her second year she was awarded a Wisconsin University fellowship in agricultural bacteriology. Nonetheless, she had less money than she had had at Vassar, and in her letters to her parents she mentioned finances more than she ever had before. She let them know when $25 would help in paying her rent, explained in detail why she spent $32.50 for a "practically new" Remington typewriter, and repeatedly asked for permission to buy a car, which would enable her to go birding in the mornings. She often told them that she couldn't possibly come home for vacations, and urged them instead to come and see her. She was aware that the Depression was beginning to have an impact on them. In a birthday letter to her father, Polly expressed her hopes that business conditions would improve the next year so that he could enjoy it. She worried about their working too hard and urged them to take some vacations, suggesting things that didn't have to cost too much. She was well aware that she had three younger siblings in college or on their way.

In many ways Polly's more than four years in Madison were years of expanding social awareness. She had always been open and curious about the world. Now she became more conscious of political and economic conditions. These conditions were becoming impossible to ignore. Evidence of the Depression was everywhere. After the bank closing on March 6, 1933, Polly wrote home that many stores were accepting farm produce in payment of bills and barter, not wages, was the payment offered in newspaper want ads.

The antisemitic developments in Germany appalled her. "Did you note in this week's *Science*," she wrote her parents, "that 26 Jewish professors have been dismissed from leading German universities on April 25—including Franck & Freundlich—making a total of 42 well known scholars who have lost their positions. . . . Good Lord! And so many here sympathise with these measures!"

She began to question the efficacy of capitalism, which she likened to a dinosaur that needed fuel to survive when all fuel had disappeared during the Ice Age. Identifying herself as a socialist, she asked her Republican father, "Of what use is personal strength to a hungry dinosaur? About as much as ambition to succeed today is to a man who is out of work. Then why preserve it in this form?" She teased her mother about speaking to the DAR, saying they would not have invited her to speak had they known her daughter was a "rabid socialist because they wouldn't understand any other kind."

She had one experience her first year that she recounted over and over throughout her life, which she credited with teaching her something vitally important about public education and its obligations. A farmer came into the laboratory one day with questions about why his calves were dying. He asked directions to the office of Professor Hastings. Polly told him where the office was, and was then confronted by a fellow graduate student who admonished her. "That man is what you at Vassar would call a Trustee. You don't *send* him to Professor Hastings, you *take* him there." He meant that a public university, unlike a private college, had the obligation to respond to the concerns of all citizens. Polly said she flew out the door, escorted the farmer to the professor's office, and was invited to stay while the professor analyzed the samples the farmer had brought with him and answered his questions.

She developed new interests. She went to lectures by Carl Sandburg, painter Grant Wood, and Frank Lloyd Wright. She saw Walter Hampden perform *Cyrano* three times, heard the Madison Civic Orchestra perform the *Messiah*, and heard Maurice Chevalier even though she had to ask her brother David who he was. She kept up her interest in birds. She described for her parents "one of the finest duck spectacles" she had ever encountered when "two splendid black and white golden-eyes" battled one another for some five minutes, time she actually monitored with a watch, describing the whistling note raised by their wings. It was, she said, "one of the most prolonged battles which I have ever seen between two animals which were neither backed by human ambitions nor hunting food."

In the course of her graduate school years Polly had another confrontation with her formidable mother. They had a disagreement over Sinclair Lewis' feisty heroine, Ann Vickers, that was more than literary. Ann, who shared Polly's social conscience and unconventional feminist attitudes, also engaged in some free sexual behavior that shocked Polly's mother. "Do I remember you're saying that you considered Ann Vickers a vulgar woman?" Polly queried. "Sometimes your conception of 'vulgarity' scares me. At least I must confess that I would consider Ann an unusually fine woman and incidentally believe the book to be the best which Sinclair Lewis has accomplished, excepting always *Arrowsmith*. He is conducting a campaign which is more than merely destructive, against the one personal sin that truly disgusts me—hypocrisy."

And then there were her clothes. This issue never disappeared. It was as if Polly and her mother were continually doing battle over Polly's childhood question of what kind of girl she was going to be. Now Polly's lack of money gave her mother the excuse she needed to keep on sending the clothes Polly didn't want. In the first years Polly tried to be polite. "The clothes arrived—thank you Mother. I seem to have about four evening dresses and very little occassion to wear any of them. The white dress will prove useful." But her impatience grew, although not until she was nearly twenty-five and in her final year of graduate school did Polly directly tackle this contentious issue. She finally sent a stern letter, exhorting her mother to stop, once and for all, sending all this stuff. "Let us consider the facts." Polly then listed six "facts"—beginning with her mother's "right and privelege" to give gifts, but explaining that often the gifts are not needed. "You see we are emotionally ashamed of excess property." Fact 5 was perhaps the most important. "When we are stocked by you, we can not enjoy the experience of getting things for ourselves. In certain cases—especially sport clothes—this is a considerable deprivation. It means that when we see 'the perfect outfit' in a window, we cant even try it on because we have too many unworn out clothes at home."

She then suggested a compromise—asking her mother only to send clothes "once in a great while" when she sees something "very extraordinary." But not even this letter could settle the issue once and for all.

In between bouts of exasperation, Polly had episodes of resignation. "OK—on the clothes situation. I guess we both understand each other. If you can't get rid of the red & white striped one, I can make it do, as I said before." She finally decided that sending occasional bulletins was the better part of valor. "Mother, did I tell you that I had my heavy white woolen skirt dyed. It is now a beautiful wine-red and with it I wear a new silk blouse, wine-red with white polka dots. I mention this mostly to protect your pocketbook the next time it is tempted in my behalf." "Tiffanies, the store you liked Mother, had a slashing sale today. I got a good looking one piece everyday dress and a print which is rather dressy and can be worn to teas etc thru the spring as well as now. Also a pair of every day shoes. (Seal skin). So, Mother, resist all temptations that you may encounter. My wardrobe is absolutely complete with the possible exception of an evening dress. and *please* dont buy one of those in my absence." But it didn't end there; they never stopped tangling over this issue.

In her second year Polly took a room with a family, which she preferred to the more sterile graduate student digs. "I do enjoy living so comfortably," she wrote her mother. "I enjoy studying in a comfortable chair by the fireplace with a nice platter of grapes from the garden beside me. I enjoy the mixture of ages which you get even in a small family, and miss in a graduate school, and I enjoy meeting many of the Blankenships friends. To be quite frank, I also enjoy Mrs. B's surprise and gratitude at finding the boarder which she dreaded, a welcome addition to the family."

Much as she enjoyed graduate school, Polly was impatient to get on with her own work, to begin structuring experiments to test her own hypotheses and answer her own questions. She understood, however, that she had entered a new world with different stakes and sensibilities and that she had to be careful. She told her parents that "a big shot" had published findings she disagreed with, and although she didn't doubt the accuracy of her evidence, "I'm not going to publish a statement which will antagonize the big shot and everyone else who has been teaching his gospel,—until I'm absolutely, positively sure I'm right."

Her own ideas beckoned her, and she was also impatient with the courses she was required to take. She had never been very tolerant of college professors—even of elementary and secondary school teachers —who demanded a regurgitation of facts, which she found childish and uninteresting. There was one exception, Professor Karl Link, who wanted his students to be well educated and culturally knowledgeable not only about bacteriology but also about art and music. She had harsh assessments of her other graduate school professors. "One could stand a lot," she wrote her parents, "if they were only good at what they profess. Now a golf professional or an actor may not be an admirable person, but he probably knows a good bit about golf, or acting, but many professors not only are insipid people but they are ignorant and stupid. Moreover, there is no one to tell them so, or to warn their students. This is called academic freedom."

Her real education, she felt, came from her fellow graduate students, who challenged and questioned one another. "Those were the examinations that counted, (she wrote years later) also the best instruction, leading on to probing discussions by means of which we each developed our ideas. . . . I did wonder, sometimes, whether the other women graduate students sensed the excitement that I and many of the men took for granted, ill-defined as it was."[2] Polly welcomed this sense of camaraderie among the graduate students and her feeling of being accepted by her male peers. At Vassar she had encountered a different reaction, an awareness that some men were uncomfortable with a woman they saw as smarter than themselves. She had been friends with a Haverford ornithologist, whose company she had enjoyed on many weekends and bird walks. But when he asked her what she majored in and she said physics, "he got a funny look on his face and said he got a D in physics. I remember thinking that was the end of this friendship," Polly said many years later.

Despite her feelings of contempt for many of the faculty, her fellow graduate students turned to her for help in dealing with them. The students asked her to represent the Agricultural College on a committee to ensure that further retrenchment by the administration would be done as wisely as possible. They also looked to her continuously to intervene with their difficult senior professor and ultimately dean, Dr. Edwin Fred. They started calling her Joseph because she could interpret the pharaoh's dreams. She wrote her mother that she felt like a social worker. Fred used her, too, as something of a go-between, helping him to figure out what was going on in the graduate school. At one point he gave her a questionnaire on living conditions. "He wanted to take an unofficial census, and thought that the best method of getting a quick cross-section of the community would be for me to put the sheets on our living room table, and let anyone fill one out who came to the house. So maybe I better not try to tell you how hard I'm working etc. etc.—Evidently that is not the impression I leave with our dean."

Her impatience with the faculty and her desire to pursue her own work led her to push aggressively for permission to finish her course work for the degree in fewer than the usually required three years. She was well prepared in bacteriology, but she was less well prepared in chemistry, physics, and math. Nonetheless, she managed to talk her way out of many courses, and to complete her course work in just one year. She completed her dissertation and her oral defense at the end of 1933, when she was twenty-three years old.

Professor Fred evidently had a higher opinion of her than she had of him. At the start of only her second year, he pressured her to give a major paper, based on her master's thesis on inhibiting the reproduction of bacteria, at the December 1932 meeting of the Society of American Bacteriologists in Ann Arbor. Polly had misgivings, because she felt the work was incomplete. "But," she wrote her parents, "if he persists it would be very bad to refuse—especially as he is president of the Society this year. His wishes, however, just don't rate beside the work itself—so we'll continue to refuse to commit ourselves—a state which can be maintained until about the 5th of November." Nonetheless, she worked feverishly to get the work finished to her own satisfaction. "Work is slow but we hope honest. I am full of good resolves about not doing carelessly the experiment which should be done carefully, and not doing in elaborate detail the experiment which should be merely a rough approximation previous to further attacks. Why are people so dumb? Why must people eat oatmeal?"

"The main trouble is that the stuff I'm doing now has to be looked at often during at least twenty hours, so that it is hard to work in enough sleep. So far I've neglected the work for the sleep with disastrous results as my inconclusive data—tonight reviewed—amply illustrate. For the next two weeks I'll start a stagger system—stay up tonight late—go to bed tomorrow very early etc. etc."

The weeks leading up to the meeting were intense. Except for one evening at a basketball game, her days went from 8:00 A.M. until about 11:30 P.M. "with 2 hours out at supper time. The rest is pure lab work—cutting most classes etc, but getting results, and having a splendid time."

Years later, Polly's own assessment of that work was very critical. "The theory behind it was attractive and the first experiments supported it. Some of the later experimental results were ambiguous but at that time I had less confidence in my laboratory techniques than in the theory: less interest, I'm afraid, in the 'truth' than in the approval with which the work was greeted. I did not realize this clearly at the time but never again published preliminary results prematurely."[3] About twenty-five people from her department went to the meeting. "Everybodies just whetting their appetite to see me taken for a ride—if I can believe them—and you can—about half way."

Her paper attracted considerable attention. The editor of the

Journal of Bacteriology, who was also head of the Yale bacteriology department, told Polly he had never heard a better paper by a young student and asked that his journal be allowed to publish the paper, which it did the following year. Dr. Leslie Webster of the Rockefeller Institute asked to see her, "saying that he was interested not in what I had done, but in what I planned to do next. Had I ever thought of working at the Rockefeller Institute etc, etc." She was ecstatic.

But in the days following the meeting she thought about the real importance of what she had experienced. At first, she admitted, foremost in her mind was all the praise she received. But barely a few days later, she was thinking more about the shoddiness of much of the work and the pomposity of many of the experts. "In retrospect," she wrote her parents, "the meetings leave rather a bad taste. The transient effects of flattery having worn off, one reviews them in the light of common day, and can not but be disgusted with the sloppiness of most of the reports, and of the work which they describe. In the first place, most reports are merely a little 'additional data'—in the whole meeting one encounters only one or two new ideas, only one or two nice pieces of synthesis. Now 'additional data' is all very well, if recognized as such, but the trouble is that the average student who has collected a little, feels that he has a piece of research and is ready to pass on. He makes little attempt to relate it to the whole, thereby often overlooking the significance of his own conclusions. The result is a mass of inarticulate if not apparently conflicting findings. New hypothesis are tested not by a logically consistent structure of previously discovered facts, but by whether Dr. So & So agrees or disagrees."

Polly still wanted what she had wanted a year before—the opportunity to pursue her own research. "I want to go somewhere where I can do about three years work without being bothered by any short-time ambitions—moreover I now know exactly what piece of work I want it to be. If that R [Rockefeller] offer comes—" Though she was wary of being unrealistically optimistic, she still concluded that all the attention afforded her meant that "I may be able to choose pretty much what I want for next year."

She returned to Madison with high hopes and immediately plunged back into her work. She had no more required courses, but she decided to audit a course in pathology, which she thought she would need especially for the Rockefeller job. It proved to be a fortuitous decision. Another student in the course was Henry Bunting, and his father was the professor.

When they met, Henry was a second-year medical student. He had grown up in Madison, the son of two doctors. He had New England grandparents on both sides of his family. His maternal grandparents were from Bangor, Maine, where his grandmother had been a musician and his grandfather practiced medicine for fifty-seven years. Family lore has it that Henry's mother told her father she was going to be a nurse and he responded, "If you are determined to do a damn fool thing like that, for heaven's sake, be a doctor." She went to medical school at Johns Hopkins, which was where she met Henry's father. Henry's paternal grandfather was a Connecticut farmer and educator, who founded a school, but then was stricken with tuberculosis and settled in Wisconsin for his health. Both of Henry's paternal grandparents were enthusiastic naturalists and communicated this love to Henry.

And it was this enthusiasm that led Henry to Polly. One of his friends, observing that both of them kept bird glasses in their cars, decided they should be introduced.

Soon after, Polly began referring to Henry in so many letters that finally her mother responded with thinly disguised exasperation: "Of course I am interested in the birds thee is banding, but who is this Henry Bunting?" Polly responded, "Among your complaints of late, I remember one (very nicely expressed) to the effect that descriptions of Henry Bunting were not as detailed as descriptions of the pin feathers of the geese. Did you not think that the fact, in itself, was significant?

"He is just over 6 ft—very slender—somewhat stooped, wears his hair almost cropped & is rather puckish looking. Dresses quite carefully—and is rather particular about little courtesies—eg—if we are going birding Sunday afternoon, he always telephones about 10 min before he calls for me. This is not done to the exclusion of spontaneous visits, upon other occassions (etc), when calling up would be inconvenient.

"His room is very much like Daves—all full of pictures & things. Tool bench–tennis stringing outfit, beetle collections, bird books etc. etc. etc. He plays the flute—likes good music. He is devoted to his slightly older sister who is now married, and living in New Haven. She too was a junior phi bete etc etc—in Greek & Latin & comp lit. In fact Dr, Mrs, Henry & Elizabeth all use a Greek dictionary with facility and frequency.

"He is a quiet, kindly sort—very well liked by his classmates in spite of his interests, and his superior scholarship, and his general abstinence. How's that?" No one ever thought she did wrong in marrying him.

By the end of 1935, she and Henry—although never officially "engaged"—had made plans to cast in their lots together. His sister, Elizabeth, referred to their understanding as "the situation" between them, saying she understood she was not allowed to use the word "engagement." She just wanted to know what books Polly had so that she wouldn't give Henry any duplicates for Christmas—unless Polly preferred that she give him slips of paper marked, "This is good for a saucepan set in 1937." Henry left Wisconsin in September of 1934 to go to Harvard for his last two years of medical school. His departure only made Polly more determined to finish her degree with dispatch.

Despite her lively social life and her serious romance, her professional work never stopped being central. After the Ann Arbor meeting, she spent several months refining and rewriting her paper and getting it ready for publication in the *Journal of Bacteriology*. At the same time she embarked on a different strand of research with a graduate student in chemistry, Carl Baumann, into the properties of carotin, a substance chemically related to Vitamin A. She and Baumann were trying to answer a number of questions related to the synthesis and production of carotin by bacteria, questions of particular interest to one of the senior professors, Harry Steenbock. He was in a position to get money for further investigations, so Polly spent the spring of 1933 deciding whether or not she was sufficiently interested to pursue this research. She recognized that it made practical sense since she worked well with Baumann, Steenbock supplied excellent equipment, she had already done a lot of work, and "some of the uninteresting parts embrace techniques which its high time I encountered." She eventually decided to turn the carotin studies into her Ph.D. dissertation and to postpone the other work that interested her more. She was only twenty-two years old, not always as diplomatic as she later became, and couldn't always resist pushing her own point of view. When she found herself in what she called a "high powered" carotin conference with the two senior professors, Fred and Steenbock, she informed her parents that "Polly kept forgetting herself as usual and telling her betters how stupid were most of their ideas. Some people never learn."

She spent the spring of 1933 doing "the manual work of preparing media, inoculating cultures, harvesting crops, & recording data . . . but its seldom indeed that research proceeds so smoothly. The point is that the field is practically unexplored & Baumann has his technique in excellent shape as he has been studying carotin for two or three years. We shall probably carry along all these lines of research for a while—working on one problem while bacteria & rats grow for another."

Between 1933 and 1935 she published four papers; her doctoral dissertation, one with Baumann, Steenbock, and Fred, one just with Baumann and one just with Steenbock. In April 1933 Baumann presented their work to the American Society of Biological Chemists in Cincinnati, and their paper was published in the *Journal of Biological Chemistry* later that year.

She was paid enough as a research assistant to be almost self-supporting. Given the continuing state of the economy, this mattered to her.

Her parents were concerned that by agreeing to the carotin research she was allowing herself to be taken advantage of by the professors and was not pursuing her own work, which would be more likely to get her a position. Polly assured them she wasn't going to allow the research to drag on, and if it did she saw no reason why she couldn't drop it at the end of the 1933 summer. But, she told them, "plans must be adapted to work, not work to plans (within limits)."

Professor Fred advised her to try for fellowships at Yale, Harvard, or Chicago, saying that there was much to be gained academically by finishing up her work at another institution. But he was giving her mixed signals, saying one day that if she wanted the fellowship at Yale, "letters should be written almost immediately," but then postponing her predoctoral exams so that she began to worry that trying to get anything for the 1934–1935 year would be impossible. "Incidentally you will be amused to know that Fred approached me with 'You did take alot of stuff like philosophy didn't you?' because Clark said your bacteriology was all right but did you have any culture? I told him you'd had all that in college—but if you'll make out a list of those courses, I'll just give it to Clark."—"So I made a list to prove I took culture in college."

By the beginning of 1934, when she was not quite twenty-four years old, she had her Ph.D. in hand. It had taken only two and a half years from start to finish. The date, Polly said years later, "had special significance to fellow graduate students: it was the first doctoral degree we knew about that was awarded after the full repeal of prohibition." So they celebrated by "someone trying to improve the ambient air with a nasal spray loaded with gin. Eventually the police, prodded by annoyed neighbors, gave us a very helpful warning telephone call and the party broke up."[4] Not surprisingly, it was one of the details of graduate school life that Polly didn't include in any of her many letters to her parents.

While she continued as a research assistant working twelve to fifteen hours a day, she was also seriously looking for jobs. She did not want to stay in Madison; and since she continued to receive appreciative comments about the Ann Arbor paper, she kept hoping that a job offer was not too far away.

She was aware that jobs were scarce for everyone, men as well as women. When one of her colleagues was fortunate enough to get one, everyone rejoiced. She wrote her mother asking for help for a friend. "Janet is a thoroughly competent secretary, as well as a decidedly better-than-average-tho-not-brilliant bacteriologist. Dr. Nerke doesn't need anyone, does he? or any of the other hospitals with which you are connected. Enough money to live on is requisite.... Teaching jobs are almost hopeless these days." Her roommate, another doctoral candidate, began taking education courses "inorder to be equipt to teach in a state high school—anything for a job. Betke has landed herself an excellent technicians job at the P & S in N.Y."

Nevertheless, Polly believed she had reason to be hopeful and kept receiving tantalizing bits of encouragement. The chair of the Yale bacteriology department contacted her, saying that although he had no current openings for research assistants he hoped eventually she would come to Yale. Another hopeful sign, she wrote her mother, was "2 new jobs for chemists. One got a job last week, and another was approached today. The news has spread quickly among our group of perplexed souls, and everyone is feeling much happier."

In another letter to her mother she wrote: "I heard of a splendid job in the east for the year after next and thereafter. My informant says that those in charge have been considering me, and that they have promised to come to Madison this summer to see me. My informant is quite confidential, but I can say that its just the type of job I would want."

She kept up her letters to her parents; she knew they were anxiously awaiting news. "About the hypothetical job. You see 'the people' haven't contacted me directly as yet—if they ever will. But its at Wellesley. The head of the Bacty and Botany depts retires in about another year. They want a bacteriologist to take her place. They wish to keep the bacteriologist in charge of the department. Facilities for research seem to be good and of course summers are free. Presumably they are coming west to see me this summer. But you musnt say a word to anyone!!"

Then came another possibility that looked even more promising. "Letter from Miss Benton says she is getting married to a widower with a 15-year old daughter." Women's colleges didn't permit female faculty members to be married so Benton was leaving. "Now don't go jumping to conclusions. This does not mean a job at Vassar. They will undoubtedly ask the girl who did so well in Miss Benton's place last year. She is in line, and I happen to know that Miss Benton doesn't think I would be any good as a teacher. I disagree with her, but put more weight in her opinion than in my own." Polly made light of Benton's assessment, but it must have hurt, since she had worked so closely with Benton while she was an undergraduate, had admired her, and had even roomed with her at the Ann Arbor meeting. None of this prevented Polly, years later, from paying tribute to Anne Benton's bacteriology course when, as president of Radcliffe, she delivered a major address to the American Society for Microbiology.

Henry came home for the summer, and Polly kept on with her work for Steenbock.

He encouraged her "to publish the paper in the English journal *The Biochemical Journal*, which is very nice because that is undoubtedly the most widely read biochemical publication in the world. I hope that we can send it off this week."

At the start of 1936 Polly was still in Madison, continuing with the carotin research. In spite of Benton's lack of encouragement, Polly believed she had reason to hope that the Vassar job would come through. MacCracken notified her Wisconsin professors that she was being considered, which they interpreted as an announcement of her appointment. She knew better and waited through January for official word, sending frequent updates to her parents. "As yet there is no word from Prexy. Now I must stop and write Prexy to tell him that things can be managed from this end."

"Still no word from Prexy. I imagine that Miss Roberts did not get back until this Monday and that I shall hear tomorrow. This morning when I went to the lab to give Steenbock the fruits of yesterday's writing, I found that he had told everyone of my job, so I guess there is no doubt about it from this end. I wish Prexy's letter would come so that *all* doubt would be removed."

"If I dont hear from Prexy on Monday, I shall notify him of the fact."

Five days later a telegram finally arrived. Despite all the assurances and assumptions, the job was not offered to her. It was one of the few occasions when Polly permitted herself to express real discouragement. "I cant tell you how sorry I am," she wrote her parents. "Prexy's telegram came last night. The delay was due to stupidity on the part of the local office, not of the college. (You remember that I wired Prexy Tuesday morning)." She said Prexy was still hopeful for the next year. Her mother was furious, feeling Prexy had "let her down," but Polly sprang to his defense. "The fault is with my enthusiasm, not his."

Despite Webster's encouragement both before and after the Ann Arbor meeting, he never came through with a job offer at the Rockefeller Institute either. The Wellesley job didn't materialize. There were some tentative inquiries from Bennington, but then "a very wishy-washy letter from Leigh arrived Monday—so that's that. Perhaps it will work another year. Yale doesnt interest me because the equipment for my work would be so limited. The wise thing undoubtedly seems to be to stay here, if Steenbock will have me. The work is extremely interesting & promising. Baumann leaves for Europe next year & I'm sort of next in line on the carotene work—the one who has picked up the laboratory details which never get into print. It seems to be the place for me—if they'll have me. I'm sorry, too, in many ways, but believe that the balance lies here."

But then she had second thoughts. Henry was in the East. Her family was in the East. It was cold in Wisconsin. She had a distressing amount of delayed dental work to be done. Her own work wasn't going well; she needed to know more genetics. So she approached Steenbock about leaving. But he said he really wanted her to stay, he had a particular job he wanted done, and had no one else to do it. "So I guess that's that," she wrote her parents stoically. "I shall start work at once.

"Please send me my heavy shoes, my new dresses, and other odds and ends which I may have left home, including my skates."

Her parents, however, telephoned and urged her to come home. She conferred with the chairman of the agricultural bacteriology department who didn't think she could accomplish much on this new project in the semester remaining on her research grant. "This was the decisive advice." She returned to Steenbock, who agreed she could leave.

"I shall stay here until the end of the semester—i.e. about Feb. 1st. In these two weeks I shall study the literature and leave my best analysis of the situation and of promising lines of research."

Her spirits revived. "We had about a foot of snow last night. This afternoon I hope to go skiing altho it will be a bit soft. It will be just my luck to leave Madison the year that all the snow is here and none of it in the east."

"I am having a very busy time taking stock of myself and my future ambitions that I may spend this vacation as enjoyably as possible," she wrote her parents. "I have always felt that things one does when one doesnt have to do anything, are the most important things one ever does. All I ask of you is that you make it easy for me not to *have* to do things. . . . I am most afraid of people and activities. . . . You will understand if my way of life seems unsocial, that it is a matter of self-preservation. Needless to say, I do not consider my family 'people' but rather a part of myself."

She spent the last few days in Wisconsin reading some difficult German articles for Steenbock, saying goodbye to her uncle and aunt, packing up her books to be sent by freight (they guaranteed a five-day service for $1.70 per one hundred pounds.) It was frigid, not getting above zero for days on end. She had her car checked and rechecked, especially its heater, and arranged to drive with a friend, Lee Kline, who was investigating the possibility of a job in Washington. Her parents were worried about her driving across the country in the dead of winter. She did her best to reassure them.

Dear Dear Mother and Dad:—

 Please have some confidence in me!—(Mothers letter has just come asking questions about driving etc.) I think I have answered all of them. Fortuneately Lee is all that you could wish in a companion—he is an excellent driver as I know, having driven to Detroit and back with him. We shall be in no hurry—and do not plan to drive after dark. All this is true—I hope indeed that it will be comforting.

 But stop —treat this question objectively, scientifically (Yes I know one must recognize the strength of emotion—but one can also allow for them)—I am in Madison. I want to go to New York. The direct, sensible way of going is in my car. I take all reasonable precautions—see that the car is in good shape—adjust my plans to weather and so forth—and drive home as intelligently as I can. True there may be some risk—but that need not be a bad thing. It is by overcoming real obstacles and dangers in the course of simple, direct and independent living that one enjoys the privalege of being a young, healthy adult. There is nothing flighty about this trip. No one but you thinks of it as such a difficult undertaking. Are we in this generation to dissipate our abilities only against ridiculous obstacles? Can we know danger only by going skiing, riding to hounds, playing hockey or driving when we are drunk? Of what use is all the physical and mental discipline of my 26 years of education if I can not be trusted in this perfectly reasonable undertaking?

 It is not as tho I am looking for delay or frozen fingers! I have been driving for 6 days with the weather at -20 F—I know something about my problem—and shall behave accordingly. It is not as tho I was travelling by ox cart!—etc etc!

 So if either of you have anything more to say—stop first and answer these questions. What is life about? What makes it worthwhile? And if you can start on a substantial philosophical base—and still fit your excessive concern into the picture—I shall certainly be interested in seeing how you do it.

 I cant help being your capable, independent daughter.
 Believe in me
 And my love.

5

Niches as Well as Nests

Polly's trip east in her little Ford coupe turned out to be a "blizzardy drive." By the time she reached New York she had determined that the best use of this unanticipated free time would be to study genetics, which she believed necessary for her research. Neither the economic state of the country nor her failure to find a job nor the fact that she and Henry had agreed to be married caused her to reconsider her plan to pursue a serious career in scientific research. Other women with firm marriage plans might shelve professional plans, but Polly saw no reason to do that. "Women as well as men want and need their niches as well as their nests," she said years later.[1]

Just as she was settling in to not having a job, she received an unexpected phone call from Bennington, the women's college in Vermont. A family friend, Mrs. Ingersoll, who had been interested in Bennington from its beginnings, heard that the college needed a biologist. Polly had been turned down earlier by Bennington, of course, but a professor had left unexpectedly and now they urgently needed someone to teach the second half of a physiology course and a course in genetics. The second semester was about to start, and they wanted to know if Polly could begin the following Monday, in less than a week. "I had never taken either genetics or physiology," said Polly, "and I told them so. They said they thought 'with my background' I could manage, and I said, 'Well, I had been planning to be in Williamstown for the weekend, where Henry's sister lived, so I guessed I could start Monday.... It was so exciting driving up, not knowing where you were going or who was going to be there and see a whole new world.... It was wonderful to begin in the winter with all that nice snow."

Bennington had opened only four years earlier, and its first class was going to graduate that June. It had grown from its 1932 beginnings of eighty-seven freshmen and nineteen teachers to, by 1935, a student body of 250 and a faculty of fifty. When Polly arrived, it still had what she called "a pioneering zeal."

It was one of several colleges that had come into being as a response to the difficulties that progressive secondary schools were having in placing their graduates in colleges. The schools were teaching adventurous curricula, incorporating learning outside the classroom, but most colleges were still locked into more traditional programs.

Bennington's classes were small, friendly, and informal, never relying on textbooks or secondary sources. It wasn't a Bennington thing to bone up for exams.

It had more flexible criteria than some of the Seven Sisters for admitting students and hiring faculty. The president wanted professors who had life experience outside academia, and who were good teachers.

They also had to serve as advisers, which Polly quickly discovered took an inordinate amount of time. She immediately found herself with a half-dozen officially assigned advisees, but during her first week about twenty-five students dropped in to see her. She complained in a letter home that she couldn't possibly keep them all straight. At one point she had seventy reports to write for students in her class, and eight students whose work she was responsible for documenting in detailed summaries.

The atmosphere, though, was relaxed and informal, which was different from the more traditional women's colleges. When Polly delivered a speech to the Wellesley faculty, she was amused that two faculty members who had worked together in the same department for a great many years still called one another "Miss Snow" and "Miss Lindsey." She found the number of elderly spinsters on the Wellesley faculty stultifying. The Bennington faculty, on the other hand, was young and some were even married.

Bennington had the added advantage of being in beautiful countryside with opportunities for the exploration and sports that Polly loved. She persuaded the authorities to open the tennis courts a day early after a rainstorm, seeing that they had dried and been marked. She coached field hockey, and invited the Williams men to play, which created a mixed team. She took to the Vermont hills for skiing. "Everyday they post on the bulletin board the 'wax for the day,' she wrote her parents. "One begins to wonder whether perhaps one is at Lake Placid."

Her teaching schedule, however, would have been demanding even for an experienced teacher. She taught human biology and physiology for thirty-five students, Monday, Wednesday, and Thursday mornings from 9 to 1; genetics for about ten students, from 2 to 3 Monday afternoons; and bacteriology with about eight students, on Fridays from 9 to 1. She struggled a bit at the beginning, not only preparing for lectures and labs, but also organizing the courses—but she never seriously worried that she had made a mistake in accepting the job. Her convictions about how scientific learning takes place meshed with the Bennington principles of hands-on involvement. When she suspected that she had intestinal worms, she took a sample, looked at them under the microscope, confirmed her diagnosis, and showed one to a student who happened to be in the laboratory.

She told her students frankly about her inadequate preparation, explaining that her background in genetics was, as she put it in a letter to her parents, "very holey." She told them that they would all be learning together and that they needed to find out first what they all already knew. "They didn't think they knew anything, but, on being questioned, discovered that they did know that dogs had dogs and cats had cats. We worked on from there.... Did black cats have black kittens? and so forth."[2]

Given her awareness of her shortcomings, Polly was somewhat startled on the first day of class, when two faculty members asked if they could audit. One was Barbara Jones, an economist whose reputation was known to Polly, and who came to be very important to her later. The other was Julia McCamy, an anthropologist. "They said they had both audited genetics the year before but 'hadn't gotten much out of it.'" Rather than caving in to worry about what they might think of her, Polly instead used their presence as an opportunity to get help with her teaching.

This was a faculty that cared about teaching and talked about it when they met at meals. That cross-fertilization between disciplines was stimulating, and after graduate study in a large university "it was great to live and work in a small college where one could see the poetry books from the science section of the library and get to know creative faculty from other disciplines."[3]

Being a science teacher in a college that was primarily interested in the arts also turned out to have unexpected benefits. Polly had greater freedom: "plenty of input and concern but few specific demands or restrictions," she remembered years later. She had many ideas about how to teach science, and now she had the chance to test them. By the time she left Vassar, Polly had come to believe that the problem with most college science courses was that they did not expose students to the real excitement of science. They were so tied to transferring information about what was already known that they failed to communicate to students the exhilaration of discovery. "I believed that to know what science was about you had to know what scientific research was like and you had to learn that from trying your hand at it.... Learning the names of the bones of the body or how plants utilize light ... may be informative but does not necessarily convey an understanding of scientific methods. This was my opportunity to try to give non-scientists an awareness of the essence of science.

"I converted the laboratory exercises left by my predecessor into demonstrations that I performed during the 'lecture' periods and then helped each student find some investigative project that she would like to carry out herself. They found all kinds of interesting topics: What percentage of the freshman class is left-footed? Can spiders hear? How much variation is there in the number of petals of common buttercups? ... Genuine scientific frontiers lie close at hand. Classes were lively. ... One fascinating thing to me was that six or seven of those non-scientists later went into careers in science or medicine, which was not my objective in planning the courses."[4]

At the end of her first semester Polly retired to Northport for part of the summer, to catch up on her reading and to do some serious thinking. She studied the nutrition of the fruit fly, kept track of the birds and the flowers, observed the height and time between waves as they washed up on the shore, and read. She set up daily schedules, penciling in HB—Henry—most days from 10:30 to 1. She posed some questions to herself: "How is the size of earth measured? How far down is life found? What are people's ideals at different ages? How much do they think about? Problems of youth—sex. ... Moths do it back to back," and she added a little sketch.

She thought about the scientific field she had chosen and welcomed the realization that, at least at the moment, it was a peripheral one, removed from the center stage of scientific inquiry, where competition would not be so fierce. She wrote in her journal: "Here is a new field an unexplored field—a field where I should have time to think a field that matters to me And while the sun begins to lengthen the Autumn shadows no preacher shall I be—but a searcher."

She discovered—despite the misgivings of Anne Benton—that she was a good teacher, actually better than good. "She was absolutely first rate," said Yvette Edmundson, one of her students, "open and clear and logical and interested. When I came back to teach at Bennington, I found myself using her phrases and her cadences. I didn't mean to, but I did."

It was research, however, not teaching, which interested Polly the most. As soon as possible she rearranged her schedule to make time for it. By her second year, the fall of 1936, she manipulated her conference hours so that all of her official work was completed in the mornings, leaving her afternoons free for research and her evenings for study.

While her professional life was proceeding smoothly, so was her personal life. It became clearer and clearer that she had found a soulmate in Henry. During Polly's first half-year at Bennington, when Henry was finishing the Harvard Medical School, they managed to meet often wherever the countryside looked interesting. Henry figured out that if he left Boston and she left Bennington at the same time, they could meet at a midpoint, usually the French King Bridge in Greenfield, Massachusetts, in two hours and ten minutes. That bridge was often the starting point of their adventures, walks and hikes, birding and frogging. Polly chronicled their encounters in detailed letters to her parents.

"Yesterday Henry & I met at the French King Bridge just east of Greenfield—at 10:00 AM. We climbed around the river bank until noon —ate in Greenfield and then walked all afternoon. Supper from 6:30–7:00—home by 9:15. It was a beautiful winter's day—not a cloud in the sky—temperature just above freezing—rather a sharp wind. In spite of the week of thawing there was lots of snow—much more than is left here at Bennington. For some strange reason we saw almost no birds."

"Henry and I met at the French King Bridge in a drizzle. For an hour or so we sat in the car while he gave me the lesson on interuterine development which I handed, after valuable editing, to the physiology class yesterday morning. Then we walked around a bit, and finally as it began to stop raining, found a place to eat. We are now cooking at least one meal out of doors to get some experience in camp-cooking. We are bound to need it someday. Everything but our baking went well, and we have some theories as to what was wrong with that. In the afternoon a warm sun fought its way out through the clouds. We climbed a small mountain, lay in the sun a while, caught a snake and studied its rate of respiration under different conditions, found pine warblers singing and yellow palm warblers chucking, wandered down the mountain, chased an obscure sparrow that got away, listened to the peepers and frogs, watched the stars come out, heard a few measures of the Hermit's song and finally reached our cars and left for home."

On other excursions they "specialized in bear scratches and cancerous growths on birches and beeches—collecting much data of little significance." Once, they treed a porcupine. Polly climbed up after it to see what would happen, and was surprised when the animal released its quills.

One day they drove to Deerfield to see her cousin Miner Crary, who was a student in the preparatory school there. While the students were in church, Polly and Henry, seeing various track-and-field equipment arranged on an empty field, ran hurdles, high jumped, broad jumped, and shot-putted until Miner reappeared.

Then, as his final exams approached, Henry brought his medical books to Bennington and prepared for serious study. The Bennington students got to recognize him and, when they knocked on Polly's door and saw him there would say, shyly, "Maybe you'd rather I came back next week." "I couldn't disappoint them," Polly wrote her parents. In spite of his studying and her work load, they still managed to get outside and enjoy the changing seasons. They celebrated the arrival of May and summer with warblers and thrushes coming in droves in the night. She thought she and Henry should "go dizzy trying to take them in."

Henry graduated from Harvard in May 1936 and left Boston May 30th for Baltimore and an internship at Johns Hopkins. Although they had intended to get married as soon as possible, Hopkins did not permit interns to change their marital status during their appointments. An intern could come married, but couldn't get married. "The faculty thought young doctors should be wedded to medicine." Although Henry's father was a great friend of those in power at Hopkins, they were unwilling to make an exception. So Polly signed on for another year at Bennington.

In the intervening year Polly enthusiastically involved herself in some of the traditional rituals of being a bride despite her refusal to be formally "engaged." She spent time choosing a silver pattern and a few months before her wedding went to a museum exhibition of silver, "to take a look before committing myself on this difficult question." She inspected Tiffany's monogram designs before picking one for her glassware.

Henry's schedule at Hopkins was so busy that Polly joked in a letter to her mother, "it looks as if we could be married some time on July 1st, if Henry can get a few minutes off at noon, or something." In fact, they were married on June 22, 1937, in the beach house at Northport. All the guests as well as the bride and groom played endless games of tennis throughout the weekend. Polly wore a simple, street-length white dress and a corsage, and Henry, a dark suit. Her hair was pulled back. A photograph shows them both looking serious, straight at the camera, not touching one another.

For the next academic year Polly was hired by Goucher College, then an all-women's college in the suburbs of Baltimore, and one of the few that would hire married women. She was an instructor in the departments of physiology and hygiene. Goucher lacked the rural countryside of Bennington, but did have riding, walking and running trails. Polly found tennis courts and accepted the invitation of the Goucher riding instructor to spend some of her small amount of spare time riding.

Their first home was a three-room railroad apartment, all the rooms in a straight line. It had lots of closets, which was fortunate, given the seven cartons of wedding presents deposited there by American Express. The house was on a slight hill overlooking the bay, next to a large field.

They arrived in the evening of June 30, 1937, and went to see Polly's Vassar friend Leal, who was now married to her childhood sweetheart, Barry Wood, a Harvard all-American who had appeared on the cover of *Time* as the embodiment of the scholar-athlete. Although pregnant, Leal was working on a Ph.D. in biology at Johns Hopkins, much to the consternation of some of her professors; and Barry was a medical student.

After visiting the Woods, Polly and Henry went to their own place on Cornwall Street. Their bed hadn't arrived yet, but the store had sent a substitute and they slept on the springs.

The apartment suited them just fine—there was "all the sunshine one could want on the roof outside our bedroom window"—and they quickly invested in a ladder so that they could climb up for sunbaths. Polly followed the comings and goings of the Henslow's sparrow that sang continuously from the corner post. The interior decorating was less to their taste. "I could wish for less melody in the wallpaper.... Every room has a calendar on the wall and a linoleum rug. We are gradually eliminating all of these."

Polly spent her first month in Baltimore getting settled. She enjoyed her new identity. Her letterhead said "Mrs. Henry Bunting, 303 South Cornwall Street, Baltimore, Maryland." And she enjoyed setting up her house, her nest. The day after their arrival she spent two hours at Montgomery Ward buying odds and ends and pricing stoves. She bought an ice cream maker. She called Bastille Day "basic improvement day," and spent it with hammer and screw drivers putting poles, nails, racks, hooks, pegs, and shelves in the closets. They converted her father's "famous box with its screwed-in top" into a telephone table and set up her flat trunk as a linen closet. She asked her mother to buy her all sorts of unnecessary but nice accessories for serving meals: a dozen luncheon plates, a little glass pitcher for maple syrup or sauce, or a small serving dish for berries."

She took considerable pride in her housewifely skills, writing her parents often about her culinary achievements—the meat loaves, macaroni, apple pie and sauce, and leg of lamb that she was preparing to last for several meals and the cheese souffle with pimento cheese "which came out exactly right" although she cheated by using a quarter teaspoon of baking powder. She and Henry entertained frequently, "about five people in to meals per week," mostly unmarried doctors who were colleagues of Henry's.

They saw a fair amount of both of their families. Henry's older sister, Elizabeth, came down from Massachusetts with some regularity. Polly's brother Gardner, a newly minted lawyer, was working in Washington at the labor board while also preparing for the New York bar exam. Polly chided him a bit about neglecting his studying for what she called his "flossy social life." She kept in touch with her younger brother, David, now a teenager, putting in small notes to him in her letters to her parents. David was always interested in music, and Polly asked for his help in ordering records to add to their growing collection. He came down for visits from time to time, and Polly reported to her mother how helpful and "domestic" he was.

"Well this housekeeping game is a push-over," Polly wrote her mother. "Nothing to it, not the way I do it." Polly's landlady was responsible for the serious housecleaning, but Polly washed windows, darned stockings, re-dyed old sweaters, and when a friend sent her a table cloth and napkins as a wedding present, she and Henry's mother hemmed them. She didn't take offense when her mother-in-law sent her a bag for her sewing as a Christmas present.

She didn't, however, allow these mundane chores to occupy her exclusively. Two weeks after her arrival in Baltimore, she was in the laboratory at Goucher about five hours a day, "by far the most research I have done in a long time." She wrote her parents: "Tomorrow morning, after a very long nights' sleep, I shall inoculate a series of bottles which will have to be doctored every hour for at least 48 hours & possibly longer. I shall take them and an armful of books home to the kitchen where I shall watch developments and do some good reviewing in the field of bacteriology. When the cultures have calmed down a little, I shall put in a period at the library. With this armchair preparation I should be able to cope with the semester much more adequately."

She was surprised to find that the college gave her a full-time assistant and a student to wash dishes. And even more valuable from her point of view—no classes on Friday, Saturday or Sunday—"A good 3 days for research every week!"

Once classes began, however, her schedule was so full that she had to give up her own work. In addition to lecturing and correcting a large share of the ninety-five quizzes of the hygiene course, she had to deal with twenty-five students—"a dismaying number," in her section of the hygiene class. She had to have conferences with what she diplomatically called "the less successful students," a significant number of whom were in her physiology class.

By November she recognized that it was impossible to continue research. She didn't have the same kind of freedom she had had at Bennington and was appalled by the Goucher sophomore comprehensive exam crammed with exactly the kind of detail she believed impeded real learning. "It would seem to me to interfere terribly with ones education to have to pass such a thing." In spite of her convictions, she realized that if these students were to do well, she was going to have to stress the exact points on which they were to be examined. Nonetheless, she continued to have them do some challenging work. By February her bacteriology class was giving rabbits intravenous injections and later in the year were running tests on unknown samples sent in for diagnosis of syphilis.

Her time was eroded even more by her obligation to participate in Goucher social functions. She attended affairs at the president's house, helped cut down bushes and clear a riding ring for the May Day performance, and even performed a parody of a Goucher girl learning to ride, in which she repeatedly fell off her horse. She remarked wistfully in letters about the lack of time for her research, but she accepted what she knew was expected of her.

Through it all she managed to keep up with her reading—studying calculus on her own and finishing books on the physiology of elephants, on leprosy, on Madame Curie, and tuberculosis. When her Goucher term ended on June 15, 1938, she treated herself to a real indulgence—*The Yearling*.

Henry, too, was extremely busy. He had decided to move to the Baltimore City Hospital because there was a particularly fine doctor there and because research opportunities were better. His $6-a-month residency began July 1, just days after he and Polly arrived in Baltimore. He stayed at the city hospital a full year, working long days, usually leaving home before nine, and often not returning much before midnight. He was frequently sick. Polly kept track of what she mostly described as colds, and she didn't worry. They spent Henry's evenings off reading or walking, or listening to phonograph records, or writing up laboratory exercises while he examined some specimen—sometimes mosses and lichens he had collected—under the microscope. They went to hear the Philadelphia Orchestra conducted by Eugene Ormandy, getting there an hour ahead in order to get good standing-room spots.

In their professional lives Polly and Henry supported and complemented one another. When Polly needed to demonstrate for her class the dissection of a cat, which she had never done and wasn't sure she knew enough about, Henry came and did it for her. When he needed it, she helped him with his tremendous pile of X-rays. And they continued to share each other's enthusiasms. "Last night," she wrote, "we had a very exciting time. We were examining material from a lung abscess with the dark field microscope. I suddenly realized that the field was full of protozoa—fellows that looked like this (small drawing). It seemed awfully strange to us to find them in the lung, and today I have quite unsuccessfully examined the literature for other examples. We made some transfers to laboratory media which we are now going to examine."

It was the kind of cooperation and collaboration that she came to see was not typical of other married couples. For the first time Polly had the opportunity to closely observe the lives of suburban women, and she was surprised by what she saw. In a revealing letter she wrote her parents: "Lots of fun watching the people around these parts, particularly the women. Thru my landlady, Nora Coates, brought up at West Point and proud of it, I pick up a good deal. Every one of these neat little brick houses has at least one woman who doesn't seem to have enough to do. If they did all of their own wash etc. they could keep busy, but they dont. Most of the time they spend visiting with each other or yelling at their kids, just out of boredom. I suppose that once when one did ones own baking and so forth, the job of housekeeper was a taxing one demanding plenty of intelligence but it certainly has degenerated, without these people having realized it. They all talk, I hear them out the back window, about how hard they have to work, but in reality they wander aimlessly about looking for amusement. Their husbands have cars but they are not allowed to use them. The fact that I use ours has already called for comment from Nora: 'My your husband must be a generous man.'" For the present, these observations led Polly to no insights, but she filed them away in the back of her mind.

Whenever Polly and Henry could find the time, they set out to explore the surrounding country—one weekend to northwestern Maryland "where the colors should be fine," one weekend to Harper's Ferry and the Appalachian Trail where the dogwood was brilliant red, another time to the north bank of the Susquehanna where they "found a fine bit of wild country." One weekend when they had to attend an evening event at the president's house and couldn't take their usual country excursion, they got up in the dark at 3:30 A.M., met their milkman, and drove to Hawk Mountain to watch the hawks until late in the afternoon. On a summer evening they thought nothing of driving twenty miles to the Severn River below Annapolis to swim and have a picnic. Most often they went to Carroll Island. Even empty marshes were beautiful to what she called their "city-full eyes."

When they couldn't get away, Polly found as much of nature as she could wherever she was. While waiting for Henry at the hospital, she paid attention to the mockingbirds, which were "singing so loudly outside that here in the inner room with the typewriter going I can hear them." She and Henry subjected the field between the house and the hospital to intensive survey, enabling them "to keep track of the summer if only to a slight extent. Almost every time that Henry comes home he brings some new grass or bug which we look up and record."

By the summer of 1938 Henry was back at Hopkins, finishing up the last two months of his internship. On weekends he could be in charge of two wards and the accident room; Polly, who had a summer job working in the Hopkins lab, often had to track down blood donors. It was the kind of hands-on experience she found particularly valuable. Every Monday morning, when the lab assistant collected serum for his Wassermann tests, he let Polly bleed guinea pigs from the heart, and sometimes a sheep. "One can read and read about these things but no amount of reading is the equivalent of actual experience," she wrote her parents. "I certainly shall be a broader if not a better bacteriologist after this month." In many ways it was a productive summer, but when it finally ended she wrote to her parents, "It's been a good month but we hope that we never have to spend another summer so far away from the country."

Life at this point was quite wonderful for Polly. She wrote to her father not to worry about them financially. They had money in a joint savings account and in individual accounts as well. "We feel very comfortable and settled, but decided yesterday that we couldnt be, because we couldnt figure out any adjustments that we'd made; and all the books and all our friends have always told us that a lot of adjusting was going to be necessary."

6

A Garden Not a Racetrack

After Henry's internship and residency, he decided to follow in his father's footsteps and become a pathologist, which meant another residency, this one at the Yale Medical School. Yale awarded him one of the more lucrative fellowships ($1,800) funded by the Jane Coffin Childs Memorial Fund for Medical Research.

Polly hoped to return to her research and received two offers—a $600 fellowship and a part-time job for the same amount with Professor Leo Rettger of Yale's bacteriology department. He wanted her to maintain his acidophilus cultures, which he was sending to companies making acidophilus milk, a mixture used to ameliorate various intestinal disorders. Professor Rettger offered her the job, but then surprisingly tried to talk her into accepting the fellowship instead, assuring her that it afforded "greater dignity." Polly understood instinctively that something more was going on than a concern for her status. The fellowship, she discovered, would come from the university, whereas the salary would come from the professor's own department and Professor Rettger apparently had not informed the dean about his acidophilus business. It all looked, as Polly wrote her parents, "a bit shady." She was amused that Rettger's letter urging her to accept the fellowship was written longhand while all his other communications to her had been typewritten by his secretary. She typed her response saying she preferred his job, and kept a carbon copy. Academic politics amused her.

There were several reasons she preferred the job. Unlike the fellowship, it was part-time, and she thought the small stipend inadequate for full-time work. She also wanted time for all the domestic chores that she accepted, without question, as her responsibility. Even more important, she felt she would be freer to do her own work if she had no fellowship. She had already seen in graduate school the way money could dictate the problem to be studied, and she wanted to avoid that pressure. With this job, Professor Rettger had promised her what she wanted most, access to a laboratory.

Once Polly had her $600-a-year job, Yale reduced Henry's stipend from $1,800 to $1,200, which Polly and Henry thought was quite fair. Even though the country was coming out of the Depression in 1938, the Depression mentality was still pervasive, and it seemed reasonable to them for the university to use that sum for another graduate student.

Polly's job didn't demand much—about three hours a day—transferring cultures, working on practical problems that arose in connection with their industrial use, and on the fifteenth of every month, shipping them out to the commercial companies that depended on Yale to supply their cultures. But the job was invaluable because it afforded her a way of "incorporating" herself into the Yale bacteriology department. "This job," she wrote her parents, "gives me legitimate status with very little responsibility," access not only to the laboratory, but also to seminars, Yale libraries, and courses. Above all, it gave her what young scholars at the start of their careers needed most and what so few, particularly women, had: time, freedom, and support to do their own independent research while graduate training was still fresh. Too many women, she said, could show only what they had accomplished under a senior professor, not what they could do on their own. "That was the break that few married women had in my day," she said years later.

This was the first time Polly could organize her life totally around her scientific work. Other than teaching a graduate evening course in bacteriology, which Professor Rettger wanted taught, her schedule, even the pace of her life, were determined by her experiments. Henry too was involved with his research, and they moved easily in and out of each other's laboratories, discussing their work, waiting for the conclusion of each other's experiments. "Henry is humming around with test tubes and rabbit blood," Polly wrote her parents, "so a good time for a letter." That first fall they stayed close to their labs nearly every night to check experiments that had to be tended between 8:30 and 10 o'clock, going out for supper at 11. When a doctor friend of Henry's asked what he did about his wife when he worked these long hours, Henry said, "Well, tonight she's across the street in the library reading articles for me."

She had been thinking about heredity and evolution since childhood, and now she began to focus on the ways in which bacteria transmitted their characteristics from one generation to the next. "By what mechanism did each species reproduce its kind with such uncanny speed and precision?" she asked herself. Within each tiny cell, she reasoned, there must be an elaborate organization to enable such variations to occur.

In the 1930's these weren't questions that were at the forefront of scientific research. Quite the contrary. "Requests for grants were turned down with unusual alacrity," Polly said, and friends tried their best to talk her out of pursuing such apparently unproductive lines of inquiry. "I thought it was good to go into a peripheral field . . . because there would be time to work on things and develop them; you wouldn't be in the midst of 55 highly trained people who were trying to beat each other to get to a certain point, in which case you wouldn't get there first." Madame Curie had reasoned in the same way, Polly said. "She decided to go into radioactivity because it was not of interest to many other people and research would not move too fast. She was very conscious that with her daughter, she couldn't work as fast as a full-time man."[1]

Polly knew that she too was going to combine work with a family, which would necessarily mean that her career could not proceed along an uninterrupted trajectory. There would be stops and starts. But being a woman, she believed, also gave her an advantage; she would not be the one responsible for supporting the family. Henry had that burden, so she could take her time. "I was never very interested in my scientific career," Polly said years later. "I was doing science because I enjoyed it. I never expected to be a top professor somewhere or to make any remarkable discovery."

This unambitious attitude might have come about because of her Quaker roots, which taught modesty. "You're not supposed to make a big thing of yourself. You're not supposed to be flashy," her children remembered her saying. They also remembered that she was very severe about "bragging." You never, ever brag. That is not done. Aiming for a fancy career would be like bragging.

But there was also the reality of what women in academia—not only in science, where it was particularly bad, but in all fields—could expect in the thirties. They faced formidable obstacles. They were relegated to low level assistantships, which rarely allowed them to pursue their own research. Good work as an instructor almost never led to promotion to a higher rank. Rather than being stepping-stones or entering wedges, instructorships for women were usually the upper limits of their careers.[2] Not only could they rarely expect to be professors, nepotism rules were firmly in place and if one partner were fired it was never the husband. Years later Polly wrote in a short autobiographical sketch that she had been "allowed" to do research in the Yale bacteriology department.

There is not a trace of bitterness or even of frustration either in her recollections of these years or in the letters she wrote at the time. What mattered to her was having the opportunity to do her own work. She did not even notice her title. As long as she could get grants for her research, it did not anger her that she could not sign for them; they could be awarded to her, but she had to be vouched for by a professor—always male. Later she crafted a poetic image. Life didn't have to be a racetrack, she said. It could, instead, be a garden.

The work that absorbed her now she had begun before she came to Yale. Since graduate school, Polly had been intrigued by *Serratia marcescens*, a bright red strain of bacteria that threw off pink-and-white mutants and sometimes caused blood-red spots on foods. She wanted to find out at what rate these changes occurred and hoped to do so through the use of color; color variants are easy to detect and easy to count. She grew cultures in a carefully controlled environment and discovered that the rates of variation were remarkably constant. In generation after generation a certain number were of a different color, so something in the previous population was bringing about this deviation in the next generation. She concluded, therefore, that these were heritable variations, analogous to genetic mutations in higher organisms. She was excited by her discoveries. "Its such fun when one has at last achieved a satisfactory technique," she wrote her parents, "for one can just 'turn it on' and reap the rewards."

She could not believe that so many strains of *Serratia* would have developed such elaborate mechanisms for color changes unless it were advantageous under certain conditions and disadvantageous under others. So she began to experiment by changing the environment. "I'd learned to question micro-organisms," she said, "rather than second-guess them; I'd developed sufficient confidence in the experimental approach to be intrigued by unexpected results, results that must be telling me something I didn't know."[3]

She published two papers in the *Journal of Bacteriology* in 1940 and two in 1942—the first two describing the variations in color and their rates of change and the second two describing the effects of the environment on the color variations. She berated herself for writing so slowly. Although she didn't produce a large volume of work, she was listed in all the editions of *American Men of Science*, the Who's Who of scientific achievement, which, in a sign of the times, included the biographies and descriptions of the work of a few women. In 1972 it became *American Men and Women of Science* and continued to list her. And Nobel Prize winners Salvador Luria and Max Delbruck cited her work in their seminal 1945 paper on inheritance in bacteria. Today her papers are still cited as background confirmation for studies people are continuing to do.

Nonetheless, Polly never considered her scientific endeavors to be of any significance. "Mine was one of the steps, one of the useful little bricks," she said. "Although the work had its own importance for the moment it wasn't something of lasting importance."

"That's an unduly modest assessment," said Anne Lacy, for many years professor of biology at Goucher College, who was a Yale graduate student during these years. "Polly was one of the first people to find mutations in bacteria. I always felt she didn't get enough credit for her work. I always mention her in my classes."

Polly wanted more than just to do science. As important to her as the research, was the place she and Henry chose to live. After a year in suburban Baltimore, they were determined to live in the country, where they could walk on dirt roads, observe birds, and plant gardens. They drove in arcs around New Haven, looking for for-rent signs or even for-sale signs, and eventually they found a rural enclave between Waterbury and New Haven named Bethany. The town of Bethany was more than the backdrop—it was an essential component of their lives.

Although many Connecticut towns were suburban, Bethany was sheltered from the encroachments of development by several nearby reservoirs and the water company's ownership of thousands of acres of woods. It was protected further by a town ordinance forbidding any commercial structure or sign within the town. It had no movie theaters, no town square or central gathering place, but was instead spread out with the town hall, library, and firehouse separated by sections of country roads. Until the late 1950's, it didn't even have street lights. Cows grazed on the hillsides. When Polly and Henry first moved there, it sported one general store, two gas stations, and two paved roads that went through the town, parallel to one another. Twice a day a bus traveled past an old airport, which stayed in use until 1966. And it took them only twenty minutes to get from this perfect spot to their labs in New Haven.

Bethany's population was unusual. There were only about a thousand people, a mix of Yale professors and farmers who had lived there for generations and, coincidentally, a large contingent of Vassar women, whose husbands were working in New Haven. The Vassar women, who had not known one another before settling in Bethany, "were doers, movers and shakers," said Susan Bonner, who grew up in Bethany and whose mother was one of the Vassar contingent. "They were all doing things that were the purview of women—having babies and canning beans, but they were also fixing cars, hauling wood or chopping firewood. The men were doing the typically male things; the women were doing both and because they were highly educated and literate they did it with a flair."

A farmer named Frank Zaica confided in Polly how much he and his farmer-friends admired her and her friends. They all wanted to get married, he told Polly, but they couldn't find girls who didn't hold their noses every time they went into a barn. It was amazing to him to find girls who kept goats, chickens, and cows and in Polly's case bees, and didn't mind shoveling manure. He knew nothing about these women except that they had gone to this place called Vassar and he wanted to know what they learned at that place. Polly said later she thought Frank's comments were a great compliment to liberal education, which had taught them to adapt, "to do what fitted into one's life at a specific time and place."

Friction between the old inhabitants and the newcomers were unknown in Bethany. Everyone raised money for the PTA, participated in Gilbert & Sullivan performances, grew gardens, joined 4-H clubs, became volunteer firemen, and met at the county fair and the fireman's carnival. They all used the front hall of the house nearest the pond as a skate exchange. Everybody went to town meetings about zoning and planning, and the people who were elected to offices were a mixture of the people who had been in the town for generations and the Yale newcomers, women as well as men. When the Buntings gave their New Year's parties, they invited the whole town—Yale professors, farmers, carpenters, the mayor—and everybody came. One Sunday when Polly and Henry were sitting down for Sunday chicken with guests "the rather new milk delivery boy arrived. 'Won't you join us?' Henry asked—and to all of our surprise he readily accepted. We really felt quite flattered," Polly reported to her parents.

Polly and Henry weren't the only people moving in. On Sundays, Polly heard the sounds of axes, brush scythes, and children laughing as families came to clear the few acres they had bought. She described these families as "poor but very self respecting," and noted that for the most part the head-of-the-house built the house, unaided. "The rooms are small," she wrote, "but the materials are good and it is all payd for!—so different from Cornwall St.," the home of the suburban Baltimore matrons with too little to do.

Polly and Henry found an unfinished stone house on Northrup Road that had been built by a young couple whose business had moved them to another state. It didn't have electricity, finished floors, or even a real front door. In the beginning they had to carry water from their neighbors. The rent was $35 a month. It had a big stone fireplace and sat on a sumac-covered hillside, right on the edge of oak woods. A stream babbled just below. There were what Polly described as "good woods" right in their backyard. "I dont know how we could ever find another place where we could live in such comfort so near to the open woods and hills," she wrote her parents. She urged them to bring old shoes when they came to visit so that they could all go walking together.

They moved in with their Coleman stove and other camping equipment and so little furniture that the house had what she described as "a pleasant airiness." They set up their card table in the living room for a desk and used her father's old student lamp for light. The light it gave was so beautiful, she said, "we shall miss it when electricity comes." By mid-September the hand pump was working, so they could stop hauling water. A month after that, the electrician spent three days rewiring the entire house and installing fixtures. They got home one night at midnight and found light. The first thing they did was put the Tchaikovsky 6th Symphony full blast on the phonograph, and then they made a roast chicken. By the end of the year the plumber connected the radiators and installed the hot water system, and they hooked up the Sears Roebuck Cold Spot refrigerator.

Meanwhile they were busy painting, washing windows, and tackling the rocks that made the entranceway bumpy. Polly got a good workout wielding a twelve-pound crowbar on the small rocks, but concluded that dynamite would be needed to move the biggest ones. Even though they knew they wouldn't be living there permanently, it seemed natural to them to make the place as beautiful as they could. They began a twenty-by-twenty-five-foot garden almost immediately, planting winter rye and winter vetch. They found flowers in the woods and transplanted them. They planted two bushes in front of one of the "more conspicuous cellar windows," and raked their front lawns to remove the old grass, glass, and paper that "marred their beauty."

Their wonderful stone house, however, had one unexpected drawback. It was infested with cockroaches, one of nature's manifestations that even Polly found repulsive. But she managed to turn her revulsion into a philosophical reverie in her journal.

> The cockroach campaign goes on in the kitchen. I begin to understand more of the war mentality. Here are these creatures which do one really very little actual harm. In fact I have always been rather fond of them—they have added a dash of interest to many a weary laboratory hour. When they first invaded the house it was rather friendly and, indeed, for a long time they did no apparent harm. However it wasnt "the thing" so we began to

hunt them. And gradually they increased, dug in, and began to litter up the place. We chased them with pyrethrum but barely scratched the surface. Now we just chase them—with spatula, or bare hands. Our tactics consist merely of killing them on sight any & everywhere, particularly the women and children. In the day-time we run the vacuum up and down the available cracks. How we hate them! Kill em, Kill em—but still they really do us very little harm.

Is it actually to their benefit to multiply so rapidly? Were there just a few I should let them alone as I let spiders alone. The old question.

In early December 1938, after Polly and Henry had been settled in Bethany for a few months, Henry met with his boss, Professor Winternitz, to discuss his future. Henry wanted to know if he could count on staying at Yale or if he should apply elsewhere. Winternitz told him that everyone in the department was delighted with his work and with the way in which he had fitted in and that they hoped that they might make future positions attractive enough to keep him indefinitely. They hoped he would consider himself a permanent member of the department. Polly and Henry were jubilant. It was so much better than just being given another fellowship. "(And such an easy drive from N.Y.)," Polly noted parenthetically in a letter to her parents.

So Polly and Henry began to establish their small farm. They bought two Saanen goats and baby chickens that gave them milk and eggs and some meat. They already had bees and their vegetable garden. They purchased a small knocked-down chicken house, which they converted into a goat house, and built a chicken house out of the crates that had brought a rabbit colony to Yale. They got a government-printed handbook on barn building, and built a small barn, mixing cement, and boarding in the sides with old crate box lumber. It was their most ambitious project and Polly described it as fun, but admitted that it was rather hard work. "We werent too experienced—neither our muscles nor our minds, but we followed the government direct as carefully as we could and we shouted loudly at each other in our best Italian."

Polly and Henry kept banding and studying birds and in the spring of 1940 had the most exciting birding experience of their lives. They banded two of the six chimney swifts that were found about a year later in the jungle on the Peru-Brazil border. Until then no one had known where chimney swifts wintered and, for Polly and Henry, it was wonderfully satisfying to have contributed to that discovery.

Polly continued to schedule every minute, wringing out every last ounce of time. In a letter to her parents she described what was apparently to her a fairly ordinary weekend day. "Today I went walking early, then had breakfast, washed some windows, baked macaroni & rhubarb pie, cleaned my winter blouses & skirts with gasoline, moved a bunch of cedar trees, had lunch, did a little reading, went for a long walk, made a little strawberry bed and built some more wall between us and the Mooneys—had supper, did the dishes—and feel rested and in fine shape tonight."

Bethany gave Polly some of the same pleasures she had loved at Northport, her family's country retreat. She organized her work life to give her as much time as possible in her glorious surroundings, getting up early to squeeze in an hour or so of skiing on the Bethany Gap hill, and when spring came, leaving the lab early enough to have an hour of daylight for walking or working around her place. Sometimes she weeded the garden topless, Band-Aids over her nipples. Waking up to the bird songs made each day start for her with a kind of excitement. Although the nature descriptions in her letters were shorter, more contained and controlled than those of her college and graduate school days, they were still an intrinsic part of her running commentary on her life. She noticed, always, the birds, the weather, what is blooming. Describing nature seemed to get her adjectival and lyrical, at times even a little overwrought, but even in her most extravagant descriptions, she was always precise. "The frog croaked three times . . ." she wrote her parents. She listed fifty-four birds she had seen with checks to indicate whether she had seen it "sometimes" or only "occasionally."

She was profoundly happy, often expressing in her journals her gratitude for her life and the joy she and Henry took in one another's companionship—especially in light of what so many were suffering in the war that was being fought so far away. She didn't take the good times for granted or allow them to slip by unnoticed. "Sunday in the hills around Brattleboro was unbelievably lovely. . . . We wandered about all day—listening and watching—scarcely able to believe in our good fortune—not able at all to conceive of events along the Meuse—real as they had been the night before."

From the start, Polly and Henry were part of the community. In addition to his position at Yale, Henry became the Bethany town doctor—at times the town's only doctor. He treated everything from aches and pains and dog bites to the serious illnesses that sent people to the hospital in New Haven. When their neighbors down the hill realized they couldn't get to the hospital on time, and that their baby was going to be delivered at home, they called Henry. "He came down the hill in his mackintosh, and Polly brought a box to put the baby in. It said 'Connecticut Red Apples on it,'" Jacquelyn Mattfeld remembered. Henry's day sometimes began as early as 4:15 A.M. Sometimes patients showed up at the house. When a child who had been bitten by a dog arrived at 8 after Henry had already left, Polly dressed the leg. Other days he wouldn't be home until 10:30 or 11, because he was making house calls on his way home from the hospital. People trusted Henry, but often in a cautious way. Once, when he went to treat a farmer who had done odd jobs around their place, Henry opened the top drawer of the bureau to find what he had suspected would be there—all the many pills he'd given the farmer over the years that had never been taken.

Although contrary to Yale policy, Henry charged his patients something; he knew that was the only way proud, independent farmers would feel right about accepting his services. People paid in various ways. The milkman showed up with two bottles of heavy cream. Other people brought eggs or a big load of manure for the garden. And at Christmas there were numerous bottles of alcohol.

Because she was the doctor's wife, people tended to trust Polly too, and turned to her for advice and help. She came to see that every town needs a central place to go for information about available resources, so she found out all she could about social service agencies and programs in New Haven. She became one of the organizers of the Public Health Nursing Association and served on the board of directors for seven years. When Mrs. Schon fell and hurt her elbow, it was Polly who drove her to the hospital for X-rays. From time to time Polly dropped in on the elderly Miss Fox, the woman who had established the professional visiting nurse service during the World War I. She seemed lonely.

Polly and Henry's social life was as crowded as it had been in Baltimore with friends coming and going for quick visits, for dinner, for weekends, for the opportunity to enjoy some country. Polly, who in so many ways was an intensely private person, always liked bringing people together in her home. When friends turned up she often put them to work, having them help with building a stone wall or spading the garden, or transplanting some bushes. If they all went swimming, she could whip off her shirt and plunge right in. She didn't slow down for company, but instead included them in whatever she was doing. "Our guests seem to come here primarily to catch up on sleep—which most of them seem to need rather badly," she wrote. Perhaps her breakneck pace wore them out.

Among her visitors were her parents. She often asked them for advice—whether it was a question for her father about his recipe for brandied peaches or how deep a water pipe should be or for her mother about what wax to use on the floors. She didn't ask her father for money, but from time to time he sent generous checks. And her mother helped in other practical ways. She sent material for curtains and bureau covers; brought roasts or pies baked by the incomparable Nora; and sent labor-saving appliances, such as an electric mixer and a pressure cooker, which Polly used often.

The packages of clothes kept coming too. Polly did her best to stop them, once again begging to be permitted to wear enough things out so that she could have an excuse for shopping for herself. "Of course there are two sides to the question," she wrote her mother. "Just remember *my* side of the case next time you feel tempted and dont yield unless . . . you feel yourself in the hand of superior forces." She never won this argument and never gave up trying.

Polly had every intention of keeping right on with her scientific work. But in the spring of 1940 she announced to her parents that she would have to refuse a fellowship she had applied for even if it were granted, because she was pregnant with her first child.

During the first few months, nausea almost incapacitated her. She was so sick that Henry took care of much of the cooking and housecleaning, and brought her orange juice first thing in the morning before she got out of bed. Her mother came and helped, cleaning the refrigerator and even the woodwork, bringing stew and pie and sherry.

Polly chronicled the progress of her pregnancy in her journal, keeping almost clinical notes of when the nausea started, how her weight increased, and which activities she could continue. She struggled on with her acidophilus job almost until the end of April, but finally called it quits to "ease my conscience," determining to "substitute an equivalent period in the summer" when the nausea would not be so debilitating.

Staying home was not a trial. Polly was never bored and had no difficulty enjoying her solitude. The sun, the birds, the dog John, the flowers, happily filled her days and her mind. "A perfectly beautiful day here," she wrote, just two months before her baby's birth. "The house is all clean, the beds made, the dishes washed and the last lot of clothes soaking. By eleven o'clock I shall be all thru with the chores and shall have the rest of the day in which to amuse myself. Perhaps I shall get some ferns and things to plant around the rock in the back yard. Certainly John should have another bath and anti-flea treatment. The bees should be looked at—and the warblers. The chicken 'house' needs a little repairing:—I guess I'll be able to amuse myself all right. Of course there are windows and things too, but I'm afraid they'll wait a while longer. A sun bath is more to the point." She mused in her journal, "I be in the sun, and read, and sleep, and eat and am reminded of the buffalo boys in the Mowgli stories who drove the buffalo out to the wallows every morning and 'one single day was as long as most people's whole lives.' My days, like theirs, pass happily, timelessly, with sleeping and playing in the sun."

But as the pregnancy drew to a close, she became impatient. She wrote her mother, "This stage is rather like a honeymoon—exciting and all that but you'd much rather settle down to the real business & fun. I certainly look forward to the day when I shall come home from that hospital!"

7

A Busy Life

Polly and Henry's first child and only daughter was born November 14, 1940. They named her Mary. While Polly was still in the hospital, her mother's mother, the grandmother who had been her tutor, died. Unable to travel to Brooklyn, Polly wrote her mother a warm letter of condolence, expressing her heightened sense of what it meant to be both a mother and a daughter.

> Last night, after the lights were out and little Mary had been taken back to the nursery, I didnt feel so very far away from you. Many were the thoughts that ran about the room, in and out of mind, singly and in troops. How very glad I was that you had been with Nana all of Thursday. And it was contentful to know that she had known of little Mary's existence in this life....
>
> It was strange, a little earlier in the evening, to look at my Mary and to realize that some day I would be telling her about *my* Nana, who had died so soon after she was born. Here was a specific message, stored up, but special for her, some day. I suppose there will be lots of messages that will be saved from now on.

Polly and little Mary came home to Bethany on November 27th, after a full two weeks in the hospital. In accordance with the practices of the day, the new mother had very specific instructions from her doctor. She was allowed to be up one hour, three times a day, the first week; in the second week, she could be up all day, but had to take a morning and afternoon nap. She was permitted out for short walks in the third week and was allowed to drive after the fourth week. She obeyed all these instructions, but by four and a half weeks she was cleaning the stables.

Two days after they came home, the pediatrician paid a house call—doctors still did in those days—and since it was too icy to drive up the hill, he parked at the bottom and walked up. He arranged for a nurse from the local visiting nurse service to show Polly how to bathe

the baby. During the first visit, Polly only watched. The next day, the nurse watched. Henry cooked the Thanksgiving turkey that year, together with rice and cauliflower. "What laughing days these are," Polly wrote her parents.

Polly approached the raising of her little daughter as she had everything else—scientifically. She noted every detail of Mary's development, taking notes on her feeding schedule and the quantities of everything she consumed, how many teaspoons of pablum or banana or ounces of orange juice, the numbers and consistency of her bowel movements, her hours of sleeping and waking, when her eyelashes grew in, and when she shed her first tear. Each of Mary's visitors and her reactions to them were duly recorded. The hour-by-hour schedules that always filled Polly's journals were still there, only now they chronicled when Mary was outside and when inside, when asleep and when awake. Rather than approaching the normal infant difficulties, such as spitting up and nervousness in the bath, as developmental stages to be gone through, Polly saw them as problems to be solved. She posed questions to herself and posited possible answers, setting up controlled experiments, and as she had done in an entirely different context, took data. "All of this burping business seems wrong. . . . Several factors seem to be involved. Activity, especially on her stomach is certainly conducive to the trouble . . . Program: Collect data on no & quant of burps." When Mary cried in her bath, Polly asked, "Could it be that the soap irritates?" She noted that on December 10th Mary had a diaper rash. "Try: 1.using only oil for 3 days, 2.sleeping at night without diapers, 3.using very little soap in bath."

In her frequent letters to her parents, Polly never jotted down perfunctory remarks like "the baby is fine"; she wrote detailed descriptions of exactly what Mary was doing. "Today's accomplishment was a sudden understanding of the problem of dipping a spoon into a dish," Polly wrote her parents when Mary was eight months old. "The notion came to her quite suddenly at supper tonight. She was lifting her first spoonful of cereal to her lips when she paused, thoughtfully lowered it to the dish, took a new spoonfull, and then brought it to her mouth. After that she dipped & lifted until the dish was empty. All I had to do was to keep the spoon upright at times."

Polly had always wanted to raise children, and now Mary became her primary interest, leading her to make a major change in her life. She decided not to return to the laboratory but instead to stay home and become a full-time mother. She wanted to get to know Mary and, as she put it, "watch this process." There was also a practical reason. The war was beginning to affect daily life, and gasoline was becoming scarce. They had only enough for Henry to go back and forth to New Haven. They were on different schedules, and it would have strained their resources if she had had to drive in at different times.

Neither her frequent letters to her parents nor her journals betray any trace of intense struggle over this decision. She sized up the situation, decided what to do, and then, without fanfare or prolonged introspection, just did it. "I didn't agonize about it," she said. "I thought about it. It just looked like a fun thing to do for a few years. It was the most interesting thing I could think of at that point." She did not worry whether she would be able to return to her scientific work, whether she would lose her place in the hierarchy. She wasn't a climber of ladders. "At each point I was doing the things that, on balance, looked most interesting to me," she said years later. "I think that when one is making one's own decisions on these things as they come along, conflicts are minimized. It's when one thinks one is being pushed into something, that one has problems. . . . I wasn't caught in a debate about whether to have an eminent scientific career, or have children. Eminence did not attract me . . . I wanted an interesting life."[1]

She also welcomed the prospect of becoming more involved in their small farm. "I realized that if I hadn't been living in the country where there were so many things I loved to do—if I had been living in the city with—as I imagined it—extra time on my hands, I might not have done it so completely. The confinement of a small apartment would have been very difficult for me."[2]

Her days were now filled with a succession of chores. She canned enough produce to last through the winter. When she described "rather a canning day," it was no exaggeration—"13 quarts stewed tomatoes, 6 quarts tomato juice bottled, about 20 glasses grape jelly, 7 quarts grape juice bottled, and several quarts pulp for ice cream." Extracting the honey was another responsibility—sixty pounds at a time going into jars, while another sixty pounds waited in two large kettles. As sugar became scarcer, and sugar rationing more likely, there was a great increase in the demand for honey.

She handled the carpentry needed to keep the various buildings in good order and took care of the increasing number of animals. The goats, Rita and Sookey, were in residence. There were seven hens, giving an average of 5.3 eggs a month, and Polly rigged up a lamp bulb warmer in the cellar for an additional sixteen baby chicks. By the end of May a mother hen hatched nine chicks from nine of their biggest eggs. When a goat needed to be bred, Polly was known to put it in the front seat of the car, right next to her, and drive down New Haven's main street.

She never gave cutesy names to the animals in her life. The succession of dogs all had human names—John, Bob, Mitzi, Nicky. The first goats, too, were named Henry and Andrews, family names no less. A horse who was blind in one eye was named Judy.

Although she spent considerable time and energy thinking about her animals and figuring out strategies to make them more comfortable and productive, there was nothing sentimental about Polly's attachment. She and Henry raised their animals, and then they butchered and ate them. On one page of her journal Polly placed some lovely photographs of baby Mary reaching out for two sweet little goats. On the next page is the notation, "Killed the kids." She nurtured the little chicks until they could produce eggs and then killed them for meat all winter long. "The big rooster has been succeeded by his son," Henry wrote to Polly's parents—"thus the old order changeth."

The chores that required neither skill nor imagination were onerous to her, particularly "the ironing menace," she called it. She bought a machine called an "Ironrite" and noted wryly in a letter to her mother when the salesperson was coming to demonstrate it that she had the week's laundry sprinkled and ready. "If I'm stupid enough I may get most of it done free."

Ultimately she found ways of making all her chores interesting by treating them as scientific problems that could be solved through precise observation. When one of the goats was not eating well, she decided to record the exact amounts it consumed each day. When certain plants weren't doing well, she asked, "Too much sun? Too little water?" She diagrammed the gardens, illustrating exactly what was planted where, recording the type of seed planted, when lime was applied and when the beets, carrots, spinach, and lettuce were harvested. She kept precise notes on the composition of the animals' feed. She made diagrams for each beehive and kept records, asking herself, "What is the meaning of this mold? lack of ventilation?" When mice invaded the cellar and ate the corn and beans, she recorded that too. Keeping detailed notes aided her memory, which she was always trying to improve, but, just as important, she believed in data, in record-keeping. She wanted to know, not to guess or surmise.

But no matter how she struggled, she could not cram more than twenty-four hours into each day. Time was her most intractable enemy. Within a month of Mary's birth, Polly realized how easy it would be to fill her days with repetitive chores that gave her no sense of accomplishment. "The great problem at the moment is that of utilizing the long days to best advantage," she wrote in her journal. "The greatest danger seems to be neglect of studies in favor of little jobs."

From childhood, she had always known how to use even snippets of time productively, often beginning a letter on one day when she had a minute, and picking it up a day later, or an hour later, when she had another; she continued this practice in Bethany. She recorded each of the day's activities to see how long it took and if, by any chance, she was overlooking some minutes that could be used for scientific work. She set up columns for AM, PM, and a brand new category—PPM. She kept rearranging the order of chores, trying to carve out blocks of uninterrupted time. "I now milk early while Henry feeds Mary. This lets the night milking come before supper & frees the evenings."

She thought it might be possible to preserve one hour a day for study. To see if this hypothesis was workable, she wrote at the top of a page in her journal "Data for Dec. 16," and underneath noted exactly what she did in each time slot. This showed her she had five hours that were not taken up with Mary, animals, or cooking, and could be spent on "other non-routine jobs"—things that had to be done, but not necessarily every day—including housecleaning, laundry, reading, mending, exercise, gardening, visiting, setting bird traps, spreading manure, working on the barn, darning, baking, doing accounts, and writing letters. It would be possible, she concluded, to preserve the 8 to 9 P.M. period for science. On the days she failed to meet this goal she marked "st.-1" in the margin of her journal. On the days she found more than an hour she noted that too.

She had banished lab research from her life, but it wasn't possible for her to banish the problems that interested her from her mind. And so she decided to start working on some scientific papers again. By the time Mary was a year old, Polly had organized her routine so that she could get to the library for three hours on Thursday nights. She was relieved to find no references to *Serratia* that she had missed. "No one is even interested in the problem at the moment." But she continued to be interested and concentrated on getting a paper ready for the December 1941 meeting of the Society of American Bacteriologists in Baltimore. There was to be a roundtable on the genetics of bacteria. In early September 1941 she listed in her journal eight "tasks" to be done, the eighth being "Write paper"; it came after "distribute manure, move chicken yard fences, spade garden, paint barns, make shelves in house, paint in house." By mid-November, with the meeting about a month away, the paper was moved to the top of her list, but the farm chores had not disappeared.

Through it all, she and Henry never stopped entertaining friends. Guests would arrive with entourages of children in tow. When Polly didn't have enough space inside she just moved everyone outside. She enjoyed these occasions. "These parties greatly stimulate my domestic instincts," she wrote her parents. "The house is all clean—even the windows. The large bouquets of asters and other fall flowers decorate the living room and there is a little bunch of silver red, sweet fern and pale lavender asters in the guest room."

More and more, the war was eroding Polly's sense of tranquility. The draft was instituted in 1940. Henry's medical research into treatments for gas poisonings kept him from being drafted, but she was worried about her brothers, and in letters to her parents kept asking about their status. They were now both married, but her younger brother, David, was drafted into the Navy. Fortunately he was stationed in Washington and he and his wife, Laura, who had been a student of Polly's at Bennington, came to Bethany whenever they could get away. Henry's family visited too, as did Polly's parents, aunts, and uncles. Polly welcomed all of her extended family to Bethany, remarking in a letter to her mother that, compared with the rest of the family, she and Henry were very settled.

She didn't take their good life for granted. Her journal entry for December 6, 1941: "Home after an afternoon out-of-doors with Henry and Mary. Excellent hard cider, a good supper, our home, a pleasant life—how easy, natural and pleasant it all seems. How strange to think of its rarity in our world. Can we keep it? For how long? The entry for December 7, 1941 reads: "Some of it has gone already. This evening when we returned from an afternoon of shopping and sawing in the Water Co. woods, where it costs us $1.00 to cut ourselves a cord of wood, Harry Greene called to tell us of the bombing of Pearl Harbor. "*December 8, 1941* This noon while Mary & I ate our luncheon in the kitchen, we heard the President request both houses of Congress to declare war on Japan. It wasnt much of a speech, but my head went down beside the loaf of bread and I cried—not knowing quite why—until Mary objected."

This is the only time Polly ever mentions crying. Witnesses to some of her life's tragedies insist they never saw her cry, and she said about herself that crying was not something she did—except this once, when it appeared as if her world was teetering on the edge of catastrophe.

Nonetheless, at Christmastime she delivered her paper to the American Society of Bacteriologists, arranged for it to be published, and returned as quickly as possible to the farm.

The war had already created a number of practical problems. Gasoline had become scarcer. All excursions, from family outings to grocery shopping, as well as the necessary farm work, had to be carefully organized. With so many men off fighting, Henry's medical practice in town became more demanding. The labor shortages complicated both the work on the farm and the acquisition of supplies. For a couple of years Polly was able to have groceries delivered, but by the end of 1943 the stores had no one to deliver or even to pack orders. She and Henry found it increasingly difficult to find anyone to help with the farm, and they could barely finish all the chores even by 8 PM. And by February 1942 she was pregnant again and dealing with the same debilitating nausea as before.

Still the routine had to go on. "The first warm & sunny day we have had in a long time," she wrote to her parents. "Mary and I scarcely came in from milking and milking. We examined all the bee hives, painted things, pruned things, & splashed in lots of mud puddles." By the summer Mary was much more independent and Polly celebrated, "I can enjoy considerably more reading & writing. Sunday morning Henry & I must have worked here at the desk for a couple of hours with almost no interruption; and this afternoon I went up to the picnic ground, where there was a fine breeze, and read 'Bacteriologic Reviews' all afternoon." She managed to publish two papers on her *Serratia* work in 1942.

The summer's serenity, however, was short-lived. At the end of July they received the disturbing news that the owner of their lovely stone house had decided to return and was evicting them. Polly moved into high gear, contacting eight different real estate agents covering towns from Orange to Branford. Houses were difficult to find, and for a brief moment they considered abandoning their much-loved country life and moving to town. "We can get a 1st floor flat in a poor section of town for $45 a month," Polly wrote her parents, "but how we'd hate to do it!" They were lucky. They found what Polly described as "a quite elegant" house in Bethany that had been built only a year and a half before, whose owners needed semi-caretakers temporarily while the war was on and they were away.

During the last two weeks of September, in her seventh month of pregnancy and with a two-year-old, Polly set about moving. It was more complicated than an ordinary move, because in addition to their furniture and belongings they also had to deal with all the animals, beehives, plants, and various animal buildings. "It wasnt easy," Polly confessed in her journal. "Pictures had to be put away as there is no provision for them at the new house. Dishes etc had to be de-cockroached, (We spent as much time getting rid of cockroaches as we did on the actual packing & moving). The bees (7 hives) presented a problem; warm nights they wouldnt retire completely so we had to wait for cold nights before moving the stronger colonies."

Charles, named for his paternal grandfather, was born October 31, 1942. This time Polly's hospital stay was shorter and they were home in a week. Mary wanted to know if having a baby hurt, and Polly noted in her journal that she told her "it hurt enough for me to think 'ouch' but not enough for me to say it."

Childbearing didn't slow Polly down for long. From the hospital she wrote her parents that she was "seriously expecting" them for Christmas and it would be fun if Gardner and his wife, Barbara, could come too. Even from a distance, she remained involved in her siblings' lives, keeping her eyes open for second-hand clothes for their children, recommending doctors and treatments for Winifred's sick son and for Gardner's recurring sinus infections. David and Laura were constant visitors.

But none came to celebrate Charles's first Christmas. Instead, it turned out to be a sad holiday. Winifred, who had been pregnant at the same time as Polly, lost her child and Gwy went immediately to be with her in St. Louis. And without warning, Henry was stricken with tuberculosis.

He had not appeared to be at all sick. He had been working hard and late not only at his job, but also during the move. He had taken apart the barns, helped carry them over in pieces, and reassembled them on a cold rainy Sunday. Barely ten days earlier he had moved the drain into the new goat house, set up the indoor milking stand, and fixed the floor in the feed house. Colleagues and friends of Henry's had had the disease in previous years, but there had been no reason to suspect that Henry was susceptible.

On Christmas Eve he left for the TB sanitorium in Wallingford, Connecticut. Polly permitted herself only one terse sentence about this event at the conclusion of a journal entry for January 12, 1943, three weeks after his departure. The entry began with news that the goat, Gracie, was bred on December 26th, continued with news of Charles's weight, his ability to roll over easily from front to back, his responsiveness to people, his interest in biffing his strung up toys, his enjoyment of hot cereals and pablum. And then, almost parenthetically, "HB went to Gaylord on Dec. 24th." Fifteen empty pages followed; she wrote no more for nine months.

During the first three weeks in the hospital, Henry was not permitted even to sit up in bed, but he still managed to scribble letters. They were filled with detailed descriptions of all he could see outside his hospital window—"the cold freezing drizzle" and the sun lighting up "the gorgeous crystal landscape," icicles "twinkling musically" as they dropped off the trees. In one letter to Polly's parents he let them know how much he appreciated her: "her good sense, individuality, humor, balance, and what a good mother she is. Nor can I calculate what she has done for me, what a good influence she has been, how she's limbered me up mentally and changed my point of view about so many things, giving me a better sense of values." Previously Henry had always spent his free time outdoors "or making something with my hands." Now he was determined to use this enforced free time to make up for some lapses in his education. This would be an ideal opportunity to catch up on nonmedical reading. He brought his complete Shakespeare and Homer with him. He read Benjamin Franklin's *Autobiography*. He listened to the classical radio station from New York, putting on earphones to shut out the noise of the hospital and the other patients. As soon as sitting up was permitted, he sketched. Like Polly, he worked to make the best of a bad situation. "If I can't do my war work," he wrote Polly's parents, "I might as well take a real vacation, even though it seems selfish whenever I think of it in that light."

Despite having a two-year-old, a two-month-old, and a farm, Polly didn't miss a beat. Two days after Henry's departure, she not only bred one of the goats and cared for her two children, she also took in the children of friends. When Henry's sister suffered a miscarriage, Polly looked after her nephew, Johnny Fine.

Though rationing was in force, visiting sick relatives was considered a reason for getting extra gasoline and Polly managed frequent visits to Henry. It was the middle of a New England winter and snow and ice made the thirty-five-mile round trip difficult. Henry commented on the difficulties in his letters to Polly's parents; she never mentioned them in hers. She brought in a succession of part-time babysitters, and friends filled in on some weekends.

During the three months of Henry's hospitalization, Polly's letters to her family continued without interruption. Even reading between the lines, it would be difficult to guess that her husband was in a tuberculosis sanitorium. "Jan 18th: This week has been a pleasantly full one for me," and she described taking care of friends' two little girls because their father was spending a weekend at a camp for conscientious objectors. "The children will be in good hands while I visit Henry but I dont believe that the wood-pile will grow much." In the same letter she reported that Mary had learned to ride her bike. In another she described Mary's finding a photograph of a distinguished gentleman in the magazine *Better Homes and Gardens* and crying "Ce Granddaddy." Only occasionally did she reveal that she was a bit distracted. "I wish that I could remember just when I had written last. Was it to you or to Madison or to Princeton that I repeated such & such?" And in a rare admission that these were trying times, she wrote to her parents, "It was a great treat for all of us to have both of you here—one appreciates a visit these days." One indication of how busy she was is the absence in her journal of her usual records of the children, the goats, the gardens, or the bees.

Henry returned home on March 15th, the day on which Polly had planned to bring in a whole flock of new baby chickens. She postponed the chickens. "I guess I rate," Henry wrote her parents.

Polly noted his return in her journal with a single sentence: "Henry back from Wallingford March 15, 1943."

In the months following Henry's return, their usually packed lives assumed an almost meandering pace. "Sitting on the front porch," Henry wrote Polly's parents, "I can watch the straggling flocks of robins flying across the valley or the bounding dancing group of siskins bob in and out of sight; red shoulder hawks cry in our little valley and soar overhead; and the grouse thumps just back of the house." He spent his time observing the children and did everything he physically could with both Mary and Charles. He wrote detailed descriptions to Polly's parents of what they were doing.

> Charlie is now jumping back and forth from knees to hands on my bed. You've got to watch him all the time now as he can progress forward as well.
>
> M. is doing very nicely with her natural history. I taught her termites this morning—there are several nests within the fence rails lying on the ground here. She can spot beetles, spiders, bees, ants, flies, worms & caterpillars by their proper names as well as of course all the local four legged things and snakes too.... I have yet to see some natural thing she hasn't been interested in or mechanical gadget for that matter. All this plus her handling herself so well gives me much satisfaction because it assures me she will get so much more enjoyment out of life than if she didn't have these must-be-satisfied-itches. The other night it was very hard to get her to sleep after she had heard & asked what a cricket was without go getting the cricket. The next day P. found her one and the day after she found one herself.

With Henry at home, Polly's life was somewhat easier. He didn't need any special care, and she was able to leave the children with him when she ran errands or worked in the garden. Her days had what was for her an almost leisurely pace. One day she was actually able to sit on the porch and write a letter at 10:30 in the morning. "I generally finish up in the house by about 11 AM—then we all go outside while the dinner cooks. I go to the mail box, gather wood, clean stables or do some such until noon when I feed Charles & then the rest of us. Charles plays until 2 when Mary & Henry sleep. Then I go to the garden or tackle some special out-door or indoor job until 4 when I waken Mary & give C his orange juice. Mary & I do the chores, I put on supper, give baths & feed Charles. Then we three eat & by 8 o'clock Mary is back in bed & the kitchen picked up. Then Henry & I read until about 10. The reason it works so well is (1) because Charles is so dreadfully good and (2) because Mary naps & sleeps so well—and isnt much trouble these days anyway. . . . If I have Mrs. Hewins once in a while for ironing & cleaning I shall manage very comfortably."

She was still grappling with a familiar enemy: "The old time problem," she called it in her journal. She had tried, yet again, to set up hour-by-hour schedules, but then, for the first time, she seemed to accept the fact that life had become fundamentally different. After the schedule, she wrote, "All of which is nonsense because children dont work that way—nor husbands." In early December, while she treated herself to a haircut at the Roger Sherman Beauty Parlor, her first real excursion after Charles's birth, she admitted giving up another of her almost sacred rituals. She wrote her mother that she was going to invest in a stack of postcards, "because regular letter writing just doesnt work out."

By May, Henry was able to take short walks. Polly cleared an old path through the woods along the stream—"7 minutes worth of walking," as Henry described it. Sometimes he just walked around the garden and watched Polly working in it. As the summer went on, they were able to go a bit farther—blackberrying on the hillside, up to the field where Polly had found a towhee nest that Henry wanted to photograph. Pretty soon he was able to wash dishes and take more care of the children. Friends still dropped by for a visit or a swim, and Polly would thrust the rooster in the oven, make a ton of rice and gravy, and serve supper to all who had gathered. One rainy day Henry put Mary on her pony and led her into the woods where they found a lady slipper, a very rare lily. "And that was one of those special moments I've never forgotten," Mary said many years later. As the summer ended, Polly was finding life "very easy & pleasant these days for there are no pressing jobs to be done . . . and I find time each day for some bacteriology."

Henry returned to work part-time on September 1, 1943. "I can truthfully say," he wrote Polly's parents, "that this is the first vacation I have been glad to say is over." He came home at noon and rested in the afternoon, but by the end of the month he was already "writing furiously trying to finish a group of papers summarizing their research."

By the end of 1943, with Mary three and Charles one and Henry recuperating, the pace picked up once again. Polly took on one more chore, canvassing her neighborhood for War Bond and Stamp pledges. Although no more hour-by-hour schedules appear in her notebooks, many of her letters and journal entries are filled with detailed accounts of ordinary days, as if, once again, she were trying to examine them to see if there were any pockets of unused minutes she might be missing. "The way we run:—up between 6 & 6:30 with one child or the other. Feed Charles & prepare own breakfast. Henry shoots a rat & feeds the goats—then I milk & by 8 AM he is off to work & I start picking up the pieces. . . . Evenings not always as free as they might be—eg ironing etc. but not so bad either—certainly the best yet." She never stopped trying to find more efficient ways of operating. They constantly experimented with different schedules adapting themselves to the children's changing capabilities.

A full year after Henry was hospitalized, he finally appeared to be cured. Only then did Polly allow even an acknowledgment of the strain of his absence to appear in her journal. Characteristically this acknowledgement is oblique. She refers not to her own, but to Mary's anxiety about Henry's health.

"December 22, 1943—One can not help thinking, this week, of the events of a year ago, but it isnt something that one talks about very much. Yesterday morning Mary came to breakfast remarking—'My dolls are all sick today. If they dont get better I may have to take them to Wallingford.' We thought it curious. That night Henry was later than usual. He wasnt home at her supper time. 'Where's Daddy? Do you think he might be sick, Mother?' He had a slight cold—'I hope not,' I answered quite casually.

"And then the door opened & he came home—she flew off the stool into his arms. 'My Daddy came home. My Daddy came home.' Then we knew.

"The next morning at breakfast: 'Mother—why couldnt I go inside to see Daddy at Wallingford?' 'Remember when we got Gwy & went to see Daddy? Remember when we saw the baby in Wallingford' (I didnt) etc. etc. One finds out a lot from those like Mary who share their thoughts fairly freely." Polly, herself, was never one of them.

Dwelling on past pain was simply not something she did. Her way of dealing with the sadness in her life was to ignore it. When people she had been close to died, she noted their loss only perfunctorily. She wrote warm, compassionate letters to her parents upon the deaths of their parents, but in her journals she didn't comment on her own sense of loss. In the journal entry for October 23, 1941, she noted the death of her grandfather in a single sentence at the end of an ordinary day's entry about Mary's progress in walking and the rash over her nose. "Mother called this morning to say that Granddad had died last night—suddenly and peacefully." When one of her graduate school roommates died in her twenties, Polly wrote one short sentence—"Frankie died on Monday"—at the end of a routine letter to her parents which was mostly about dinners and her growing record collection.

Henry was well enough by the summer of 1944 to go with a group to Central America to look into the causes of tropical diseases that were afflicting soldiers. The government program required that after the trip he spend two months in Washington engaged in intensive study. Polly was pregnant again, but there is nothing in either her letters or her journals to suggest that she thought her condition should make him change his plans. She noted in her journal on May 26th that Henry had left on the 8:50 bus for New York, New Orleans, and ultimately Guatemala. Then "Millers over for lunch. Planted 10 rows field corn & mowed some lawn after they left."

Henry's recovery from TB seemed complete, but by November 28, 1944, he was again in the hospital—this time with pneumonia, which began with a sinus infection. He was back home in a few days. Polly didn't hover over him. She kept track of the health of each member of the family, noting details of even trivial things such as the children's colds and stomach upsets. None of it alarmed her; it was just part of her running record of their lives. And this third pregnancy was no exception; with more precision than an obstetrician, she kept a record of her weight changes, and noted when the nausea first appeared.

She also kept track of the weather. As the winter progressed and the snow got deeper, Polly recognized that getting down the hill from their house might be a problem, especially if she were in a hurry to get to the hospital. So she left the car parked on the highway. When labor began, Henry was at work in New Haven, so she skied down from the house, left her skis stuck upwards on the side of the road, and drove herself to the hospital in New Haven.

William Henry Bunting was born at 9:30 P.M. on Wednesday, January 17, 1945. He weighed ten pounds, and his mother described him as "well filled out" with "large open hands & feet—unsquashed head & not too red."

Life with three children didn't prove much different from life with two. One new chore, however, had been added: bringing in the hay— two tons of it. Polly borrowed a friend's truck, which happened to be without working brakes, and filled her barns, and also the barn of the neighboring farmer who helped. Henry threw himself into this task, working at it hard, "like an athlete," a friend remembered. Friends joined them for wonderful haying parties, sharing the work and the barbecue that followed.

By summer Henry was too busy even to take off a July weekend to go to Northport. "His lecture schedule is heavy," Polly wrote her parents, "& for the first time since the war began he's got a research program of his own going & he's awfully eager to follow up on it as much as he can."

Everything, however, turned upside down with the war's end in August, when the owner of their elegant home returned from the Navy and announced that he and his bride would be moving into the house. Once again, Polly and Henry began looking for a place to live. They got a babysitter at seven each night and went "tramping." They had always enjoyed exploring, but now they were under considerable pressure to find a place quickly that they could afford and that would be big enough for their growing family. And they were competing with returning veterans for scarce housing.

Luckily they found the perfect spot, on unpaved Hilldale Road, fourteen acres on a hillside that sloped down to a big meadow, surrounded by an apple and pear orchard and dense woods. There was no house there—they would have to build that—but it was pure Bethany country; Polly wrote her mother that they liked it so much they would rather have less of a house in this beautiful, tranquil spot than more of a house closer to the main road. Polly borrowed money from her parents to pay for it and was scrupulously careful about paying it back—$50 per month. Her father offered more lenient terms, but she stuck to their arrangement. Soon after, the road was resurfaced and widened to sixteen feet. Polly was relieved it was not to be wider.

Polly and Henry intended to move in mid-March. Henry was slated to take his final medical exams in Chicago just a few days before—the ones taken after many years of specialization to make him an accredited pathologist. Then their landlord changed his plans and decided to move in on March 1; the Buntings had to get out two weeks earlier than planned. Polly took the change in stride. In the midst of packing she gave her last dinner party.

And she still struggled to find time for intellectual endeavors. "Gradually the old discontent creeps up even on the emergency of moving. Therefore attempt once more ½ hour reading-study periods each day. Emphasis—goats' nutrition." She whittled her daily hour down to thirty minutes, but she didn't give up.

Easter was spent "moving our farm buildings onto the place. The goat house was taken to pieces, scrubbed with Turner water, piled on Tucker Downs' truck & taken to its new site. We also picked up a fine outhouse which the Coons no longer wanted. Next Sunday a gang is going to help us with the hay barn which we can then move intact. The fences & other odds & ends have been removed from the Turners so that episode is almost ended."

At the same time some exciting professional opportunities developed. Yale agreed to give Henry a year's leave with pay enabling him to do research at Harvard and MIT. And out of the blue, Polly was asked to give a paper at a major conference in the fall of 1946, which was to be held at Cold Spring Harbor, the preeminent Long Island laboratory, which for more than fifty years had been a gathering place for leading scientific researchers.

Cold Spring Harbor was an informal, rustic place, with summer cottages, roll-down tents, and primitive plumbing, but the relaxed atmosphere belied the intellectual excitement that took place there. It was a mecca for microbiologists. It was at the 1953 symposium that James Watson presented his and Francis Crick's double helix model for the structure of DNA. Before the war Cold Spring Harbor had been the site of yearly summer symposia, where some of the brightest lights in science gathered, but wartime shortages of gas and rationing of food had necessitated the cancellation of the meetings from 1943 through 1945. With the war finally over, the 1946 symposium was scheduled to include papers on the new work being done in Polly's chosen field. Polly, the only woman on the program, was invited at the insistence of Salvador Luria, who was in charge of the event and who, twenty-three years later, in 1969, won the Nobel Prize for his work on the genetic structure of viruses. At the time of the 1946 symposium he was a professor in the bacteriology department at Indiana University.

Luria had seen Polly's papers on *Serratia* and said that hers was the first good bacterial genetics that had been done prior to his own, in fact the only work before his that he considered real bacterial genetics. "We simply can not hold the Symposium without her," he said.[3] No one in the science world knew where Polly was or even who she was, but Luria tracked her down. At first Polly said she couldn't present a paper; she had been out of the laboratory for five years and was totally involved with her three small children. But Luria insisted. As it happened, "everybody else had had to go off for war work," Polly recalled years later. "I had been busy with children. I wasn't as far behind as I might have been."[4] So by the middle of April, in addition to moving buildings and children, Polly was also working on her paper. She got a babysitter every Wednesday night at six so she could have at least one long evening a week in the library. Henry took off the last few weeks of June to care for the children so that she could work uninterrupted.

When the program for the symposium was officially announced, Polly wrote her mother with pride, "26 speakers from many countries & laboratories. Mary I. Bunting (the only woman) from Bethany, Conn. looks awfully odd."

Writing this paper posed special difficulties because—partly to save money, partly because housing was so scarce, but mostly for the adventure—they had decided to spend part of the summer camping out on their newly acquired hillside. They converted their goat house into their main residence, having taken it apart, scrubbed and painted it—the "walls white, tops of tables & bunks, the bureau & cupboards a fine dark blue & floor & legs of things red—all done with left over paints." They placed the goat house in their orchard where it served as kitchen (with a two-compartment icebox), dining room, and, when the weather was bad, the children's play space. The children slept there too, and Henry rubbed some good insect repellent on them each night to protect them from mosquitoes. Polly and Henry slept out in a tent where the view was best.

"There wasn't room in the 10 by 14 foot goat house for all of our clothes, tools, cooking equipment, etc. but a nearby 'building' made from a large crate served nicely. Cardboard boxes on shelves on three sides, each brightly labeled, kept us organized and there was space in the center for a cozy dressing room." They had already acquired an outhouse, and they built an outdoor fireplace to do much of the cooking.

But just as they began camping, Mary came down with German measles and a 102 fever, so they temporarily abandoned the hilltop and moved to Henry's parents' house in New Haven to "await developments," as Polly put it. Once Mary recovered, they resumed their adventure.

Their first night actually ensconced in the goat house, Polly wrote letters by the light of the kerosene lantern while sitting at what she called their "eating bench." Mary pretended she was riding in a covered wagon, and Henry was off rehearsing his policeman's role in the *Pirates of Penzance*. The boys slept while a thunderstorm poured down outside, but the house remained warm and dry, "really very gay & cozy," Polly assured her mother.

By the first week in June, the weather was better. "We're all enjoying camp life—perhaps 'Mother' the most—everything seems so convenient & so easy—with clothes, food, cleaning reduced to a minimum. The kerosene stove works very smoothly—we even have our full breakfasts with hot cereal & pancakes. And fortunately the water is very soft so one gets fine suds even without heating it. I get an hour or

A Busy Life

two after lunch each day for writing & reading & the telephone never interrupts. The children have been on a water coloring binge & of course there's nothing like the out-of-doors for that."

Polly finished her paper and delivered it to about eighty experts in the concrete auditorium, Blackford Hall, which always smelled a little moldy. "It was exciting," she remembered. "There was the sense of getting acquainted again," among scientists who had been separated by the war.

"It was during that symposium that Polly took a walk with some of the other participants and had a conversation about what to call the new field. They settled on 'microbial genetics' because it included yeast and other organisms," said Evelyn Witkin, professor emerita of genetics at Rutgers, who was working with Luria. "That's how the field got its name, from that informal discussion." It was at this conference that "the new field of microbial genetics found its voice," Polly said years later.

Once the conference was behind her, Polly and Henry turned their attention to his coming sabbatical year. With so many veterans returning, housing was scarce everywhere and Polly and Henry doubted they could find a place to live in the Boston area. They considered using the farmhouse in Northport as their "headquarters," but then Polly was invited to teach a bacteriology course at Wellesley, taking the place of a professor on sabbatical. She agreed on condition that she could teach part-time and that they could find a place to live. They found 8 Waban Street, a house a few blocks from the Wellesley campus that they shared with several students who had the second floor.

Without her collection of Bethany neighbors and friends, Polly was without a babysitter. She believed she would have an easier time finding someone if she allowed a young mother to bring her own children along while looking after Mary, Charles, and Bill. She was right. She found lots who were "eager to get out of their homes and make a little money."

Even so, there were chaotic times and the children, young as they were, had to adapt to a crowded schedule. It was, as Polly wrote her mother, "a busy life." When their regular sitter became sick with a rheumatic heart condition and had to leave suddenly, they improvised and reorganized. "Some days Bill went off with Henry to a friend's house & Charles spent the afternoon in lab with me—which both boys thoroughly enjoyed. Other days students baby-tended during my actual teaching hours & I did a bit of laundry & cleaning between classes. Henry gets the dishes done each morning while I'm getting Mary & Charles off to school which is a big help—we make beds as we climb out of them." Mary was just five and attending the Wellesley nursery school, which was a short block away. But she also had the responsibility of bringing the family's groceries home in a wagon attached to her tricycle.

By December, Polly was pregnant for the fourth and last time. It was her most difficult pregnancy. She caught pneumonia in December, and to pay for extra help her parents sent a check, which she returned. "I'm much too well & this establishment is much too easy." After all, she didn't have the farm, the gardens, or the animals. Although she got better, the nausea didn't; she didn't feel really well until after the baby was delivered. She noted this only in her journal, never in her letters, and she kept right on with her teaching and with everything else.

Polly and Henry were looking forward to their return to Bethany and began making plans for building their home—their dream house. They pored over architectural books. They made drawings, drafted plans, consulted with Polly's parents, and asked for advice from her father's bankers. In January, Henry reserved cinder block, cement joists, and sheet metal for furnace ducts. "All subject to change—depending on what contractors say when we show them the plans." But as the months rolled by, there was one delay after another. Their contractor was honest and experienced, but known for his slowness. And even though he was an old scoutmaster and had a crew of former Boy Scouts—"excellent & loyal young fellows," Polly described them—the unrelenting demand for housing made it possible for workmen to press for higher and higher wages. Then in May, carpenters and painters in the New Haven area went on strike. Building materials kept going up and finally became so expensive that their contractor told them he could no longer make predictions about costs. He advised against building the house.

Always good at improvising, Polly and Henry decided to build just the cellar and hoped that prices would fall enough in a year to enable them to build the upstairs. Her parents were aghast. Polly tried to reassure them. "We've thought over your objections. . . . They all seem to be based on the notion that we shall be uncomfortable. After being in similar quarters that our friends, the Johnsons, used all last winter we are convinced that should not be the case. And we would so enjoy being rid of the complications of using other people's houses."

Setting up house for a family of what would soon be six in a forty-by-fifty-foot cellar required careful planning. They investigated every aspect, from the type of roofing paper they could use later on farm buildings, to the masonry and the sorts of space heaters that would be adequate: Army surplus space heaters for warmth and a Franklin stove "for cheer."

"We'll paint the inside with white bondex & the outside of course where it comes above ground." "The extra white paint & the bathroom in the cellar are both features we shall probably always be glad to have." "It was my idea to put in an open fireplace even if we had to put up the entire chimney to get it to draw. Then we could paint signs "1949 goal" etc along its length. However I'm afraid that was not considered practical. Betty Janeway suggested that a little holy water and a milk bottle with a slit in the top should be left outside the front entrance (beside the cellar bulkhead)."

As their time in Wellesley was ending, workmen in Bethany dug out the cellar with a bulldozer in about two days and promised to get the walls up by June 1st. Polly and Henry made plans to leave Waban Street at the end of the last week of June. It had been an extremely productive year for Henry. He published nine papers in 1947 alone.

For Polly, however, though the year had been productive, it had been too frantic and unfocused and had filled her with dissatisfaction. As she prepared to return to Bethany and a new baby, she pondered the future. She was much impressed by a somewhat philosophical article about the nature of science in the magazine *American Scientist* written by G. Evelyn Hutchinson, a zoology professor at Yale whom she knew. It was "the most inspiring column I have ever read," she exclaimed to her journal. She wrote "Hutch" a fan letter, but more importantly, summarized for herself what she found most noteworthy about the man himself: "Hutchinson is one of those rare individuals, so fortunately balanced, so beautifully constructed that the motions of his daily activities keep him wound up and the ill effects of environmental hazards are not able to reach or affect the mechanism."

Her own "environmental hazards" were the considerable demands on her time. While she read students' final papers and exams, she tried to figure out, once again, if there was a better way to manage her time. She prepared the family's future financial budget, which she hoped was realistic, and tried also to lay out what she called the "time budget."

"If Birge as pres of Wis could manage 1 hour/day in the lab—Best to try for that 1 hour after lunch & limit it to reading at least for the next half year. *Now* to make the reading count! How best?"

Attending the Cold Spring Harbor conference and then being thrust back into the classroom reminded her how intensely she loved science and how hard it was to combine research with caring for small children. As her Wellesley year came to a close, she read and reread an extraordinary article "Needed: Prestige for Mothers" by Rene Spitz, a psychoanalyst, which was printed in the *Vassar Magazine* of May 1947. Spitz argued that "Agrarian society seems to provide the ideal setting for woman—one in which she can adapt, develop and enjoy all her capacities, functions and desires in harmony with anatomico-biological patterns of the race. *The pattern guarantees the satisfaction of woman's instinctual urges, both on the level of her so-called sexual drives and on the level of prestige* [Spitz's italics]. In contrast with this we find that in industrial society neither of these urges can be properly satisfied." He bemoaned the requirements of an industrial society that directed more women into paid jobs, robbing children of the time and attention they needed, discouraging mothers from breast-feeding, turning children into "liabilities while in agricultural society they were assets." He blamed all the ills of society—divorce, juvenile delinquency, lack of purpose of the younger generation—on "the failure of western society to adapt the agrarian family pattern to an industrial civilization."

Polly took this article very seriously, reminding herself in her journals to read it yet again. She was thinking a lot about her role as a mother and ruminated in her journal in an unusually subjective tone. For the first time in Polly's musings there is a sense of urgency and a sense of her own mortality. "36 is half way. One ought to be pretty well wound up—discouraging to find oneself behaving as if one were almost run down—as if the internal mechanism had almost ceased to function, even tho the gold case may still look fairly impressive. Now or never—before rust completely & irrevocably destroys the fine metals—and those not so fine. The machine ran once, after a fashion & I dont know that any essential part is actually missing or beyond repair."

But she was pregnant, and they were far from settled. During the summer the children went down to Northport, while she and Henry bunked in the homes of friends and worked to make the basement habitable. They wanted to be sure they would have a good cement floor and since they didn't yet have a well, water for mixing it posed a problem. The fire department came over one Sunday with the pumper full of water, and lots of friends gathered around to pour the floor.

Polly prepared the walls until John arrived on August 25. Ideas about childbirth had changed in the few short years since Mary was born; this time Polly was home in three days and was planting the garden in four weeks. While she was in the hospital, Henry partitioned the bedroom and bathroom. It took them a few weeks to get pipes hooked up for their stove, and by that time "there had been a pane of ice ⅛" thick on the roof that morning so it was about time."

By the time John was three weeks old, the older children were back from Long Island and Polly rejoiced in her journal. "At last the family is gathered under one roof—and that roof is ours." She and Henry had been married for ten years, and this was their first place of their own—not rented, not borrowed, not temporary. They were home. By the first week in October Polly recorded in her journal, "Finally found my own clothes!" Even more important, they paid the last bill by October 17, the last and largest, and then "really owned the place." "I really think we've done all right," she wrote her parents, "we're comfortable, we're not in debt, and we havent sacrificed the size or quality of our future home because of present conditions."

8

The Best Years of All

They lived in the basement for two and a half years before they had saved enough money to begin building the rest of the house, and it took them nearly two more years to finish it. The work went slowly because, to keep down the costs, they did much of it themselves, with a little help from Mr. Bangberg, whom the children nicknamed Mr. Bangboard. He had two paralyzed fingers that stuck straight out, and the kids marveled at how he could continue to hammer. Polly considered taking a year off from work, but she didn't. She squeezed in the insulating and the floor finishing and the painting—the window trim red because "it rather warms the place up and pulls the house down to earth." The first day they really lived together upstairs as a family was Christmas Day 1951, and they celebrated, reveling in their comfortable living space with its windows overlooking their hilltop.

Soon after, Henry's mother died following a stroke, and Henry's father moved in with them. Henry and his father enjoyed an unusually close relationship, "one of the strongest bonds" in Henry's life, Polly said. Henry not only loved and respected his father, he also admired him as a teacher, a doctor, and a mentor. They realized what had been a long-standing ambition for both of them when they published a scientific paper together. When Dr. Bunting moved in, a friend suggested that he was so old he might be a burden. But Polly said that no matter how old someone was they could always contribute; since Pop couldn't go far, he could always be home for the children. For Chuck, his grandfather was an idol. He loved listening to his stories of his boyhood in Lacrosse, Wisconsin, growing up on the banks of the Mississippi. He reminded Chuck of Mark Twain; he even wore white linen suits as Mark Twain had.

Polly was still trying to juggle time slots. A year after returning from Wellesley, she extricated herself from some of her volunteer activities.

Then she added a new one. She began to collaborate with Henry on a weekly newspaper column called "The Countryside" for the *Amity*

Star, a weekly tabloid that was written, printed, and published by friends. The paper detailed the comings and goings of the town—the card parties and fashion shows, the Bethany Athletic Association's banquets for the basketball team, the firemen's balls, the "Ladies Society" gathering to hear the director of a New Haven nursery school discuss "The Joys and Problems of Child Rearing," the sixth-grade pageant on the "American Way of Life" depicting contributions "which different racial groups make." It ran photographs of children sledding on the Buntings' hill and photographs of the PTA Junior Fashion Show models—elementary school girls in party dresses, white gloves, white socks, and Mary Janes.

The Buntings' first column appeared May 24, 1951. Like almost all those that followed, it was full of information, but also tried to help readers increase their enjoyment of the natural world. Almost all of the columns, many of which were written primarily for children, posed questions that could be answered only by careful observation. "Have you ever caught a firefly? Which part of him does the flashing? Is the light hot?" In another column they asked, "Nests of red shouldered hawks are located in conspicuous places—Can anyone tell us where one is?"

By this time Polly and Henry were not only involved in Bethany's social life, their sense of civic responsibility also led them to become involved in its politics. They attended town meetings about budgets, where everything from snow plowing to the school music program was argued about. As a member of the zoning board, Henry found himself participating in knock-down, drag-out fights. Polly learned a great deal about politics from these meetings. She got practice negotiating with opponents and navigating the sometimes treacherous backwaters of political infighting—experience that was to serve her well.

Another way Polly exercised her sense of civic responsibility was by being a leader of 4-H, the national agricultural education program with the motto "Head, Heart, Hands, and Health," which had been part of rural towns since the turn of the century. In Bethany, 4-H was partly social, partly civic, and partly a service organization where you could learn how to make clothes, how to plant a garden, how to make pies, and participate in the county fair. When the annual county fair was on, it was the major story in the local paper, warranting banner headlines. More than two thousand exhibitors turned up.

Polly had taken on a group of 4-H boys during the war, after they had been left leaderless; and when the war ended she just continued, smuggling in Bill even though he was underage. He named the group "Hide, Fur and Feathers." They engaged in the usual activities, but they were young boys and also enjoyed some pranks. One of the group's more memorable ones was to "borrow" Mary's pony and, without anyone knowing, to breed her with a male pony they had located. When Mary's pony began to look a little chubby, she thought it was just getting ready for the winter. But one morning she went out to the field and saw what she thought was a Great Dane. It was a new little pony.

All 4H clubs were supposed to have a community project. "I had suggested worthy causes like eradicating poison ivy along the highways," Polly said many years later. "They didn't buy it. Then a couple of them noticed that the town bulldozer was preparing to dig a hole in a swamp near the school to make a place for the fire engine to fill its tank. Why not make a big pond, big enough for ice skating in winter and swimming in summer. There was no such place near the center of town." Peck Pond, as it was eventually called, came to be a real center for the kids of Bethany. But it took extensive research, fund-raising, political maneuvering, and the involvement of many more groups than just Polly's band of 4-H boys. Polly eventually formed a twenty-one-person committee to handle the growing number of details. She started as its secretary, but three years later the group was still handling details, and she was the chair. They published regulations in the *Amity Star* asking people not to disturb the plants or animals. "Bathing is permitted," the regulations stated, "but no washing with soap."

"Peck Pond certainly was a success," she said, "but the first summer the principal of the school and I had to be life guards whenever it was open. He had found out that only one child in the 8th grade and half of the seniors in the school knew how to swim."

Years later Polly said she got more satisfaction out of the creation of Peck Pond than anything else she did in Bethany. She remained involved with it as long as she lived there, keeping track in her journals of the numbers of people swimming, and working to encourage people to contribute time and money so the pond could keep going, and the site expanding for more uses. Eventually it included a wildlife sanctuary. The pond is still there, "for the benefit of the citizens of Bethany" the sign reads. "That's a long time for something like that to last," Polly said.

Another of Polly's community activities was even more complicated and time-consuming: the establishment of a regional high school for the towns of Bethany, Orange, and Woodbridge.

While their children were small, Polly and Henry had been pleased with the Bethany school. It was a four-room brick building with classes of about fifteen to twenty children—two grades to a room. But the school became overcrowded and it only went to the eighth grade. As her children got older, the prospect of sending them to the infamous Hillhouse High School in New Haven, the only high school in the area, was not appealing. For farm kids to travel to the "big city" was a traumatic experience. Besides, Hillhouse was overcrowded too. Even worse, there were muggings in the halls.

In the past, students from rural areas hadn't gone on to high school in significant numbers; they had gone to work on their family farms after elementary school. Rural school boards hadn't felt pressure to supply the elaborate buildings and trained staffs that the expanding high school curriculum had come to require. By the early 1950's, however, Connecticut was becoming more densely populated, so there were more high school age students in rural areas, transportation improved, farming began to give way to mechanization, and the demand for more education and job training sharply increased. At the same time high schools began to include many forms of job training and extracurricular activities, such as sports and clubs; students wanted to participate in the full life of the school and not worry about coordinating their school schedule with that of the bus.

When the contingent of Bethany children with Yale-affiliated parents was approaching high school age, many thought it might be time to build a high school for Bethany and two nearby towns, Orange and Woodbridge. The three towns set up a joint twelve-member Temporary Regional School Planning Committee with Polly and Pete Treffers, a neighbor and friend who was chair of the Yale microbiology department, as part of the Bethany contingent. Through the fall of 1952 Polly attended school committee meetings, town meetings, PTA meetings, all in connection with this project.

The School Planning Committee completed its work and made its report within a matter of weeks, recommending the establishment of a regional high school. In the referendum that followed, the three towns voted to support the project. So Regional High School District No. 5 came into being and the three towns elected representatives to the Regional Board of Education, a nine-member board that elected Polly secretary.

The school itself still had to be created and this proved to be extremely complicated and expensive. Townspeople had to be convinced to approve a $1.8 million bond issue. The board had to find a site and select an architect, develop plans, choose contractors, hire a superintendent, and develop a budget. Polly was involved with every aspect of this undertaking.

After many vicissitudes the thirty-room school, with Mary and Charles among the students, opened on September 27, 1954. The furnaces weren't working, but Polly wrote her parents, "the students are working hard and not complaining." Polly even suggested that it was just as well that all was not perfect. "Perhaps it is psychologically very good to start in a bare working nucleus & watch the improvements come. I'm sure if we had handed the community a complete school there would have been many more adverse criticisms."

The establishment of the regional high school was the most significant achievement of Polly's Bethany years. It enabled her to serve her community, to make things better, always of great importance to her. But the experience also served her personally, by helping her to hone her organizational and political skills; by requiring her to practice patience and diplomacy; by increasing her understanding of the financial aspects of education; by forcing her to speak in public and discover that she could do it. Above all, her achievement in helping establish the regional high school soon became an unexpected credential; it proved beyond any doubt that she was interested in and committed to public education.

When Polly looked back many years later, she was to say about these Bethany years, "Living was easy; I had returned to research on a part-time schedule. The children had their 4H projects. We all had many friends. I think those were the best years of all."[1]

9

Heaven on Earth

Before the new high school even opened, Polly was faced with the cataclysm that changed her life profoundly and irrevocably. It stole upon her without warning. In an ordinary letter to her parents, dated March 24, 1954, she commiserated with her mother about some indisposition, and gave the usual rundown of the illnesses of each of the children. And then on page two—"Actually Henry is the one who has been suffering lately with awful headaches. They have been present more or less continuously for about a month & have been very severe during the last week. When a wave comes on he gets faint & nauseated etc. & really feels rottenly most of the time.

"He is checking sinuses etc. & trying all sorts of things now & feels somewhat better today than he has during the last few days. I'm glad to say that he is sleeping well.

"Now I'll go look for him & drive him home if possible."

Three weeks later, on April 15, 1954, barely a month after his forty-third birthday, Henry Bunting was dead of a malignant brain tumor. The scientific paper he had published with his father the year before was his last.

Most of their friends and colleagues had not even known he was sick. "Nobody knew anything about that," said Mary, who was thirteen at the time. "That's the way they did things then. They didn't talk about death." Henry's older sister, Elizabeth, who lived another fifty years, never forgave him for not telling her. Even his doctor, William Winternitz, whose father was Henry's boss at Yale, and with whom Henry had set up ski jumps on their hillside, did not expect him to die. Henry even refused to allow the young doctor to order X-rays. He felt sure what they would show, and he wanted no surgery. "He would not go to the hospital," said Winternitz. "He was adamant. He did not want anybody messing with him. I couldn't get him to go where we could do X-rays. I was just trying to treat him symptomatically. I was working on sinuses. In the last week or two when he began to get nauseated, I gave him a new drug that was potent against nausea. Imagine me, a young internist, attending this highly respected and loved figure without knowing what was going on."

Henry had diagnosed his own condition, but at first he didn't even confide in Polly. She did not realize how serious things were until they went skiing and he became so nauseated from the pain they had to stop so he could vomit. "I didn't realize how significant and how severe the headaches were," she said, "but he did. He just didn't think anybody would be helped by talking about it." She didn't talk about it either. As close as she came was to say to young Bill Winternitz, "there is nothing Henry can't have" if it could help, and to ask once if Henry should go to the Mayo Clinic. But she never even suggested to the doctor that she knew he was dying.

The children didn't know what was happening until it was all over. The night before Henry died they saw an IV attached to his arm, but they didn't know what that meant. The doctor had been coming periodically, but he had been doing so for quite awhile, so they didn't attribute any importance to that. Chuck awoke in the middle of the night and saw red lights flashing outside the house, but as the town doctor Henry was sometimes called out in the middle of the night. Bill remembered in the preceding weeks, Henry's pressing the cold water tanks they kept in the car for fire-fighting against his head. The cold gave some relief. "Before Dad died," Bill said years later, "I often faked being sick—mostly because I disliked school so much. I was amazed it was so easy to fool Mother. In retrospect, she was just giving me time with Dad, and Dad time with me."

Bill Winternitz's telephone rang about midnight. It was Polly telling him that Henry had stopped breathing. "I raced over there. I did a tracheotomy. I did everything I could think of. I called Ned Shutkin, another doctor, who came and helped. We called an ambulance. That was a wild ride to the hospital. We did artificial respiration which we knew wasn't going to do any good but we couldn't stop. He was gone. If we had been less involved emotionally, we would have recognized that. I couldn't accept it. That night was a defining moment in my life, one of the worst nights of my life. When I was chastising myself, saying maybe I'm responsible, Ned Shutkin said, 'You're not God,'—for which I was grateful."

Polly followed the ambulance in her car, and when they left the hospital at about five in the morning she drove Bill Winternitz and Ned Shutkin back to her house, where their cars were parked. "She was completely unemotional," Winternitz remembered, "no crying, no hugging, nothing but a thick feeling of depression in that car. No one said much. It was as if we had come home from a long drive to New York, home from somewhere routine.

"I picked up my car and went back to my office in New Haven. I didn't sleep. I didn't do anything. Then one of the pathologists came to my office to tell me what he had found—a wildly growing brain tumor that would have been untreatable. That was very important to me."

The children awoke the next morning to see their grandfather in his pajamas. They had never seen him in his pajamas before. Mary asked, "Grandpa, are you sick?" "Mother then pulled me away so Grandpa didn't have to answer," Mary said. "And she told me that Daddy had died that night. And he was already gone, which was the other amazing thing. It just ended. I was 13. When we finally went back to school I remember sitting in the school bus—Chuck and Bill and me—all in the same seat that normally only two people sat in. I remember just feeling I was so different from everyone else on the bus. I didn't know anyone else whose father had died. I just remember the three of us sitting on that bus, holding on for dear life."

Eliza Janeway, Polly's Vassar roommate, called as soon as she heard. She offered to come right away. But Polly said, "No, we're getting along all right. We're doing all right."

Henry was cremated and his ashes buried in Bethany. A week later, on April 22, a memorial service was held in the Dwight Memorial Chapel on the Yale campus. The more than one hundred seats were filled, and people crowded in and were standing anywhere there was space. Polly and the children cut apple blossoms to fill the chapel. Henry had always loved his orchard, and the apple blossoms were at their height. The Reverend Sidney Lovett, the university chaplain, conducted the service. H. Frank Bozyan, an assistant university organist, played. Professor Thomas C. Mendenhall, a lifelong friend and master of Berkeley College, where Henry was a fellow, spoke. He emphasized Henry's generosity of spirit and his total indifference to material things. "They tended to come between him and others, to diffuse that warmth which he gave off so lavishly. Polly has told me of a letter, written years ago when they were newlyweds and his family was urging him to buy a house. He resisted, saying, 'The only kind of possession that has ever seemed real to me is appreciation; in this sense my holdings are very considerable and all my titles are clear.'"

People did what they could. Gardner gave them a TV. Neighbors brought food, so much that Polly told a friend she could not get another thing in her freezer. A painter who had done some of the painting on the house came by and asked if he could help with some chores, like taking down storm windows. Polly thought that was a much more sensible response than sending flowers, of which they got many.

"I remember her hugging this wonderful man, Mr. Wong, who lived in Boston," remembered Mary. "He was someone they got to know during the Wellesley year. He would come and visit us on his way to see relatives in New York City. And he would always bring this pistachio ice cream my father loved. And I remember his coming sometime after Daddy died and driving in with his pistachio ice cream, and Mother having to tell him Daddy wasn't alive, and that man broke down and cried and Mother held him. And it was a moment—I felt so badly for her and for him and maybe for everybody."

Polly behaved characteristically. Although a close friend described her grief as so profound she was "in another state of being," neither her friends nor her children ever saw her cry. The stoicism and self-discipline that had never permitted her to dwell on sorrows drove her now. Within days of Henry's death, Polly returned to the laboratory, returned to delivering eggs from the farm to those in the medical school who had ordered them.

Polly's deep feelings of closeness to Henry remained as long as she lived. His photograph—of a serious, young man with intense dark eyes—was on her dresser into her old age. And on what would have been his eightieth birthday she wrote everybody in the family a letter about him, wishing he had been alive to see his children and their spouses and his grandchildren.

Polly did everything possible to keep up the pattern of life she and Henry had established together. The following December she gave a New Year's party for her children and their friends—thirty-nine teenagers—and wrote her parents that they were "all at their best, singing, dancing & visiting." Henry had always taken each of his children on a special trip for their birthdays. The January after Henry's death, Polly drove Bill and three of his friends to the Mystic, Connecticut, marine museum. "It was a good day," she wrote her parents, "—the trip promised Bill 364 days before."

Her parents respected her independence and allowed her time to adjust. "I think the Bethany family is bravely facing the future," Polly's father wrote to Winifred, who was still living in Kansas City. "I have a little the feeling that the labor of so big a place and so many activities with animals and crops and gardens will be burdensome in connection with intellectual pursuits. But they will work things out." Polly remembered overhearing her father reassuring her worried mother, "You must respect the independence of the widow." Polly thought that was something he'd learned from his experience as a lawyer helping widows. They needed to feel they were going to make it. "Which I had never thought of in those terms at all," Polly said, "and therefore remembered it."

"Polly thrived on being busy," said Winifed. "After Henry died I think this business of keeping occupied wasn't just financial necessity."

Financial necessity, however, was certainly part of it. She said years later that she knew her family would have supported her if she needed them, but she wanted to manage on her own if she could. She wanted to take care of her own children. She applied to the high school to teach, but in spite of her Ph.D. and years of research, she was turned down because she wasn't certified. She had given occasional guest lectures at Yale and had always found her work there rewarding, but now she had to make a living. There was no question of her becoming the principal advisor on doctoral dissertations. She didn't have a teaching appointment, and she had no illusions about the likelihood of being offered one. It was not something any woman could expect; Yale was a closed society. There was an unwritten law.

Years later Polly said, "I was worried about staying at Yale. I was very much afraid that they might make a position for me, primarily because of my husband, which wouldn't be good for anyone."[1] She needn't have worried. Such an offer never came, in spite of the efforts of her good friend Pete Treffers, who was chair of the microbiology department. He tried to cobble together a job for her, half-time teaching in the master of arts in teaching program, and the other half teaching an undergraduate course in microbiology. Treffers wrote to the provost of Polly's excellent work, and of the teaching she had done without pay. He outlined the need for an undergraduate program in microbiology, which she would be eminently qualified to teach. The provost turned him down by return mail, citing financial reasons and maintaining that his refusal "implies no reflection on the merit of your candidate ... but is one element in an over-all directive to prevent any expansion in the course offerings of the F.A.S." [the faculty of arts and sciences].

Polly continued with some of her community obligations, attending meetings of the nurses association and meetings on the regional high school. She showed up regularly in the laboratory, working almost full-time. Bill Belser, a graduate student with whom she published several papers, said, "She felt strongly that she had a job to do and she did it." Sometimes she brought John, who was seven, with her. When speaking about this time years later, Polly would say only, "My hand was somewhat in but my research was second rate."[2]

Henry's death brought to an end the life she wanted and had assumed would always be hers—doing research that interested her, living in the kind of rural place she loved, bringing up her children in the way and in the place she and Henry had chosen together, in the home they had built with their own hands. With Henry's death that world ended. She always had country places to retreat to and gardens to tend, but never again was her life to assume this shape, this pace, that she found so congenial and so satisfying. The life that had afforded her the satisfactions she cherished most was over.

It was her volunteer community activities rather than her scientific research that propelled her into an entirely new life. Six months after Henry died, on October 14th, Polly's old friend from Bennington, the economist Barbara Jones, who had audited Polly's first genetics class, called to say she had some business at Yale and would be close by: Could she drop in for a visit? Jones spent the night, and Polly told her about the work she was doing for the regional school: selecting an architect and a superintendent, lobbying for the bond issue, addressing town meetings.

Polly knew that Barbara Jones's husband, Lewis Webster Jones, was the president of Rutgers University. She did not know that Douglass College, the New Jersey state college for women affiliated with Rutgers, was looking for a dean. "It was years before I realized that she had come up to see what shape I was in," Polly said, "and would I be a good person to put on the list at Douglass College. And the things we talked about were just the right things." Although Polly had only been a volunteer, her work on the regional school had given her significant experience with public education and shown her commitment to it. "So I guess she went home with a good report. A while afterwards some of the trustees at Douglass College came to see me, but it took me a long time to make that connection."

Polly had never even considered academic administration, but when the offer came, the job looked very attractive. "Perhaps the time was ripe for a woman who had been married and had children." And she badly needed a paycheck.

But the decision to take the job was a difficult one. Douglass was in New Brunswick, New Jersey, a city, and going there would mean abandoning the rural life she and the children loved. They had known city kids, kids from New Haven, who seemed to them, in Mary's words, to be from "a different space." Going would also mean for Polly herself permanently giving up her scientific research and embarking on an entirely new career. She asked her children what they thought. "Mary spoke up. 'Mother, this is a decision that you'll have to make, and not us,' which was right and she carried the day with the others."

Polly sized up her options and decided they should go. Rather than clinging to hopes that could no longer be realized, she changed direction entirely and embraced a new challenge and an entirely new life and never looked back.

"It was very difficult to decide what to do," Polly admitted years later. But she finally arrived at what for her was the decisive argument. "I recognized that the children thought the whole world was Bethany, and that was not necessarily the best way for them to think about the world. It seemed to me that the worst thing I could do for them then would have been to reinforce the notion that heaven on earth was in just this one spot where they had happened to be born. When one had an interesting challenge, one shouldn't be afraid to take it. There were good people wherever one might live."[3]

Part III
The Second Life

10

A Sightseer in a New Land

Polly was officially appointed the third dean of Douglass College on March 24, 1955, exactly one year to the day since writing that restrained letter to her mother about Henry's illness and barely eleven months after his death. In announcing the appointment, Rutgers President Lewis Webster Jones said he had chosen her with the "unanimous agreement" of separate faculty and trustee advisory committees and said he believed she was "an admirable choice." He also found it necessary to state that she was "a charming lady" and "one of the rather rare individuals who have successfully combined a distinguished career in research and scholarship with the responsibilities of her family." The photograph in the student newspaper was of Polly with all her children.

The stage had been set for her a few months before her appointment when, with much fanfare and celebration, the college changed its name from what it had been for its first thirty-seven years—New Jersey College for Women, abbreviated to N.J.C.—to that of its founder and first dean, Mabel Smith Douglass. More than a thousand people, including the governor of the state, gathered for the event, which was held in the college's elegant chapel. The name change symbolized a fundamental shift in character from a kind of ladies' institution into a real college. So even before Polly's arrival change had already begun; she noted in her first convocation speech, "It was an auspicious time to come to Douglass."

New Jersey College for Women came into being because of the prodigious efforts of Mabel Smith Douglass, an elegant, blonde, Jersey City matron, whose sense of justice was fired when she discovered that women were not permitted to attend the state university. With no organizational experience—she had never even held a job—she launched her crusade and proved to be a brilliantly effective and indefatigable crusader.

Her Jersey City neighbor, James T. Fielder, happened to be the governor, and through him she got an interview with President Woodrow

Wilson to ask for his support in setting up the new college. She gave hundreds of addresses in high schools, clubhouses, private homes, and Grange halls. She was, nonetheless, rebuffed by philanthropic foundations, so she appealed to the women of the state and organized a one dollar subscription drive for a first building. She wasn't able to raise enough money; and when she collapsed from exhaustion in 1915, others in the State Federation of Women's Clubs took up the cause. After seven years of nonstop political activity and pressure, their efforts succeeded when the Rutgers trustees agreed to establish a "coordinate college of the state university," though Rutgers would not assume any financial responsibility for it. All its funding had to come through its own efforts.

In spite of its shaky start, the college survived and prospered. When its first class of forty-two students graduated in 1922, it already had a Phi Beta Kappa chapter. Barely ten years later, more than a thousand students were enrolled, the land and buildings were worth many millions of dollars, and the library, which when the college opened had consisted of only twelve books sent over from Rutgers and housed in the registrar's closet, now had over six hundred.

When Mrs. Douglass became its first dean in 1918—like Polly—she was a young widow with children. She hoped ten or maybe fifteen students would apply, a respectable number since only 3,416 girls had graduated from all of the state's public high schools that year. Instead, fifty-four young women began classes in ivy-covered Carpender mansion, where they also lived. There were sixteen faculty members. The curriculum included all the standards of the liberal arts as well as teacher education and home economics.

The doors were almost immediately closed, however, when Spanish influenza struck and all the students had to be sent home. But fifty of the fifty-four returned and managed to survive the winter even though they had to study in coats and galoshes, huddled around small coal stoves and oil heaters, since there was no other heat in their living quarters.

The home of Drury Cooper across the street served as infirmary, dining hall, and second dormitory. Presently a gymnasium was added. Since it was built of World War I surplus boxes, in which airplane engines were to have been shipped to Europe, it was supposed to be only temporary, but the packing-box gym ended up housing the physical education program for the next forty-three years.

Between 1923 and 1926 the state gave funds for three more buildings called Science, Recitation, and Botany, but then the generosity ended; not a single classroom or student building was built with state funds until Polly's time. But private benefactors came forward, and the campus spread out on a hundred acres of sprawling New Jersey woods. Most of the land was donated by James Neilson, an old neighbor whom Mrs. Douglass called "Our Fairy Godfather," and when he died in 1937 at ninety-three he left his colonial-style mansion to the college.

More than buildings were established in these early years. The college's ethos and traditions were put in place as well. An honor system, which governed all aspects of student life, remained for many decades. And perhaps most significant, the small houses, which Mabel Douglass built instead of dormitories, continued to survive. Mrs. Douglass couldn't borrow enough money to build big dorms so she made a virtue of necessity and instead built twelve residences on a horseshoe-shaped drive figuring that, should the college not survive, these houses could be sold as private homes. Even after enrollment burgeoned, and large, conventional dormitories had to be built, life in the individual houses proved so satisfactory that the college eventually built even more of them.

When she came to Douglass in 1955, Polly had been there only twice before. She told everybody who questioned her that she would have no plans for the place until she had time to look and learn. She spent the summer learning. She shuttled back and forth between Bethany and the guest room of the dean's house, conferring with her predecessor until she took over herself on July 1. The fall Douglass alumnae magazine described just how busy her summer had been. "She's investigated every nook and cranny of the campus; she's met with trustees, faculty, administrators, department heads, student leaders and alumnae officers. She's studied reports and recommendations and read, read, read.... Matters of curriculum, budget, student enrollment and undergraduate life, faculty and staff, personnel, physical plant, community and public relations have been just some of her concerns." Years later Polly described herself as "a sightseer in a new land."[1] Although college campuses were familiar territory—she had spent a good part of her adult life on them—she was unprepared for administration. She had never taken education courses, had never expected to leave teaching and research, and had never given serious thought to administrative concerns.

Bill was in Europe with family friends, and the other three children were in Bethany with their grandfather. The neighbors down the hill, whose daughter Henry had delivered at home, became like an extended family, and helped. Polly managed to find time to write Bill jolly, frequent letters full of hints of things he should look for ("Did you know that our American robin is really a thrush?—the genuine robin you can now see—"), motherly admonishments ("Very not vary, otherwise your spelling is much better than in your first letter. Keep it up!"), along with news of home—Mary's riding ribbons in the rodeo, Chuck's two-night scout camporama.

She had a vastly different style from that of her predecessor, Margaret Trumbull Corwin, who was very much of the old school and whose administration was filled with what one administrator called "a stodgy group of maiden ladies." Dean Corwin was herself a maiden lady with no academic credentials, who before coming to Douglass in 1934 had spent fifteen years as secretary of the Yale University graduate school. She was described by one long-time home economics professor as "a white-gloved woman."

Propriety mattered to Dean Corwin. Hats and gloves were required at college functions, and when the girls ventured into town they were instructed to dress and behave like ladies. Reserved and formal, she kept the dean's house orderly and immaculate. She had all the seniors for luncheon in small groups—definitely a hat and gloves occasion. They sat at the polished dining room table while she introduced her favorite subjects: something current that she wanted their reactions to, or a book she encouraged them to read.

She was, from all reports, a kindly woman, but she ran a tight ship. When the student newspaper printed the names of nominees for the following year's staff without having submitted them first to her, she shut down the paper for almost a year. Faculty meetings began with the college secretary taking attendance, "making you feel like a kid in the 6th grade," complained one professor. This procedure might explain why, shortly after Polly's arrival, a professor wrote her a note asking permission to miss a faculty meeting, explaining that he could not get back on time from a professional meeting in Atlantic City.

Dean Corwin described her college as "a campus devoted to plain living and high thinking,"[2] attitudes that had a chilling effect on some faculty who felt she was running the place like a girls' finishing school. A student who was caught sneaking back into her dormitory room after hours, admitted under Dean Corwin's questioning that she had been in New York with her fiancé. Dean Corwin then asked whether she had slept with him; apparently the answer was "yes," because the student was put on probation for the term. When a sociology professor who found out about this sarcastically suggested at a faculty meeting that perhaps the catalog ought to list "virginity" as one of the requirements for graduation, Dean Corwin was reported to have told him that, so long as she was dean, he would never be promoted. When a married, part-time female faculty member was called back to fill in for a colleague sick with pneumonia, she explained to Dean Corwin that she was pregnant but would be willing to help out for a few months. "Dean Corwin gave this nervous little giggle and said, 'Well, times change. I guess you will be the first pregnant woman—at least the only one I know about—at Douglass.'" Polly, on the other hand, saw an opportunity when a friend of hers became pregnant. She made sure to have her come to speak to a class "to show that pregnant people could be scientists."

No wonder that Polly's arrival, as a vigorous, informal, young woman, with children and serious academic credentials, signaled to many people on the Douglass campus that a new day had come. Dress, to her mother's despair, was still not one of her priorities. She had no difficulty forgetting white gloves. And when she spoke to a New Jersey women's group, she noted instantly that she was the only person in the room without a hat. For future occasions of this sort, she decided, she had better wear one. She ran up the stairs to her office, which startled some long-time employees who were accustomed to more sedate behavior on the dean's part; she ate yogurt for lunch before yogurt was fashionable. When she went walking on the campus in the early morning, she wore sneakers and almost always had at least one child in tow and often at least one dog. "The dynamic dean," the students called her. They noted in their yearbook that she played hockey and tennis and went ice-skating and parked a big, old, tan-and-cream station wagon in the driveway. When a blizzard shut down the campus, Polly realized the milking machines at the Agricultural College wouldn't be working, so she went over and helped milk the cows. The fall dean's tea for new faculty, which in the past had been a formal affair, was now an occasion for "a bunch of little kids and animals," according to the recollection of a faculty member hired in 1958. "It was kind of startling—livestock running around. I sat down on the couch and it had no bottom." When a Rutgers student invited her to supper at his fraternity, she shocked him when she declined in favor of "coming over later for a beer."

In a gesture to the students who entered with her in 1955, Polly put on the small round hat, called a "dink", which identified first-years. She, too, she told them, was "a freshman," just starting out. When time came for the faculty show, she played the part of an alien and put on a hat that beeped.

The day after she and the children moved into the dean's house, she was finishing some errands when she saw a distressed twelve-year old boy in a neighboring backyard. He had an ax in his hand, a look of agony on his face, and six chickens in a coop nearby. She asked him what was the matter, and he explained that the police had said it was illegal to have these chickens in town; his father had told him to kill them, and he didn't know how. Polly told him she had killed lots of chickens so she put down her bundles, caught the hen, showed the boy how to hold the wings and legs so that they wouldn't flutter, and finished the job on the chopping block.

11

A Great Cultural Change

Polly's arrival not only ushered in a new era for Douglass College, but also a new era for the Bunting family. They drove down from Bethany looking, Mary was convinced, a little like Okies. Mary's pony, Beauty, was in the back of a friend's open truck, tied down, with so much furniture packed all around her that the terrified animal tried to get out. With difficulty they managed to get her to the Agricultural College.

Life for her children, Polly was well aware, would be far different in almost all respects from the years that had gone before. She tried hard to find ways to ease the pain and the shock. One way was to preserve as much as possible of the children's country life. She bought a little farm in Califon, about twenty-five miles from New Brunswick near the Raritan River. She convinced the Agricultural College that they could use Beauty for a scientific experiment of dubious importance—something about the efficiency with which horses utilized their nutrition. They kept Beauty and measured her urine and feces, but the real purpose, of course, was to have the pony close enough to afford Mary some comfort. The Buntings adopted a stray dog that had turned up in one of the dorms and named her Claudia; they housed prairie dogs, Clarence and Josephine, in the basement, which had a dirt floor; during at least two summers Polly adopted a goat from a dairy so that John could milk it and get a taste of the goat experience he felt he had missed.

Nonetheless, the children all found the adjustment to New Brunswick profound and difficult. "Cataclysmic," was the way Bill described it. Until that moment, he said, "it really had been about as idyllic a childhood as one could imagine. It was downhill after that." As adults, they all agreed that Bethany had been the defining experience of their lives—that all the choices they later made were determined by having their childhood in that place. "Bethany was the most important part of our lives," said Bill. "I think we're all still trying to live in Bethany." And indeed, a few weeks after their arrival Bill did go back to Bethany for a long visit. He stayed several weeks with old family friends, went to school with them, but then decided that even if he didn't like New Brunswick, maybe he belonged with his own family after all, and he came back. Mary informed Polly that she would stay only through the first year to help Polly get started in her new job, but then she was going back to Bethany. Polly said, "Thank you. I'll need you the first year. You just stick by." Mary stuck by until she left for the University of Vermont four years later.

One of the first things that bothered the children about New Brunswick was the house they moved into. It could not possibly have been more different from their handmade Bethany home. Built in 1900, the dean's residence, an elegant, three-story, red brick mansion, was one of the fanciest houses in town and had belonged to one of the most prominent families. It had pillars, large windows, a dumbwaiter, and a butler's pantry with a marble sink and a door with huge iron hinges that swung both ways to make traffic into the dining room as easy as possible for the butler the Buntings did not have. The bathrooms, too, were marble and tiled. It had eight fireplaces, many of which actually worked, a dining room with a parquet floor, an elegant wooden banister with beautifully carved spools on its turnings, and a closed-in sun porch with striped awnings. The backyard was huge, with a giant mimosa tree and a trumpet vine that sported big orange flowers. But it could not compare with their beloved hilltop with its unobstructed view of those much loved Connecticut hills and trees. The first day in the new house, John got lost wandering around all the floors.

There was one positive aspect of the house from Mary's point of view. It had been the backdrop of one of the great twentieth century crimes—the Hall-Mills murder case. Mary pored over William Kunstler's book, detailing how Edward Wheeler Hall, the handsome Episcopal rector, and his young lover, Eleanor Reinhardt Mills, the choir singer, were killed during a September tryst in 1922 and their bodies discovered under a crab apple tree in a lover's lane outside of New Brunswick. Hall's wife and her two brothers, William and Henry, were arrested for the murder, but were never convicted, and the case is still unsolved. Polly remembered her grandmother giving unusual attention to that murder. Somehow it was all right to devour details of that crime "because it involved the church." By the time the Bunting family took up residence, the rumor was still abroad that Willie's ghost haunted the house. And during one of the children's parties, a young guest was heard shrieking upstairs, convinced she had actually seen it.

The elegant house on the city street was only one of the things the children had to adjust to. There was also the considerable loss of their independence. In Bethany they had been able to earn their own money and weren't dependent on allowances handed out by their parents. They had 4-H projects that brought in enough cash to buy bikes, to go to fairs or to the movies, even to buy a good many of their clothes. They also raised produce that Polly bought from them. "By age nine," Bill remembered, "I was regularly riding horses all over town, raising a steer, keeping a large flock of chickens, shooting guns, and using my own axe." Chuck and Bill had both been driving tractors, but in New Brunswick they couldn't even work with a power mower until they were fourteen.

More disconcerting, New Brunswick had racial problems—actually race riots—before many other places. Bethany had been mostly white, but New Brunswick was more mixed, with a large Eastern European population and a large African-American population and tensions between them that the Bunting children had never encountered before. The racial pressure exploded in their world after Mary, who had insisted on attending the public school that was only one-third white, gave a party to which she invited both black and white students. It turned out that hers was the first integrated party in New Brunswick, and the white students who came were angry to find black students there. Afterwards, Mary found herself ostracized in school. She decided after that year to go with Bill to Rutgers Prep, which at that time was set up in a dilapidated little 1870's brick building and had a student body of children of Rutgers faculty. "It was in turmoil physically," Bill remembered, "but it was a very good, provocative school—a very lively place, and we benefited." But Mary never felt accepted. She was one of only two non-Jewish students in her class. When the other one found out she hadn't been baptized, she told Mary she would surely go to hell.

At the same time Chuck and Bill were also having trouble adjusting to their school. Polly had been told by Yale colleagues that the New Brunswick public schools were not good so she initially sent both Chuck and Bill to Pingry, an exclusive prep school in Elizabeth, about twenty minutes by grimy train from New Brunswick. It was different in every way from the country school they had attended in Bethany. There was a dress code—ties and short pants. In Bethany, anyone who wore short pants would be ridiculed; they even swam in blue jeans. Bill left Pingry after only a year, but Chuck stayed—he's not sure even now exactly why—perhaps because of the sports, out of stubbornness, or just from a feeling that somehow it made him more independent.

One of their biggest adjustments was seeing much less of their mother. Polly knew that the demands of her job might mean that she would be away from her children more than she would have liked. But she had no choice. Although she never asked her colleagues to accommodate themselves to her personal obligations, occasionally they were made aware of them. "She never dwelled on it," remembered a professor, but every once in awhile, because of a comment at a meeting, they were reminded that "this lady had children to take care of."

"A lot fell on the elders of us," Mary remembered. "Polly wasn't home a lot. . . . I do remember feeling guilty when I went off to college. I remember being very aware that part of the team was disappearing."

To make sure meals were on the table, Polly established a system: the oldest person home was in charge of the next meal. When Polly was home, she took over. If not, Mary was next in line, and so on. "And," Polly said, "there was always peanut butter and jelly." When everyone was home for dinner, everybody worked. Three pressure cookers would be going full blast. When Polly had to be out of town, the kids could eat in the college dining room with the students. And Mr. Lasagna, in charge of the dining room, would always have something special for them. In case of a medical emergency, the backyard of the dean of students' house bordered their own and the infirmary was nearby.

From time to time the Buntings had people living with them to help with various chores: students, and for a while, Marie Louise Duran Reynals, an old Yale friend whose late husband had been a colleague of Henry's. "It was nice to have another adult in the house," Polly said. They tried having a housekeeper, but that didn't work. They were more comfortable taking care of family chores in the ways they always had. "We were used to talking to each other while we were doing chores in the kitchen and weren't very good at visiting with each other in the living room," Polly said. For a while they had a maid, "but not anyone who knew how to manage the boys," according to Polly. "Mary could be a little strict with them, but she was a great help."

Polly never pressured any of the children to take part in her life at the college. But John, who was seven when they came to Douglass, enjoyed perambulating around the campus, investigating how it worked. He became something of a mascot for the students, impersonating Elvis at campus parties, serving punch, delivering mail, even running the switchboard during a blizzard when the operators couldn't get to campus. He let the family in on all the tidbits he had discovered, and after just a few bites of dinner, he'd say, "Mother, you have no idea what is going on at this place." "People began feeding him information they thought I should have," Polly said.

The students were intrigued by all the occupants of 23 Nichol Avenue. No children had lived in the dean's house for more than twenty years and the idea of this single mother, juggling a multiplicity of roles, and caring for four active children, piqued the students' interest. They were curious about the children's habits and hobbies, but even more intrigued by the idea that the dean had children at all. The student newspaper ran many articles about the children and their adjustment to New Brunswick. The kids apparently kept to themselves all the pain and reservations they felt, because the articles gave the impression that they were all delighted with their new life.

12

A Neophyte at the Deaning Business

Polly empathized with her children's disorientation. She herself was figuring out how to navigate in this new environment. Even though she had spent virtually all her adult life on college campuses, now she had to see things from an entirely new perspective. She was an administrator—*the* administrator—in charge. She had a faculty she was responsible both to and for, buildings and grounds to look after, an academic program to oversee, and complex relations with the large university across town to manage. In fact, she said years later, although her title was dean, at Douglass she was really a college president.

She was, however, without experience in administration or the ways of academic governance, so she couldn't express her ideas in what she called the "appropriate lingo."[1] She was, as the Rutgers historian Richard McCormick phrased it, "a neophyte at the deaning business," such a neophyte in fact that the first faculty meeting she presided over at Douglass was the first faculty meeting she had ever attended. Her previous positions hadn't afforded her that privilege. But she quickly put her individual stamp on the faculty meetings, introducing a new hospitality, beginning them with coffee and cookies and sometimes having students serve ice cream on hand-painted trays and staff members pour coffee from silver samovars.

She had never paid attention to hierarchy, and she carried this attitude to Douglass and dispensed with it. For example, when she found out that a new assistant was a widow like herself, whose husband had died suddenly leaving her with three young daughters, and who had never worked outside her home before, Polly took her under her wing. "She did everything possible to help my mother raise a strong family," said one of the daughters, now a chemistry professor at Rutgers.

Polly also lost no time in putting to rest any idea that she felt diminished by having given up scientific research. In her first official speech at the first convocation, she addressed this idea head-on. "The choice is not between activities but between problems, and the problems of higher education today seem to me at least as absorbingly interesting and challenging as the love-life of the bacteria.... I do not feel that I have given up research."

She did, however, manage to keep some minimal scientific work going. Her Douglass appointment included a position as professor of bacteriology, and she found time to continue research she had been doing with grants from the Atomic Energy Commission and the American Tuberculosis Association. She was able to bring those grants with her to Douglass, and at the end of 1957 she received another one for five thousand dollars from the U.S. Public Health Service for *Serratia* research that she carried on with her one graduate student, Ann Heuer. That grant was renewed and she set up her lab at the Agricultural College. She even squeezed in a minimal amount of scientific reading although she did not manage to publish any papers.

In many ways it was an intellectually stimulating time for Polly. She was encountering new problems and new concepts. She still filled her small, brown, plastic looseleaf notebooks, only now the notes were no longer lists of birds she had seen, or the condition of her beehives, or the details of her children's development. Instead, her journals became a sounding board for working through ideas, a way of having a dialogue with herself. She wrote down ideas for speeches or quotes from books she was reading, which now concerned student participation in administration, women's education, the place of public education and higher education, societal changes and the kinds of effects they were likely to have on students and on educational institutions, statistics on languages being taught, and population projections. Sometimes she copied long quotations from books that particularly interested her and then incorporated the ideas into her speeches and into her thinking. It was her method of moving into her new position, of mastering a new discipline. She was giving herself her own course and in short order was speaking knowledgeably about education in general and public education in particular.

She recognized that she thought as a faculty member first and then as an administrator. So she began looking for someone who would take care of the administrative details so she could focus on educational issues. Everyone recommended the same person, Edna Newby, a Douglass graduate who had worked in a succession of positions at the college. Polly wasted no time. She called Newby into her office and offered her the newly created position of assistant dean. "Mrs. Bunting made no bones about it," Newby recalled. "She had never had anything to do with running a college. I was to supervise admissions, registrar, placement bureau, and work closely with the business manager. I just sort of coordinated everything. I met with the heads of these departments once a month, so we knew what each other was doing and we weren't duplicating what we were planning to do." If Polly couldn't get to a faculty meeting, Newby chaired it. "I did everything from janitorial service up. I would un-stop toilets. If I went into a building to see how things were going and I heard water running, I would lift the ball up and stop it. It was a very interesting job."

They were a good combination. Newby enjoyed the picayune administrative details that Polly didn't want to deal with. "The less she saw of me, the better she liked it," Newby said years later. "And she didn't even care how much I reported to her as long as things were going well. If she could be of any help in a difficult situation, she'd be glad to step in."

A short, stocky, roly-poly woman, Edna Newby was jolly, unpretentious, and accessible. She had grown up in northern New Jersey, the daughter of a bricklayer, who lost his construction business along with their house and everything else in the Depression; her sister, then in high school, supported the family by working part-time as a bank teller. Edna was a junior at Douglass, and offered to drop out and go home to help, but her parents insisted she finish college. So she took out a loan from Douglass, which she paid off at the rate of a few dollars a month for years and years.

Except for a brief stint with the USO during the war, Edna Newby worked at Douglass all her life. She never married. She was the adviser to Douglass' small contingent of foreign students—"the mother hen and shepherd," one of them called her. More than twenty years after her retirement, her home was still filled not only with photographs of her sister's and her neighbor's children and grandchildren, but also with stacks of cards and pictures from former students.

By her own admission, Newby was no intellectual. She had no advanced degrees, just her Douglass B.A., along with a great deal of experience at the institution and great affection and respect for it. Like Polly, she had never had any courses in administration and didn't place much stock in them. They both learned on the job. "I knew what had been done and tried to keep it going that way," Newby said.

Polly, however, wanted to be more than a status quo administrator. She wanted to streamline and simplify the administration to make it easier for people to communicate with her. She wanted to hear from students too and in fact put nine students on an advisory committee to the dean. The purpose of these administrative changes was to bring about clearer and closer communication between Polly and the other constituencies of the college. She was decidedly a "shirt-sleeve" administrator.

Most important, she wanted to figure out how to make the educational program more effective. And to do this, she was unwilling to let anything go unexamined. She encouraged the faculty to reevaluate a variety of curricular issues: graduation requirements, the major, distribution requirements, small classes versus large lectures, the orientation program, reducing the load of first-year students from five to four courses, determining whether students were writing too many papers and not having enough time for reflective reading and serious thinking.

In requiring faculty to engage in this process, she was in danger of stepping on a great many toes. But in fact, for the most part, she managed to persuade the faculty that she was on their side. "She genuinely was *with* the faculty," remembered Philosophy Professor Fadlou Shehadi. "It wasn't a tactic with her, not scheming to pacify people so they wouldn't give her trouble. That was just her style. I think it came from her being an educator and caring about education. She was a good sympathetic listener, never gave the impression of being against you. Even if she didn't give you what you asked for you came out not feeling resentful."

Another reason why the faculty trusted her was that she made it clear from the start that she cared about their interests. Faculty salaries at Douglass were even lower than at Rutgers, even for men; Dean Corwin's cheerful greeting to returning faculty was always, "Welcome to another frugal year." Polly approached the problem of raising salaries with a kind of missionary zeal. She was particularly distressed that low salaries prevented faculty members from giving their own children the educational opportunities they themselves had enjoyed.[2] By the end of her tenure at Douglass, this effort had been only marginally successful. There had been raises, although not as significant as Polly had hoped. Douglass was, after all, part of a public university dependent upon state budgets.

She encouraged faculty to conduct research because she believed it was good for them and beneficial for students to witness their commitment. Without such opportunities, she thought the best scholars would leave Douglass and the best Douglass students would never go into teaching. She overturned a long-standing prohibition against Douglass faculty teaching in the Rutgers graduate program.

She recognized, however, the difficulty of carrying out research when teaching loads were heavy, sabbaticals nonexistent, and even leaves of absence difficult to finance. Douglass faculty taught nine to twelve hours each week—more than faculty at many comparable women's colleges—counseled their own students, and served on college committees. Polly tried to ensure that they could teach at least one elective, because she believed both faculty and students benefitted when faculty members had at least one course that was of deep personal significance to them."[3]

Being an outsider, with no investment in the way things had always been done, enabled her "to question precedents and traditions that had outworn their usefulness,"[4] such as the long-time requirement that students attend chapel. At her first faculty meeting she asked if requiring chapel attendance did not defeat its purpose. She was concerned, she said, not with "what went on in the chapel but with what went on in the student."

Grumbling about compulsory chapel attendance was almost as old as Douglass itself. In 1945 the New Jersey legislature had officially declared Rutgers and all its divisions the State University, and so all compulsory attendance at religious exercises had to be abandoned for fear of violating the Constitution. But Douglass had two different types of chapel services—only one of them religious—and students were on their honor to attend a prescribed number of either sort or risk losing academic credits.

Polly handled this potentially contentious issue by changing the name of the program from "chapel," which had a stuffy ring to it, to Voorhees Assemblies, after the building where they were held. She set up a Voorhees Assembly Board, which included students, giving them a mechanism for influencing the programs. She invited a wide range of speakers, hoping every student would find at least a few programs of interest. Then she added another carrot to entice more people to attend the speeches: she opened the lunches that followed the assemblies to anyone who wanted to come, rather than restricting them just to seniors. She had already established a special, for-seniors-only series of buffet dinners at her house. She published a letter in the student newspaper to announce the changes and to get the attention of the students, faculty, and staff. No "thou shalts"—rather, "c'mon—this is interesting. Give it a try." When she summed up the major accomplishments of her first year, the establishment of the Voorhees Assembly Board was high on her list.

She instituted other innovations. She brought in practicing artists to teach art, refusing to get caught up in the on-going debate about whether teaching students how to do things was too vocational for liberal arts colleges. Writing had squeaked through even in the most elite Eastern schools, but they were wary of painting or sculpture and wouldn't even consider photography or printmaking. She dismissed the whole liberal-arts-versus-vocational conundrum as nonsense, believing it should be resolved in favor of both. "It seemed to me," Polly said, "as a scientist, that if you didn't have the chance to do it, you weren't going to understand it. It always bothered me that the history of a subject would be considered legitimate, but actually doing it in the laboratory, so to speak, would be suspect."[5]

She proposed a first-year biology course, similar to those she had taught at Bennington and Goucher, which would give students unexpected research problems, such as "What proportion of the freshman class is left-footed? To what extent do ants depend upon their eyes? How many forms of life can you detect in an aquarium?" It was to be different from the usual "baby science" courses in which students only memorize what has already been discovered, and have no experience enjoying the challenge and satisfactions of discovering things for themselves.[6] "Courses designed primarily to expose freshmen to all that faculty think they should know may snuff out rather than fan their admittedly feeble flames," Polly said.

She was scrupulous about not treading on faculty toes and during her first October wrote letters to the appropriate faculty committees explaining her ideas and looking for allies. She understood that faculty members prized their responsibility for the curriculum. "Polly's approach was to sell her point to a few faculty and hope they would carry it to the whole faculty," remembered Dean of Students Marjorie Trayes. "If she tried something and it didn't work, she'd couch it in different terms and try again—emptying the test tube and starting over." She proved to be adept politically and rather enjoyed the machinations. "There was a professor of physics who was always worried about the things I was trying to do," she said years later, laughing as she remembered him. "And he'd get up and make big long speeches and I quickly learned the longer he talked the more everybody was going to vote my way. So I sort of encouraged him. It's very helpful to have people like that on a faculty."

Having established these few hands-on courses, Polly began to think about ways to enrich the entire curriculum. She decided the best way to dislodge old concepts in favor of new ones would be to encourage faculty to try new courses on a short-term basis, to stage an experiment, for a few years and a few students. She wanted them to feel free to try out a novel approach or a quirky idea and thought they would feel less inhibited knowing it was only a pilot program, that they wouldn't be compelled to face faculty scrutiny prematurely.

Since she never stopped thinking like a scientist, one of the first things that bothered her as an administrator was the subjective and irrational bases of so many educational decisions. "Faculty arguments would be based on tradition or their own life experience or an appealing new trend but not on evidence of effectiveness."[7] She wanted evidence. Shortly after she arrived at Douglass, she mused in her notebooks: "Phenomenon in higher education—that supervision is minimal, that information about personnel performance is secured furtively, that evaluation procedures are non existent."

The plan for experimental courses went through with little opposition and was adopted by the faculty in April 1956. "I think they were sort of intrigued," Polly remembered. For the next several years just about every faculty meeting had some experimental courses being proposed—more than twenty the first year. But when Polly suggested that not all experimental courses need be taught by faculty members, that some could be taught by people in the community with professional expertise, there was something of a palace revolution. A faculty committee spent a full hour trying to convince her to change her mind. In deference to the intensity of their feelings, she agreed not to solicit teachers formally. She was well aware, she said, "that the majority of proposals coming from the outside would be crackpot attempts which the Committee would have to decline." But she told them that if she heard of an interesting experiment, "and if we had money to support it, I saw no reason why the College should not benefit from a pilot plant run whether or not the course was taught by someone now on our faculty."[8] In fact, when this meeting took place, Polly had already made at least one attempt to recruit someone—William G. Avirett of the Carnegie Endowment for International Peace.

Polly collaborated and cooperated when she could, but when she believed something ought to be done, she went ahead and did it. Somehow this independent style caused very little resentment among her faculty and staff. Perhaps this was because she connected with people in a direct, personal way. When she bought her farm in Califon, she invited the whole faculty, staff members, and their families out for a Sunday picnic. As a way of enticing faculty members to stay at the student Christmas Dance, she announced that anybody who stayed as long as she did was invited to her home for refreshments after the festivities. She participated in all the ceremonial events—Dad's Day, Founder's Day, Alumnae events—carrying out the hostess part of the dean's role with her own style. When, at an alumnae weekend, the alumnae presented her with a skirt in the Douglass tartan made by a '38 alumna, Polly made a point of wearing it during the weekend. "The Dean proved to be an excellent model," the Douglass alumnae magazine reported.

She continued what she had always done, bringing colleagues together in her home. The ambience was different from Bethany, but the spirit was the same. She not only believed in the importance of handling social events in a civilized and gracious way, she enjoyed it.

Polly didn't bowl people over when they first encountered her. Soft spoken, somewhat unprepossessing physically, and an uncharismatic speaker, she had what one professor described as "a kind of refinement that insinuates itself the more you expose yourself—like radiation—it starts to penetrate."

13

Mother, Scientist, Educator

Polly wanted direct contact with students. She wanted them to feel free to come by her house and almost immediately settled upon a simple signal to let them know when they could. If the porch light was on in the evenings, it meant that she was at home, not busy, and available for conversation.

If they happened to drop by when she was having dinner with her family, she invited them in. "They often expressed surprise: 'You eat in the kitchen, too?' I was pleased to let them know," Polly said. She met with student newspaper representatives "while drinking apple cider at the kitchen table," they reported. On at least one occasion she engaged in an arm-wrestling match with a student. Polly won, but the encounter put the nervous young woman at ease. The dean's tea, with its legendary brownies, was part of the first-year orientation, and Polly made a point of speaking individually to each awkward freshman. She had Friday night buffet suppers for seniors at her house; fifteen dinners throughout the year with fourteen students at each dinner, few enough for serious conversation, but not so few that they would feel uncomfortable. There was no formal attire, no hat and gloves.

Few administrators in those days ever asked students their opinions about anything, but in the first issue of the student newspaper her first fall Polly announced that she wanted good communication "both ways." She proved that she was serious about that two-way street when students asked her to lift the ban on smoking in their dormitory living rooms and she complied. Their letter gave her confidence, she said, "that the students recognize and respect the hazards involved." When they complained that there were no quiet places to study during exams, she opened the physics building for them. She believed that student participation in running the college was an essential part of their education. She believed the college should teach more than academics.

She wanted data on which she could formulate policy, so she asked them to write down their impressions and to put them in manila envelopes and drop them off in her office. She wanted to find out how their college experience changed them, to assess the "growth of student from freshman to senior." "There is more information in a student's wastebasket than in the dean's office," she said. She asked sophomores about "sophomore slump." "Does it exist?" she asked. "For whom? How can you measure it? Or detect it? Let's study it this year ... go at it for yourself—and drop in some evening between 9:30 and 10:30 and tell me about your sophomore year."[1]

She asked them to take part in what she called "a thoughtful statewide program of public relations." As a public institution, Rutgers was dependent upon the political support of citizens, and Polly urged students to be careful about what they said. They shared some responsibility for the college's well-being, she told them, and "the most important thing you can do—and you can do it better than anyone else—is to make it clear to people what this college is—and why that thing is important."[2]

They responded with commitment to the institution. When Polly wrote an article in the college alumnae magazine about the pressures on Douglass faculty because of the continually escalating enrollment, five sophomores wrote a letter to the student newspaper offering to assist faculty members with routine tasks and asking other students to join them. The following week the "letters to the editor" section of the paper was crammed with offers of help. Polly had all sorts of ideas about what they could do, from filing and answering phones to conferring with younger students.

From the first, she observed and valued the diversity of the student body, "as varied as that of the State of New Jersey," George Schmidt wrote in his history of Douglass. It included Catholics, Jews, and all denominations of Protestants. There were students from the large high schools of Newark and Jersey City as well as from the smaller schools of the more rural western and southern regions. About ten percent came from outside New Jersey. "The melting pot was really at work at Douglass College," Polly said.[3]

But it wasn't working quite well enough to bring in many students from racial minorities, particularly African-Americans. When some faculty members approached Polly with a plan to change long-standing admission policies, she was very receptive. Although there were no quotas or other officially sanctioned restrictions, Douglass admission policies favored certain high schools with what one admissions committee member called "a middle class mix." These faculty wanted to look more seriously at students from inner city schools, to bring more diversity to the college. Polly was all in favor.

In the 1950's, conformity was prized; television portrayed a monolithic society without hyphenated Americans. Polly worked against this vision because it not only contradicted her fundamentally democratic view, but also conflicted with what she saw as the best interests of her students. Conformity contradicted the essential purposes of education, as Polly defined them: to develop "objective thinking and courageous creative action."[4] She believed that education was not to provide students with personal advancement or financial gain, but to create clear thinkers who could serve society.

In many of Polly's dealings with students, she behaved more like a parent than a dean. When a delinquent student pleaded to be reinstated, Polly wanted to give her another chance even though more experienced faculty were strongly opposed. When a student-faculty-administration committee imposed on one misbehaving student what Polly thought was too harsh a penalty, she decided to overturn it, until Marjorie Trayes, dean of students, insisted that she should not, and they had some spirited arguments; in the end Polly regretfully abided by the committee's recommendations. "Polly thought you could change a student just by being nice to her," Trayes said.

Considering herself responsible for more than students' academic life, she lectured them about staying healthy. On a day devoted to sports activities, she suggested that students observe themselves and their performance, and as she had done in virtually every circumstance of her life, gather the data. The college had physical education requirements, but far more than these were necessary, she said, to "keep a person in even moderately good physical, mental, and emotional health." "Try leading the healthy life for one week & see how good you feel—how well other things go & how much fun you can have."

Above all, she saw herself as an educator whose job was to help students gain the satisfactions from intellectual effort she herself had experienced and found so rewarding. At the same time she never underestimated the loneliness, particularly for young women, of immersing themselves in scholarship. So she tried to establish a counseling program to guide students "into the right slot." Quoting a book that impressed her, she copied into her journal: "The sense of community from which the students seemed to draw support seems to involve more than their vision of certain members of the faculty as models for emulation. It involved the experience of *being seen* by such models as being 'in the same boat' with them."[5] To these words Polly added words of her own. "The loneliness of the scholarly young woman too often has been all the more profound because she has seldom been seen as 'in the same boat.'"

When she spoke to students about the deep satisfactions of scholarship and exhorted them to aspire for more than "a split-level in the Oranges," she knew she was contradicting virtually everything they saw around them. The position of women was a subject that had never particularly preoccupied her, but now her situation was different. She was the chief executive of a woman's college. She had a responsibility to the young women who came there to be educated. Bit by bit she was being obliged to take note of those conditions in the society that prevented her students from getting the full benefits of their education.

In the 1950's, anti-intellectualism was pervasive and smart women were portrayed as decidedly unsexy. Some possible distant satisfaction seemed a high price to pay for the sacrifice of present male attention. Polly noted in one of her journals that the desire for popularity with men took precedence over all other forms of anxiety. Even parents saw their daughters' college education as preparation for marriage rather than as a way of gaining a fuller and more interesting life. College women panicked if they were not engaged to be married by graduation. "A ring by spring," was the watchword. The Douglass student newspaper listed the engagements and pinnings: they were big news.

In the postwar period the definition of femininity had regressed into an almost Victorian combination of indolence and indulgence. Yanking women away from the jobs they had successfully performed during the war and thrusting them back into full-time domesticity were necessary parts of recovering from the trauma of the war. Within two months of the war's end, some eight hundred thousand women had been fired from jobs in the aircraft industry. It took only two years, for two million women to lose their jobs.[6]

Women were to be kept far from the world of work because, according to the rationale, if they had to compete with men, they would become hard and aggressive. Such behavior would almost surely doom a woman to loneliness—or so the story went. Fiction about career women in women's magazines always portrayed them as unhappy and emotionally empty.[7] In the thirties and early forties, movie heroines like the indomitable Bette Davis had once flouted all convention and endured; in the early fifties she was murmuring in *All About Eve* that unless you can turn over in bed and see him, you're not a woman. When *Life* magazine ran a special issue on "The American Woman" in December 1956, it noted the "completely fulfilling moments of a woman's life—the first prom, the first kiss, the first baby." The first ten pages were photographs of American "girls" in various settings—Southwestern girl on the desert, Southern girl in a pink formal gown leaning against a pillar—all devoted to looks and clothes. There seemed to be no connection between the photographs and the articles that came later in the issue, about women's anxiety, depression, and dissatisfaction.

It was not expected that women who got married should work. It was especially frowned upon if that woman was a mother. The vague disapproval that Polly had encountered a few years earlier when she resumed part-time research at Yale had, by the mid-fifties, hardened into a pervasive moral position. Mothers could work if compelled to help the family survive, but a woman in such a situation could only be pitied. The only legitimate work for middle-class mothers was raising well-behaved children, keeping the house spotless, having dinner ready on time, and remaining perfectly groomed. Along with these requirements, they were expected to attain an impossible standard: movie star measurements, coiffed hair, and the necessary serenity to greet their husbands joyfully at the end of the day. Magazines and the new television situation comedies defined and reinforced the popular image; women were portrayed as perfectly competent mistresses of their households, although the farther they ventured from their houses the less competent they seemed.[8]

Women's chief contribution to the larger society was to keep America's formidable industrial machine churning; that is, to be consumers. They were supposed to buy all the labor-saving devices being manufactured: the washers, dryers, freezers, blenders, mixers, floor waxers, frost-free refrigerators, and souped-up vacuum cleaners. The ads in the women's magazines and situation comedies all pictured women standing proudly in front of brand-new appliances, many of which were designed to eliminate the very work the women were supposed to be doing. This liberation from household drudgery only served to further undermine women's sense of themselves. They no longer had work they could consider meaningful. Even inside their own homes, they had little to assuage their boredom and their sense of uselessness. Girls growing up in these homes not only saw their mothers drifting in idleness, they also saw their brothers being raised with entirely different expectations.[9] Whatever was expected of their sons, mothers knew daughters were to be educated to get married.

Educational institutions, which should have known better, embodied these same attitudes. The Harvard Business School didn't admit women until 1961. And at the School of Education a professor did his best to discourage Polly's daughter-in-law from pursuing a Ph.D. because she was about to be married. "Why would you want to earn the degree?" he asked. "You can be a wife and a mother." Members of the University of Michigan history department told Margaret Judson, a highly respected Douglass historian who had gone there to teach for a year, that they had never questioned her scholarship, but feared that the presence of a women in department meetings would inhibit men from smoking or putting their feet up on chairs.[10]

Attitudes toward women academics began to change slowly in the fifties because there was a serious shortage of Ph.D.s. But still, antinepotism rules remained in place, restricting institutions from employing both husband and wife. At Rutgers both husband and wife could not have tenure; one had to be appointed on a year-to-year basis and it was rarely the husband.

Polly did what she could to counteract these tendencies, particularly for students interested in the sciences, which in those days was almost totally male-oriented and male-dominated. Science, which required rigorous thinking, was seen as the antithesis of femininity. "It was a hard time for women in science," said Marie Siewierski, who graduated from Douglass in 1961 and is now a Douglass chemistry professor. "Even in a field such as chemistry where there was so much demand and recruiters came to the Douglass campus to interview graduating seniors, the discrimination was rampant although then no one was calling it that. When I interviewed for my first job at American Cyanamid, they said, 'At this point in the interview we would talk about the opportunity for movement into management. But since you are a woman, this doesn't apply to you.' There were very, very few women—none in upper management. Women were given routine quality-control positions. Automatically, men earned 20 per cent more, no ifs, ands or buts."

When the chair of the chemistry department told another Douglass student, who was planning on being a doctor, that she should switch to home economics, the student fled to Polly's office. "I felt heart-broken and insulted. I attributed to him powers of knowledge he did not have, as if he knew something about me that I didn't know. Polly said, 'He doesn't know everything. Go do it. Take chemistry in summer school.' I got an A in both summer school courses." And she became a physician.

Polly encouraged her students formally and publicly, but also individually. She wrote warm, personal letters to students who received fellowships. She established a high honors program and introduced it by saying, "Anyone who has watched track records knows that as soon as one person vaults over 14 feet or jumps over 6 feet or runs a mile in less than 4 minutes—others find they can. Nothing is so effectively inspiring as knowledge of actual achievement."

Her efforts to encourage graduate study had their effect. In three years the number of Douglass seniors going on to graduate school rose from four to seventeen percent."[11]

The obstacles these women were encountering at this point seemed to Polly to be part of a larger problem: the pervasive sense of inferiority she found among Douglass students. Too many of them were ashamed of their backgrounds and of their parents, especially if they couldn't speak English very well. Polly sought to show them that their ethnic differences were not weaknesses but strengths. "I felt that perhaps too much attention had been given to training students in American manners and dress," she said.[12] Some of their sense of inferiority seemed to come from the faculty. Students asked her why faculty often assumed they were only at Douglass because they couldn't get in anywhere else, when Douglass had been their first choice. Like the students, Polly found, the faculty didn't see how good a college Douglass was.

One of the first things Polly did to counteract this sense of inferiority was to invite distinguished speakers to the college who came from all different sectors of society, different disciplines and ethnic groups. They were scholars, performers, businesspeople, artists, and politicians; and many of them were women. Polly wanted to invigorate the intellectual life of the campus, but more important, to counteract the tendency to value uniformity. Her roster was impressive: Robert Frost, Margaret Mead, Ogden Nash, Allen Ginsberg, Martha Graham, Erich Fromm, W. H. Auden, Aaron Copland. Avant-garde musician John Cage and classical guitarist Andrés Segovia. Hodding Carter, editor and publisher, and Thurgood Marshall, then NAACP legal director, discussed race relations. The secretary of the New York Stock Exchange spoke to economics majors on the workings of the stock market, and Sidney Hook came on International Weekend. There was one program of traditional music of four faiths: Protestant, Catholic, Jewish, and Greek Orthodox. Students particularly remembered Eleanor Roosevelt—fortifying them against the assumption that because they were women their opportunities would be severely circumscribed. They remembered her saying, "You are only inferior if you believe it too."

During Polly's final year as dean, the students initiated something that made her feel that, as she put it, she "had won." A group of ten very able literature students proposed teaching a Thursday evening course in World Poetry, to begin with epics and go through the twentieth century. Among them, they spoke eight languages: French, German, Spanish, Italian, Serbo-Croatian, Hungarian, Russian, and Polish. Some wrote their own translations of the poems. They wanted to teach the class for credit and invited faculty to attend. "It was interesting to take that proposal to the faculty," Polly said. "I didn't really know whether they would approve giving credit or not, but fortunately just the right professor got up and made a rather nasty speech, about how this would lower standards. In a way, that sold the idea to the rest of the faculty." They voted to approve the course as described.

There was a feeling of real excitement at the first class on January 29, 1959. More than two hundred people crowded into Room 206 in Recitation Hall: students, professors, administrators, even a reporter from the *New York Times*. "It seemed to me that was just what we wanted," said Polly. "This was a unique course. At few colleges in the country could students have given that course. They were no longer ashamed of their foreign background. They valued what they alone could offer."[13]

By the end of Polly's tenure at Douglass, she could write in her annual report, "The observation that Douglass students have increasing confidence in their own abilities and in the importance of their potential contribution to the life of their times has been a great satisfaction."

Polly helped the students as much by who and what she was, as by anything she said. In her final year at Douglass the students dedicated their yearbook to her: "Mother, scientist, and educator, she may well be our pattern." Without setting out to be an example, Polly became one. For many of the students she was the first single mother they had encountered, the first working woman with a significant job. By skillfully balancing her competing responsibilities she showed them what a woman could achieve. And when Douglass students spoke of her years later, it was her courageous, independent spirit, her being a single mother who raised her children alone, had an important job, served her community—combined it all and flourished—that they remembered most and thanked her for.

14

The Tidal Wave

Years later, in describing her first heady days at Douglass, what Polly remembered most was the excitement, the sense of possibility, her belief in the promise of public education. She spoke often of the farmer with the dying calves who had come to the University of Wisconsin to consult with Professor Hastings. Polly wanted New Jersey citizens to feel, as he had, that their public university was a resource they could turn to for information and advice. "The college is an organic and contributing member of society," she wrote in her journal. "(College must be conducted for its social function—not its own benefit.)"

Although new to administration, Polly began from a bedrock of principles. She often quoted Thomas Jefferson, who spoke of "a system of general instruction which shall reach every description of our citizens, from the richest to the poorest," and John Adams, who linked education with the preservation of democracy. "The education of all ranks of people was made the care and expense of the public in a manner that I believe has been unknown to any other people ancient or modern," Polly copied into her journal.

She agreed with these Founding Fathers that education was the fulfillment of democratic ideals. "The decision of people to go to college," Polly said, "is a fulfillment of our religious and political ideals founded on our belief in the worth of the individual."[1] Everything she did or tried to do emanated from this philosophical framework, an essential component of which was that women, just like men, should have access to the full spectrum of educational opportunity.

This commitment collided almost immediately with the uncomfortable fact that a population explosion was in the making. The freshman class entering at the same time she did numbered 435—larger than any that had gone before and far larger than had been anticipated. By the following fall the dormitories were filled to capacity.

When Polly assembled figures on population growth, the numbers of students currently in New Jersey high schools, and the projected percentages of those who would be seeking a college education in the near future, she saw that Douglass was facing what she called "a tidal wave," which "poses a tremendous challenge to a culture conceived on the premise that each individual must have his chance to shove into the stream of life."[2]

By 1965, when those in sixth grade were ready for college, there would be a fifty percent increase in the number of students banging on the university's door and there would be no room for ten to twenty thousand of them. Douglass still only had room for the same two percent of female high school graduates from New Jersey that the college had admitted when it was founded. But, Polly said, times were changing, and it was anticipated that thirty-five to forty percent of those graduating in just thirteen years would want to continue their education.

A tenth grader, whose algebra teacher had told her class that by the time they graduated Rutgers would be turning down thousands of students, wrote to the university asking it to please save her a place in 1961. Polly quoted this letter often to illustrate how much students were counting on their state university. The state was worried, too. The New Jersey Department of Education published a study, "The Closing Door to College and New Jersey's Undergraduates 1954–73," which stated that "if equality of educational opportunity is to be a reality in 1973, New Jersey colleges, public and private, will have to accommodate six times as many full-time undergraduates as they did in 1954–55." Soon after, the State Board of Education sent a companion report to the governor and legislature called "College Opportunity in New Jersey," which recommended doubling facilities at Rutgers and other state educational institutions.[3]

It was clear, therefore, from the beginning of Polly's time at Douglass, that expanding the campus, in fact, re-creating it, would have to be one of her highest priorities. The college had to add classrooms, dormitories, a library, laboratories, and since many of the faculty lived as far away as New York, faculty housing.

But before any planning could get underway, however, Polly had to undertake some serious proselytizing to convince many that expansion was a good idea. Rutgers, as a public university, depended upon taxpayers and their votes; and the state of New Jersey had been unwilling to pay for any building at Douglass since 1926, except for a one hundred-thousand-dollar-garage-repair shop. Fortunately Polly's experience with the Bethany school had taught her what kind of effort was necessary to rally an apathetic public to the support of an educational undertaking. This, she recognized, was part of her job.

One of the first things she did was to contact the heads of a dozen large statewide organizations having to do with women, such as the YWCA, PTA, and League of Women Voters, and invite them to a luncheon at the dean's house. They discussed the problems of the college and the university and education in general. The gathering proved to be both congenial and productive. "No minutes were kept. There were no reporters. People could speak very freely. The general cross-fertilization of ideas and concerns proved very exciting ... we decided to meet regularly, every few months, and did for several years. They would come to the house. ... We'd have luncheon together and then go on talking informally, for a good part of the afternoon. It became a powerful group."[4]

Polly also spoke to citizens' groups all over the state—to PTAs, Kiwanis, Rotary and Lions clubs, women's groups, and educational organizations. She gave them all the same message: New Jersey was third in per capita wealth, but thirty-ninth in state expenditure for higher education. "This is your state university," she told anyone who would listen. "Support it. Let your legislators know that it matters." Ultimately, she believed, it was this public support that convinced the legislature to approve the one million dollars for the library. She was so exhilarated by this success that she stopped students all over campus to let them hear the good news. Even years later, alumnae remembered Polly running up behind them, blurting out the news that the state had just granted the money.

She knew it was crucial also to enlist support from all the Douglass constituencies, and so she set about informing them how pressing the problem was. At her first faculty meeting on September 14, 1955, she announced the unusually high enrollment along with a series of Wednesday afternoon meetings for faculty members and administrators to "think through" how best to operate given the additional students. She organized committees of faculty, staff, students, and alumnae to meet with the architect. She laid out for the trustees her bold, ambitious ideas for the future. She told Douglass alumnae that their most important job was to make sure the people of the state "have sufficient understanding of the value of the kind of education Douglass College offers."

Her fund-raising style was simple, honest, and devoid of jargon. She just went out and asked for the money. The alumnae magazine published during her first fall on the job printed the recipe for "Mrs. Bunting's Never-Fail Date-Nut Loaf" on the page with an article "Dough for Douglass." In asking the newly hired alumnae executive director for a fund that she could spend without any strings attached, she said, "If you had ever lived on a farm you would know what I mean by 'my egg money.'" Douglass alumnae responded enthusiastically to her style. Not only did they raise ten thousand dollars—a significant sum in 1958—for her egg money, they also became effective public relations ambassadors.

Even so, there were many alumnae who felt antipathy to the very idea of expansion. They clung to the image of the old Douglass—a small girls' college with a closely woven community and feared that enlarging the college would rend the fabric. They also worried that expansion would erode the commitment of the faculty, who felt a great sense of responsibility for the running of the college. "It was like a family—a family business, like a family laundry," said Fadlou Shehadi, a longtime faculty member. Enlarging the college might well mean losing what was best about it.

Polly understood those feelings, but saw no alternative. She continued to be asked whether the quality of the Douglass education could be maintained in a much larger college. Her answers remained constant. Clinging to the old ways, far from reinforcing the old standards, would be more likely to erode them. "If Douglass does not expand rapidly," she wrote in an annual report, "there will be an immediate and serious lack of opportunities for a quality education for women in New Jersey. Eventually, some other units of the University would undoubtedly take over major responsibility for their education, and Douglass might find itself not the 'honors' college contemplated but a junior college adjunct of the University."[5] Besides, Polly said, standards are set at the top and could always be maintained. They should never be marshaled as an excuse for cutting off people's chance to get in at the bottom. She said she was far more concerned "about the well-qualified we turn away than the few chances we take." "In the last analysis the real test of education is whether it can be applied to large numbers of people. The usefulness of a drug is not judged by the fact of its discovery or even by its performance in the research laboratory. It depends on whether it can be made in quantity, whether it is stable, whether it is reasonably palatable, whether the public can be induced to take it—in short, its usefulness to people in large number. . . . I believe that the same thing is true in education . . . we must make the attempt to give as much as possible to as many as possible."[6]

Privately, however, she admitted that there were dangers. The expansion might well bring about some important losses. There was much to value in the intimate community that Douglass had become. She ruminated in her journals, "Mob training & competition we know to be bad. The danger is that with the tidal wave we shall have more of it."

If some members of the Douglass community were nervous about the expansion, they were absolutely paranoid about another plan of Polly's, which she believed was also necessitated by the tidal wave: bringing about greater integration of Douglass with Rutgers. Polly saw Rutgers as a resource, a place to go for assistance, "rather than a controlling force or a threat." She had believed from the beginning that the "peculiar strength" of Douglass grew out of its relationship to the university and believed that that relationship could be used to create both economies and greater opportunities for students. She described Douglass in her journal in biological terms—as a "specialized organ" that "carries on all vital functions to some extent but has emphasized certain functions & thereby makes a more efficient contribution to the whole." She saw Douglass evolving into a different sort of institution and evolution always intrigued her.

With skyrocketing enrollments, duplication and overlapping of courses were luxuries they could no longer afford. She wanted anything offered on any of the campuses to be available to all students. "It seems quite ridiculous that at the moment a girl cannot major in geology, or that boys do not know that they may take quantity cooking," she said. Integrating Douglass into Rutgers, she believed, would afford Douglass students the intellectual and social advantages of a university along with the "opportunities for leadership which would be lost in a larger unit."[7] She understood the importance for young women of belonging to a separate institution where "they are freed from their compulsive need to concentrate on pleasing a man and encouraged to develop their own powers of critical and creative thinking."

Douglass, however, "was very, very jealous of its autonomy and its distinctiveness," said Richard McCormick, Douglass historian and former dean. "It had a distinctive culture and a very provincial culture and by that time quite an anxious culture. It was a cocoon over there." Many of the older faculty could not believe that any educational advantages that might come about with closer affiliation with Rutgers could be worth the losses. They saw Douglass as a stepchild in the university and believed too much cooperation "across town" would end by swallowing up Douglass, obliterating its "unique mission to prepare young women for positions of leadership," said Philosophy Professor Shehadi. While the faculty would gain the opportunity for graduate teaching and research, some feared proximity would create pressure too. The ethos of academe was changing. Higher education was beginning to shrug off the old gentility in favor of a new professionalism—an identification on the part of faculty members less with the institution and more with their discipline. At the same time, administrators were developing an inclination to evaluate faculty on their record of publication. Many older faculty members were feeling threatened.

It was not only those on campus who opposed cooperation, but also some very influential people off-campus. There had even been a special meeting of the Trustees' Committee in November 1954, before Polly's arrival, at which the entire position of the College in the University was reviewed. The head of the New Jersey State Federation of Women's Clubs, which had a long-standing and proprietary interest in Douglass, spoke out about the importance of "autonomy." Mrs. M. Caswell Heine likened the position of Douglass to that of a Victorian wife, subservient, without control over her financial destiny. "It took a long struggle of brave souls," she said, "to move on from this romantic delusion to a relationship between the sexes more realistic, more self-respecting and cooperative.

"What we want is a woman's college, which shall maintain its integrity as such for all future time . . . because it is only with four years of semi-sequestration, that women have the freedom to be themselves."

Polly did what she could to allay these anxieties, listening to faculty members who sought her out in her office, even organizing tours to show Douglass staff members other parts of the Rutgers campus. She kept reiterating the same ideas, such as the importance of inter-campus transportation, cooperation between departments, and economizing. When a longtime physics professor died, Polly decided it would be too expensive to modernize his laboratory properly, so she sent the undergraduates needing elementary physics to Rutgers. She was helped in these endeavors by her close friendship with both Lewis Webster Jones and his wife, Barbara. "Polly could interpret Douglass in a way no other dean could to Dr. Jones," said Marjorie Trayes, "and answer his questions and shush him when he was saying things she didn't agree with. They were good enough friends for that."

Eventually her proselytizing and politicking paid off. Opposition to integration with Rutgers decreased. More and more departments worked together to avoid duplication of courses and consulted on new appointments. Graduation ceremonies were melded together. Douglass faculty became increasingly involved in graduate teaching and more faculty from other parts of the university came to Douglass.

And slowly but surely more money was forthcoming to support Polly's building projects. So now, though her fund-raising efforts had to go on, she also threw herself into the task of implementing these projects. She determined the priorities and influenced virtually all of the decisions; involved herself in minutiae, such as the shape of the dormitory windows as well as more substantive matters of what buildings were to be built and where they were to be placed.

And priorities were constantly being shifted. In the beginning a new gymnasium was seen as essential, but it was put off after the trustees determined that the existing gym was "a disgrace" but not a "fire hazard." Dormitories presented more complicated problems. There had been no new ones since 1931, and the existing ones were full, so there would be no way to admit additional students without adding beds. It was now far too expensive even to contemplate putting up more of the small houses that had become Douglass' hallmark. But Polly didn't want to sacrifice the camaraderie, the cohesion, and the sense of belonging that came with them, so she divided the college into three residential campuses of between five hundred to eight hundred students with an experienced counselor and its own community government and programs. Faculty members were also associated with specific campuses and participated in the extracurricular life and in the advising of the students so that groups of students and faculty could get to know each other well. Each residence was to be an "academic-social-residential community," not holding cells where students only went to sleep.

She also believed that Douglass needed "a bit of glamour." It had a beautiful white-spired chapel, and now Polly wanted some new buildings that would be comparable, particularly a new dining hall. She believed eating together in a civilized way mattered. Dinner had always been important in her family, so it came as something of a shock to her when a study conducted by the Douglass Home Economics Department discovered that a sizable proportion of Douglass students were not in the habit of sitting down to any meal with their families; TV dinners and fast food had become the norm. Polly wanted the evening meal to be a sit-down occasion so that students might "appreciate the values and learn the techniques of this significant function. Such education can not be neglected if women are to be effective in family and community life and make their full contribution to the intellectual development of their time."[8]

While they waited for the new buildings, space in the existing ones had to be juggled. In determining how to do this, Polly was not unwilling to challenge some established assumptions. She sternly informed department chairs, "It is essential that we follow a policy of multiple use of what facilities we have, inconvenient as it sometimes may seem."[9] "...the territorial privileges of individual departments which cannot be justified educationally or economically must be revised."[10]

In the cause of efficiency she changed the class schedule from fifty-minute classes three times a week to seventy-five-minute classes twice a week, with twenty minutes in between to give students time to get from one place to another. She maintained that the new schedule would bring about "better utilization of class space and faculty time, greater educational opportunities for the individual student, and longer blocks of uninterrupted time for study."[11] She explained the new schedule to the students and then appealed to their pride. "Without question, the new schedule does imply greater responsibility for the individual student. If this assumption of student maturity is unwarranted, the plan is doomed to failure but we would not have adopted it if we did not feel confident that you could and would profit thereby."[12]

The fewer, longer, meetings would serve another important purpose: more commuters would be able to take advantage of what was offered at the state university since they would have to travel less frequently.

The expansion of Douglass and its integration with Rutgers were at the heart of Polly's administration. Although she set the process in motion and contributed to virtually all of the initial planning, the actual completion of many of the buildings took place after she had left. Nonetheless, the numbers and types of buildings that were added bore the stamp of her educational concepts and her ideological commitments. It took both boldness and courage for her to persevere as she did. When she began, the money wasn't in hand, but she was confident it would come. The students weren't yet at the gates, but she was sure they would come too. In the end she presided over the creation of an essentially new institution with a new library, new dormitories, new dining hall, and, even more important, with a new sense of itself.

She also obliged the Rutgers community to develop a new sense of Douglass. According to Marjorie Trayes, "When people were saying things about Douglass in a meeting that she didn't approve of, she could, very calmly and very distinctly, point out where they were wrong. She changed minds and attitudes."

And then an event occurred that would irrevocably alter her thinking and focus her attention on the cause that was to define virtually everything she did from this point forward.

15

The Awakening

Polly admitted frankly that she was "never interested in women as such."[1] As a child she had given serious thought to what kind of a girl she would be, but she had never thought of herself, or other women, in a political context, never worried about their rights or about their differentness. She always insisted—even into her old age—that she had never been denied the chance to do the work she wanted, never felt denigrated because she was female and never felt overlooked because of her gender.

Now, however, her experience at Douglass and her sense of responsibility for its students was causing some new ideas to come into her mind. A barrage of fragmentary observations appears in her notebooks: "Women as such never seem interesting because you cant do anything about it—but do differ." "What is the quality of experience in the home in suburbia—for parents? children? *Modern gadgets* have not freed Mother of routine just changed it and made it less creative." "Reading about physicist Lise Meitner—Whether or not women are as good etc etc the satisfactions are open to them—& that is the reason for entering the field."

Around this time she was invited by Arthur Adams to join the Commission on the Education of Women of the American Council on Education, a sort of clearinghouse for information on the education of women. It had been established by the council in 1953 "to document, analyze and follow the involvement of women in all the different levels and fields of learning." This appointment was significant for her because it stimulated her thinking about women's education and introduced her to people in Washington who were also thinking about it. A year after Polly was appointed she became the chair.

Then an invitation arrived, which was to be even more important. On December 6, 1957, Polly was invited to become a member of the Divisional Committee for Scientific Personnel and Education of the National Science Foundation, a committee concerned with the development and employment of scientists. It was to be a two-year term, ending November 30, 1959, but she was invited for a second term and so she served four years.

By the time Polly officially took her seat at the NSF in January 1958, the country was reeling from the Russians' launching of *Sputnik*. There was a collective sense of panic about the state of science education in the United States and a frantic search for what we could do to catch up with our enemies. A kind of hysteria was in the air—Polly remembered some legislation being proposed to force schools to refuse morning milk to any students who hadn't done well in arithmetic that day.[2] Edward Teller called it "a kind of technological Pearl Harbor."[3] "We were scared stiff," Polly remembered. Congress responded by appropriating nine million dollars for the immediate expansion of programs to improve science education and then passed the aptly named "National Defense Education Act," the first general federal aid to education legislation since the Morrell Act of 1862 had established the Land Grant colleges. "Reducing the waste of talent" became a national objective.[4]

Polly's committee was to advise the NSF on what they should do to develop scientists faster. "One of the questions we asked," she remembered, "and I think I was the person on the committee who asked this—was who are the bright young kids, by IQ kinds of tests, who do not go to college. We thought if we could find out who they were, maybe there was something we could do to help them." Six weeks later the staff had information from three different testing groups. What they told Polly's committee was that of the sixteen-to-nineteen-year-olds with IQs in the top ten percent of the nation who did not go on to college, ninety-eight to ninety-nine percent were female. It was, "earth shaking," "mind-boggling," she was to say years later. "Nearly all of the males with that kind of identified ability were continuing their education; practically none of the females were." This information galvanized her.

What happened next, however, stunned her even more. Nothing happened. None of the other members of the committee took any notice. The statistic that Polly had found earth-shattering did not even give them pause. They simply carried on with the meeting, moving to the next item on the agenda. Many years later, when she recalled that meeting, it still caused her to wonder. "The reason for identifying this pool was to develop it, and nobody got talking about how to develop the women. These were nice men—not sexist people—and they just sort of set this aside. Nobody on the Advisory Committee or the National Science Foundation staff proposed to do anything about this loss of talent. Nobody seemed to think it important. I was deeply puzzled. I felt that I was looking into a great dark cave that had been right beneath my feet all of my life without my knowing it. Beneath their feet too."[5]

Polly came to believe that not only did the committee and the staff not want to bother talking about the loss of female talent, "they even seemed to wish to conceal the facts, as if they didn't want the country to know that almost all the bright males were continuing beyond high school. I think the committee's feeling was that if Congress knew that all the males were going on, then there would be less reason to support experimental programs at the high school level." If the only students who were being deflected from higher education were the inconsequential ones, there would be less interest in, and less money for improving the teaching of science, which the NSF scientists knew needed improvement.

> I was too baffled to say anything right then. I needed to think this over: why did they have this reaction? I went home trying to figure out what was going on. These were able and good men who cared about developing scientific talent. Did they see no future for bright females, no loss in neglecting them? I think it was probably fortunate at that time that I was reading one of John Gardner's books—I can't remember just which one—and I came on a sentence that just turned the light on for me. Gardner wrote, 'a society gets the kind of excellence it values.' He was thinking about musicians or philosophers or plumbers. I thought first of baseball players in the U.S. and soccer players elsewhere. And I thought about women. Those scientists at the NSF had not valued the scientific potentialities of women. They didn't think that those women, if they had gone on, would have contributed anything. They didn't think educating them would give them a group of people who were going to make a difference. They didn't have any expectation that the women would be important. They had an assumption—right there—this unexpectation as to what women would do with their educated intelligence. This country didn't expect women to do important things. That was why so few women bothered to go on in the sciences or in many other demanding fields. That explained what inhibited women from developing and using their full intellectual capabilities. There was, I came to see, a climate of unexpectation as to what women were likely to contribute on any intellectual frontier. My divining rod had found a flood that would run with me where I was running."[6]

Years later Polly referred to this insight as her "awakening." She said it was "quite dramatic," revolutionizing her view of women. It made her realize that women had a problem whose magnitude she had not appreciated until this moment. She had not thought seriously about women's opportunities before because she had grown up believing that women had been liberated. She had seen her mother, her aunts, and her friends, like Leal, pursuing their interests. She had attended a girls' school and then Vassar, and had never been conscious of being denigrated. She had married Henry, who had always respected her and her aspirations and who himself had grown up in a family of strong women.

So even though Polly had witnessed discrimination, she had never felt its impact. She had never permitted herself to recognize it because she did not believe in complaining, in looking to blame others. Yale had refused to offer her a full-time position because she was a woman; she had been required to have male researchers sign for her grants; no matter what she achieved, she had never been promoted up the professorial ranks. All of this, however, she simply could not see as discrimination. Nor could she see it when her graduate school professors permitted her to go through graduate study at breakneck speed, not demanding of her the same grounding in organic chemistry and advanced biochemistry they had insisted upon for her male colleagues. Now she saw their permissiveness not as a testimony to her capabilities, but as another example of the lower expectations for women. They did not believe her training mattered because they did not expect her to do much.

Polly had been able to avoid confronting these unpleasant realities before, because she herself didn't care about professional advancement or titles. She cared only about the work, and she had had the opportunities she wanted. But opportunities were not enough; if no one cared what young women made of themselves, what would be waiting for them after college?

Once this insight came to Polly, it changed her life. Quite suddenly, Polly Bunting was on her way to becoming an activist.

She was still not thinking in political terms. Women were not yet an officially labeled "minority group," with laws that protected them. The language of civil rights and discrimination hadn't been formulated yet. But using her innate sense of fair play and her logic, Polly saw that what was going on did not make any sense. It was wasteful. Too much important work needed to be done to ignore half the population. As she wrote a friend years later, she never thought about whether or not women could "do it all." She just resented having women told what they could do before anyone looked to see.

"The minute I got that notion I began to see it all around," she said, "in the things people said to children. They would ask boys what they were doing and what they were going to be. And they would talk to girls about their pretty dresses. I was finding one thing after another that supported my basic hypothesis. I can remember visiting a New Jersey high school.... The guidance officer told me about a student who was 'so good that he ought to go to Harvard.' 'What about the able young women in the class,?' I asked. 'Oh, the top student in the senior class is a girl and we are glad to say that she is planning to go to college.'"[7]

She saw that the conclusions people had come to about women's capabilities were based on faulty information. As a bacteriologist, she knew that if you wanted to understand the difference between two kinds of organisms, you grew them in duplicate in a variety of different media and saw how they behaved. But men and women had been grown in different environments, so there was no valid basis for comparing their capabilities.

What also struck Polly was people's willingness to make uncritical pronouncements about the differing capabilities of all men and all women when, as she pointed out, "men and women show overlapping abilities wherever we can measure them. Some women are better than most men, even at running the Boston marathon. The point is to give each individual the opportunities that fit that person and not to judge individuals by group averages.... Most of the chatter about this topic is ridiculous. I've heard eminent scholars argue that because women have not had many Nobel prizes in a certain field, they are of no importance in the field. Well, most men have not had Nobel prizes in it either."[8]

Polly was particularly distressed that young women, from very early ages, were not only discouraged from going on in science, but were being shunted into terminal programs. "They are discouraged from taking physics in high school, urged not to take College Boards in chemistry... and in college warned not to plunge in as freshmen." And it wasn't only in science, but in other fields as well, that women were discouraged from doing advanced work. "The climate of unexpectation as to what women may do with their education has led to all the hidden dissuaders in our culture that tend to ridicule our vaunted freedom of opportunity," she said. Unless women were backed up by high expectations, "they will work primarily for approval rather than break-through and will not be at the fronts, particularly not at the unheralded fronts where they could serve so successfully."[9]

She had believed until now that women, like men, had choices about how they would spend their lives, and if few of them chose to earn doctorates, that was perfectly acceptable. Now she began to wonder how free those choices really were. Had this climate of unexpectation in which women lived from their earliest days so warped their perspectives, so stunted their ambitions, that they could not aspire? "Here was a situation," she concluded, "as complex, as un-understood and possibly as important as the genetics of *Serratia*."[10]

Polly was determined that, at least at Douglass, women would be given every opportunity. Almost immediately she set in motion a series of initiatives that were to have an impact that reverberated beyond Douglass. She decided that rather than preaching or writing, she would set up an experiment, "pick a particular phenomenon, a particular area of unexpectation and probe it a bit. . . . It would be important, whatever one tried, to demonstrate that one cared what women did with their talents, that one thought it worthwhile to assist them, that one had high expectations. No point in searching the universe for the exception, individuals who would 'prove the rule.' Better to see if one could change ordinary behavior, change, thereby, the image. Women were notoriously poor at math. Was there hidden interest & talent here?"[11]

She decided to assess the possible loss of mathematical talent among New Jersey women. She applied to the Ford Foundation for a grant and often recounted the anecdote about why she may have received it. A year or two before approaching the foundation, she was stuffing the family's Thanksgiving turkey when two young men rang her doorbell. Thinking they had come to one of the Douglass student houses, they asked if she were the housemother. She replied that she certainly was, but that she was the only one at home at the moment. "Those two young men looked so crestfallen and lonely—and a campus is lonely at vacation time—that I said, 'I'd love to have company in the kitchen. Won't you come in?'" One of them was a Rutgers freshman, the other his friend from Cornell, to whom he had promised all sorts of dates at Douglass that he was unable to deliver. Polly chatted with them in the kitchen for a bit and sent them on their way. After she received the Ford grant a year or so later, she found herself being introduced by an official of the foundation, who recounted the story of how his son had come to Polly's house the day before Thanksgiving. "Not that I didn't have a good application," Polly said, "but he may have been more willing to listen."

With the grant in hand, she launched the Program in Mathematics at Douglass by sending a postcard to many thousands of women college graduates in the state whose names and addresses came from alumnae offices. There were three questions on the post cards: "Did you take mathematics in college? Would you like to take more? Would you like to get a job using mathematics?" About six hundred yes, yes, yes postcards were returned, and so Polly began setting up a few special mathematics courses at Rutgers. When letters were sent to those six hundred asking if they would be interested in taking these courses, only a couple hundred wrote back that they were. Polly wondered what had happened to all the others and made some telephone calls. "And that was one of the times I hadn't guessed what the answer was," she said years later. "They were already doing it at places near them where they could go and take math." The postcard itself—evidence that someone thought they could do it and was urging them to try—was all the catalyst they needed.

Polly began to understand that educated women were eager and ready to take full advantage of their educations. She also began to see, however, that the pattern of their lives was so different from that of men that they needed a different educational timetable. Because of marriage, child bearing, and the requirements of husbands' employment, which often meant they had to relocate, women were often compelled to interrupt their education. Institutions had to abandon outmoded schedules that were in direct conflict with what she called "the biological facts of life." Women did not want to postpone family responsibilities; they wanted instead to combine them with education. As Polly pointed out rather wryly, women were taking seriously what legions of commencement speakers had been saying—that learning should continue throughout one's life.

In the 1950's, however, most women's colleges had rules against admitting married women and would only permit their own students who got married to stay under certain prescribed conditions: they had to attend full-time, and in some cases had to sign a written statement promising not to discuss any aspect of their marriage with their classmates. Pregnant students were automatically banished. State universities permitted married women to enroll, but they did little to encourage them.

Women's colleges stifled their female faculty members, adopting the same nepotism rules as men's colleges, which always meant excluding the wife. They impeded the scholarly growth of young mothers on their faculties by giving them only subservient positions and not affording them the time or opportunity to develop their own research, so the women had no way to progress up the professorial ranks. Polly believed that whether they admitted it or not, women's colleges saw themselves and were seen by others as finishing schools—places where education was finished—rather than as Polly thought they should be, places that "assumed their share of responsibility for the advancement of knowledge."[12] "It seemed," Polly said, "that the women's colleges were concerned with the training of girls, not the education of women."

Even organizations like the National Association of Deans of Women, of which Polly was a member, and the American Association of

University Women were not working against the climate. What Polly labeled the "hidden dissuaders" were rampant in the very organizations which should have been working to counteract them. "It was as if they were all invested in the status quo," she said years later, "perhaps afraid of rocking the boat for fear that what they had would be taken away, or maybe not interested in gaining for younger women privileges they had not had themselves."

Polly saw these archaic prejudices as absurd, especially when she gathered demographic statistics showing that the youngest child of one-half of all married women was in first grade when the mother was only thirty-two years old. And people were living longer, so that women could expect to have more years after their children were in school than before they entered. Women's colleges, therefore, had to equip women to use those years productively. She wrote in her journal: "If man has a future he will *look back with horror* on past 25-50 years— Time when all children were *forced* into school so much of the time and *adults* largely prevented from attending."

She found an apt image, which she used often in speeches, in the establishment in 1956 of the interstate highway system that fanned out across the country. These highways, Polly pointed out, were wide enough for people traveling at different speeds and had well-marked entrances and exits. Women's colleges, she argued, should afford women that same freedom. They needed to be able to get off the education highway to bear and rear children and then get on again when those responsibilities were behind them.

"How could we claim, as we did, that the test of liberal education was its ability to prepare students to continue the process through the rest of their lives, and refuse admission to able individuals who had missed out earlier and now desperately wanted their chance to catch up, wanted it enough to pay baby sitters as well as tuition. . . . The more I thought about it, the more unwise, unjust & foolish it seemed. . . . It was anti-intellectualism parading in the name of quality," she said years later. "It was high time that the educators of women showed that they valued their product."

Polly began thinking about ways to open up Douglass and make it more flexible and hospitable for such women. She suggested in a letter to a Douglass trustee that students should be able to take whatever courses they wanted whether or not the courses were in the prescribed sequences and whether or not the women were working toward a degree. Even if the established sequences were best for most students, Polly argued that they were not the only way.

The more she thought back on her own early years of motherhood and her minute-by-minute schedules, the clearer it became to her that the biggest stumbling block in the way of young mothers who wanted to return to college was the pervasive rule that all students had to attend full-time. Polly knew that women with small children simply could not adhere to that conventional schedule. They had to shoehorn their classes in between other competing obligations. But no part of the one-size-fits-all educational blueprint was more jealously guarded—at least at the prestigious schools—than the idea that only full-time study was acceptable. Even though older students for many decades had attended night school, and many engineers had worked while they attended professional school, the idea of permitting older women to take only a few courses during the day was heresy. "There was a notion," Polly said years later, "that the colleges that weren't prestigious, little colleges that started here and there, had part-time students and none of the Eastern colleges wanted to be like those little places. It had to be pure—do it right. People pay too much attention to image."

She asked some of the Eastern men's colleges why they had rules against part-time study and learned that they were concerned it would lead to "dilettantism." Polly recognized that might be a problem; she never had any patience with students who squandered their educational opportunities. But she saw no sign of that scourge among the hard-working mothers who wanted to go to college and had no other option than Douglass. They could neither afford nor travel to any other university. A public university had obligations to its citizens, she believed, that should transcend these entrenched and petty regulations and prejudices. "It seems to me that what we should be offering the people is something so much broader than what we are offering," she wrote to a trustee. "Let the private colleges worry about standards, we should worry about opportunities."[13]

She decided to do what she could at Douglass and launched another experiment: the admission of a small group of older women on a part-time basis. To accomplish this, she knew she had to convince the various Douglass constituencies that there was nothing about part-time study that would corrupt the institution, undermine its prestige, nor lead to lower standards.

She began with the trustees who had the responsibility for setting the college's policies. In May 1957 she presented a carefully worded proposal to their college committee in which she reiterated logically and eloquently all her arguments. By the end of the month the committee endorsed her recommendation.

In order to get Rutgers' President Jones on her side, she pointed out that this program might win the university the gratitude of a vital constituency. She knew from her lunches with the presidents of many women's organizations that they did not believe the university adequately met the needs of the state's women. She told Jones that they could "rally this important force" by opening classes to the women of the state.[14]

She also emphasized the economic advantages to both the university and the state. "Frequently young men who have come to New Brunswick to look at a job will drop in to find out whether their wives could complete their college work here. More and more, the availability of higher education . . . is a telling factor when people consider job opportunities."[15]

And the part-time program might benefit the college's academic program. More than half of Douglass' students were leaving after two years, mostly to get married, and Polly feared that their loss might lead to the evisceration of the academic program. The departure of so many of the older students, just when they were ready to declare a major, might eventually leave the college with too few advanced students for the more advanced courses. If Douglass had to stop teaching higher level courses, it might well end up being relegated to the status of a junior college. Admitting advanced students on a part-time basis might save the day.

Despite these arguments, many Douglass faculty and staff found part-time study an heretical concept. Edna Newby dismissed it as impossible. Douglass was and always had been a college for full-time undergraduate women. Part-time women had to go to the night college at Rutgers. As the custodian of Douglass' institutional memory, she knew it was her job to keep Polly from wandering onto forbidden paths. She was so emphatic she assumed that was the end of the idea.

But it was not. And wander Polly did, but not before the faculty engaged in some spirited discussions of their own. Faculty who had been at the college for a long time saw this idea as a break with tradition, "a radical change," remembered History Professor Thomas Weber, the abandonment of Douglass' identity as "a unified kind of defined college." Fortunately for Polly, there were enough younger faculty members who were willing to go along with her. But it took a full year after she first made her plea to the trustees. Even when the faculty finally approved the proposal, the trustees hobbled it with all sorts of restrictions and conditions. Part-time students had to meet the same admission requirements as full-time students; they could only be commuters, not residents; they must have had at least one year of college; they had to take at least six credit hours each semester and had to take courses in consecutive terms; and no full-time student who was failing could shift to part-time status without first being re-admitted by the admission committee. And there couldn't be too many. The faculty finally agreed to admit ten married women as part-time students.

As Polly had anticipated, the program was far more unsettling to contemplate than to implement. When the older women arrived on campus, they soon blended in. The faculty discovered that the first ten pioneers were dedicated students—mature, serious about their education. "It was something they really valued and appreciated, something precious to them and therefore they made the most of it," remembered Philosophy Professor Fadlou Shehadi. "They were the ones who always had read the assignments and did not party all night like the younger students. They were up with questions. They stated their views with conviction and clarity. And they contributed, enriched the class."

The undergraduates were intrigued by them and became very eager to have lunch with them and talk to them. They saw them as people who could "help them understand their future and how you did things," said Polly. They were impressed by the depth of the older women's intellectual interests and inspired by their determination. The fact that they were married—the ultimate female achievement—and still returned to complete their college education spoke volumes to the younger students. "I began to see these older women as my unlabelled deans," said Polly. "The older women," commented mathematics instructor Katheryne McCormick," were the GIs of Douglass."

By the second year, the ten students had grown to fifteen and by the third year to twenty-seven. By the fifth year, opposition had melted away, and the faculty eliminated the requirement of one year of college so that high school graduates became eligible. The percentage of those dropping out was less than among the full-time undergraduates. Some went on and received Ph.D.s. One, the wife of a chicken farmer, earned a Ph.D. from Princeton in medieval history and became a professor at Hampshire College. In her last Douglass annual report, Polly wrote, "Their presence on campus has been a stimulus and an inspiration to many of the younger students."

Ultimately the program succeeded beyond Polly's most optimistic imaginings. The numbers continued to grow until there were close to three hundred part-time students, with their own dean, their own club —called "Sophia," the Greek word for wisdom—and their own lounge containing a large portrait of Polly. They are disproportionately represented in Phi Beta Kappa. The program eventually bore Polly's name and became the most significant achievement of her Douglass years.

When Douglass celebrated the twenty-fifth anniversary of the Bunting Program on May 20, 1984, Polly, then in her seventies, came for all the festivities. In inviting Polly to this commemoration, the vice-president of "Sophia" wrote: "I have so wanted to meet you. Often I have wondered whether you know how much being back in school has meant to so many."

Polly heard her praises sung and delivered a short speech. Characteristically, she took no credit for herself, but said simply that had she been asked twenty-five years earlier about the likelihood of such an anniversary celebration, "I would have thought it unlikely—more likely the College would have forgotten it ever had a *rule against it! It made no sense!*" She did want it known, however, that Douglass was the first to have a part-time program for married women—"a bit ahead of Minnesota & Sarah Lawrence. I like to have that known."

Polly kept in touch with the program all of her life, continuing to send contributions to a loan fund for older women who needed financial assistance.

16

A Bit of Rebellion

As the 1950's came to a close, Polly had become more accustomed to her position and the responsibilities and obligations it entailed. There were fewer notes in her notebooks, as if she no longer needed to carry on an internal dialogue to work out her ideas. She had honed her message. She knew what she wanted to say and what needed to be accomplished. Her major initiatives, the part-time program for older women and the expansion, were well underway. The land was no longer new.

She had changed Douglass significantly—too significantly for some of the faculty. Some couldn't accept the transformation of the Douglass they had known. She was beginning to recognize, as Richard McCormick, the former Rutgers dean, put it, "that you couldn't push the college too rapidly into modernity. And in that sense she may have bruised some of the more stalwart characters there." The resentment against the closer affiliation with Rutgers had never fully abated, and the antagonism of some faculty only became more intense. They felt that she "was selling out to Rutgers, sacrificing some of the things we had done independently, tying us to Rutgers too tightly," remembered Marjorie Trayes.

Some faculty saw her as using Douglass to advance her own aspirations. She was unquestionably gaining a more prominent national profile, serving on the NSF committee and the American Council on Education. And she understood that what she was accomplishing at Douglass had societal implications for higher education and American women. Coupled with the faculty's resistance came the belief that, as History Professor Thomas Weber put it, Polly's "ambitions were outrunning the possibilities of the campus." She was seen as wanting and needing a bigger stage and no longer being satisfied with the deanship of a college.

"There was a bit of rebellion about Polly toward the end," said Marjorie Trayes. This might account for the almost weary tone in Polly's 1959 annual report—a "been there, done that" feeling, which was not characteristic of her. The report lacked the verve that usually characterized her writing. She even mixed up the opening enrollment figure, citing it as 1,480 in one place and later as 1,650, suggesting a totally uncharacteristic lack of attention to detail. "Each academic year has its satisfactions and its frustrations," she wrote. "This year both have seemed particularly acute at Douglass." The increase in the student body had not led to an increase in staff or faculty. And it was particularly galling to her that university decisions of vital importance to Douglass had been made without consultation, by what she called "administrative fiat." "Polly was getting restless at Douglass and Douglass was becoming a little restless under Polly," said Trayes.

The struggle with Rutgers was not new, and it might well have been exacerbated by the imminent departure of her old friend and colleague Lewis Webster Jones. From the beginning she had looked to Rutgers as a resource, but the relationship had not been without tension. Several years earlier Polly had said that too often, "Rutgers means 'they' and not 'we.'" At the start of her administration she called for a redesign of the letterhead to "give a little more prominence to Douglass College." She expressed annoyance to the Rutgers public relations department: "How in thunder can we get the name of Douglass across to the people of the state if every time we have an interesting item the 'Douglass' is deleted in favor of 'Rutgers?' . . . I hope that in the future . . . [we] can have the satisfaction of hearing that she is a student at 'Douglass College.'"[1]

In spite of her annoyances and dissatisfactions, Polly always maintained that she was not out looking for a new job; one simply fell into her lap, as the Douglass position had. During the spring of 1959, her last spring at Douglass, she was extraordinarily busy. In addition to her usual duties as dean, she organized the first Alumnae College, she went to Puerto Rico for a four-day meeting of the National Science Foundation; flew to Washington, D.C., for a meeting of the Commission on the Education of Women of the American Council on Education; delivered two addresses at the State Federation of Women's Clubs convention in Atlantic City; went to New York to take part in a special symposium on basic research, sponsored by the National Academy of Sciences; headed the Schools and Colleges Division of the New Brunswick United Fund; and chaired the University Committee on Relations with the National Science Foundation.

And then her life became even busier. She received a telephone call from the chair of the Smith College search committee. They were looking for a new president and asked if some of Smith's trustees could talk with her about the kinds of things they ought to consider. Polly thought it would be fun to chat with them and invited them down to

Douglass for lunch. But by this time she was savvy enough in the workings of academe to know that along with talking to her about what Smith needed they were also coming to have a look at her. "And I can remember the day before they came looking in the mirror and saying, 'Now if you really want this job you'd better go and get your hair fixed.'" But she decided right then that she didn't want the Smith job. She liked being in a university with varied colleagues and access to research. Women's colleges had a less cosmopolitan and charged atmosphere.

Quite a large contingent of Smith trustees did come, and among them was Paul Buck, a Harvard history professor, who had been the dean of the Harvard faculty and provost of the university. "He had an informed interest in women's education and in Radcliffe," Polly said. She told the Smith trustees frankly that she thought the best thing for the colleges in the Connecticut Valley would be to work together to build a graduate school. She made clear how important she thought it was for faculty to have access to facilities for research and told the trustees that these colleges would be far more attractive to qualified faculty if there were opportunities for teaching, at least part-time, at the graduate level. But Smith wasn't any more eager for change and expansion than Douglass, and Polly noted that her ideas were not received particularly well. Nonetheless, she thought she should say what she thought, and then if future candidates happened to agree with her the trustees would have heard it before and might take the position more seriously.

After the lunch Polly didn't give Smith or college presidencies any more thought until a few days later, when at seven one morning she received a telephone call from her friend Katharine McBride, the president of Bryn Mawr. She had heard of the Smith visit and urged Polly not to make any commitments too quickly, "which was a very mysterious telephone call at seven a.m. I thought, 'What under the sun is going on?'" Polly didn't have to wait long to find out. Within a few days she heard from Radcliffe. Would she meet with some of the trustees? She realized Radcliffe was considering her, and that probably Paul Buck, who had noted her strong pitch for universities, had planted the idea. Polly saw immediately that she had the right background for Radcliffe. She had taught at both Yale, a university, and at two women's colleges, Bennington and Goucher, and she was administering a women's college within a university, a connection similar to Radcliffe's with Harvard. Polly had not known that Radcliffe was looking for a president, looking particularly for a woman and a scholar, who could hold her own in the Harvard community.

Until that moment Polly had never given Radcliffe any thought at all. But Harvard had always been part of her world. She had been four or five when she first heard that name. She and her father had been watching a boat on Long Island Sound returning from Boston. When Polly asked her father what was in Boston, he had hesitated for only a second before saying "Harvard is in Boston." And when she asked what Harvard was, he responded, "Well, that's the greatest college in this country." "And that was the first time I'd heard about Harvard. And I always remembered it." Now she decided it was time to go up and look over Radcliffe, "sneaking in during a vacation," was how she put it. She had never been on the campus and was not very impressed with what she saw. She didn't talk with anyone, but she found the buildings pretty grim.

When it became apparent to Polly that the Radcliffe trustees were serious about her, her first reaction was that she wasn't interested. She wanted more challenges than at first she thought she would find at Radcliffe. It appeared to her that the college was getting along just fine, and she had no interest in being an administrator who just kept things perking along. In addition, she believed that public education was more important, that it played a more essential role in the lives of communities and individuals. Her children, too, reminded her of the greater importance of public education, and expressed their suspicions that she was being enticed away only because of Radcliffe's greater prestige. "I wondered about it myself," Polly admitted. But she was restless, frustrated with some of the parochial obstructions being thrown in the way of her plans. Douglass was growing very rapidly, and she was beginning to doubt if she wanted to administer as large and complex an organization as it was becoming. Administration was something she had stumbled into; although she was managing well, she saw that skills she did not have were becoming more and more important at Douglass and would not be as important at Radcliffe. She recognized that the initiatives she felt most strongly about were in place and now just needed to be overseen. Although she hadn't been actively looking for a new job, this one did look promising.

What finally tipped the scales in Radcliffe's favor was Polly's recognizing how committed she had become to improving women's education, expanding women's opportunities and changing expectations about what women could accomplish. The Boston area, with its proximity to so many educational institutions, offered valuable resources, and at Radcliffe "one would have a kind of pedestal from which to operate. What happened at Radcliffe," she saw, "would make more difference to the climate of expectation than what happened at Douglass." She decided to go.

The news of her appointment came at the beginning of June 1959. She was chairing a meeting of the Douglass College Council in Science Hall when the telephone rang. Polly answered it and returned to the meeting, which continued for another hour. When it ended, Polly told the assembled group that she had just been appointed the new president of Radcliffe College. "It would not have been good to make an announcement right in the middle of the meeting," she said. "There was more work to do."[2] She was to be the first woman president of Radcliffe since Ada L. Comstock—who had held the office from 1923 to 1943—the fifth in its history and the first scientist. Her salary was to be twenty thousand dollars, several thousand more than she had received at Douglass. It was a respectable salary in 1960, when cabinet secretaries earned twenty-five thousand dollars and the vice-president of the United States thirty-five.

The last Douglass faculty meeting that Polly presided over was on April 12, 1960. No official notice was taken in the faculty minutes of her departure. They established a faculty committee headed by History Professor Margaret Judson to begin the process of searching for a new dean. The next meeting, May 24, 1960, was presided over by University Dean John L. Swink, who became Douglass' acting dean. In chairing the meeting, Swink said nothing at all about his predecessor.

But the students were brokenhearted, particularly the class of '59. They had begun their college years when she began as dean and had adopted her as their official class adviser for all four years. One of them wrote to her that she was such an integral part of their class that any reunion would be incomplete without her. They dedicated the 1959 yearbook to her: "How she managed to dovetail her multiplicity of roles as national educator, Dean of the College, mother of four (and Claudia), and guide-confidante-friend of the student body is beyond us.... To Mrs. Mary Ingraham Bunting, who unknowingly provides the women of Douglass with day-by-day inspiration."

It was perhaps inevitable that some Douglass alumnae and students would hold it against her for leaving. A year later, when she said in a public statement that many Douglass students were the first in their families to go to college, some of them were outraged. She had made a simple statement of fact, but it activated their old sense of inferiority. They felt she had deserted them for a more prestigious place and now was looking down on them. The great majority of Douglass alumnae, however, continued to remember her with affection and respect.

For the rest of her life she returned to the campus repeatedly, for conferences, anniversary celebrations, and reunions. In 1960 she received an honorary degree as well as a farewell gift—two abstract lithographs of tree-like structures by Reginald Neal, chairman of the Douglass art department. In 1982 she addressed the class of 1957 on their twenty-fifth reunion. In 1981, when she went there to speak about older women returning to college, she spoke of her Douglass years with great affection. "One of the fine learning periods of my life began here 25 years ago when as a 'geneticist with nest building experience' I was suddenly plunged into college administration. One has a special feeling for the places where one grew and the people who aided the process. Students, faculty, deans, alumnae, and many others took me in hand here and guided my learning with skill and kindly concern, all of us recognizing that the vitality of a fine college was at stake. Would that all college presidents and deans had the same assistance today."[3]

Eventually Douglass established a professorship in Polly's name. Their final accolade was to name a dormitory after her for students in a special science and math program. Dedicated in 1988, it houses undergraduate and graduate women studying science and math. The concept behind the program was that younger women just starting their college studies in fields where women are few, could benefit by having proximity to more established scholars. It was an idea Polly believed in wholeheartedly. At the dedication on May 20, 1988, Polly spoke about the isolation women often feel in scientific fields and even referred to her own lonely experience. A Rutgers chemistry professor remembered that he was moved to tears.

Those who maintained that Polly left Douglass because she was looking for a more prestigious post misjudged her. She had a mission she was committed to. She saw what needed to be done—not for herself, but for women whose talents were being wasted and for other women coming along, trying—in her words—"to shove into the stream of life." In her new post she would have more visibility, more opportunity to promote the cause of expectations for women. When Radcliffe spoke she knew people listened. She was ready. This sightseer had made this new land her own.

On June 8, 1959, the Radcliffe trustees made the official announcement of her appointment. Virtually every newspaper account emphasized that she was a widow with four children.

17

A Kind of Pedestal

The Radcliffe Polly came to in 1960 was badly in need of her vision, courage, and feisty determination. But it didn't know it. Assured of its position as the premier college in the elite group of "seven sisters," Radcliffe was not looking for change.

The college had come into being in 1879. It was not founded, in the usual sense, but rather evolved in fits and starts, beginning as an idea of Arthur Gilman, the director of a Cambridge girls' school, and his wife, Stella, who had a daughter they thought should have access to a Harvard education. They convinced Harvard's president to permit some professors to give courses to women of the caliber they offered to men, but in a separate, small house on Appian Way. "The Harvard Annex," as it was called, was so successful that three years later it was incorporated as the Society for the Collegiate Instruction of Women and twelve years after that, in 1894, was renamed Radcliffe College after Harvard's first major woman donor. As a real college it became a degree-granting institution, offering not a Harvard degree, but one which Harvard's president agreed to countersign. By 1943, in exchange for eighty-five percent of the tuition paid to Radcliffe, Harvard agreed to allow Radcliffe women to attend the same classes as the men. The war was on; large numbers of men, both students and faculty, had left, so the measure was initiated as sensible but assumed to be temporary. Once ensconced in classes in the Harvard Yard, however, the women never left.

When Polly arrived, Radcliffe, though loosely attached to Harvard, controlled its real estate and its endowment. The group of twelve trustees who comprised the "Council" met every month and, in effect, ran the college. The much larger Board of Trustees, which met less frequently, more or less rubber-stamped the Council's actions.

The members of the Council were all Bostonians with pedigrees and longtime connections to Radcliffe. Since there were no term limits on the Council, its composition remained more or less the same through the years. Some people resigned or chose not to be re-nominated or died, but many stayed on and on. They were accustomed to having things done as they had always been done.

Polly startled the trustees right from the beginning. When she was being interviewed and they told her that she would be expected to live in the stately president's house on the elegant Brattle Street, a house not unlike the dean's residence at Douglass, Polly expressed a decided preference for living out on the fringes, in the country. They told her, "Cambridge is really country," to which she responded, "You mean, I could keep a cow?" "I wasn't planning on keeping a cow," she explained later, "I was just trying to get the definition of country straightened out a little bit. And then they all looked at each other and there was all this 'ssssss.'"

Eventually she did move into the president's house, but she went on doing unconventional things that made the trustees uneasy. Soon after her arrival, for example, she invited all of Radcliffe's maids to a fancy tea with the silver and china and all the trimmings; she wanted to let them know that she appreciated what they contributed to the college.

She ensconced her bees on the roof of the president's house, directly above the dining room where contributors and visiting dignitaries were entertained. It was a particularly good spot, she explained, surrounded by many trees and hedges and, "that hive made honey like everything." Once, she delivered a long lecture on bees and their habits to workmen on ladders painting the windows. She was tending to her hive, and they were painting and kept asking questions that she just kept answering.

And she continued the practice she had begun at Douglass, of leaving on her porch light to let students, or administrators, know that they were welcome to drop in. "She drove her administrators crazy," remembered the dean of students, Sue Bolman, "because any student could talk to her directly about anything any time. She didn't pay much attention to hierarchy."

When Bolman suggested bringing a minister into the dormitories to discuss sexual matters, Polly welcomed the idea. "The other deans almost fell on the floor," Bolman remembered. "The idea—the very idea—that these issues would be discussed at Radcliffe College!"

"I always felt I was sort of hanging on to her by the coattails," said Helen Homans Gilbert, longtime president of the Board of Trustees. "She was such a dynamo, that [the trustees] didn't really know how to slow her down."[1] Sometimes some of the trustees would implore Gilbert not to let a new idea of Polly's come up at a board meeting; they wanted more time to consider it before having to vote. But with Polly, things didn't get put off. She always had new ideas; and this constant stream of innovation, along with her habit of speaking extemporaneously, from jotted notes, made the trustees nervous. They never quite knew what was going to happen next. "Polly just moved right ahead," said Bolman. "She was sometimes very autonomous."

Gilbert was a tall, austere Boston Brahmin of the first rank, a direct descendent of John Adams. She was usually attired in tweed suits and sensible shoes. In an interview years later she claimed that the Harvard faculty didn't like Polly—they were, after all, not accustomed to "that kind of woman." That could have been more Gilbert's attitude than the faculty's, since barely three years after Polly had assumed the presidency, at least one distinguished faculty member, Paul Buck, who had been on the committee that first interviewed her, wrote in a congratulatory letter, "I could use many adjectives to describe your great achievement as Radcliffe's President, but the one uppermost in my mind today as most applicable to you is 'leadership.'" Whatever the reason—Polly's Brooklyn background, her Ph.D., or just her history as an academic woman of considerable accomplishment—her relationship with Gilbert was always somewhat uneasy.

In those days there were only three hundred or so "girls" in each Radcliffe class—a paltry eleven to twelve hundred in the entire college, compared to the ten thousand-plus men of Harvard. Sitting in classes in a sea of Harris tweed jackets, Radcliffe students were well aware of their minority status. And it wasn't only the numbers. When they were invited to a meal in the paneled Harvard dining halls or attended tutorials in the spacious, well-appointed rooms of tutors in the stately Harvard houses, it was impossible not to compare those accommodations to their own institutionally arid dormitories with all the ambience of a Motel 6. The brick structures were not only sterile, they were also seriously overcrowded. Students not paying the full tuition were crammed into economy doubles and triples. Students who were paying in full usually had somewhat larger rooms, but these were small, sparsely furnished rectangles lacking either charm or comfort. The rooms were lined up along linoleum paved hallways. One student likened it to "a home for unwed mothers."

Polly's predecessor, Wilbur K. Jordan, a remote, white-haired member of the Harvard faculty, was rarely even glimpsed by undergraduates. Of the other Radcliffe administrators, students were aware of only a few deans, also remote figures. The administration didn't even include a dean of students, which in other colleges was someone concerned with students' problems outside of the classroom. Radcliffe, it was made clear to undergraduates from the very beginning, was concerned only about what went on inside. The dormitories were overseen by "housemothers," elderly, well-meaning ladies of the Margaret Corwin vintage, who knew much about ladylike behavior and very little about anything else. When they entered and left the dining halls at dinner, the students were required to stand as a gesture of respect. The housemother's main function was to serve milk and store-bought cookies on Saturday nights for the unfortunate few who were dateless. They also served coffee from silver-plated urns after the formal, seated Sunday lunch at which all girls were required to wear skirts. All students had to participate in a work program—waiting on tables, helping in the kitchen, or sitting at a switchboard at the dormitories' front doors to answer the telephone and buzz the lucky recipient of a phone call or visitor. No such requirement existed for the men at Harvard.

The student body, like that of most of the other elite New England colleges, was almost exclusively white, middle- and upper-class, with an occasional black student whose parents were almost always middle-class or celebrities. At the beginning of freshman year the "directory" appeared with black-and-white, postage-stamp-sized photographs of the newest initiates. This booklet was snapped up by the eager young men of the Ivy League. Harvard men flocked to the red brick dorms in the Radcliffe Quadrangle to attend the annual "Jolly-Ups," where nervous freshmen circled each other with the wary insouciance of adolescents at a suburban dancing school.

No men were ever allowed above the first floor. If someone's father or uncle or brother gained permission to ascend the staircase because he had been recruited to carry something heavy, the call "Man on Floor" rang out like a siren as a warning not to appear in the halls in some scanty costume. There were "callers' rooms" downstairs, but when a member of the opposite sex was entertained there, the door had to be securely propped open. Freshmen had a 9 P.M. curfew. Older students were required to record in the big sign-out books at the front desk where they were headed, but on weekday nights everyone had to be well inside the locked dorms before midnight.

The atmosphere was one of unrelenting pressure to achieve academically, along with pervasive confusion about what all that achievement was for. The future was vague, with the promise only of domesticity, school-teaching, or assisting some high-level man. There was little reason to aspire. And condescension was rampant. Radcliffe students were barred from Lamont, the undergraduate Harvard library, to spare the boys from distractions. But it never occurred to anyone to bar the boys from the inadequate Radcliffe library in the Radcliffe Yard; in fact, many of them went there to study. Women were still not accepted in the Harvard Business School, and their numbers in the other Harvard professional schools were few. At Harvard, as elsewhere, it was taken for granted that when women did earn advanced degrees they probably wouldn't put them to much use after they achieved the only real accomplishment that mattered—marriage. For those unattached at graduation, Radcliffe offered a summer secretarial course. Everyone knew that, Radcliffe degree or not, the first question at most job interviews was likely to be "How fast can you type?"

Like other women's colleges, Radcliffe was preparing women for the world they would face; it wasn't trying to change that world. There was no protection whatsoever from sexual harassment, a phenomenon not even discovered yet. And when tutors or professors made passes at a student there was no one for the student to turn to. The adult women on campus, the deans and housemothers, were never seen as people with the power to solve problems or with the openness to accept confidences.

Classes, which had formally been integrated in 1943, were all held in the Harvard Yard, which depending on the weather was either a five-minute bicycle ride or a fifteen-minute walk from the Radcliffe dorms. Slacks could never be worn away from the Quadrangle, so students donned their straight mid-calf tweed skirts and climbed onto their bicycles struggling to keep the skirts pulled down low enough for respectability and high enough to make pedaling a possibility.

These brilliant young women were frequently reminded how brilliant and, even more important, how lucky they were to be at the summit of the academic hierarchy. But there was no advising system. They were never guided or encouraged. Radcliffe students were definitely on their own.

The attitudes of the 1950's were as securely in place at Radcliffe as they were everywhere else. When one trustee, Mrs. Barry Bingham of Louisville, Kentucky, whose husband was the wealthy newspaper publisher, came to the end of her term, she received a set of book ends accompanied by a citation: "Mary Caperton Bingham: A fit model for the haute couture of Paris, a dimpled blonde who speaks with wit and precision, she is a treat both to the eye and to the ear. In her southern bailiwick she and her husband form one of the world's truly fabulous couples. The Trustees' meetings will seem pallid without the subtly sophisticated aura which has surrounded both her person and her penetrating comments."[2]

Polly had been scheduled to begin her job officially in July, but President Jordan decided that he would prefer to leave by February 1. So during the first semester of 1960 Polly was running both Radcliffe and

Douglass. "It was certainly one of the times," she said, "when one was glad one was healthy."

She divided her week between the two colleges, commuting between Cambridge and New Brunswick, telling her Radcliffe secretary to open the mail and forward only those things that could not wait. When she was in Cambridge, she camped in the president's house at 76 Brattle Street, feeling, she wrote her mother, "more like a guest than a President of Radcliffe." She made a particular point of meeting the student leaders, to get some sense of their concerns and ideas. She addressed alumnae at a Cambridge gathering she labeled "Radcliffe Alumnae Educate A New President." She spoke to Radcliffe clubs in various cities, telling the New Jersey club that she came from their alma mater on Tuesday and their state university on Wednesday. She met with her predecessor on a fairly regular basis, usually at the Harvard Club in New York. She referred to these meetings as "a special introductory course" for "one eager and grateful president-elect." She felt, she said, "like a horse with a new rider—neither sure of the other yet."

Mary, Polly's chief support at home, had left for the University of Vermont. Chuck stayed in New Brunswick to finish his senior year at Pingry. Bill and John moved with Polly to Cambridge, where they attended Browne and Nichols, a preparatory Cambridge day-school. They took full advantage of all the enticements of Harvard Square—the movies, bowling, shops, and subway into Boston. In an interview Polly joked that she "had two boys holding down the president's house in Cambridge and one at the dean's house in New Jersey, and I told them all they had to have fresh flowers at the side of my bed whenever I arrived."[3]

Although she was running two entirely different institutions for the first half of 1960, Polly wasn't just biding her time at Radcliffe. At only her second meeting with the Radcliffe Council, barely one month after her arrival, she informed the trustees that she was "shocked" at the low level of administrative salaries and not so subtly let them know that she thought it was wrong for Radcliffe to take advantage of its situation as a prestigious college to pay employees substantially less than they would be paid at other comparable colleges. By the next meeting, although the college was facing an almost certain deficit, she had the go-ahead to raise salaries.

She also dealt with issues of communication. She established a committee to review salaries and retirements to make sure she would stay informed. She asked for a survey of all buildings and properties owned or leased by the college. She convinced the Council that it was in the best interest of trustee effectiveness for its decisions to be communicated to the rest of the board through an "interim letter." By the third meeting in May, she informed them that she was going to include students on a major planning committee. "It would enrich their education," she said.

All this time she also was thinking hard about the best way to advance the cause that was most important to her—removing the societal barriers that interfered with women's achievement. As she had at Douglass, she wasted no time in moving ahead with her agenda. She didn't even wait for her official May inauguration to put a serious proposal on the table.

18

The Messy Experiment

It was Polly's most ambitious idea yet. At Douglass she had focused on women at the beginning of their higher education, women who hadn't been able to get a foot on the bottom rung of the educational ladder. Now she turned her attention to those on the top of that ladder, highly trained women who had finished their education. How, she asked herself, could Radcliffe stem the exodus of such women from promising careers? Characteristically she determined that her best course would be to set up another experiment.

She decided to use the same approach as she had studying color variation in *Serratia*, when she had placed cultures in different media and examined how the differences affected them. What would happen, she asked herself, if a few highly trained women were in a supportive rather than a competitive environment, with time, money to free them from child care and housework, and access to all the resources of Harvard—if they had the 1960's equivalent of Virginia Woolf's five hundred pounds and a room of their own? Would such enriched surroundings lead them to be productive? Would they become "professionally visible" once again, able to complete abandoned projects or return to professional careers? She had no way of knowing if any women would be interested, if her sense of what was needed would prove to be correct, if anything of value would be learned. Nothing like this had ever been tried before.

She knew her first hurdle would be convincing the Board of Trustees. She had been thinking about these ideas since her NSF "awakening" several years before, but they were brand new to the Board; none of its members had ever considered using the college as an agent of social change. But that was exactly why Polly had come to Radcliffe, and she wanted to start moving in that direction as soon as possible. She knew she could bide her time, get to know the college, let the trustees get to know her, and politic with a few of the most influential before presenting her plan. But she was temperamentally unable to procrastinate.

Furthermore, she counted on her instincts that the trustees would be unlikely to deny her the chance to try out her first big idea. Next year might be too late. So she decided to plunge. On March 7, 1960, two months before her official inauguration and only a month since she had begun camping out in the president's house, she laid out her revolutionary concept to the Council and then a few weeks later at her first meeting with the full board.

She recommended establishing a program to be known as the Radcliffe Institute for Independent Study. It would offer a stipend of three thousand dollars to twenty women from the greater Boston area who had interrupted promising careers or creative work to raise families. The money was to pay babysitters and housecleaners, giving the women free time during one academic year so they could return to "sustained intellectual creativity." They were to have access to all of Harvard's facilities "from libraries to laboratories, from museums to computers; the companionship and guidance of renowned authorities in a hundred fields, the chance to renew their commitment to their profession." These women had to have either a Ph.D. "or evidence of an equivalent level of achievement." (Some of the non-Ph.D.s in the first group laughingly referred to themselves as "the equivalents.") There were to be no restrictions about age or fields. What mattered was "evidence of past accomplishment and the promise of purposeful activity."[1] The program was to be flexible and open-ended, without courses, requirements, or obligations. It was not to be a program for women working for degrees. It was to be a benevolent environment. Too often, Polly said, educational programs were designed as racetracks, when what was really needed were gardens. Years later she said, "Microbial geneticists have come to recognize the value, in early explorations, of what they call the messy experiment. It can reveal hypotheses that might otherwise be missed."[2] The name she chose, the Radcliffe Institute for Independent Study, expressed her commitment to offering individuals the opportunity to do whatever they wanted to do.

Polly urged the trustees to see the Institute as an integral component of Radcliffe's commitment to educated women, a symbol of Radcliffe's belief in women's accomplishments, an example to show that what women did with their education was important. She wanted it to help change the climate of unexpectation. The Institute was not to be a rival of the undergraduate program, but an enhancement of it, affording undergraduates the chance to participate in research and attend seminars. Even more important, it was to give undergraduates the chance to see first-hand the rewards of committed intellectual work. Polly hoped it would lead them to see a purpose and a future for themselves and help to dissipate their confusion about the purposes of education, which tended to be particularly intense in coeducational institutions dominated by male faculty members.

It was the last item on their agenda and the trustees were stunned. Helen Gilbert said years later that what startled her was "the whole enormity of the project." She would have liked about three weeks or a month to think it over. "But that didn't happen with Polly."[3]

It's not hard to understand the trustees' concern. It was an experiment whose objectives were outside the traditional scope of an undergraduate college. Its outcome was most uncertain. Its assumptions were contrary to the prevailing attitudes of the time. No one could foresee where it would lead or even if it would survive. And it was clearly going to be expensive.

As Polly anticipated, none of the trustees wanted to turn her down flat. Nonetheless, they were extremely nervous about the possibility of the Institute's siphoning money from their ten-million-dollar Ten Year Plan. As diplomatically as they could, they expressed their reservations. But Polly found herself with a most welcome, totally unexpected ally. David Lilienthal, a trustee, who had been head of the Tennessee Valley Authority and the first chairman of the Atomic Energy Commission, instantaneously and enthusiastically endorsed the idea as important, in its way, as the establishment of the college itself. He expressed pride that such a proposal should emanate from Radcliffe, and warned the trustees to stop petty questioning, which could undermine the effort to raise the necessary money. He urged them to recognize and affirm the fundamental importance of the concept. In his memoirs Lilienthal relished having ignited what he called "staid Radcliffe." "It was an hour of triumph for an idea, an idea that was not mine but President Bunting's, but that perhaps needed my intense emotional support to get through the Trustees. . . ."[4]

Lilienthal appreciated her right from the start and characterized her in his journal with telling accuracy. "No one has less of the superficial, glad-hander surface so often seen in a college president," he wrote. "A twinkle in her eye, when she disagrees a cloud comes over her face, and you know exactly what her disagreement or qualification is. With a farm girl manner when she is in motion, not 'feminine' in the conventional sense."[5] When Lilienthal resigned from the Radcliffe board two years later, Polly wrote him: "We are all greatly aware of our debt to you for your strong support of this venture when it was just a gleam in some of our eyes."

After Lilienthal's speech, the trustees gave their grudging permission, but not exactly their blessing. They prohibited Polly from approaching any traditional Radcliffe supporters for money; she would have to find new contributors herself. "It was an interesting way to tie my hands," Polly was to say years later. "It rather amused me. I thought of it as a challenge from the old curmudgeons."

She was not a complete novice as far as serious fund-raising was concerned. She had experience rallying voters to pass bond issues and arousing enthusiasm in alumnae groups. But this was the first time she had to appeal, personally, to individuals with great wealth. She proved to be very adept at it, and undoubtedly this was yet another thing that shocked the trustees. "Radcliffe was conscious of its New England antecedents and the necessity of doing things with propriety," said longtime trustee Mary Bundy. "It really wasn't done to ask for money. You did it terribly discreetly, in a very quiet way."

Polly, on the other hand, came right out and asked for it. She had always had a healthy respect for money, from her childhood when she had shoveled her grandmother's walk to earn money for books. She had learned, as she grew older, how crucial money could be to achieve her purposes; but she was never impressed by it for its own sake and never intimidated by those who possessed it. She approached them as she approached everyone else—directly, without fanfare. "She had a good way of describing her visions of what could be for Radcliffe," said Mary Bundy. "She was putting it together in her own mind as she went along, so it was always fresh and took the listener with her—the listener was drawn into the creative process. Quite magnetic."

In her fund-raising efforts Polly did not do what college presidents routinely do today. She did not enlist the forces of a development office or ask for extensive research. She thought carefully about where the likeliest sources of money were to be found and then went to them. Her first prospect was Agnes Meyer, widow of the publisher, Eugene Meyer, and mother of Katharine Graham, who later became the publisher of the *Washington Post* and who Polly, erroneously as it turned out, believed had gone to Radcliffe.

Polly knew Agnes Meyer to be "a strong woman with an original mind" and had reason to believe from Meyer's remarks at a recent Barnard College conference, that she might appreciate the concept of the Institute. Polly called her for an appointment, was invited to lunch at the Meyer's elegant home in Mount Kisco, New York, and received a promise of fifty thousand dollars. When she left that house, it suddenly came to her as she stood on the front steps, "Now I'm really going to have to start that Institute."

Polly learned a great deal from this encounter because after she explained her concept Meyer asked her how much money she wanted.

The question took Polly by surprise because she hadn't come with a specific amount in mind. "I discovered then what became my philosophy: that it was up to me to describe what we wanted to do and what it would cost . . . but that it was up to the donor to decide what he or she wanted to give."[6]

Meyer's fifty thousand dollars was a good start, but it wasn't nearly enough, so Polly spent most of the summer of 1960 on the hunt for more. She thought next of John Gardner at the Carnegie Corporation, and wrote to him: "There is something about the education of women in this country that reminds one of plants cultivated under conditions permitting excellent early vegetative growth but few flowers and less fruit. There is a marked discrepancy between the abilities demonstrated by female students in our schools and colleges and their later intellectual achievements." Gardner proved to be very sympathetic. He told her it "was refreshing to have someone from a woman's college who was looking for support for a promising new program," rather than just complaining about not getting enough. Carnegie gave a five-year $150,000 grant.

Polly's next surprise was a request from Laurance Rockefeller that she pay him a visit, "a nice switch, donor seeks solicitor." Rockefeller had already decided to make women's concerns one of his causes perhaps because his mother, like Polly's, had been involved in the YWCA. One of Polly's Vassar roommates was now married to Laurance Rockefeller's brother, John D. Rockefeller III, and Polly believed she spoke to him about this new experiment. In the end the Rockefeller Brothers Fund made a five-year grant of $250,000.

Laurance Rockefeller proved to be vital to the Institute for many years. "He was truly interested, raised questions, followed the details, and was on the advisery committee. He gave more than money—he gave his mind and his point of view and his name," Polly said. When Lillian Hellman, another member of the advisory committee, questioned whether all the effort and money were worth it—after all, so few people would be helped—it was Rockefeller who supported Polly's contention that the potential impact of the Institute went beyond the number of people who were directly helped by it. It could serve as an example to other institutions throughout the country.[7]

The enthusiasm of these foundations rubbed off on the Radcliffe powers-that-be. "Once you get the right folks showing support," Polly said many years later, "you look a lot better to the home team."

But no one—not the home team, not even Polly herself—was prepared for the sensation caused by the announcement of the Institute. On Sunday, November 20, 1960, the *New York Times* ran the story by veteran education writer Fred Hechinger on page one. Newspapers as far away as Omaha, Nebraska, where Harvard doings are not always big news, also ran a story. The following Sunday, the *Times* ran a second story in which Hechinger described Polly as "soft-spoken" and "hard thinking" and called the Institute "a rescue mission to help intellectually displaced women."

The response was overwhelming. Louise Donovan, Polly's assistant, remembered that the Monday morning after the *Times* article "the phone never stopped ringing." An extra person had to be hired to answer the calls. "Half of them," Donovan said, "were from women with a baby crying in the background. A number of them said things like, 'I know I am not qualified, but I am so thrilled that someone recognizes this problem and that you are doing something for women.' There were some of 'how do I get an application' but there were more saying 'thank you for recognizing what the situation was.' It was very moving."

By December 1, more than 160 letters of congratulations and inquiry had been received, some from as far away as New Zealand, India, France, Belgium, Saudi Arabia and Japan. By the end of December, barely a month after the announcement, 120 applications had been received even though formal application forms hadn't even been printed yet. Among the applicants were doctors, lawyers, and Ph.D.s. They ranged in age from twenty-five to fifty-six, married, widowed, single, with and without children, living in twenty-one states and five foreign countries with their projects ranging from Christian art to regional planning, cellular physiology to U.S. naval history. Eventually nearly two hundred women applied for the twenty part-time fellowships. "A superior group of women is already lined up waiting impatiently for the Institute's doors to open," wrote one of Polly's assistants in a December 2, 1960, memo. The letters and calls came so fast and furiously that statistics became outdated almost as soon as they were compiled. "At first appraisal it is going to be a delicate and difficult task to choose the first appointees . . . from such an embarrassment of riches."[8] Polly's divining rod had struck a new flood—one deeper than even she had suspected. She summed it up with a Quaker phrase. "We spoke to their condition."

Overnight, Polly found herself where she had only dimly conceived of being—on that pedestal—where she could proclaim the ideas she had been articulating softly for some time. She was invited to contribute an article to the *New York Times Sunday Magazine*, which *Reader's Digest* ran in a condensed version. *Newsweek* and *Life* came calling. Houghton Mifflin solicited a book. *Time* magazine put her on the cover. The climate of unexpectation was suddenly big news.

What mattered especially to Polly were the letters from women

1. Polly with her brother Gardner at the children's table in the dining room at 363 Adelphi Street. *Courtesy of the Bunting family.*

2. Polly astride Wedding Bells, the pony she invited into the family's Northport, Long Island, house. Her brother, Gardner, is waiting for his turn to ride. *Courtesy of the Bunting family.*

3. At Vassar in 1930, Polly competing in the long jump. *Courtesy of Peter H. Wood.*

4. The Vassar Sophomore Party Committee in 1928. Polly, *second from the left*. Her roommate, Blanchette Hooker, later Mrs. John D. Rockefeller III, *last on far right*. Courtesy of Peter H. Wood.

5. The Vassar Junior Class Hockey Team in 1929. Polly, *seated second from left*, is next to her roommate and closest college friend, *seated far left*, Leal Hutchins, later Mrs. Barry Wood. *Seated far right*, another roommate, Blanchette Hooker, later Mrs. John D. Rockefeller III. Courtesy of Peter H. Wood.

6. Polly's sister, Winifred Warner; Polly's mother, Mary Shotwell Ingraham ("Gwy"), with Polly's grandmother, Alice Gardner Shotwell ("Nana"), holding Winifred's baby daughter, Mary Ann Warner. *Courtesy of the Bunting family.*

7. Polly Bunting, 1933, twenty-three years of age. *Courtesy of the Bunting family.*

8. Polly and Henry Bunting on their wedding day in June 1937, at the beach house in Northport, Long Island. *Courtesy of the Bunting family.*

9. The Ingraham family, late 1930's. *Left to right*: Harold Warner, Polly's brother-in-law; Winifred Warner, Polly's sister; David Ingraham, Polly's youngest sibling; Laura Ingraham, David's wife; Henry Andrews Ingraham, Polly's father; Mary Shotwell Ingraham ("Gwy"), Polly's mother; Polly; Henry Bunting; Barbara Ingraham, Polly's sister-in-law; and Gardner Ingraham, Polly's brother. *Courtesy of the Bunting family.*

10. Fall 1938, Polly and Henry in the doorway of their first Bethany house that they rented for $35 a month. *Courtesy of the Bunting family.*

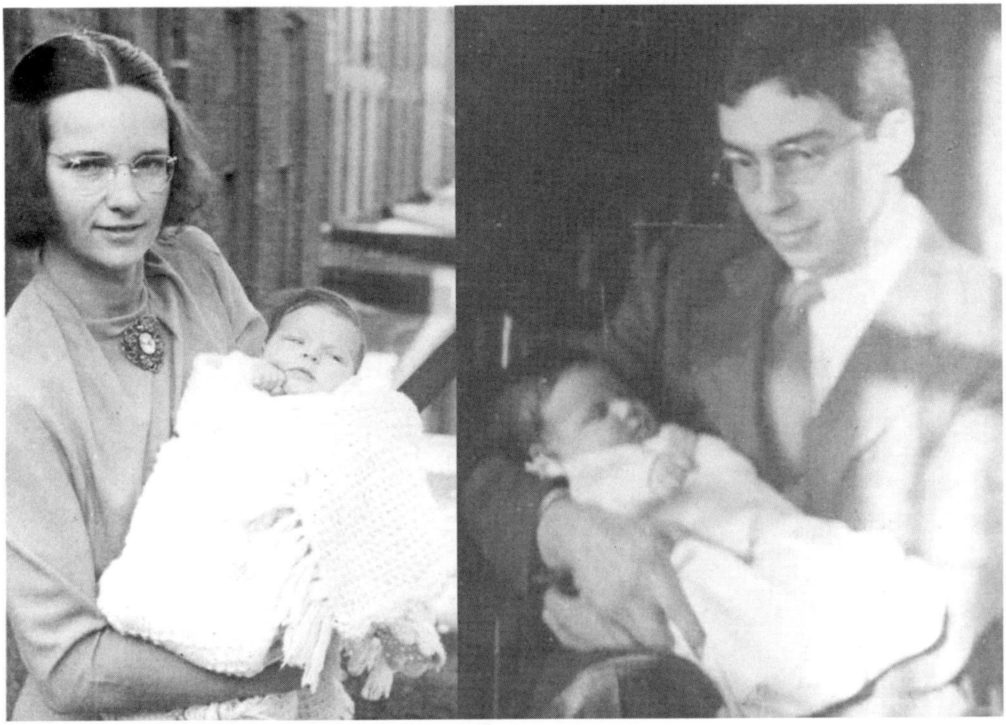

11. Polly and Henry holding their baby daughter, Mary, 1940. *Courtesy of the Bunting family.*

12. The basement—the first phase of their Bethany house—which the six Buntings lived in for two-and-a-half years. The big windows afforded the children splendid views of the field mice running through the tunnels the mice built whenever it snowed. *Courtesy of the Bunting family.*

13. Polly and her four children, *left to right*, Chuck, John, Bill, and Mary, in front of the finished Bethany house in 1955 shortly before they left for Douglass. *Courtesy of the Bunting family.*

14. At her first Douglass "Campus Night" in October 1955, Polly identified herself as a first-year student by wearing a "dink," the small, round hat, and holding the pine tree sign. *Courtesy of the Associate Alumnae of Douglass College.*

15. At Douglass, John, *center*, and Bill, *far left*, joined students at one of Polly's Friday night dinners. *Courtesy of the Associate Alumnae of Douglass College.*

16. At Douglass, Polly breaks ground for the new library-study center, April 16, 1959. Watching her, *second from left*, is Rutgers President Mason Gross, successor of her old friend, Lewis Webster Jones. *Courtesy of Special Collections and University Archives, Rutgers University Libraries.*

17. May 19, 1960: Polly's inauguration day at Radcliffe, with Helen Gilbert, longtime president of Radcliffe's Board of Trustees. Polly's predecessor, Wilbur Jordan, is at left. *Courtesy of the Radcliffe Archives, Radcliffe Institute, Harvard University.*

18. The Ingraham family gathered for Polly's Radcliffe inauguration. *Left to right*: Polly's nephew, Sandy Ingraham; Mary Bunting; John Bunting; Polly's niece, Alice Ingraham; Bill Bunting; Polly's father, Henry Andrews Ingraham; Polly; Polly's mother, Mary Shotwell Ingraham; Polly's brother, David Ingraham; Chuck Bunting; Polly's brother, Gardner Ingraham; Gardner's wife, Barbara Ingraham; David's wife, Laura Ingraham. *Courtesy of the Radcliffe Archives, Radcliffe Institute, Harvard University.*

19. Polly and her four children (*left to right*: Mary, 19; John, 12; Chuck, 17; and Bill, 14) when they came to Radcliffe. *Courtesy of the Radcliffe Archives, Radcliffe Institute, Harvard University.*

20. Polly with her freshman seminar at Radcliffe. *Courtesy of the Radcliffe Archives, Radcliffe Institute, Harvard University.*

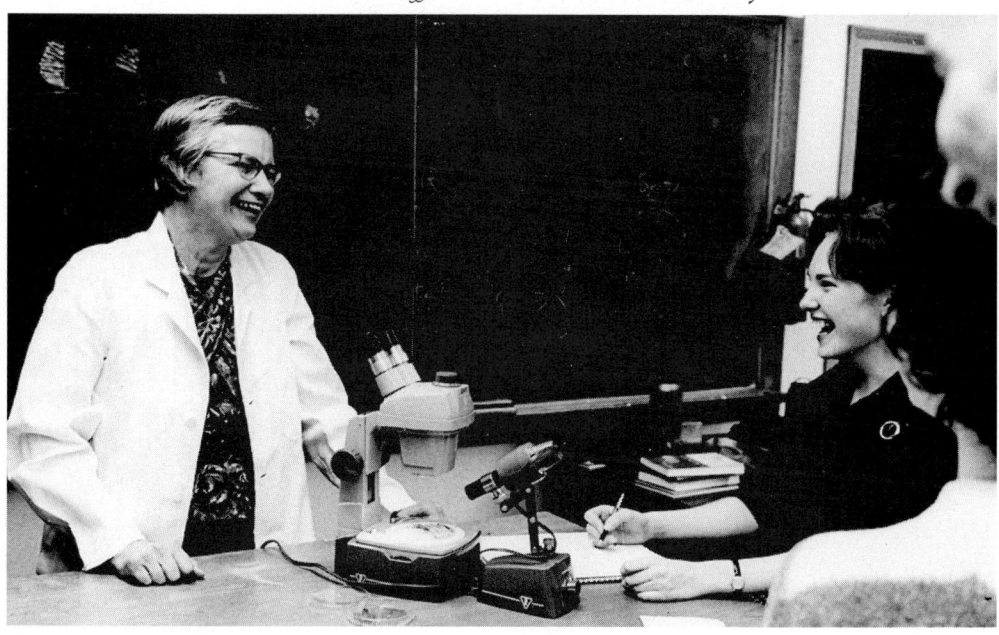

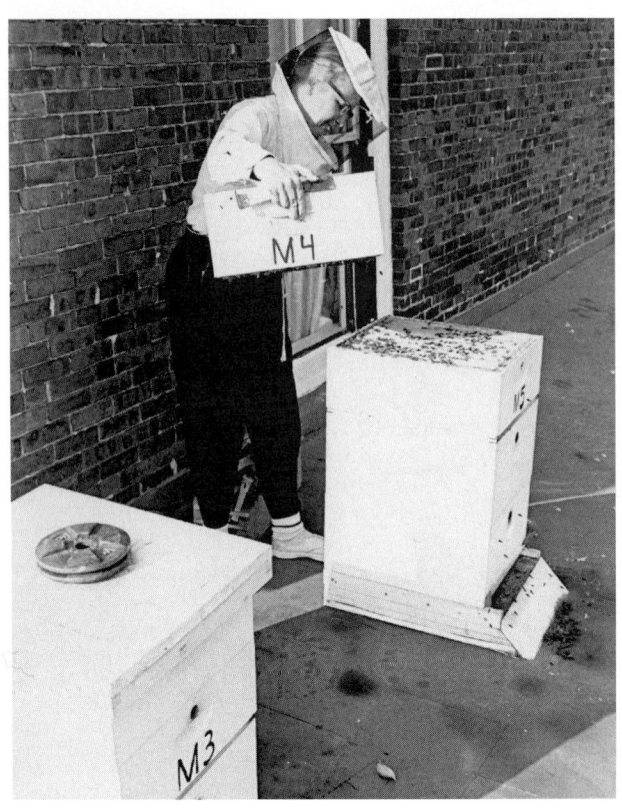

21. Polly with the bees on the roof of the Radcliffe president's house at 76 Brattle Street. Even well into her sixties, Polly managed to carry these sixty-pound "supers" from the roof down to the cellar, ducking through a window, stepping on a toilet cover, climbing down the narrow back staircase, through the kitchen and down the cellar steps. *Courtesy of the Radcliffe Archives, Radcliffe Institute, Harvard University.*

22. Polly often joined Radcliffe students in their dormitories for meals and after-dinner conversation. *Courtesy of Lynn Millar, Radcliffe Archives, Radcliffe Institute, Harvard University.*

23. In the Cabinet Room of the White House, June 29, 1964, President Lyndon Johnson shakes Polly's hand after her swearing-in for the Atomic Energy Commission. *Courtesy of the Radcliffe Archives, Radcliffe Institute, Harvard University.*

24. After the turmoil in Cambridge in 1969, Polly enjoyed her customary August holiday with her daughter Mary and granddaughter Laura at Mt. Shuksan in Washington State. *Courtesy of the Bunting family.*

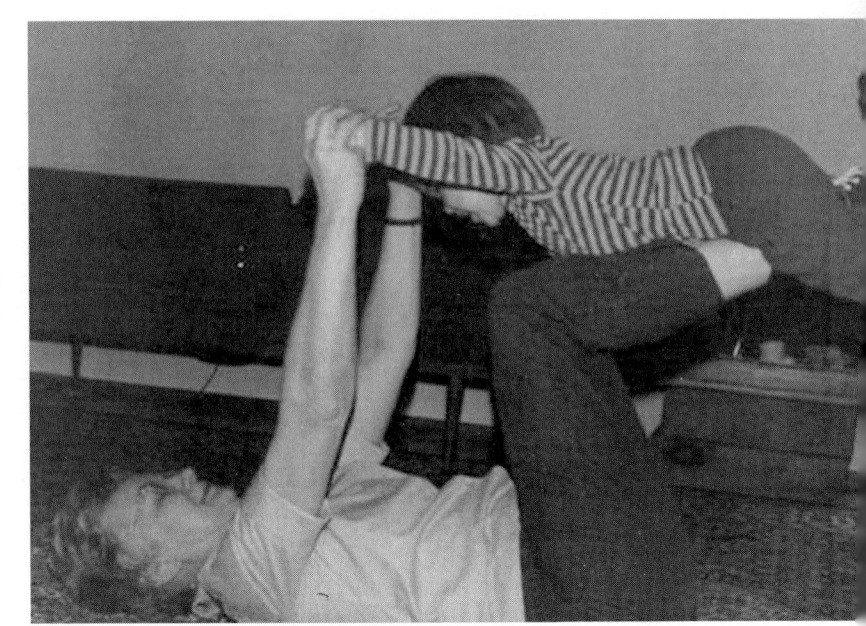

25. Grandma Polly with granddaughter Laura, May 1970. *Courtesy of the Bunting family.*

26. Polly in 1972, her last year as Radcliffe's president. *Courtesy of the Bunting family.*

27. Polly after her retirement, 1980's. *Courtesy of the Radcliffe Archives, Radcliffe Institute, Harvard University.*

28. Polly after her retirement from Princeton when she began living full-time in her home in New Boston, New Hampshire. *Courtesy of the Bunting family.*

29. Even in retirement, Polly often attended discussions with fellows at what was then the Bunting Institute. *Courtesy of Lillian Kemp, Radcliffe Archives, Radcliffe Institute, Harvard University.*

30. Polly with her second husband, Dr. Clement Smith, a neonatologist and retired member of the faculty of the Harvard Medical School. *Courtesy of Lillian Kemp, Radcliffe Archives, Radcliffe Institute, Harvard University.*

31. Polly's eightieth birthday at the Bunting Institute. *Courtesy of Victoria Gewirz, Radcliffe Archives, Radcliffe Institute, Harvard University.*

32. Polly's last house in New Boston, New Hampshire. *Courtesy of Patricia M. Armstrong.*

33. Polly, 85, with one of Bill's oxen on his farm in Maine. The ribbon around the horns was from the just concluded ceremony at Radcliffe, naming one of the rooms in Radcliffe's administration building, Fay House, in Polly's honor. *Courtesy of the Bunting family.*

around the world. She kept them among her personal papers. They came from women in all walks of life and all levels of education. There was a letter from a newly widowed surgeon in Australia writing to ask if Polly thought there was any place she might still fit in. A particularly eloquent letter came from the wife of a dairy farmer on a 280-acre Ozark farm in Maples, Missouri, with a grade school education and what she believed was a talent for dress designing. "How can I find out whether or not I'm kidding myself?" she wrote Polly. "Many times I have been tempted to leave my family so great is my frustration. . . . Must my life's only goal be that of my husband, to be a successful farmer? I feel I can give so much more of myself if only I could get started in a field suited to my abilities. . . . Help me if you can, please."

Many letters were from Radcliffe alumnae grateful that their college was once again appearing to express confidence in them. Polly copied portions of these letters by hand into her journals. Perhaps their most surprising quality was the intensity of the emotion in them. "To know that inspiration, encouragement and intellectual companionship are to be available to women, other mothers like myself perhaps, who have been struggling along in a frighteningly lonely atmosphere to complete creative work, is suddenly to see the sun breaking through the clouds at last!" "Your program of advanced study for women who have left academic life means more to me than I can say. My concept of my own life has been altered & enlivened by the thought that someone thinks I might still be able to contribute something, somehow, despite the fact that I have a home with 4 children in it."

There also were the women who stopped her on the street to tell her that just the existence of the Institute had given them courage to return to work, to try something new, to be something more. Polly particularly remembered the woman from Exeter, New Hampshire, who told her she had been slipping into Cambridge for years, not telling anyone where she was going, to work at Widener Library.

But not everyone was enthusiastic. Surprisingly to Polly, the staunchest opposition came from Radcliffe alumnae who lived in Boston. Many of them even refused to allow income over which they had some control to be used for the Institute. At the twenty-fifth reunion of the class of 1936, a group of Boston alumnae performed a satirical song in the Radcliffe Quadrangle: "terut, terut, we are the girls of the Institute." Polly watched from a folding chair, her hands in her lap, a thin-lipped smile pasted on her face.

The Bostonians had never liked her. They disapproved of her informal style, her inexpensive dresses, and absence of makeup. Some even approached one of Polly's former Vassar roommates, urging her to tell Polly she ought to dress better. The friend declined. They saw the Institute as something that "would belittle their Radcliffe, their undergraduate Radcliffe." "When I described it at their meetings I could hear them muttering in the cloak room," Polly said. She came to understand that the Institute made them feel threatened. It was as if the college's president was belittling the choices they had made to be wives and mothers.

This, however, was a complete misunderstanding of what Polly believed. She had never doubted the value of women's traditional roles. She wanted to expand, not limit, women's choices. She did not see the validation of some women's right to choose a profession as the invalidation of others' right to stay home. The novelty of the Institute came precisely from its acknowledgment of the complexity of women's lives. Polly was not out to overturn the accepted order of things; she just wanted to rearrange the pieces.

She wanted women to be aware of how many years they would have after their children were raised. They would need something to make those years satisfying, and so it made sense to keep in contact with the professional world, even if the contact was peripheral. Women could have it all, she was saying—just not all at once. The pattern of their lives required them to pursue objectives sequentially.

In fact, she had a traditional view of marriage; she never suggested or even implied that men should share the housework or child care. One of the first statements of the Institute's purposes set out the sharp distinctions in the roles of men and women. "A woman, educated or not, when she marries is dominated by her biological role of childbearing and child-rearing and by her psychological role in relation to her husband.... The husband as the primary source of income must put the requirements of his own career before those of his wife. And even the most intellectually ambitious woman cannot quarrel with this if the preservation of her marriage is important to her."[9]

As a response to the anger she had aroused in the Bostonians, Polly set up an alumnae committee to advise her on how the college could better prepare women for their lives as mothers and community volunteers. But the alumnae never did the assignment and kept coming up with schemes that sounded more and more like the Institute. They never believed Polly wanted from them what she said she wanted, and the committee finally just melted away.

The Institute began its life in the fall of 1961. Its first home, rented from Harvard, was 78 Mount Auburn Street, a sixteen-room yellow clapboard house with shutters on the windows. It was old and creaky—"a rabbit warren of tiny rooms" with an "antiquated heating system," which "could be relied upon to honk, rattle, wheeze, gasp, at timed intervals."[10] It was crowded and somewhat dowdy, but had a cozy, family-like feeling. Years later Polly referred to it as "the incubator," a safe and comfortable place that worked so well "scholars were reluctant to move." The upstairs bedrooms became studies, usually shared because there weren't enough. Some fellows were assigned the attic rooms, and those who couldn't be fitted in anywhere were assigned stalls in Widener Library. The house was home to the Institute for six years.

There was no whiff of bureaucratic formality, in large measure because of Polly's inspired choice of the first director, a Douglass political science professor named Constance Smith. Smith gave up a tenured position to sign on to Polly's risky enterprise. She had the impeccable academic credentials Polly knew would be required to give the fledgling undertaking credibility in the Harvard universe. Smith was a Phi Beta Kappa graduate of Wellesley and had a Harvard Ph.D. Equally important, she had all the qualities Polly knew the Institute needed: broad intellectual interests, along with administrative and fund-raising abilities. Above all, she had the kind of sympathetic understanding that could give "young, and not so young, talented but momentarily insecure women the courage to continue to invest in themselves in spite of the indifference or occasionally the hostility of family, friends and academic institutions . . . someone who could create an oasis for intellectual and creative women."[11]

But Connie Smith was far from an obvious choice. Like Polly, she had had no administrative training or experience, and even though the first Institute was geared toward young married women, Smith was single and childless. Nonetheless, Polly sensed that she was the right person for the job. The fellows were devoted to her, describing her as "a center and a soul" under whose "loving eye" each of them blossomed. Her office door was always open; she supplied homemade goodies at the Tuesday seminars. And when a woman felt her project was going nowhere and wanted to careen off in a new direction, Smith listened and supported her. If a woman was hesitant about asking for help from a scholar at Harvard or elsewhere, Smith used the Institute's clout to approach this eminent person. "At the Institute, we had a kind of garden," said Polly, "and Connie Smith was a marvelous gardener. She could sense what each plant needed to flourish and flower."[12] She presided over the Institute until she died, very young of cancer in 1970, almost exactly ten years after the first newspaper announcement of the Institute.

In the beginning the fellows were chosen by a Radcliffe committee with help from Harvard faculty who assessed the significance of the proposed projects and the likelihood that the applicants could handle them. Polly wanted to be sure the Institute scholar would have no problem relating to the faculty in her field, so unless at least one professor found her project interesting, she would not receive a fellowship.

The first applicants were impressive, not "malcontents" or "complainers," but "highly skilled and energetic women with rich and full lives who feel simply that with such help as the Institute will offer, their lives can be even fuller, their contributions even greater."[13] The original plan was for all fellows to come from the Boston area, but it had to be abandoned because there were so many excellent applications from far away. They represented a wide range of fields and presented a panoply of projects. The variety made "an illuminating comment on women's potential for creativity and scholarship, for there is scarcely a discipline that is not represented."[14]

In keeping with Polly's conviction that learning could and should be lifelong, there was no age limit, and from the beginning fellowships were given to women even in their seventies. Most, however, were in their thirties and married with children; two thirds of them were in the arts and humanities. The majority already had Ph.D.s, but the first group also included a poet, Anne Sexton, who had never gone to college at all and was near the beginning of her distinguished career. There were artists and scientists, lawyers and social workers, academics and writers.

There was a sense of mission and excitement among the first fellows. They were well aware that they were trailblazers and were intensely grateful for this rare opportunity—this rescue operation. The writer Tillie Olsen, one of the later fellows, described it as "the gift of enabling circumstances;" the photographer Elsa Dorfman, more "like a booster rocket." Just like the older women whom Polly enabled to resume their education at Douglass, the first Institute scholars were indefatigable workers. They stimulated and supported one another, took leisurely coffee breaks and long walks along the Charles, participated in the colloquia and dinners that became an essential component of the Institute. They had "enough time to explore, to vent our doubts, to strengthen our resolve," remembered one of the first fellows. Most of them used their modest stipends for baby-sitting and household help. Anne Sexton, however, used some of her money to convert her back porch into a study and the rest as the down payment on a swimming pool that filled most of her backyard. Barbara Swan, a painter, bought a dishwasher after reading in a magazine that it would save five hundred hours of time. Another used some of her stipend to pay the parking tickets she received after leaving her car outside Widener Library.

One of the first discoveries was that being selected was a significant benefit all by itself. It legitimized the work. Apparently, even more inhibiting to women than the press of competing responsibilities was the absence of professional recognition. Anne Sexton said the fellowship immediately "made what I was doing more respectable to my husband."[15] Many scholars said that prior to their Institute appointments they had suffered from a feeling of guilt from doing anything "on my own, of my own." One scholar described herself as suffering from what she called "the Jane Austen syndrome. Most women hid their work under their embroidery."[16] Another fellow said she had had to pretend to her critical neighbors that she was taking bridge lessons instead of pursuing her library research. Anne Sexton said, "You always have a guilty feeling that it's selfish, because everyone says, 'Why isn't it enough to be a wife and mother?' I still remember my mother-in-law saying, 'Why aren't your husband and children enough—why don't you make it a hobby?' But if you get this amount of money, everyone immediately thinks you're respected, and beyond that, you're contributing."[17]

The fellowship program was the heart of the Institute, but Polly did not intend for it to be the whole. She wanted some full-time "Resident Fellows"—women who were already well established and could use the time for their own research. Their presence in the Institute, she believed, could be an inspiration and a comfort to the part-timers who were venturing out after a long hibernation and could exert a subtle but powerful force on the "groping" Radcliffe undergraduates who were not convinced there was any future waiting for them. Polly hoped the older women would provide some of the benefits supplied to Harvard men by close association with the tutors in the Houses.

Beyond that, Polly hoped the Institute would be a resource for all women, even those not formally affiliated with Radcliffe. She wanted guidance to be available, to give women practical advice on how to use their "time, talents and training most effectively." In 1964 Connie Smith compiled a 150-page directory called "The Next Step," of educational, vocational, and volunteer part-time opportunities for women in the Boston area. It also contained material intended to help talented women anywhere evaluate their abilities and work out ways of using them. Approximately ten thousand copies were sold. It prompted women in Washington, D.C., England, and New Zealand to compile directories of their own.

As the years went on and other needs presented themselves, Polly brought more programs under the Institute umbrella. When she received letters from women in medicine explaining that they needed not independent study but the opportunity to continue their training part-time over a prolonged period, she recognized another manifestation of the climate of unexpectation. Women with young children were barred from most medical residencies. One young mother told Polly that she had been turned down repeatedly by all the major Boston hospitals. She described "a totally barricaded door." Polly decided to open it. Fortunately Charles Janeway, the husband of one of her college roommates, was now the top physician at Children's Hospital in Boston, where there were a good many women in pediatrics, several of whom had been in touch with Polly. Polly convinced Janeway to allow them to work part-time, in exchange for the Institute paying their stipends. And then, in yet another serendipitous happening of the sort that so often characterized Polly's searches for money, Dr. John Bowers, an executive of the Macy Foundation, unexpectedly turned up in her office asking her to chair a conference about how to attract more women into medicine. Polly said she didn't need a conference; all that was necessary, she knew, was to enable women to work part-time so that they could complete their advanced training even if they had a child or two. Bowers said, "If I give you $25,000 a year for three years to do that, will you chair my conference?" Polly said she'd be delighted, and the Institute was therefore able to help fifty medical women complete their training at their own pace. This breakthrough moved Flower Hospital in New York and a few other places to change their rules. "It was never easy for the hospitals or for the women," Polly said years later, "but in the end society profited. When one considers the motivation of the women who enter medicine and the investments that they and society make in their training, the casual manner in which they once were dropped, after years and years of education, seems as inexplicable as it was inexcusable."[18]

Another group that contacted Polly were women graduate students who needed help changing the continuing prejudice against part-time study. In 1967 Polly secured a grant from the Charles E. Merrill Trust and made funds available to part-time graduate women who were attending universities in southern New England, other than Radcliffe or Harvard. The Radcliffe trustees were uneasy about giving students money that had been donated to Radcliffe, and then permitting them to use it at other institutions. The trustees thought such a maneuver was illegal. Polly thought it probably was too, but it was enabling women to move forward and was contributing to altering the climate of unexpectation. And besides, Radcliffe never got caught.

Once it became clear that the Institute was a fixture of Radcliffe, not a temporary experiment, Polly began pushing for a more permanent setting, one physically nearer to the Radcliffe undergraduates. In 1967 the Institute abandoned its cozy yellow house and moved to the top three floors of the library in the Radcliffe Quadrangle. There was now room for staff offices, a conference room, a big colloquium room with a dining alcove and kitchen, space for fellows' studies and studios for music and art. On May 4, 1987, it moved once more to a three-building complex at 34 Concord Avenue.

In 1978, at the Radcliffe Centennial, the Institute was renamed the Mary Ingraham Bunting Institute. Polly accepted the honor with grace, but said later she never liked to call it that and thought "putting it all on one person was downplaying it." Far better, she said, to keep Radcliffe's name in the title and have it remain "a Radcliffe thing."

In many ways the Institute was enormously successful. Women flocked to it. During its first four years, 324 women, of whom 150 held advanced degrees, were turned down for fellowships. By 1987 the Institute was responding to nearly five thousand inquiries yearly and processing about 550 applications for the nineteen available fellowships. In the 1992–93 year they received more than seven hundred applications, from across this country and from points around the world, from women struggling with careers as artists and from others who held secure positions at prestigious universities. The Institute also served as a model for other programs, and the Institute staff were often called upon to be advisers to those setting up similar enterprises.[19]

But not all of Polly's initial plans worked out. She had hoped there would be many full-time Resident Fellows to serve as role-models for the part-time associates and undergraduates. But there was never enough money for this. Only two were ever appointed.

The close connections with Radcliffe undergraduates didn't materialize either. Unlike Douglass, where the older and younger women were thrown together in the same classes, at Radcliffe it was more difficult to create occasions for their meeting. The fellows were, for the most part, busy mothers who wanted to use their time for their own work rather than spending it in the Radcliffe dorms talking to undergraduates. And the undergraduates weren't that interested in them. Occasionally a student would comment that she was excited to meet an older woman who was really interested in her work, but "for many Radcliffe students a working mother was no novelty. What they needed to give point and purpose to their college experience was not casual social contacts with professional women but the opportunity to observe them in positions of responsibility and honor in the academic hierarchy. This was rarely possible at Harvard."[20]

The guidance component dwindled too. In the beginning about two hundred women, other than the regular applicants, came to the

Institute for information and advice. But as more continuing education programs developed around the country, there was less demand for advice from Institute staff. They did help develop a nationwide roster of women Ph.D.s and women holding the rank of assistant professor and above. Polly herself kept notes in her journals of job openings at various colleges, universities, and organizations and whenever possible tried to recommend a promising applicant for the right position.

And in Polly's view there was another reason for dissatisfaction. She wanted the Institute staff to come up with concrete information "on the very questions which gave rise to the creation of the Institute itself . . . what are the nature and qualities of the educated woman's motivations and ambitions, her response to the difficult role of individual and wife? What changes might be made to the undergraduate education of women . . . to stimulate the educated woman to plan her life so as to use her education more satisfyingly and to build on it indefinitely?" The staff did conduct a number of studies into Institute scholars' social backgrounds and aspirations, labor requirements for women, opportunities for women in various professions, the life pattern and expectations of the wives of Harvard graduate students and all married women graduate students at the university and of all Radcliffe graduates with medical careers. But these investigations did not yield the kind of cutting-edge research Polly had envisioned. Ironically, the research proceeded very slowly because most of the qualified researchers were women who were combining professional work with domestic responsibilities and who preferred to work part-time.

The most nagging and persistent problem of the Institute remained its funding. Even though it cost less to maintain an Institute fellow for two years than to educate an undergraduate for one, finding adequate funds continued to be difficult. Shortly before her retirement from Radcliffe, Polly told a conference on women, "With all its success, the Radcliffe Institute's future is precarious. The number of women who have sought its assistance is very large, the number who have offered financial support is beginning to grow but is still very small."[21] Although the Radcliffe trustees soon recognized that the Institute was an integral part of the college, they maintained, with some justification, that Radcliffe didn't have adequate resources for its undergraduate program and therefore couldn't give the Institute the substantial financial support it required. The Institute continued to have the responsibility of raising its own funds, and so it continued to face financially precarious conditions.

In spite of these difficulties, the Institute succeeded in what was Polly's primary objective: to contribute to the gradual dissipation of the climate of unexpectation, to show the world and women themselves what they were capable of. In her last official speech at the joint Harvard-Radcliffe Baccalaureate on June 13, 1972, Polly came as close as she ever had to taking a modicum of credit for some of the significant social changes that had transpired on her watch. "I do not know to what extent the Institute has contributed to the marked change in the national climate of expectation that is taking place, but that change is most welcome," she said.

The Institute was Polly's first major initiative at Radcliffe and one of the most significant of her achievements. She believed it was the cornerstone of her legacy. But after the death of Constance Smith and Polly's departure from Radcliffe, it changed considerably. Polly's purpose had been to offer the advantage she valued most and felt democracy owed all its citizens—opportunity—to "hitherto undistinguished women who had been trapped by family responsibilities and other circumstances... people who weren't so different from other people."[22] But by the 1990's that purpose seemed to have faded away, perhaps because society had changed, perhaps because Polly's democratic fervor is not shared by many at prestigious colleges. Whatever the cause, it became more of the "race track" and less of the "garden."

Even when Polly was at Radcliffe's helm, there was pride in the accomplishments of the Institute fellows. Anne Sexton's Pulitzer Prize was mentioned often. But Polly never confused such accolades with the Institute's purpose. Shortly before her retirement from Radcliffe, she expressed enthusiasm for the achievements of Institute fellows, but her words reveal her real priorities. "Virtually all Institute Fellows, some 300, have continued in their chosen fields with growing effectiveness and personal satisfaction, and their families seem to have thrived."[23] Effectiveness, personal satisfaction, and thriving families, not success.

In later years, long after her official connection to the Institute had ended, Polly was circumspect about how she regarded its transformation. Always realistic, she never wanted or expected people or institutions to remain stagnant. But she always dismissed ambition as a goal for herself. She often said that the fringes offered an opportunity to pursue whatever one found interesting, rather than exile from the mainstream. She carefully structured a cooperative rather than a competitive environment in the Institute's early years because she believed competition interfered with, rather than stimulated, creativity.

But Polly kept her opinions about the Institute's new priorities strictly to herself. After her retirement from Radcliffe, she often came to the afternoon colloquia and to the brown bag lunches at which the fellows talked about their work. She was always invited to the first meeting of the new scholars and recounted how the Institute had been born, how she had experienced her awakening at the National Science Foundation, and what her aspirations for women had been. It was always an exhilarating moment—the fellows filled with admiration bordering on reverence. At one such meeting, late in her life, they all rose spontaneously after her short speech and applauded enthusiastically for a long time.

Polly kept in touch with the Institute until her last days, even coming to the thirty-fifth anniversary celebration just a few months before her death. Marian Parry, an artist and former fellow, presented her with a watercolor of an open door, to symbolize "the doors Mrs. Bunting has opened for all of us." Polly was grievously ill, frail, and bent from osteoporosis, but when the Institute Director Florence Ladd thanked her for being there to witness "the success of your experiment," Polly answered clearly, "It is my pleasure."

19

A Geneticist With Nest-Building Experience

While the Institute had a disappointingly small impact on Radcliffe undergraduates, Polly's second major accomplishment, the transformation of Radcliffe's sterile residential Quadrangle, affected them significantly.

She had been unaware how impoverished the lives of Radcliffe's undergraduates were until she met with student government leaders shortly after her February arrival. She wanted to know what they thought ought to be done, what ideas they had, what they needed. She was shocked to find that they didn't seem to have any ideas at all. To each proposal of hers they answered only that such things couldn't be done at Radcliffe; there was always a rule against them. Here were these brilliant kids, she thought, picked from all over the country, and they didn't think it was possible to make any changes. And these were the people who were being educated to be community leaders. She saw that although she was not intimidated by Harvard, the students were. The climate of unexpectation had seeped into the consciousness of even the most gifted. She puzzled over what she could do to empower them.

She began with a modest strategy: giving each dormitory one dollar per student to spend in any way they chose. She put no restrictions on what they could buy, but they had to make the decision as a group and they had to tell her what they bought. It was her scientific habit—to set things in motion and then to step back and watch what happened. She never would have predicted what did happen. These high-powered, intellectual, brilliant Radcliffe women bought the traditional tools of domesticity, vacuum cleaners and sewing machines.

The students were sending her a message, and she got it. The message was not, "We have such a low opinion of ourselves as women that we think we can only clean and sew." The message was, "We don't think that the satisfaction we sometimes take in doing old-fashioned things will stand in the way of our being good scholars." They were protesting against Harvard's condescension, its telling them in countless ways that they would be valued only to the extent that they gave up being women, that there should no longer be any room in their lives for the time-honored things women had always done. They were asking Polly to endorse their refusal to go along with the insulting assumption that anyone who did "women's things" was unworthy of the great learning available in a great university. They wanted to go on being smart, but on their own terms.

No attitude could have been more likely to arouse Polly's sympathy. She had raised children, cooked and gardened, killed chickens and goats, and even done manual labor. She knew that one learns from all these things, that life itself teaches too. As soon as she could, Polly made sure that all dormitories had vacuum cleaners and sewing machines and small kitchenettes.

She began to see that the problem at Radcliffe was the mirror image of the problem at Douglass. At Douglass the students had little confidence in their intellectual capabilities, while at Radcliffe they had confidence in little else. They weren't even sure that life had other dimensions. The emphasis at Radcliffe on the exclusive value of academic work to the detriment of everything else only added to their confusion. "Radcliffe really didn't respect other aspects of life," Polly said.

So Polly set out, by her own example, to legitimize the things women had always done. She invited students to lunches and dinners at her home with the silver and china and beautiful flower arrangements that in many instances she created herself. "The old-fashioned, first-class way" was how one of Polly's administrators described these occasions. She knew there weren't going to be home economics courses at Radcliffe, but she insisted that "learning to give the right party can be one of the more important things that a woman can do." When some students approached her about changes they wanted in the requirements of the English department, she told them to give a party, invite the right professors and talk to them.

Had it been up to Polly, the curriculum would have included many more courses about child development. Many alumnae had told her they felt ill equipped to bring up their children. She knew she could have nothing to say about what Harvard was teaching, so she found her own way to introduce the experience she thought students needed. As soon as she could, Polly put apartments for young couples into the dormitories. By 1965 there were nineteen children living in Radcliffe houses. Polly thought Radcliffe was the first college in the country to have small children running around the dormitories. She was convinced of the importance of this step when she saw how attentively students observed the children and their parents' handling of them, how much they enjoyed seeing little kids peddling tricycles down the halls. On November 22, 1963, when President Kennedy was assassinated, a young mother in one dorm said she kept her two-year-old son up from his nap because all the students seemed to want to see him.

In her May 19, 1960, inaugural address, Polly expressed many of the ideas she had honed since her "awakening." But she also used this address for a more specific purpose. To an audience that consisted of the president of Harvard, faculty and administrators, the Radcliffe Board of Trustees, the Harvard Board of Overseers, representatives of twenty-six colleges (not Yale, however, still a male bastion, it did not send a dignitary) she gave notice that under her leadership, Radcliffe College would be in the vanguard of changing the entrenched idea that "it really doesn't matter what women do and that it isn't important that they be excellent at anything." She did this with characteristic humor and in plain English. She described herself alternately as "a myopic biologist diverted from the study of heredity and variation in microorganisms,"... "a deviant bird that may have had too much fun on the range to worry about early nest building, but certainly did not feel frustrated later when cooped up with the chicks." It was, she said, "as a geneticist with nest building experience" that she chose to examine both the role of higher education and the predicament of women. Even though laws no longer prevented women from pursuing a multitude of activities, "American women seem somewhat like a dog I knew, who long after the front fence had been removed, ran down the road to the place where the gate used to be, before turning into the yard."

Of course "the woman in our society who seeks to combine her multiple roles," faces difficulties, but "length of life opens new possibilities," which "can be realized only when plans are well laid and doors kept open. Women will continue to wish to pattern their lives differently from men, but with a little ingenuity on the part of the women and a little flexibility on the part of society, including educational institutions, the logistics can be accomplished. Differences in pattern need not dictate differences in purpose." Radcliffe, she maintained, had an important part to play in changing this attitude. "Cultural change is a flying wedge directed most readily from the front."

It was a sunny day and a festive occasion. Some old friends were there: Mason Gross, who had succeeded Lewis Webster Jones, from Rutgers; Tom Mendenhall from Bethany, who had delivered the eulogy at Henry's funeral and who was now the president of Smith; and Katharine McBride from Bryn Mawr, the person who first telephoned Polly to hint that Radcliffe was seriously considering her. All of Polly's children were on hand as were her parents, her brothers and sister, and Henry's sister. There was punch and coffee and tea and little sandwiches in Agassiz and then a fancy dinner across Brattle Street at the graduate center. In between dinner and dessert the student cast of *Kiss Me Kate* entertained the dignitaries.

Soon after, the *New Yorker* ran an article on three new college presidents. The two profiled men were referred to as Mr. and Dr., while Polly, who had a Ph.D., was called throughout the article "Mrs. B."[1]

The festivities didn't distract her for long. She was already working on the Institute, and now she addressed herself to the vast discrepancy between the living quarters at Harvard and those at Radcliffe. Harvard had built its colonial-style "houses" by the Charles River in the 1930's with a large grant from the Harkness family. They were modeled after British universities, with landscaped courtyards and paneled common rooms, where senior and junior faculty mingled with undergraduates, offering both formal and informal advice on matters academic and personal. They shared meals in large dining halls, attended teas in the master's quarters, congregated in tutors' suites. It was where students from varied backgrounds could work on a variety of projects. There was a civilized, collegial atmosphere, where students could see themselves as junior partners in an important enterprise. Harvard officials had said often that at least one-fourth of a student's education occurred in the house.

The Radcliffe dormitories, on the other hand, were the antithesis of intellectual or cultural centers. Nothing went on there. Students returned each evening to the sterile, barren Quadrangle only for sleeping and eating. And not only did the dorms lack the elegant architecture and cosmopolitan ambience of the Harvard houses, they were located too far away, both physically and psychically, from the collegial life of the university. "Radcliffe students were commuting to Harvard classes from crowded barracks," Polly said.

And they *were* overcrowded. Radcliffe dormitories had originally been designed with only single rooms, but enrollment had increased nearly fifty percent in the preceding twenty years, and the percentage of students living at the college rather than commuting had tripled. Building had not kept pace. Single rooms had been converted to economy doubles with bunk beds, doubles had become triples, common rooms had become bedrooms, and increasing numbers of students had to be assigned to a variety of makeshift off-campus houses that were expensive to maintain. One of the deans called it a "housing nightmare."

It wasn't fair, and Polly was determined to change it. She believed that concentrated study required privacy, quiet, and sometimes a place to cry. Each student needed—literally—a room of her own. Polly knew that these dormitories, devoid of intellectual stimulation or adult presence, were a constant reminder to the students that they were less important than the men who went to Harvard.

There was, however, no rich benefactor to endow a Radcliffe house system, and there was no money with which to embark on major building or remodeling. Nonetheless Polly was determined to do what she could. So in the summer of 1961 she announced that one group of dormitories would be North House, another South House, and another East House, and then she differentiated the houses by painting the doors different colors: blue for North, reddish-orange for East, and yellow for South. When the students in South House complained they didn't like yellow, she had their doors repainted green. Students in North House made their own comment by wrapping a banner that said "Bleak House" around the North House clock tower. "How they got up there I never knew but I welcomed their assertiveness. It was the kind of communication that we needed at Radcliffe," Polly said.

Polly had to cope that summer with a personal emergency. Bill, now sixteen, and always enamored of the sea, had set out the preceding September on a sailing ship, which was used as a floating prep school, giving a small group of teenagers a year of college preparatory courses along with the opportunity to learn some seamanship. In May the ship was overwhelmed by a fierce storm in the Gulf of Mexico and sank in minutes. Four of the fourteen students, the wife of the captain, and the ship's cook were drowned. Bill was one of the ten students, along with the captain and two teachers, who was rescued by a passing Dutch ship. He returned safely to Cambridge. This experience did nothing to lessen his love of the sea.

When the Radcliffe students returned to campus in the fall, a group of them came to tell Polly that a house system was much more than having the doors painted. She enjoyed the idea that they thought she hadn't figured that out. She took advantage of the opportunity to ask them what more they thought it should be.

Polly knew all about the Harvard houses from old friends like Barry Wood, the husband of her Vassar soulmate Leal, and knew long before she assumed her presidency how significant they were in the lives of Harvard undergraduates. With such a good model so close, Polly wondered why no one had thought to duplicate it at Radcliffe. There must have been some reason, some obstacle that she had not yet discovered, she thought. So she pored over past board of trustee minutes to find out what it might have been. She found, to her surprise, that the issue had never come up, not even during the 1940's and 1950's, when many new dormitories were built. Apparently no one had thought it mattered under what conditions the women lived. Even though many of the trustees had been Harvard graduates or Harvard parents, they had never compared the conditions under which the male and female students were living. And the women had been, and still were, paying the same tuition as the men.

"It was not because it was considered inappropriate for college women that Houses were not developed at Radcliffe when they were introduced at Harvard," Polly wrote, "but rather . . . because the education of women was just not thought to be that important. And unfortunately that was the way many students . . . interpreted the decision."[2] "It was just taken for granted that the women were lucky to be at Harvard at all. . . ." "It made me realize that there was more to be done at Radcliffe than I had guessed when I took the job."[3]

Polly informed Harvard's president, Nathan Pusey, and Harvard's dean, McGeorge Bundy, that she intended to create a house system at Radcliffe; Pusey invited her to appear before the Harvard Board of Overseers to inform them of her plans. It was the first time that any officer from Radcliffe had ever spoken to the Overseers. After she spoke several of them, who happened to be parents of Radcliffe students, told her they had never before thought about living conditions at Radcliffe.

At Douglass, Polly had learned how useful it was to be an outsider. It was even more useful at Radcliffe, where ingrained habits had been reinforced by a reverence for Harvard-imposed traditions. But she had no allegiance to the worlds of Boston, Cambridge, or Harvard. Nor had she come up through any administrative ranks; she hadn't been schooled in the way administrators were supposed to proceed. She felt free to make up solutions as she identified the problems. And she had the courage to face the Radcliffe trustees and politely point out to them the things they should have thought of and hadn't.

One of the chief ingredients that was present in the Harvard houses and missing at Radcliffe was faculty. Polly knew that they were the key to what she was trying to achieve. In order for young women to develop self-confidence, Polly believed that it was essential that they be in contact with adults they admired who expressed sincere interest in them and their ideas. But Radcliffe couldn't afford to sacrifice rooms in the already overcrowded dormitories. It was impossible to give up even two economy doubles for a spartan accommodation for an unmarried tutor, much less to provide more spacious accommodations for senior faculty. So Polly recruited faculty to be associated with the new Radcliffe houses even though they couldn't live there. They would still have the responsibility for transforming the dormitories into more lively and livable places.

For the first time, respected members of the Harvard faculty were giving time and thought to Radcliffe. Two years after Polly had arrived at Radcliffe each House had a member of the Harvard faculty and his wife as nonresident Heads of Houses. promptly christened Masters by the students. The Masters then recruited Faculty Associates; and, for the first time, interesting speakers appeared at the Radcliffe Quadrangle for dinner—Norman Thomas and Eudora Welty, among many others. At one of the first dinners, one of the Masters was surprised to discover that many Radcliffe seniors did not know one another. He determined to make sure that students in all the classes in his House were at least introduced, and proceeded to set up a series of dinners. The Masters' wives invited a variety of women from around Cambridge to come for lunch—wives of faculty members, graduate students, fellows at the Institute, authors, even the Master's secretary, who happened to be both a Radcliffe graduate and a lawyer. Bringing people together had never before been a goal at Radcliffe. Students had the opportunity to see women pursuing different kinds of lives, even those with advanced training constrained from using it.

The Masters had to use their imaginations and ingenuity because money was not plentiful. Where Harvard's masters had seven thousand dollars for programs, Radcliffe managed to increase its allocations to the houses from twenty-five to fifty dollars per year. Polly had to struggle to come up with the money for even the guest meals. Nonetheless she persevered, because she knew that fundamentally changing the character of the Quadrangle was central to her goals. And despite the obstacles, in a few short years, the presence of faculty became so much a part of life at the Radcliffe Quadrangle that students took it for granted. In much the same way that their absence had been an accepted aspect of life before, now seeing them around the dinner table was commonplace.

Polly found another inexpensive way to make improvements. She reorganized the Radcliffe administration, putting a dean in each of the three houses instead of having one for freshmen and sophomores and one for juniors and seniors with offices in the remote administration building. Academic advising had been nonexistent at Radcliffe, and Polly's hope was that as the deans became more accessible and actually got to know the students they could offer more effective advice. As one student said, "You feel as if you are being cared for, instead of processed."

Another change Polly made to improve students' lives without spending much money was in the area of physical education. The physical education requirement for first-year students had long been an irritant. Polly noted a trifle sarcastically in her annual report that perhaps one reason Radcliffe students had so little interest in exercise was that they got enough just walking to class. It also might have had something to do with the fact that the gymnasium had been built in 1898 and hadn't been changed much since. So she eliminated this requirement. As someone who had always been physically active and enjoyed it, she saw the requirement, two hours a week for one year, for what it was—a nuisance that was too insignificant to bring about physical fitness. As she had done at Douglass when she abolished the chapel attendance requirement, she took away the punitive stick and replaced it with a carrot. Doing something that had never been done before at Radcliffe, she asked students what kinds of activities they wanted in their gym. When it turned out they had lots of interests, she expanded the offerings, bringing in instructors in dance, fencing, and swimming. She kept the gym open later, and participation in physical activities increased geometrically.

She tried to respond to students' requests if they were reasonable. When students asked for a phone in Agassiz and television sets and books for the dorms, she somehow found the money and let them know that over five thousand dollars was spent for the things they wanted.

She not only hired a dean of students, she also enticed the retiring chief of psychiatry of the Beth Israel Hospital in Boston, a distinguished European doctor named Grete Bibring, to conduct an elective seminar for sixteen Radcliffe students at her home, across the street from the Radcliffe Quadrangle. The course was neither group therapy nor sensitivity training, but instead a serious discussion of women's education. It offered students the opportunity to talk about the purpose of their education and their plans for their futures with a woman who had had a successful career.

She concentrated on the aspects of students' lives over which she had control. She expanded lunch hours, so that students who needed more time to get back to the Quadrangle after morning classes could make it; she offered box lunches for students who had morning classes and afternoon labs; she opened the graduate center, which was much closer to the Harvard Yard, for buffet lunches, which also gave undergraduates the chance to rub shoulders with graduate women; she added fruit to the formerly starchy offerings in the automatic machines. Ingenuity and creativity filled the gaps before the serious money started arriving.

She made it clear to students, as she had at Douglass, that she was interested in hearing their ideas and concerns. One student wrote her a postcard asking for curtains on the bathroom windows and shower curtains "with bright patterns."

Since budget problems dogged Polly throughout her Radcliffe years, and since she knew that her visions were expensive, she kept up relentless fund-raising. She was on the road, traveling the country to speak to Radcliffe clubs, to visit foundations, to talk to anyone who might have money to contribute. Her journals are filled with the records of her travels, with impressions about individuals she encountered—often appreciative but occasionally dismissive—thumbnail sketches of their backgrounds, and the names and interests of their Radcliffe children; she even included the menus of some of the endless dinners. No impatience or boredom comes through in her journal scribblings, although she admitted that she kept giving the same speech over and over, just calling it by different titles.

Fund-raising was made even more difficult by changing social attitudes that tended to shock older alumnae. They questioned the advisability of giving money to what was beginning to look to them like a den of inequity. Polly's task was complicated further when, at the end of 1963, the dean of Harvard undergraduates, John Monro, announced with dismay that it had come to his attention that Harvard students were misusing permission to entertain women in their rooms "as license for wild parties and sexual intercourse."[4] At the same time, Radcliffe students were agitating for more hours during which they could entertain male visitors. When Polly went around the country soliciting funds, she had to answer repeated questions about the so-called sex scandals and the lessening of restrictions at Radcliffe. She informed group after group that the media stories about bacchanalian rites were exaggerated.

She kept searching for money because she knew that relieving the serious overcrowding in the dorms was essential, and that could only happen with more buildings. Although she had been very involved with the building at Douglass, she still saw herself as a neophyte and thought it made sense to convene a conference of more experienced people to be sure Radcliffe didn't repeat mistakes that had been made elsewhere. So at the end of her first full year she brought together twenty experts: architects, anthropologists, deans of students, psychologists, sociologists, health experts with and without M.D.s, and a few members of the Radcliffe staff, trustees, and student body. She wanted answers to some long-standing questions: What was the optimum size for a college house? Could you create an environment which would encourage connections among students and between students and faculty?

The conference, however, did not produce the results Polly had hoped for. It might have been the heat and the absence of air conditioning, but she left the discussions discouraged. "Something was lacking," she remembered years later. "No exciting new ideas had emerged, no real excitement about old ideas, either. We were in trouble."

Her perception that the conference had been a failure made her glum, so she set out for the country hideaway she had bought in New Boston, New Hampshire, to recharge her batteries and clarify her thinking. Country chores always helped her, and—as she was to recount more than a decade later—inspiration came to her as she held a scythe blade to the grindstone to sharpen it. That task reminded her that she needed to hold her mind to the problem of the Quadrangle with the same tenacity.

Polly said she realized in that moment that no matter what she did at the Quadrangle, Radcliffe students would still be commuting to Harvard for all of their classes and most of their extracurricular activities. What was necessary to enliven and deepen life at Radcliffe was to draw more of Harvard to the Quad. She asked herself how it could be done. "One did not try to push Harvard; one would have to attract it,"[5] she concluded. To make the Quadrangle more than a place where students ate and slept, to make it appealing to both Harvard and Radcliffe students and to faculty, it would have to have a place to study, to gather socially, and to hold meetings. She realized then the answer was to move the Radcliffe library to the Quadrangle.

The anecdote about the grindstone made her insight seem like an inspiration of the moment but, in fact, building a library close to the dormitories was part of Polly's thinking from the start. She had mentioned it to the Council nine months earlier, and in March 1961 the architect working on the college's Long Range Plan told the Council which specific corner of the Quadrangle he had in mind for the library. When Polly put together a proposal for donors that month, called "Creating a House Plan for Radcliffe," a library in the Quadrangle was an integral component.

Perhaps what came to her as she sharpened her scythe was the shape and scope of that library, a building that would be far more than—as one student was to say years later—"a barn for books." Since Polly's objective was to draw more of Harvard to Radcliffe, she decided to incorporate something she knew was in short supply at Harvard: faculty offices and conference rooms. "They would be excellent bait; they would change patterns of movement in just the right way."

The idea of the Radcliffe Houses clustered around an academic center proved to be the catalyst that ignited interest in all the Radcliffe constituencies, although everyone was still convinced that additional housing had to be built first. But then a surprising thing happened. "Almost everyone seemed to be more interested in the proposed library than in the proposed house. In spite of all our arguments, donors asked more questions about the library. Students started pointing out that the library would be for all of them. It would make life at the Quadrangle better for everyone. They had gotten along for many years in the crowded dormitories."[6] The architect kept producing sketches of the library while they were waiting for his ideas about the house. In the end it was Mrs. Susan Hilles, a major Radcliffe donor, who tipped the balance. One evening, when she and Polly were having an informal supper, she said, "When you are ready to build the library, let me know. I would like to give to that." It soon became evident that what she would like to give would cover at least half of the estimated cost. That was considerably more than what was in hand for the house, which was an even more expensive project. "My priorities shifted fast," Polly said. The preliminary plans were approved in the fall of 1963.

The library was a two-year project. But before either the library or the fourth house could be built, Polly received another unexpected invitation that would take her far from Cambridge and introduce her, temporarily, to an entirely new world.

20

It's Hard to Say "No" to the President

It was a quiet Saturday morning in March, and Polly was sitting in the living room with her children when the telephone rang. "Is this Mrs. Bunting? The president wants to speak to you." She thought, "Of all the jokers at Harvard, I wonder who's pulling this one?" And then she heard a familiar voice. "Mrs. Bunting?" "Yes, but I'm not sure who I'm talking to." "Well, this is Lyndon Baines Johnson. I know you are very much interested in opportunities for women," he began, and then went on with a series of questions to which he already knew the answers, since he had clearly been well briefed. He also may have remembered Polly from their work a few years earlier when he was Kennedy's vice-president and chairman of the National Advisory Council for the Peace Corps, and she the vice-chairman.

"You want women to be able to move forward into top positions," he continued, and she had to say, "Yes, Mr. President" a number of times before he arrived at the purpose of his call. Robert E. Wilson, a former oil company executive, had resigned from the Atomic Energy Commission and Johnson wanted Polly to finish the unexpired term, serving until the end of June 1965. If she agreed, she would be one of five commissioners and the first woman ever appointed to the AEC.

The AEC had been founded after World War II to ensure that the enormous power of the atomic bomb would be put in civilian, not military, hands. Its first meeting was at the beginning of January 1947, presided over by its first chairman and Polly's old ally, David Lilienthal. From the outset the AEC oversaw basic research into the nature of the atom and managed not only the various nuclear laboratories throughout the country, but also those in universities conducting basic nuclear research. Even though the AEC never had responsibility for the development of weapons, it did have responsibility for even that research which was eventually used by the military, and it was supposed to oversee the handling and storage of weapons.

Another of its responsibilities was to assess the advisability of nuclear tests. Since the signing of the Nuclear Test Ban Treaty the preceding year, nuclear tests were restricted to those conducted underground. The commission had to decide which tests should be made, to determine what they were likely to prove or disprove and assess the quantity of radiation that should be permitted to escape into the atmosphere.

It was a large and complex organization with a budget approaching nearly three billion dollars a year and approximately 7,300 employees.[1] Its operations extended to virtually every state of the Union, and it had cooperative programs with nations and organizations on every continent.

Polly understood immediately the political implications of the president's offer. It was his first appointment to this important commission, and it was an election year. He wanted to demonstrate his support for women. Polly saw that, from LBJ's point of view., she was an ideal choice. Not only was she a woman and a scientist, she had conducted considerable research in the fifties on the effects of radiation on *Serratia* with grants from the Atomic Energy Commission. In addition, there had been some conflict between labor and business over whose representative would fill this vacancy. Since Polly was not a member of either constituency, her appointment would not alienate anybody.

Johnson told Polly that he hoped still to be president after November and then he would be able to offer a five-year appointment, a full term. Polly wasted no time with coyness or even diplomacy. She said she couldn't consider leaving Radcliffe for five years, but would be very interested in working on the commission for one. Frankly it would serve both their interests if she came for just one year. She would gain the visibility she wanted for women, and he would get the political capital from the appointment during the election year. "Fair enough," he said. "Come for one year."

Polly believed it was a good time for her to step away from Radcliffe. Her major initiatives were in midstream; her top staff were experienced and competent; and her children were old enough to manage without her supervision. Mary, having graduated from the University of Vermont, was in graduate school in social work at Smith, Chuck was in his senior year at Amherst, Bill was a sophomore at Harvard, and John, a senior in high school, could board at his school. Since Mary would be living in the Brattle Street house, the boys would still have a home to go to during holidays.

Polly asked Johnson not to say anything until she had a chance to discuss his offer with the Radcliffe trustees who were meeting the following week. She laid out for them all the pros and cons of her accepting the position. On the negative side would be a certain loss of momentum in the various projects at Radcliffe and the possibility of alienating some alumnae. On the positive side would be the value of the appointment as a symbol; the wider contacts that would be gained; and the increased understanding, on both sides, of the problems of education and of government. Finally, she said, "It is hard to say 'no' to the President."

The first reaction of the Council members was astonishment. They were amazed that the president of the United States had made a personal phone call to Polly and unnerved by the prospect of losing their president for an entire year. Once they regained their equilibrium, however, they recognized how Radcliffe's prestige would be enhanced by such a significant appointment. In the end it took them less than an hour to approve Polly's leave—although, as the minutes of the meeting reveal, they did it with some "reluctance." But the meeting did not go entirely Polly's way. She recommended that, in her absence, the college be run by a committee chaired by Wilma Kerby-Miller, one of Radcliffe's deans, working closely with Helen Gilbert. Instead, the council chose Helen Gilbert to be acting president and Kerby-Miller academic vice-president.

"The trustees' decision was an interesting one," Polly commented years later. "Everyone knew Helen Gilbert and admired her.... The year would be instructive for her as well as for me." It was as close as Polly ever got to admitting that she and Gilbert did not see things the same way. Publicly Polly said she was pleased with the arrangement. In any event, since the trustees had rejected her recommendation she had to accommodate herself.

The AEC was another of those unexpected twists in Polly's life. Only a few weeks earlier, on a fund-raising trip, looking down on Zion National Park she wrote poignantly in her journal: "Monday, 3/10/64 —Henry would be 53 today & we would have been still in Bethany." A week later the President called.

Her AEC appointment was announced on page one of the *New York Times*. Much was made of the fact that she was to be the first woman commissioner, a point frequently repeated throughout her term. When she was the speaker at the monthly Government Information Officers luncheon, the person introducing her crossed out "Dr." from his prepared remarks and substituted "Mrs." And after introducing her as the first woman and the first biologist to serve on the commission, he added, "I suspect that she is also the first Commissioner to have spent a number of years as a Four-H Club leader."[2] Although this type of recognition was exactly why Polly had taken the job, she felt a little

It's Hard to Say "No" to the President

ambivalent about it. When the publicity people identified her in their annual report as the first woman commissioner, she crossed that out and wrote "the first biologist."

After the announcement of her appointment, letters of congratulations poured in, from individuals and organizations—two bulging file folders full. There were telegrams, postcards, and letters—handwritten and typed—on engraved stationery, fancy letterheads, little "informals," lined notebook paper, even one Hallmark card, "On Your New Venture." Radcliffe Trustee Gerry Piel wrote, "The atom has needed your attention ever since they smashed it in 1939." And there were notes from ordinary people who didn't even know her, touched by the significance of a woman vaulting over yet one more barrier.

On March 30, Polly flew to Washington, where a heavy snowstorm kept her circling for almost two hours. She was met by an AEC car and driven to the Germantown, Maryland, headquarters, where the Berkeley physicist, Chairman Glenn Seaborg took her to lunch with the other three commissioners whom he called the "brothers": John Palfrey, from Columbia; Gerald Tape, a chemist; and James Ramey, a lawyer with many years of experience in the field of nuclear energy. The day in Washington was busy, with lots of preliminary meetings, and Polly kept notes in her journal on where people sat in an effort to keep straight in her mind who everyone was.

After her return from what she called her "initiation," she wrote a letter to Seaborg. "Although I am not at all clear as to what my contribution can be, I have a greater awareness of all that I shall learn through my association with the AEC." She asked if, rather than beginning her term immediately, she could begin July 1 so that she could take "a neat year's leave of absence from Radcliffe. . . . I am particularly mindful of the senior class, which entered with me. They would like to have me sign diplomas and preside at their commencement." It was arranged for her to serve as a consultant until she was sworn in at the end of June. The Joint Congressional Committee met on April 26 to consider her appointment, but they didn't think she had to be in Washington for that meeting. On April 27, 1964, a telegram from Senator Leverett Saltonstall informed her that she had been confirmed.

It was a busy spring; obligations at Radcliffe did not lessen. She continued to travel the country in search of money and still kept track of a multiplicity of details. Her journals are filled with snippets: Blue Cross costs going up; repair and tuning of pianos; union negotiations for waitresses, maids, and maintenance men; leases for the various small houses rented by Radcliffe to students; concern about an elderly woman being evicted from a Radcliffe-owned property at 83 Brattle Street.

She was sworn in by President Johnson on June 29, 1964, in the Cabinet Room of the White House. The entry in her journal is sparse. "Monday—June 29 Picked up by Burke . . . 11:10 to White House to take the oath—" She then listed the few of her family and friends who were present. "Quite a wait for J." The appointment, the president said, reaffirmed American policy "that the power of the atom should be used for human progress and peace." He said he hoped that "wives and mothers of every land will find in this appointment a reaffirmation of that American determination." After a few years in public life, Polly knew to wear a hat with a short veil that just covered her forehead. "It certainly wasn't worth anyone's time & money" to come to Washington especially for the ceremony, Polly wrote her mother.

She found an apartment in what she called "a rather swanky apartment house on Cathedral Avenue." She furnished it, however, with orange crates and an army cot and bureau from Goodwill. She invested in only one piece of new furniture, a card table, because she needed some place to write her letters. No matter how busy, she always made time for them. She didn't think there was any need for much furniture since she figured her job would call for a lot of homework, but not a lot of entertaining. Although she moved in at the end of June, she didn't even have a phone until the beginning of July. She found it "rather fun camping out again. . . . I found the contrast of rising from my army cot and being called for by the chauffeured limousine of the Atomic Energy Commission rather amusing."

She set up these spartan accommodations for herself not only because she saw no point in making a fuss for such a short time, but also because she was short of money. Her salary from the AEC was $22,000, exactly the same as she was getting at Radcliffe. In the *New York Times* this was erroneously reported as $22,500, an error Polly made a point of correcting in a letter to her mother, indicating how significant a sum $500 was to her at that time. The salary, she explained, was not enough to cover the additional expenses incurred by her living in Washington; $1,800 rent for the apartment and $1,240 for John's room and board at the Cambridge School. Her mother offered help, $3,000, just the amount she needed. Polly wrote a grateful letter accepting the assistance. She seldom accepted financial help from her family, but this time she felt she had to. The new job, she said, "will demand some personal sacrifice financially, which I do not wish to pass on to my children."

As she had predicted, the job entailed prodigious amounts of study, which even she found demanding. But her journals attest to the fact that she caught on fast. She filled pages with detailed scientific information, formulas, proposals, observations from visits to nuclear laboratories, questions as to who decides which experiments are conducted, who determines which scientists receive support. It was a little, she was to say years later, like returning to her college physics major. She relied on her assistant, Richard Donovan, who had worked for the commission for many years, to brief her before and after meetings.

Being the only woman commissioner didn't affect her working relationships. She was accustomed to working with men. "They're people too," she was to say years later. But working under a woman commissioner was a great change for the staff. Polly enjoyed watching them adjust, particularly those who had been in the military and were accustomed to answering "yes, sir" or "no, sir" whenever they wished to show respect. She knew she had finally been accepted when they forgot to be embarrassed and just went ahead with the discussion.

Polly fit right in. Gerald Tape said she brought civility to the discussions. "She was a great listener," said Toni Joseph, the only woman among the four young interns working at the AEC. "She had a way of phrasing things so as not to be threatening. She had the facts, stated them without being argumentative. It didn't take long for the other commissioners to defer to her."

During her year at the AEC, Polly paid particular attention to the interns, recent college graduates. All the commissioners were cordial to them, but it was Polly who took them out to lunch and asked the real questions about their backgrounds and how well the experience at the AEC was serving them. She worked hard to establish a program that would enable them to go back to college for masters' degrees and then return to work at the AEC. "We young interns loved her," said Toni Joseph. "She saw us as her Radcliffe in Washington."

The commission had two or three meetings a week at 1717 H Street, a few blocks from the White House. Once a month they went to Germantown to meet with staff members in a huge office with a beautiful oval table. They also did a lot of traveling, mostly to universities and laboratories around the country, where the research authorized by the AEC was conducted. To Polly, those trips offered attractions beyond the labs. While in New Mexico at Los Alamos, she wrote in her journal: "Blue skies at last—Beautiful snow decorated mountains in every direction—Pinon & other pines—Robins."

The commissioners also attended conferences on nuclear energy in Europe. The first one for Polly took place at the end of August in Geneva: the Third United Nations Conference on Peaceful Uses of Atomic Energy. The next year she went with all the commissioners to Poland for a conference "designed to keep channels of communication open." While there, she made what she called "a splendid deal" with the person showing her reactors. For every half hour she spent looking at reactors, he would spend an hour taking her to see cathedrals and art galleries. "I wasn't the kind of technical person who could derive much from seeing reactors," she said.

There was one area Polly did feel herself especially qualified to assess, the biological impacts of radioactivity. She had observed that if a reactor was located near a river, the water used to cool it would flow into that river and adversely affect the fish. She insisted that steps should be taken to guard against the pollution. At the very least, she believed, the AEC should make clear to the public what the potential hazards were. Ordinarily Polly was sensitive to her status as the new kid on the block, and thought carefully before she raised questions at meetings, but on this issue she argued openly with the other members of the commission. They contended that warming, since it was thermal and not atomic, did not fall under the official aegis of the AEC; state offices were supposed to watch out for heat contamination. Polly's answer was that the reactor had been set up by the AEC and that they knew it was doing damage so they had to do something about it.

She did not win her point, but a few years after she left, when thermal pollution became a much greater national concern, Seaborg told her that she had been right and the commission should have been more forthright. Even after she left the commission, she continued to pay attention to this issue and took copious notes about it in her journal.

She had known from the start that any impact she might have at the AEC in just one year would be limited. She did bring about one major change, however, but it had nothing to do with atomic energy. She used her time in Washington to further her major cause: improving the lot of women.

The AEC was not a particularly female-friendly place. Even though about one third of its employees were women, Polly was one of only three with a Ph.D., compared with 161 men who had the degree. Part of the reason for this was that the AEC had a policy never to hire anyone part-time, with the result that a lot of talented women with the right qualifications couldn't work there. This was just the kind of situation that aroused Polly's interest, and she decided to try to change it.

She began by suggesting to the head of the AEC's personnel department, Arthur Tackman, that he make part-time positions available. He immediately rejected the suggestion, explaining that each position he filled counted as a full-time position; establishing part-time slots, therefore, would reduce his staff. Polly suspected Tackman was not much interested in women's rights, but she knew that Johnson was.

Every Friday morning, Polly learned, Tackman had to send a letter to the White House stating how many women he had hired or promoted to upper-level positions. Tackman was interested in getting "his Brownie points from the President." He didn't like sending in blank pages. So Polly proposed that the next AEC budget contain a number of part-time positions specifically justified as an experiment for recruiting professional women. Given Johnson's expressed interests, it was approved and Tackman found some fascinating women lawyers, scientists, and writers who could work not only in Washington, but out in some of the laboratories around the country. He began to get quite a reputation in Washington for this program's success, and was often invited to explain his system to other agencies. Typically, Polly allowed him to take credit for the idea.

As time-consuming as Polly's job was, Washington was far from all work and no play. She became a favorite lunch guest of recent Harvard and Radcliffe graduates, many of whom were working for newspapers, who "kept thinking they would get some big scoop," Polly said. But they never did.

She was invited to countless receptions—a particularly amusing one for "distinguished ladies" hosted by a Ford Foundation offshoot. "What a jam!" Polly noted in her journal. Commissioners invited her to lots of dinner parties, where there was good conversation about education and women and increasingly about the very disturbing war in Vietnam. When she participated in a weekend conference for returning Peace Corps volunteers, she was surprised to find that it was the war they talked about more than anything else. There was even a nice dinner at the Bundys', where she found both the Johnsons. "LBJ was settled on the porch and in a fine relaxed mood," Polly wrote her mother.

Polly found the time to keep up with Radcliffe, going there, as she had arranged with Seaborg when she began the AEC job, about one weekend a month. She dealt with questions from members of the staff, answered letters, and checked up on her children. She consulted with Max Abramovitz, the architect working on Daniels Hall, the first segment of what was eventually to be the fourth house. She wanted to keep informed about all the specific details—from the dimensions of the living room to the location of the individual thermostats. There were also a few college policy decisions to be made. Radcliffe students were clamoring for longer hours in which to entertain men; Polly recommended that they not be extended beyond those permitted at Harvard, and the council agreed. There was a two-month trial dining hall exchange between Harvard and Radcliffe, which worked well. Since neither institution was out of pocket, the innovation was accepted on a regular basis. The only troublesome issue concerned the School of Education's proposal to buy the old library in the Radcliffe Yard, which Polly vigorously opposed. She was already planning for the Institute's move there.

The new library progressed on schedule. Helen Gilbert presided over a disastrous ground-breaking ceremony where virtually everything went wrong. It turned out to be a dismal, sleeting day; the Harvard/Radcliffe Gilbert & Sullivan Players, who were to serenade the important invited guests with a special song composed for the occasion, never arrived and the smiling faces of students who were supposed to break the ground with ribbon-bedecked shovels were obscured by their masses of windblown hair. Even the balloons, which were to have ascended majestically to the heavens, ended up getting caught in the trees.

Of course Polly was constantly in touch with her family. Since her father's death two years earlier at the age of eighty-four, her seventy-seven-year-old mother was struggling on her own. Polly tried to prevail upon her to hire someone to stay with her in her apartment. The vigorously independent Gwy resisted—not wanting to give up either her privacy or the money—in spite of Polly's argument that taking on a live-in companion would relieve her children's anxiety. "I'm reminded of my own feelings about collision insurance," she wrote. "Before the children began to drive I never carried it. I took my chances—but when they started & I thought how badly they would feel if they damaged my car it seemed worth while to carry insurance for their peace of mind. Then if anything happened I could say, 'insurance will cover it.'"

Polly's own children did fine. When she arrived for Thanksgiving, having been held up for over an hour by traffic jams at the Washington airport, she found pies and turkey ready and the four children "lying on the floor by the fire." The one elaborate family event was Mary's wedding to Reiner Decher, an MIT graduate student who became a professor at the University of Washington in Seattle. The wedding took place the day after Christmas in the MIT Chapel, and Mary handled all the arrangements, even the decoration of the house. Polly's one obligation was to locate a minister, a somewhat tricky assignment since the Buntings didn't have any church connections. Quite suddenly she remembered Steven Crary, a cousin she hadn't seen since he was a little kid "bouncing on a horse," who was now the chaplain at Brown. Polly called and explained her predicament to him; and like all members of the extended Ingraham family, when called upon by a family member he responded. He performed the ceremony and, Polly said, "did a very nice job." In March, Bill—still enamored of ships and undeterred by his earlier near catastrophic experience—took a leave of absence from college to be first mate on a sailing ship.

So her Washington year drew to a close. It had a festive ending, an elegant lunch for eighteen guests that Lady Bird Johnson gave in Polly's honor at the White House.

Polly left Washington, but President Johnson kept appointing her to commissions. Less than a month after her departure, she was back at the White House for a conference on education, chairing panels on both graduate and undergraduate education. In 1966 Johnson appointed her to an advisory panel on easing the shortage of doctors and to another national advisory council on regional medical programs. She stayed in touch with the AEC serving on their Advisory Committee for Biology and Medicine, which met several times a year. And people she had come to know from the commission stayed in touch with her. Her assistant, Richard Donovan, sent her a poinsettia plant at Christmas.

Polly didn't often speak about the year she had spent hob-nobbing with the powerful. It had been interesting, but as she wrote to her mother, "a sabbatical." The official photograph of the commission—all of them sitting around the beautiful oval table with the American flag in one corner—was displayed only in a corner of a bathroom in her last apartment.

21

We Believe in Education for Women

Polly came back to Radcliffe when the college was relatively peaceful, but the country was beginning to roil. While she had been away, both the fight for civil rights and the anti–Vietnam War movements had been gathering force. The Civil Rights Act had been passed in June 1964, the day after three young civil rights workers had been murdered in Mississippi. Student activists were making their appearance at Berkeley, and in March 1965 Johnson had authorized the bombing of North Vietnam. Although not yet at a full boil, the movements that shaped the decade and rocked the world of higher education were simmering.

The women's movement was also beginning to have its effect. The formal establishment of the large feminist organizations was still a year or so away, but the erosion of the "climate of unexpectation" had begun. The 1965 Institute annual report noted that people no longer questioned, as they had when the Institute was founded, why it was necessary to pay special attention to women of education and talent. Now the basic purpose was accepted and questions focused on the "implementing details."

Some things were even changing at Harvard. Polly spoke at the annual meeting of the Harvard Club of New York, the first time women had been included.[1] She succeeded in convincing the dean of the Graduate School of Arts and Sciences to administer Radcliffe funds for part-time women graduate students, something Harvard had never countenanced before. Although Harvard had permitted part-time graduate study, it had never offered such students any money. Polly believed that even though the funds were Radcliffe's, having Harvard administer the money gave legitimacy to the part-time program.[2]

Polly began to note in speeches that a dramatic change seemed to have occurred quite suddenly in both the aspirations and expectations of young women. She appreciated the contributions of the women's movement and recognized the part they were playing in changing attitudes. But, ever uncomfortable with confrontation, she resisted being drawn into the militant brand of feminism. She had never favored separatism, even opposing professional societies for women. Now she believed she could work for Radcliffe more effectively, and encourage people to look more objectively at the programs and recommendations she was making, if she were not perceived to be a member of the movement. In response to a request for a review of a book about women's liberation, Polly wrote: "Too close association with the women's rights movement is more of a liability than an asset in getting people to look objectively at specific recommendations and programs that I am trying to implement.... I think discretion is the better part of valor for the sake of the cause we're both so interested in forwarding."[3]

Capitalizing on the forces in motion and on her own increasing celebrity, Polly took advantage of every opportunity to forward the cause, reiterating in speech after speech what by now had become the chief components of her message: part-time opportunities for young mothers; flexibility in scheduling; extended time periods for completing degrees; financial support for part-time study. She had become a recognized spokesperson, and even though speech-making was never something she enjoyed, she accepted invitations when they came, tailoring her message to her audience. To the ladies luncheon of the U.S. Chamber of Commerce, she touted the advantages adult education could bring to communities. To a group of psychiatrists, she urged abandoning their commitment to "sleepless internships."

She recognized that many disparate forces were bringing about a societal shift that she had not anticipated would happen so fast. It was difficult to unravel the strands and determine exactly where the force for change was coming from. "Whether the profound changes that interest me are being administered or whether they are just happening is debatable," she told Radcliffe alumnae. "I once saw an ant walk from New Haven to New York in 2 hours—down the corridor of the New York–New Haven train. One couldn't deny she'd been working at it but she'd had things going for her too."[4]

Whatever the causes, the effects were clear. They showed up in many specific ways. The number of Radcliffe students leaving college to get married began falling precipitously. The Radcliffe dean, Kathleen Elliott, reported to the trustees that for the first time, Radcliffe undergraduates, like Harvard undergraduates, were thinking of college as preprofessional training. Approximately one-tenth of the class of 1966 was applying to medical school, more than one-tenth to law school. And most of those not going directly into graduate or professional study "had less conventional but no less ambitious ideas." In fact, just as high a proportion of married as unmarried seniors were going directly from college to graduate or professional school. To keep up with the times, the name of Radcliffe's job placement office, which had been called the "Appointment Bureau," was changed to "Career Planning Office."

"Either the 'climate of unexpectation' that once dissuaded them is fast disappearing or it no longer affects them," Polly wrote. "In any event, today they are planning their lives in a new way. They assume marriage and family responsibilities but they also assume graduate or professional education leading to significant creative contributions."[5] They were doing, in fact, just what Polly had been urging them to do, looking at their lives through a long lens and preparing themselves for the years after their children would be grown. "In the past, the fact that their full involvement was long years ahead tended to discourage them from aiming high; now they see that it frees them to set their sights high indeed. They have time."[6] When for the first time ever, the governor of Massachusetts took part in the 1966 Radcliffe commencement, she said she saw his presence "as further evidence of a new awareness of the important roles that today's college women are planning to play in our society."

Always a realist, Polly saw that, although moving in the right direction, much remained the same. So she kept the two old summer courses that had been fixtures for generations: typing and shorthand was one and publishing procedures was the other. "Revolutions have a ragged edge," she said years later, and women college graduates still needed preparation for the low-level jobs which would be all many of them would find. These courses were fully subscribed, and not only by Radcliffe graduates, but by women from many other colleges as well.

Radcliffe students had only to look at Harvard to understand the tenacity of the old attitudes. In one class Polly's son Bill heard a distinguished Harvard professor inveigh against "pushy women," a slur Bill felt was definitely intended for him to report at home. Advisers were still discouraging married women from finishing their doctorates, and undergraduates were routinely urged to skip graduate school. Although female graduate students were generally in their late twenties and thirties, they were, nonetheless, referred to as "girls," not only by the male world in which they moved, but also by themselves. It was understood that no matter how capable, they would never be offered positions at Harvard. They watched male classmates who had accomplished less being offered the positions they wanted, while they were told that anything beyond teaching at a community college, or at best a women's college, was unrealistic.[7]

Antipathy to women was at its worst in the sciences. The few women courageous enough to venture into this male bastion not only lacked support, they often had to cope with outright hostility. When one female physics graduate student became pregnant, her adviser called her in to his office and announced, "It has come to my attention that you are not serious about science." When she insisted that she was, he told her that in order for a woman with children to get ahead in science, she would either have to attach herself to a man, run his lab and help with the training of his students, or make herself an expert in something so minute that no one else would be interested in it. But then, he added, "your husband probably wouldn't like that." "It wasn't something we ever discussed again," she said.

Polly looked at the situation with double vision. She heard what the students told her, saw that there were practically no women on the Harvard faculty, and understood that barriers and prejudices still stood in their way. But as always, she chose to look on the positive side, and to celebrate the progress that had been made. She kept focused on the task she had set for herself, improving the educational experience of Radcliffe students. An important part of that, she continued to believe, was integrating Radcliffe more and more into the larger university.

An essential piece of that effort fell into place in the fall of 1966 when the new Hilles Library opened at the Radcliffe Quadrangle, in close proximity to the Radcliffe dormitories. The library was an unqualified triumph, a strikingly beautiful building, open and spacious, with large windows on all sides. It embodied her vision of what mattered in education. It had well-insulated small conference rooms for "noisy study," because Polly thought women didn't argue enough when they were studying together, but instead went off into corners by themselves to brood. She knew that science students, in particular, needed lots of reference books close at hand, so there was one room that housed science books, where these students could gather and talk.

Most startling of all, Polly put a snack bar on the fourth floor. Food "was one of the things that libraries were not supposed to have," but she had always seen academic work as part of a full life and for her, food always stood for more than nourishment. Even so, she never anticipated how important the snack bar would become until she tried to close it on Sundays to save money. A delegation of freshmen came to her office to tell her that Sunday was the loneliest day of the week, and the one friendly, comfortable place where they could go alone was the Hilles snack bar. They implored her not to shut it then, not to shut it at all. As a member of the Radcliffe class of '67 wrote to her, the "secret success" of the library, "is the snack bar. Don't take this as an insult to intellectuality," she wrote, "but I think it's about time official Radcliffe realized that we are *females* as well as mental demi-gorgons, and we *love* boys." The snack bar, she said, is "a great place to meet people." As always, Polly listened and kept the snack bar open.

Hilles Library succeeded even beyond Polly's most optimistic expectations in its effect on the Harvard community. "It changed the evening traffic pattern on Garden Street," she said, in exactly the right direction, up toward the Quadrangle rather than away from it. The twenty faculty offices and seminar rooms were bait for the faculty, and hordes of Harvard students descended on the building to study. "It seems they like nice surroundings too," Polly told alumnae. So many Harvard students came, in fact, that during exam periods, men had to be kept out in the early evening to permit the women to find seats. These numbers greatly aided Polly in her push to encourage Harvard to finally admit Radcliffe students to Harvard's undergraduate library, Lamont. "At last," Polly said, "Radcliffe had something, in addition to women, that appealed to Harvard."

Hilles was also important for Radcliffe students. Mrs. Elliott described "the stablest and steadiest fall term" she could remember, and believed part of the reason was the elegant new library that gave students a feeling of excitement about and identification with Radcliffe, which was new. The college appeared to be less an appendage and more a full-fledged part of the university.

Polly opened the college in 1966 by announcing that "the Hilles Library and Daniels Hall (the first dormitory of the fourth house) signify more than wonderfully pleasant & convenient places for undergraduates to live and work: they are the keys to Radcliffe's future." They were also significant achievements for her. In six short years she had transformed the center of Radcliffe College, making it both more a piece of Harvard University and more a college for women.

Polly was now involved with a multiplicity of administrative responsibilities: choosing an architect for the remaining units of the fourth house; filling administrative positions—freshman advisors and financial aid director—trying to entice Harvard faculty to serve as masters for the Radcliffe houses; and dealing with minutiae that she recorded in her journals: the kinds of windows to be put into the new house, the need for curtains in faculty offices, the placement of book chutes and pencil sharpeners, and the cost of air-conditioning Agassiz for the summer. She also stayed very involved in admission decisions, exerting her influence at a fundamental level, clarifying what sort of student body she believed Radcliffe should have. She wanted interesting people, not just successful test-takers. And there were the usual fund-raising trips. She combined one with a visit to John, now a student at Beloit, a small liberal arts college in Wisconsin. She took him out to dinner with Meredith, the young woman he had met freshman year, who became his wife.

Given all her responsibilities, Polly decided it was finally time to relinquish her last connection to scientific work: she gave up teaching her freshman seminar on problems in microbial genetics, which she had taught for eight freshmen from almost the beginning of her time at Radcliffe.

It was one of thirty freshmen seminars that Harvard had introduced in 1960 for credit but not for grades, designed to give entering students the opportunity to work directly with senior faculty. These small, intense seminars, different in tone and purpose from Harvard's usual fare of large, impersonal lectures, meshed perfectly with Polly's convictions about the way science should be taught. Students should be encouraged to devise their own research projects, she believed; they should be given a sense of what it was really like to do research.

She loved the teaching and the opportunity it afforded her to stay in touch with experimental science and to show another group of students the way into a discipline she loved. But she realized that the gaps in her scientific knowledge had become too big. It was time to sharpen her focus. As she did with every transition in her life, she sized up the situation realistically and moved on without looking back.

Although she was without this natural and easy avenue into students' confidence, she remained an accessible advocate for all women in the university. She let them know where money for graduate school was to be found, guided them through the application process, even wrote letters of recommendation for them. And she was willing to use unorthodox methods to help them. One year, Polly received an invitation to tea from the women graduate students in bacteriology. "Someone said Mrs. Bunting had met every student but us," said Eva Kashket, at the time, a bacteriology graduate student at the Harvard Medical School and now a professor at Boston University. "So I wrote and gave her about fifteen different dates. I didn't think she would come, but one day soon after the phone rang and she was actually on the phone. Not a secretary. She, herself. She said she would like very much to come and asked if she could bring someone with her." About fifteen people squeezed into the Kashket's apartment in Brookline, and waited. The mystery guest turned out to be a Radcliffe senior, Diane Jacobs, who had asked Polly for advice on a career in microbiology. Polly knew it would help her to see other young women doing the thing she wanted to do. "Mrs. Bunting told us that growing female bacteriologists was like growing bacteria," remembered Eva Kashket. "In order to do it you had to have a nourishing environment."

When Kathryn Voelker Holmes was applying to Rockefeller University, Polly, without any explanation, asked her to be the all-college social chairman and organize two dances, a position that had never existed before. It wasn't until sometime later that Kathryn understood that Polly felt the Rockefeller admissions committee might be favorably impressed if she appeared to be "some kind of campus leader." They were impressed enough to admit her.

When Deborah Batts, now a federal judge, told Polly that Harvard Law School was too expensive and she was going to accept a less prestigious school, Polly said that choosing a law school was too important a decision to be based on money and found her a fellowship and a campus job to help cover the costs.

Katherine Beer, who got married and moved to Montreal after her sophomore year, went to see Polly after a few years in order to find out if there was any way to complete her missing credits. What Beer remembers is the convolutions Polly went through to work around rules and regulations to make it possible. "And I asked, 'Why are you doing this for me? Why are you going to all this trouble?' And she just looked at me and answered, 'Because we believe in education for women.'"

Polly helped with words too. More than thirty years later, an alumna remembered Polly's convocation speech, which acknowledged that just about every entering student was convinced she was the admission office's one mistake. It was true, Polly said, that they were all likely to find at least twenty-five others in their dorm alone who excelled at everything each of them had previously excelled at. But, she told them, "there is something special about you. And what you need to do in your four years here is to hold on to that."

Throughout her presidency she kept up the porch-light signal and invited small groups of students over for meals or just to talk. She kept track in her journals of those who came, from time to time jotting down their names and comments. "Pat Tomas & Carol Rappaport—Happy roommates in Holmes dropped in for a good chat." Sometimes, she served them Drambuie—another small rebellion. Students couldn't have the sherry in the dorm that was offered to faculty and house mothers; they had to have tomato juice. If a student she knew happened to be passing by the president's house, she might invite her in to ask her opinion of the plans for the new house or to get her reaction to something she was thinking about.

She paid particular attention to those having difficulties. In her journal she reported a one-hour conversation with a student who was having trouble writing papers and was considering dropping out of college. Polly quoted her in her journal, "I'm not sure I want to be patched up." She kept notes about meetings with a student who was on probation, and kept close track of the legal progress of a student indicted for transporting weapons in New Hampshire. Whenever a student was in difficulty, she tried to find out if there was an adult anywhere in the system who knew and cared about her. Always conscious of her inadequate memory, she kept lists of the names of students she wanted to remember—student government officers, house presidents, or those who had particularly impressed her at a dorm meeting or dinner by a wise comment they had made or good question they had asked. In her speeches she often used direct quotes from students, which gave her speeches an authentic ring.

By 1965 and 1966, students were demanding more involvement in the formulation of college policies. Polly welcomed their activism and tried to show them how to focus their energies constructively. She urged them to submit ideas for new courses, to give thoughtful advice to younger students, to bring lively tutors to dinner in the houses. She recognized that there had been a fundamental shift in the relationship of students to colleges, and preferred it to the reluctance and passivity she had found when she first arrived at Radcliffe.

She celebrated this emerging sense of entitlement on the part of students. She even had no difficulty accepting the new words that were defining entirely new concepts, students as "consumers" and the college as the "vendor." But neither she, nor anyone else, imagined the turmoil that was brewing.

22

Radcliffe Sticks to Its Knitting

During the next few years, as outrage against the war in Vietnam intensified, administrators in higher education found themselves in an entirely new universe. Students, who in the recent past had been excoriated for their passivity, were taking over buildings, yelling obscenities at visiting dignitaries, and holding huge, noisy protest rallies.

For those in Fay House, Radcliffe's administration building, the sound of students marching and shouting outside the windows became familiar, but never routine. "They all had on those T-shirts with the clenched fist," said Polly's assistant, Louise Donovan. "I can see those in my mind's eye. And so we all did our work as well as we could and some people carried home the most important papers every single night."

Radcliffe, at first, remained what it had always been. The gracious living expected in institutions educating young ladies was entrenched, bolstered by long-standing routines and regulations. There were still sit-down dinners, sherries in the living room, demitasse after dinner, ten o'clock sign-outs, skirts required and slacks forbidden except at specified times and in specified places, as well as assumed standards of courtesy and polite address, particularly when younger people were communicating with the older and wiser. Harvard had a dress code too. Jackets, shirts, and ties were required in all the dining halls and by some professors in their lectures.

Even though students across the country and all over the world had been making trouble for some time, administrators in Cambridge hoped the time-honored Harvard house system that gave undergraduates access to graduate students and faculty might immunize the university from the worst. Polly believed that it did make things go better for a while. But nothing was enough.

The first Harvard incident occurred in November 1966, when Robert McNamara, then secretary of defense, accepted an invitation to address both graduate and undergraduate students. As the cabinet member most responsible for the odious war, McNamara was an irresistible target. When he left Quincy House, one of the Harvard residential houses, about a hundred young people surrounded his car and began rocking it back and forth. "We were confronting the monster," remembered Donna Lieberman, one of the Radcliffe demonstrators and now director of the New York ACLU. Her sister, Judy, now a professor at the Harvard Medical School, described it as "fun," but McNamara feared that someone might get seriously hurt, so he wrenched open the door of his car and climbed on its roof saying he would answer questions. But the crowd became noisier and uglier, and McNamara, believing he was in some danger, climbed down and escaped through one of the Quincy House doors that was held open for him by a university policeman. With the help of a Harvard undergraduate, Barney Frank, later a prominent Massachusetts congressman, McNamara made his way through an underground tunnel to the Harvard Yard.[1]

Six months later, on May 10, 1967, Polly was faced with the first Radcliffe student protest. She had been busy fund-raising, as usual, throughout the spring, trying to raise money for Radcliffe's new house and renovation of the older dormitories. And on May 9 she recorded excellent news in her journal—a $2.5 million Ford Foundation challenge grant to be matched three for one in three years. But before she had time to savor the good news, she received word that twenty-three students who objected to Radcliffe's policy permitting only a few seniors to live off-campus in non-college housing were staging a hunger strike. They saw the prospect of more on-campus dormitories as a threat to their desire for more privacy and independence. They decided to express their opposition by starving themselves.

Polly met with them in the small off-campus house on Linnean Street—one of those scheduled for demolition to make way for the new dormitory—where they had established themselves. In her journal she wrote that she tried "to elevate the cause," to explain to the students how to go about effecting change in an appropriate way. She scribbled in her journal: "What does one do when a decision goes against one? Try to 'destroy 'the college—or oneself *before* formulating a reasoned statement of the case? Should an anti-intellectual approach be an early resort in an academic or any other community?" She wanted the students to learn something from the incident. "She wanted there to be no humiliation," remembered Sue Bolman, the dean of students. "We must find a way to protect their egos," she told Bolman.

Nonetheless she disapproved of using such serious tactics over what she felt was a trivial issue and, in spite of receiving urgent letters from concerned parents, Polly decided to let the students go hungry for a while. Doctors at the Harvard Medical Center agreed with her that as long as the students had water, they wouldn't do themselves permanent harm. "If they start fainting," they told her, "we'll come pick them up for you."

The strike went on with growing intensity. Its leaders badgered trustees with phone calls, invited the media to watch them set up their headquarters, and sent an open letter to the Alumnae Association decrying Radcliffe's monolithic housing policy which "stunts the educational growth" of students "who outgrow the limited residential options offered at Radcliffe." The *Crimson*, the Harvard student newspaper, joined the fray with outraged editorials accusing Polly of "squashing reform." In spite of Polly's long-standing and well-known accessibility, the protestors insisted they were as concerned with the administration's indifference to student opinion as they were with housing policy. They said they wanted "a voice in Radcliffe." Polly pointed out to them that students' views about the new house had been solicited, but that those students had all graduated. And until that moment, the current students had not shown any interest; they hadn't come to meetings or even gone to see the plans that were displayed in the Hilles Library. Polly also tried to make them understand the economic realities faced by the college; Radcliffe could not afford to do without the room-and-board fees of so many students.

She also took seriously a 1942 policy of the Harvard faculty that required undergraduates to live in a Harvard house, excepting only those who lived at home or who had secured the dean's permission to live elsewhere. Polly said that faculty policies with "educational implications" applied to Radcliffe. And she agreed with this one, believing in the educational efficacy of students living together on campus in a community of concerned adults rather than alone in isolated units. Establishing a house system comparable to Harvard's was the cornerstone of her vision for Radcliffe, and she was not about to have it derailed by the actions of a handful of disgruntled students.

Although the hunger strike took up a lot of her time, Polly's journals make clear that it didn't obsess her. In a May 15th entry she refers to a letter she had just received from the strikers along with a five-page, single-spaced "History of the Hunger Strike" (in which the students refer to themselves throughout as "girls.") But on the same journal page Polly recorded notes about a landscape exhibit on campus, lists of other possible exhibits for next year, notes on an AEC review of civil rights, and little blurbs on students—where they were from, their majors, their dorms—whose parents she was about to approach for money.

In the end she agreed to form a faculty-student committee to study the housing issue and to present a report to the Radcliffe Council. On

June 5, 1967, the leaders of the hunger strike appeared before the Council. In a more than two-hour meeting devoted almost solely to student housing, the trustees made no effort to conceal their disapproval of the strike as a tactic, their resentment of students' harassing phone calls, and their conviction that they were not, in fact, protesting the lack of attention of the administration to their concerns, but rather their inability to get the answer they wanted. The trustees saw the strike as an adolescent temper tantrum, not, as the students called it, the inevitable conclusion to two years of legitimate struggle. They rejected the demands and made clear that, in the future, serious matters needed to be resolved carefully "in an atmosphere free of coercion."

Indirectly, however, the hunger strike got the students what they wanted because it led Polly to examine why off-campus living cost the college so much; off-campus students did not pay anything toward their use of Radcliffe facilities such as the library, gym, or career center. So Polly rearranged the fee structure, adding a third component to be paid by all students regardless of where they lived, a practice now in place in many schools. The year after the hunger strike, with the new required fee and with two of the off-campus houses being demolished to make room for the new house, all seniors were given the option the hunger strikers had fought for. Ironically too few took advantage of it to make a dent in the overcrowding of the dorms Polly was trying so hard to alleviate. So the bunk beds in the overcrowded rooms remained.

The students' attack on administrative inattention may have had an effect on Polly, because over the summer she thought about additional constructive ways to involve students in the formulation of college policies. She decided to form a committee similar to one she had established at Douglass and invited house presidents and elected student government leaders to join her and some top Radcliffe administrators to make recommendations to the Council. Called the Radcliffe Policy Committee, this group was to play an important role in the stormy days that lay ahead. It also made clear to Radcliffe students that, unlike at Harvard, they did have access to their administration.

While the hunger strikers had been concerned with limited Radcliffe issues, it was the war in Vietnam that fueled the next big campus protest—Harvard's first major sit-in—on October 25, 1967. Several hundred students, concerned about the use of chemicals in Vietnam to defoliate trees, contaminate food, and kill peasants, barricaded recruiters from the Dow Chemical Corporation inside a room in Mallinckrodt Laboratory, where they were conducting interviews. For almost seven hours the students prevented the two men from getting out and anyone else from getting in touch with them. As with all of the

Harvard protests, Radcliffe students were very much involved. Polly believed they participated in greater numbers than their proportion in the student body because they "had all sorts of feelings of guilt with respect to the war," knowing that they could not be drafted.

Polly first heard about the sit-in from Dean Kathleen Elliott, who telephoned at noon from Mallinckrodt, where she had been summoned. Polly required Radcliffe deans to rush to protests because they knew the students by name and could identify those who were participating. (Dean Elliott had a pair of shoes reserved for such occasions, which she called her "uprising shoes.") Polly wanted to be sure that students were accurately identified and held accountable for their actions. Elliott and another Radcliffe dean collected the university identification cards of the Radcliffe students sitting on the floor in the hallway.

Although Radcliffe students had to obey all Harvard's rules, the colleges were still administratively separate and had different ways of handling discipline. At Harvard, discipline was handled by an administrative board on which no students served; at Radcliffe, four students and five administrators sat on a Judicial Board. It was now up to this board to decide what punishment, if any, the Radcliffe offenders would receive.

It was a thorny question of principles. Those sitting-in did not think they had done anything wrong. The 1950's standards of courtesy hadn't yet given way so the occasion had been relatively decorous. One of the protestors, Mary Goethals, now a high school science teacher, described it as orderly. "We were totally nonviolent and compliant and good," she said. Some of them even left to attend class and then returned.

There also had been no physical contact with the Dow recruiters, which made the sit-in less serious than the interference with McNamara. Still something bad had happened, and students on the Judicial Board, though they respected the commitments of the protestors, struggled with their knowledge that they had to do something about it. Polly's concern was with the psychological effect on the students on both sides. They were confronting this kind of moral ambiguity for the first time. Judicial boards had never been set up to handle complex political questions, which were entirely different from matters of behavior on which society agreed. "It was just *not* something that a group of involved young people could handle," Polly said years later. "It was quite damaging to some of them." One of the students on the board said she left college early one year because it all got to be too much.

The Harvard faculty was divided, too. Distinguished professors wrote Polly lengthy letters pleading for leniency, because they knew and liked the Radcliffe students involved, or because lenient treatment had been given to those who had harassed Defense Secretary McNamara. Threatening a public official with violence, one professor maintained, was surely more serious than engaging in a "Ghandi-like sit-in."

In spite of her sympathy for the students, Polly saw the situation differently. She did not see what the students had done—imprisoning two guests of the university, restricting their personal freedom, and not allowing them to be heard—as belonging to the tradition of American civil disobedience. She took this matter very seriously. Her journal notes make clear how seriously. She recorded all the particulars in greater detail than she usually expended on administrative matters: the number of identification cards collected, the times and places of the meetings of Harvard's Administrative Board, the facts she presented to the Radcliffe Judicial Board, her polling of the Council on honoring the recommendations of the faculty on discipline, her meetings with individual protestors. It especially distressed her that the students did not seem to understand the importance of freedom of speech and movement, that they had given so little thought to "this aspect of their heritage."

But as she had done at the time of the hunger strike, she kept to her schedule. Over the weekend she went off to a meeting in Racine, Wisconsin, to discuss the "survival" of liberal arts colleges and the possibility of establishing a national lobby to promote their needs and virtues. She returned to Cambridge on Sunday—four days after the sit-in—to face a rally at the Radcliffe Quadrangle expressing solidarity with the Dow protestors. That evening she held a meeting in Cabot Hall, one of the old brick dormitories, to impress upon Radcliffe students what she believed was at stake. Although she usually spoke extemporaneously, she thought this occasion so important that she wrote in her journal the points she planned to make. She told the students that she agreed with their opposition to the war and wanted to oppose it in whatever ways she could. But she also told them that ends, no matter how worthy, did not justify trampling on time-honored freedoms. She explained how deeply she felt about preserving civil liberties: and the "Test comes when it is for a person with whom one disagrees." And she warned them that "the laws of the land pertain at the University and if the University fails to act, outside authorities would have to do so."

Finally, on November 4, 1967, the members of the Judicial Board announced their decision. They placed the students on probation. There were, however, some students whose identification cards had not been collected at the sit-in, but who had come to the administration later and voluntarily turned in their cards saying they were just as guilty as the students being charged. The Judicial Board refused to penalize this group. They did not want to promote what they called "mass self-accusations," which can lead to "hysteria, manipulation and subtle pressures." Polly thoroughly agreed with this decision.

After dealing with the Dow protestors, Polly retreated to her country place in New Boston and enjoyed the winter snows. "Snow deep around but oil had just been delivered & all was comfortable," she wrote in her journal. "Wonderful to see the stars again. Gemini especially impressive."

The protests complicated one already difficult aspect of Polly's job: raising money. In the small black appointment book she carried with her, the college's deficit was listed under "D." In 1968 it was $89,982. A year later it had ballooned to $246,074. The deficit was exacerbated by the relatively large number of students who took leaves of absence or withdrew from college altogether. Dining halls and dormitories were generating far less than was budgeted. Also, the percentage of admitted students who decided to attend declined from eighty-eight percent in 1968 to seventy-three percent in 1969 as did applications from National Merit winners (down to thirty-five percent from eighty-three percent in 1969). Some financial aid applicants had to be moved to the waiting list, whereas only a year earlier, Polly had assured the alumnae that no students were being turned away because they couldn't pay.

Hovering over all this was the necessity of raising the money to match the Ford Foundation grant. This, Polly admitted, "was not too easy." Donors were reluctant to contribute, both those who wanted the college to take a firmer stand against the "radicals," and those who wanted the college to give in to their demands. "You'd go into the office and they'd have the door shut and no secretaries around and they'd want to know what is really going on," Polly said years later. "It was hard to get the conversation back to the needs of the college."

The protests particularly complicated fund-raising for the new house, especially after 114 graduating seniors refused to contribute to the annual fund because they maintained it was wrong for money to be spent on a new dormitory rather than on scholarships. The trustees seriously considered postponing the project, but Polly convinced them that students who were living in precisely the kind of conditions the new house was designed to fix should not be permitted to derail a long-range plan that was in the best interest of future students. And in the end she prevailed largely because she was able to convince Ailsa Mellon Bruce to substantially increase her contribution for the house, eventually named Currier House, in memory of her daughter, a Radcliffe graduate who had died with her husband in the crash of a small plane.

Over and over in her talks with prospective doors, Polly kept emphasizing how vital it was for "liberal friends" to remain loyal. To withhold their contributions and their moral support during such difficult times would hand the radicals an important victory, for nothing would please them more than to see the university weakened. In speech after speech, in letters to sympathizers and to outraged alumnae, Polly kept reiterating the responsibility of Harvard and Radcliffe to abandon neither their students nor their principles. They had to continue to educate their students, even those who were behaving in uncivilized ways. But it was an uphill battle. Polly was able to keep her equilibrium by seeing the disruptions for what they were, a momentary aberration. She summed up her attitude in a June 4, 1969, journal entry when she was preparing a fund-raising speech. "Keep focused on programs and the future," she wrote. "Radcliffe sticks to its knitting."

Meanwhile she kept up with the diversions that had always sustained her. She still kept her bees on the roof of the president's fancy house. One morning, in the midst of all the furor, she realized they were getting ready to swarm: a new queen was about to depart with her drones.

> I remember telling the cook to keep an eye open. About the middle of the morning she called my office and said that the bees were beginning to leave. She sounded quite terrified. I was busy at the moment and said, "You just talk to them, Flora, and tell them to come down on a handy tree. I'll look in just before I go off to a luncheon meeting." Flora called up a little later and said, "They've come down right on the dogwood outside of the kitchen window. They are just hanging there." So I said, "That's fine, you just keep them there, and I'll be over in half an hour." About that time two rather special alumnae from Pittsburgh, whom I hadn't known, arrived and wanted to see me. Of course I wanted to see them and invited them in. We talked for fifteen minutes or so. Then, knowing that my luncheon meeting was looming, I told them that I was sorry but I had a swarm of bees I had to hive and I would really have to leave. One of them looked at me and said, "Oh dear, what are they protesting about now?"[2]

In July, Polly took the sort of vacation she enjoyed the most—flying to Seattle to join Mary, Reiner, and their infant daughter, Laura, for ten days of hiking and picnicking. Once again her journals were filled with lists of birds, descriptions of views and sunsets and the food cooked out in the open.

During these years things never calmed down completely or for very long. Polly aways carried the telephone numbers for the police and fire departments at the back of her small black pocket calendars.

The most distressing part, however, was that she found it increasingly difficult to communicate with the students. She was, after all, a member of the administration, and she was often in the position of defending its policies. Increasingly as these difficult years went on, she was seen as one of the enemies. She kept her porch light burning and continued to go wherever the students were, trudging up to the Quadrangle for meals in the dorms even though many students were unwilling to sit at her table, and when they did, they were just "formal." She spent hours meeting with students whenever and wherever they would come: in her office, in her home, in the dorms, at lunches and teas, in formal committees and informal gatherings. Whenever possible, she engaged them in discussions, to hear whatever they were willing to say and sometimes to explain some action the college had taken. In her journal she grasped at whatever shred of optimism she could. She kept track of her encounters and listed the names of students she talked to. In those turbulent times a congenial conversation warranted a special note in her journal: "Sunday, Dec. 15, 1968—to North House where a Lindsay McDonald had a very thoughtful discussion of her "Utopian college"—'To think I've had a whole hour to talk with the pres of the college about my thing'—then to South House for Chanukah and for Christmas carols." "Now and then there was some openness with students one already knew quite well, such as friends of my children or students whom I'd known in my seminars, or student leaders who had some key responsibility. There were precious moments when we could talk, but on the whole we were cut off . . . and it was hard to understand what was on their minds when we couldn't communicate." She relied on information from adults the students would talk to: the cooks they worked with in the kitchens and the architects working on the new house. Students were willing to tell them what they wanted because they were seen as neutral. Polly called Ronald Gourley, the architect remodeling the older dormitories, "an unlabeled dean."

None of this affected Polly's sympathy for students or her faith in their fundamental decency. She was more willing than many to give them leeway. She understood that they had come of age during traumatic times and that they had arrived at college disillusioned and edgy. "They cared very much about the war," she said years later. "In the back of their minds was the analogy with Hitler's Germany, where, as they saw it, because people did not stand up in time, awful things happened." Many had also been part of the fight for civil rights and "had seen that direct action had gotten things done that government and religion and education had been too timid or too self-centered to attempt and in the process it had altered their basic ways of thinking about human potentialities and rights." And college had always been the time when students were supposed to critically examine their assumptions and their values. She didn't personalize the conflict; she understood that authority, not she, was the target.

Polly's children saw signs of the pressure she was under, but said she didn't get "frazzled." Bill was a Harvard undergraduate, and Chuck was at the Harvard Graduate School of Education, so they could observe first-hand what was happening. They were concerned, but realized, as Chuck put it, that Polly "knew what she was doing." When the family got together, there was "no moaning and groaning," said Mary. "It was very matter of fact."

Trying to stay ahead of the game as well as she could, in February 1968 she organized an official weekend conference for trustees, students, and administrators so that they could talk directly, face to face. Although Polly believed that the February conference did a great deal to lessen the antagonism between the students and the adults, nothing seemed to be enough.

Even freshmen felt emboldened. Rachel Ritvo, a freshman in 1968 who described herself as "a shy kid," nonetheless thought nothing of organizing an "eat-in" to protest the exclusion of Radcliffe freshmen from the dining room where Harvard freshmen ate. By that time Polly had restructured the food service so that Radcliffe students didn't have to trek back to the Quad for lunch. They could pack themselves sack lunches with food put out by the food service. But the only dining room available to them was in the graduate and commuters' building, and the freshmen saw no reason why they should be segregated from their Harvard classmates eating in the Freshman Union. When Rachel and a group of Radcliffe students entered the Union, she confronted the Dean of Freshman F. Skiddy Von Stade, "a polo playing prep school type with a paunch" as she remembered him. He responded that it was beneath a Harvard dean to even talk to a student who would be so rude as to come in where she was unwelcome. "I may be unwelcome to you, Dean Von Stade," Rachel said, "but I am sure my Harvard classmates would welcome me." Eventually Radcliffe students were admitted to the Union.

Polly had reservations about student power, but none about student involvement; when Radcliffe students proposed scrapping the existing student government and replacing it with a stronger organization, which would be known as the Radcliffe Union of Students, she welcomed the idea.

The first RUS constitution called for the inclusion of four students on the Council as regular nonvoting members. The Council turned this down flat for reasons Polly found unconvincing, a reflex reaction to the break with tradition rather than anything substantive. She went back and forth between the students and the trustees, explaining, cajoling, rephrasing, presenting the students' case in the most unmilitant light and the trustees' rejections in the least antagonistic, arranging dinners and meetings between students and trustees using—as she always had—hospitality, food, and good humor to bridge the widening gap. She wanted the students at the table both because she believed it beneficial for them and because she thought their perspective would be helpful. A year later, under her patient guidance, although students hadn't been given everything they wanted, they were members of trustee committees and attended many Council meetings. After a while Polly thought the trustees got to like having students at meetings; in any event, she said, trustee attendance improved.

But the atmosphere in the university did not grow any less tense. Polly called the 1968 academic year the "year of eruption." Students reacted to the disorder around the country—the race riots, assassinations, and the escalation of the war in Vietnam—with outrage. It seemed to many of them that their world was collapsing around them. They were both exasperated and incredulous that the university maintained a business-as-usual attitude in the midst of what they saw as a desperate emergency. In a break with tradition Radcliffe students demanded to have a student speaker at graduation to express their opposition to the Vietnam War and their solidarity with their Harvard classmates who might resist the draft. Polly wasn't happy; no student had ever spoken at a Radcliffe Commencement, and she liked ceremonies to be handled with traditional decorum. But as they phrased it—"it wasn't a request." And she made concessions when principles were not at stake.

The next protest occurred when Polly was attending a conference on higher education in North Carolina at the beginning of December. She received an urgent telephone call from the deans that about twenty African-American students were sitting in the hall of Fay House and refusing to leave until they met with her. They were protesting Radcliffe's failure to enroll more African-American students or to hire an African-American for the admissions office. A black perspective in that office was essential, they insisted, because Radcliffe was almost totally middle-class and ninety-seven percent white, and had made little effort, they said, to seek out girls from lower-class backgrounds where there were likely to be more minority candidates. They wanted to meet with any prospective candidates and to be assured that no one would be hired unless they approved. If the college would agree to subsidize their travel, they were willing to go to inner-city neighborhoods to recruit. They wanted a firm commitment that Radcliffe would admit at least thirty African-American freshmen in next year's class. According to the *New York Times*, it was a fairly "decorous" protest, compared with others occurring elsewhere, and they thought it worth mentioning that most of the "girls were wearing slacks."

Radcliffe's African-American students had been pushing their demands for months. They had begun working with the admissions office the preceding summer and had presented their demands to the Radcliffe Policy Committee in November. Polly herself had met with a group that had unexpectedly rung the bell at Fay House one Saturday afternoon when she was working alone in her office. As she remembered it, she went downstairs to see quite a big group, "a militant group" of black students she did not know. She didn't think it would be a good idea to let them into the building, where all the records were stored, so she suggested that they find a room in one of the other buildings. "It was kind of a cold day. I said, 'if you wait here a moment while I get a coat we can find a room and have a good talk.' And I had to make that decision, do I lock the door when I go up and get my coat or do I trust them not to come in? And I trusted them and they waited perfectly nicely. They hadn't taken over the building. You have to make those decisions and hope for the best, but I realized—if I had locked that door the whole relationship would have changed." They had a lengthy conversation, but then nothing happened, and the students were justifiably disappointed.

The students were unaware that long before their agitation Polly had been trying to increase the number of African-American applicants to Radcliffe. Her financial aid director had helped set up a local Center for Opportunity for Education, which advised and recruited students from schools in disadvantaged areas of Boston. She was also trying to establish closer relationships with some Boston junior colleges in the hopes of increasing the number of African-American transfer students from disadvantaged backgrounds. But there were some real stumbling blocks. Many of these students required considerable financial aid, and Radcliffe was always short of money. And many also needed remedial programs and reduced course loads that Radcliffe could not offer because it didn't control its academic program.

The African-American students had legitimate grievances, Polly felt. They had been patient, and she knew she had not paid enough attention or acted quickly enough. So as soon as she received the call, she left the conference and flew back to Cambridge, arriving about seven hours later. She found a large contingent of African-American students lining the downstairs hall in Fay House and observed that some of the members, largely white, of the militant Students for a Democratic Society, tried to join, but the black students rebuffed them. They wanted their own protest.

Polly delivered what she described as the very long statement that she had written on the plane. "I remember it seemed to last forever, but at least I think it showed them that we were concerned, that it wasn't a trivial response." She said she had intentionally written it down to indicate how serious she was about increasing the number of African-American students at Radcliffe. She promised to include students on a committee to interview candidates for the admissions office. "I said that I wouldn't appoint anyone that they didn't approve and we wouldn't appoint anyone I didn't approve. Either one of us would have a veto."[3]

She said that college staff members and students would be sent to inner-city schools in Boston, Philadelphia, and New York, and that five thousand dollars had been obtained for recruitment. But she refused to agree to admit a fixed number. Although she said that guidelines could be useful, "quotas imply giving a higher priority to numbers than to individuals and I think this would be retrogressive for the College and unfortunate for the students accepted. Every student coming to Radcliffe should know that she was wanted for qualities and promise that we saw in her as a person. She will have worries enough without adding the suspicion that she was accepted only to meet a quota."[4] In addition, she believed it morally wrong to promise an outcome she could not control. Nevertheless, she thought a minimum target of thirty was reasonable, and "I hope that our efforts will be successful, and that we may even exceed the goal." With that, she was relieved to get the students out of the drafty hallway and back to their dormitories in time for supper. She was impressed by the restraint and dignity with which they had conducted themselves, and she was glad about the amount of good conversation which had taken place between them and the staff while they waited for her return.

Two days later Polly sent a letter to alumnae emphasizing her determination to recruit African-American students more actively. Although she said all, including the students, agreed it would be wrong to admit anyone who "would be hurt by the experience," the applications of minority candidates would be considered according to a somewhat different set of standards. SAT scores "must be interpreted differently for students whose educational opportunities have been limited." She asked for increased donations for financial aid and for "making our policies known in your area." And she ended the appeal with a somewhat evangelical ring. "May our efforts prove sufficient to the tasks before us."[5]

The following week the students issued a statement expressing appreciation for the "expediency and thoroughness" of the earlier meeting and their hope that "the spirit of cooperation, communication and innovation" will be a "permanent part of our relationship." Polly was gratified by the constructive approach toward goals about which these students cared deeply, and by their expressed appreciation for the administration's efforts.

Whether it was the more aggressive recruiting, the efforts of the students, or just luck, they not only met the goal of thirty black students for the next year, they exceeded it. For the first time ever the percentage of black students at Radcliffe was the same as the percentage of the black population in the country, a higher percentage than at Harvard or any of the Seven Sisters. Polly gave credit, too, to the publicity engendered by the sit-in. She believed the media attention given to the demands of the African-American Radcliffe students might well "have encouraged other black people to say, 'that might not be a bad place to go.' It's interesting the way some things that look awful turn out to have a silver lining," she said.

Radcliffe continued to attract more and more black candidates. Two years later the number of applicants had increased to 350. The problem was finding adequate financial aid for them. Polly noted in her journal that the thirty-seven were eleven percent of the class but received twenty-seven percent of the aid.

Polly's dealings with the Radcliffe black students had been constructive, but for the student body as a whole the atmosphere of confrontation remained. Harvard students were objecting to the presence on the campus of ROTC, which in their view signified the university's support for "an imperialistic war." They wanted the university to stop giving ROTC either academic credit or free use of Harvard buildings and wanted ROTC instructors to be denied faculty status. In addition, they objected to Harvard's gobbling up of low-cost housing for the university's purposes, the policy of withdrawing scholarships from students on probation, and Harvard's closed system of governance. Like the Radcliffe students, they wanted to be included on governing boards, but Harvard's system was more complex and Harvard's hierarchy far less flexible.

Students for a Democratic Society (SDS), the most militant and radical of the protest groups, had staged a number of mini-protests against ROTC. They disrupted a closed meeting of Harvard's Student-Faculty Advisory Council, where a Radcliffe student had greeted Harvard's President Pusey with an obscenity. They requested permission to attend a faculty meeting when ROTC was on the agenda, but faculty meetings had always been closed and their request was denied. Not taking "no" as the final answer, the students sent Dean Franklin Ford a letter demanding that the December 12 faculty meeting be open to all students. When they were refused again, SDS decided, in a very close vote, to force their way into the meeting.

Faculty meetings were usually held in University Hall, a long, four-story stone structure well inside the venerable Harvard Yard—in an elegant former chapel with high ceilings, chandeliers, and oil portraits of former Harvard presidents on the walls. The administration, suspecting some kind of demonstration, but being unsure what form it would take, decided to move the meeting to Paine Hall, the music building across the street, which they thought would be easier to protect. They turned out to be wrong. On December 12, for the first time ever, students disrupted a Harvard faculty meeting; about two hundred students forced their way into Paine Hall. Dean Fred Glimp ordered them to leave, but they refused and sat down in the hallway. Glimp then cancelled the meeting, warning the students that their action "would be regarded as a serious disruption of the faculty's business." At approximately 3:05 P.M. the protesting students surrendered their university identification cards. Twenty-five Radcliffe students were among them.

In spite of the disruption, nothing was done about ROTC until the following February, when the faculty withdrew all of ROTC's special perks and reduced it to just another extracurricular activity. But they did not abolish it altogether; they felt the opportunity to prepare for military service should be available to undergraduates who wanted it. It was still more of a compromise than President Pusey would have liked. He thought it made no sense to take away support for ROTC because of "an unpopular war."

In the days following the sit-in, the student newspaper, the *Crimson*, weighed in with editorials deploring the "semi-secret" running of Harvard and urging student representation on faculty committees and student presence at faculty meetings. "If the Administration cannot present real arguments for closed Faculty meetings, then the rules should be changed."[6]

Polly had no voice in matters of university governance. Her only responsibility was to determine what punishment should be meted out to the Radcliffe students who had participated in the sit-in. She set about it immediately, informing the students that they faced a conference with the dean in their house and an appearance before the Radcliffe Judicial Board. Harvard put thirty-four students on probation and rescinded their scholarships, but after seven meetings the Radcliffe

Judicial Board decided on a more unconventional punishment—"a more constructive form of penalty than traditional probation," Polly called it. They offered the students a choice between immediate probation or participation in a panel discussion on the governance of the university. Students choosing the panel would be responsible for publicizing it and would have to recruit representatives of varying opinions, particularly on the question of the role and responsibility of students.

Most of the students agreed to the panel, but they wanted to appear as a group rather than as individuals. Ten of them even showed up in Polly's office one morning, unannounced and refusing to give their names, insisting that since they had engaged in political action as a group they should be judged as a group, not weakened by being separated. Polly insisted once again that each individual was responsible for her own behavior and had to be judged individually. But she told the students they could submit a joint statement.

Then there were other complications. Shortly before the panel took place, Polly received a letter from Robert Finch, then Secretary of Health, Education and Welfare, informing her of a law denying various federal loans to students who have "contributed to a substantial disruption of the administration of such institution."[7] Polly disapproved of "repressive legislation" as a way of dealing with student protests, taking matters out of the colleges' hands, but she had little choice. Radcliffe was required to rescind some scholarships.

The students mismanaged the panel, which was held on March 24. They did not adequately publicize it, so most of the members of the Judicial Board were unaware when it was happening and couldn't attend. The students did not submit the required statements or do the extensive research. They resented Polly's effort to divert the discussion from ROTC to what they maintained was a peripheral issue, university governance. But she held her ground. "When the students agreed to the panel," she said, "they knew what the topic was." Their failure to participate adequately meant automatic probation.

Eventually this decision provoked Radcliffe's most serious disruption. But this did not occur until after Harvard University was almost turned upside down. On April 9, 1969, a beautiful, unusually warm spring day, the unthinkable happened. SDS students invaded the university's main administration building, University Hall, forcibly evicted the deans, ousting them out of their offices, physically forcing them down the stairs and out of the building. For the first time ever, students actually manhandled officers of the university. All traces of the fifties veneer of good manners were permanently stripped away. Although opposition to the war was their primary motive, the students were also protesting Harvard's expansion. They wanted the university to stop forcing people out of university-owned apartments to make way for additional medical school facilities and the Kennedy school of government complex.

Polly was in New York trying to raise money when word reached her of what had happened. After making notes in her journal of various fund-raising meetings she had had, she jotted down without buildup or fanfare: "April 9—Wed. At 12 SDS took over Univ Hall."

Even students within SDS were taken by surprise, because there had been a large meeting of more than a thousand students the evening before in Memorial Hall, where the vote was against taking over a building. But at noon, members of the most radical wing of SDS grabbed the microphones and announced that they were going in. Many of those who had voted against seizure felt betrayed and stayed outside, but others thought they had no choice but to bound up the steps in support of their comrades.

Morning classes were just ending and soon a crowd gathered, but most of the students in it were booing the SDS speakers holding the bullhorns. "The mood of that crowd was anything but friendly," reported Government Professor Stanley Hoffman. An hour later, under a long-standing contingency plan, President Pusey convened, at his home, a meeting of the Executive Council, an advisory body that included Polly and the deans of the ten faculties of the University.[8]

The majority of students were still keeping the spectacle at a distance, threading their way through the crowds to the library to work on term papers. Rachel Ritvo, a freshman, was in the Yard when the students went into University Hall, but when five o'clock came, she knew she had to return to the Radcliffe Quadrangle for her work assignment—answering the dormitory telephone. "It never occurred to me not to go back to the Quad to do my bells."

Inside University Hall, students chained the doors shut. The most radical had known well enough in advance what they were going to do to come equipped with chains, keys, and bars. They began to get organized, voting against allowing any marijuana or any members of the press other than the college radio station (WHRB) and the student newspaper. But some journalists were already there and others were admitted later. In some parts of the building the atmosphere was almost festive. Students who had come in as a gesture of support were unaware that elsewhere other students were encamped in administrative offices, rifling files, and removing confidential letters and records, some of which were later published in an underground newspaper.

Outside the building, students were expressing their disapproval. In the middle of the afternoon some undergraduates burned an SDS effigy. From a window of Weld Hall, one of the freshman dormitories in the Yard, at top-decibel level, came the music of Bach's Third Brandenburg Concerto, played on the Moog Electronic Synthesizer. The weather was still balmy.[9]

Many of the protestors assumed there would be some kind of negotiation—"we'd stay overnight, we'd eat, maybe other groups would come in, we'd go off to class." One student left through a window to play in an Eliot House volleyball game and then returned once the game was finished.

But whether from panic or on the advice of those who had studied the recent riots at Columbia, Pusey had already begun to put machinery in motion to bring the occupation to an end. Sandra Walker, a student representative on the Radcliffe Council, remembered her consternation as she watched police forces gathering outside the Harvard Yard—the incongruity of seeing the massive amount of force outside these old academic buildings, which had until this moment been the scene only of classes and conversation, and knowing the fragility of the young people inside. She had an eerie feeling as she watched officers getting out of cars and putting on riot gear. She went directly to Fay House and tried to tell the deans what was going on. "They didn't actually say, 'There, there dear,' but one of the deans did say, 'The best minds in the world are working on this.'"

In the early hours of the following morning, without consulting the faculty, Pusey ordered the police to evict the students. "The feeling was that the disruption would get worse and worse, drawing ever more dissidents to Cambridge, unless it was stopped," Polly recalled years later. "Whether that was true, we shall never know, but the decision was made to call in the police. They came and they acted with considerable brutality. There was a lot of resentment."[10]

Reporters from the college radio station were on hand with a tape recorder when, at about 5 A.M., Dean Glimp informed the students through the bullhorn that they had five minutes to vacate the building. The students joined arms behind the chained doors and sang and chanted, "Hell, no, we won't go," and according to one demonstrator, shook in their boots. Katherine Kaufer Christoffel took off her glasses because she was afraid they might get broken in the melee. The police, about four hundred of them, in light blue uniforms, black boots, helmets, and jodhpurs, waited only three minutes before they cut the chains and rushed into the building. "To this day I have a vivid memory of their being about nine feet tall," said Katherine Christoffel. They began hauling people out. "Some people went limp but most of us just ran down the stairs between the two lines of police on both sides of the outside steps. They were clubbing us as we went down—not hard, but they were definitely hurting us. I think their intent was to bruise and scare, which they succeeded in doing," recalled Carlin Meyer, now a law professor in New York. One student jumped from a second-story window, something that forty years later President Pusey still remembered. But there were no life-threatening injuries, just some cuts and bruises, as the students were hauled into paddy wagons and taken off to the police station to be booked and put into jail cells. Polly wrote in her journal, "20 men 2 women by our health service—bumps, bruises, cuts." Pusey maintained years later that the dean of the medical school was on hand to be sure that no students were seriously hurt. Franklin Ford, the dean of the faculty of arts and sciences, however, suffered a mild stroke soon after the takeover.

At the station a shaggy-haired young man who had been inside University Hall stepped forward and began identifying people, picking out those who had spoken up and who appeared to be leaders. The students had thought he was one of them, but he turned out to be a police informant. Then the students were bussed off to jail. Some were released in an hour, others were kept overnight. Katherine Kaufer's glasses were lost; she was in jail and unable to see.

Polly's journal entry was, "Thur April 10 1969—Glimps report Masters—10:30—Fac Club . . . 200 inside, 1000 outside no talking point—no focus . . . Ugly situation—wanted to resolve it with least possible violence . . . Many leaders left before arrests." She was angry that outside agitators who she believed had come to Cambridge to "get Harvard" had left University Hall when they knew a police invasion was imminent leaving the younger students to face the consequences. The fact that the police had not waited the full five minutes, which WHRB had recorded on tape, was brought out by many of the students when they had to appear in court and resulted in the case against many of them being dismissed.

The police action itself was over in twenty minutes, but the repercussions were long lasting. What came to be called "the bust" galvanized the student body in support of the students who had taken over the building. For the radicals, those were heady days. Meeting followed meeting. "The big lecture halls were packed with students, graduate students, hangers-on—like a celebratory event," one of the protestors remembered. "It was like a festival. Very exciting. A lot of spirit and spontaneity, the feeling that we were taking charge." Students decided to vent their resentment against the bust by boycotting classes. At the same time, the Harvard Corporation issued its own statement suggesting that they might shut down the university to prevent any more building takeovers.

Polly was in a difficult position. As a member of the administration, she was obligated to support its decisions whether she agreed with them or not. She sat at the table at faculty meetings with President Pusey and the deans, but she restricted her comments to Radcliffe concerns, and the University Hall takeover was a Harvard matter. Publicly she supported the administration's stand, but in the private musings of her journal she revealed her misgivings. "Why didnt we convene faculty? to make decision," she wrote, clearly meaning the decision to call in the police. In her view the students were misguided young people whose passions had gotten the better of them. What they needed most was guidance and more education.

"My greatest worry now," she wrote in a letter, "is the backlash that student disruptions have helped to release. They didn't understand that use of force would backfire.... Somehow we've got to keep working for the goals of idealistic young people while teaching them the techniques that are dependable.... To me it is very sad and very dangerous that in reaching for a better society so many are willing to forget the importance of freedom of speech, courtesy and other safeguards on which our civilization depends. Choice of weapons is vitally important at every level."[11]

She believed there were distinctions to be made among the students, and she resented the oversimplification of the press and of some of the university's critics, who seemed only interested in the antics of the group she respected the least: Students for a Democratic Society. She deplored their slovenly appearance, the disrespectful way they talked, and the violence they were willing to use. "Their intolerance, acceptance of guilt by association, and uncritical analyses of many situations are counter to the values of a liberal education,"[12] she wrote to a Douglass faculty member. To another correspondent, she expressed her dismay at the radicals' "deliberate distortion of the evidence, guilt by association and related forms of dishonesty and discourtesy."[13] "Burning books," she told an alumnae gathering, "is not less worrisome when it is done by students. Loss of faith in reason will not solve the problems of our sophisticated society."[14]

She believed that although some SDS supporters genuinely opposed the war in Vietnam, most were interested primarily in aggrandizing themselves and manipulating other students. "We found, as we worked with the SDS group," she said years later, "that if some of their demands seemed quite reasonable and we met those demands, they immediately produced new ones. They didn't want issues to be resolved; their leaders wanted disruption to go on and on."[15]

They didn't like her much either. SDSers dismissed Polly as just another tool of the establishment, allied, as one put it, "with the big boys" bent only on punishment. They saw her as a remote, authoritarian figure whose feminism was outdated and whose reactions to the protests were purely defensive. They saw themselves as fighting a war to end a war and thought her reliance on what one of them dismissed as "Roberts Rules of Order" was condescending and, under these extreme circumstances, irrelevant. They took themselves far more seriously than she took them.

Having raised children, she said, enabled her to see the students as teenagers, who blurted out something nasty and then beat a hasty retreat. While this attitude helped her, it infuriated the radicals. They resented being perceived as trantrumming toddlers who deserved to be sent to their rooms. "To treat us like that and to say, 'I'm the Mom, now cool it, time out' was not respectful. What we were about was substantial."

In the days after the bust, the Harvard faculty took control. Divided between opposition to and support for the police action, they elected an evenly divided committee. Called the Committee of Fifteen, it broke up into three groups: one to look into the causes of the takeover, another into the way the university was governed, and the third to determine what punishment should be meted out to the offending students. One Radcliffe undergraduate was elected to serve on the committee, but Polly had no part to play. Although the Radcliffe students could have been brought before the Radcliffe Judicial Board, Polly felt this would be unfair. She believed that all the students who committed the same offenses should be disciplined in the same way and by the same body. She convinced the Judicial Board and the Council to ask Harvard to assume that responsibility and sent Pusey a letter formally making the request. "I hope this is all that you need from us to effect this action," she wrote. "It has been quite a struggle to bring us all to this point."

Once the transfer was made Polly no longer had any say and many of the Radcliffe students felt she had abandoned them. But she did what she could to help them. When some of the fiercest SDSers were put on probation and quite illegally returned to their old jobs as kitchen assistants, she turned a blind eye. "We knew they were young people who, at that time, weren't talking to their families or any other adults. They were talking to the cooks and waitresses in the dining hall, and it seemed to us more important for them to have that contact and to be earning a little, and be able to live, than it was for us to be too rigid."

More disturbances followed on the Harvard campus. Objecting to Harvard's expansion was one of the reasons students had given for occupying University Hall, and about two weeks later 120 demonstrators crowded into the planning office in Holyoke Center and partially destroyed scale models of future Harvard buildings. They shouted down the planning officer when he attempted to answer their questions and left after an hour of unpleasantness. One lunchtime, about forty students confronted Polly's assistant, Louise Donovan, filling her office with megaphones and, as she put it, "blasphemies." They wanted an appointment with Polly, and Donovan kept asking for their names so she could make one. "They would never give a name and repeated this in various languages." One of the young men shouted, "Are you trying to intimidate us?" Donovan thought that was very funny since there were about forty of them crowded into her small office and she was all alone. Trustees sent her flowers, but Polly didn't take it that seriously.

A week later, Pusey announced the appointment of a committee to "undertake an in-depth study of the University" and promised to relocate tenants in buildings demolished by Harvard. The statement recognized that "the increase in numbers of students and faculty in recent years" has made present channels of communication inadequate.[16] In September a committee of Overseers, including Radcliffe's Helen Gilbert, recommended the creation of a university-wide Committee on Governance with representatives from all the constituencies of the university (excepting only the Radcliffe alumnae). It was not lost on Ellen Messer, the Radcliffe student who served on the committee, that the kind of student-faculty-administration communication Harvard was struggling to bring about was already well established at Radcliffe. She sat at those meetings marveling at what was passing for progress.

Many people hoped Pusey's gestures of conciliation would calm the protestors. But Polly, always a realist, had no such illusions. "I'm afraid we're not out of it yet," she wrote to one of Radcliffe's longtime trustees, Thomas Cabot, "but perhaps we're better prepared than we were a few weeks ago."

With that letter in the mail, she took off for a weekend in New Boston. She left Cambridge early Saturday afternoon on what was a lovely spring day and on Sunday "burned weeds and planted lettuce." It was fortunate that she had a peaceful weekend because two days later it was her turn to be the focus of the students' rage.

Until now, although radical Radcliffe students had been taking part in the various protests, Polly herself had been out of their direct line of fire. They didn't see Polly as "a player" and some of the less militant saw her as benign—ineffective and inconsequential—not an adversary.

Even though some of the radical Radcliffe students felt embittered about Polly's turning them over to Harvard after University Hall, they did not perceive her as an important enemy. Harvard was the object of their anger.

Now they suddenly remembered that shortly before the University Hall takeover, she had put the Paine Hall protestors on probation. Posters announcing an impending protest began to appear—"Bunting Strikes Again!" "FIGHT Radcliffe Probations Rally at 11:00 A.M. March to Fay House—Confront Bunting!" One of the posters had an odd misspelling—turning Fay House into Faye House—not a mistake a Radcliffe student would be likely to make. This reinforced Polly's suspicion that outside agitators were involved.

On April 29 about seventy-five students, men and women, gathered at Memorial Church in the Harvard Yard and marched up Garden Street with banners and shouts, to confront Polly.[17] The *New York Times* reported that the march was led by Naomi Schapiro, "wearing a blue sweater and print skirt." Whenever women were involved, the *Times* found it necessary to report what they were wearing.

Because of all the publicity and because it was so close to the University Hall episode, Polly had no idea how many people might show up or who they were likely to be. The Paine Hall panel was a complex Radcliffe issue that most people probably wouldn't understand or be interested in, but Polly knew that any protest would attract the standard SDS contingent from Harvard and elsewhere.

To add to her concerns, she had been having bouts of faintness, which her doctors wrongly thought might mean heart problems. Nothing, she thought, would be quite as embarrassing as fainting before a mob of ranting students. She discovered a little later her indisposition was only minor and digestive, but she didn't know that at the time and the specter of keeling over was definitely on her mind.

Instead of staying barricaded in her office, she decided to wait for the students on the steps of Fay House, in full view of the Radcliffe Yard. It was a lambent spring day. Vivid white blossoms were on the dogwood tree, a few students were stretched out on the grass, and she always preferred to be outside. So that is where they found her. But they didn't recognize her, so they pushed right past, swarmed into the building and up the wooden stairs to her office. From inside the building, Polly could hear, "She isn't in here," and then, "She's down at the front door." Before they rushed back downstairs, they managed to scatter some papers around her office, which one of the Harvard seniors stopped to pick up. Alice Dodds, Polly's secretary, thanked him.

Back downstairs Polly immediately recognized some Harvard graduates, "SDS pros," as she described them, who had been hanging around Cambridge for just such occasions. They launched the protest with some fiery speeches, followed by milder ones by Radcliffe students. But quickly the event was taken over by students who looked very young and who Polly deduced were most certainly Harvard freshmen. At that point she thought, "Sure—They'd have been in their dorms when University Hall was taken over and they'd watched it and they hadn't had the courage to go out and so here, on this nice day, this mild, civilized protest at Radcliffe, they were going to be part of the modern world. Daring young men would slide around in front of me, and with touching effort, say something nasty. I remember one rather stout chap who set himself squarely in front of me, yelled 'PIG,' just once and backed away. Watching their faces, as I could, I felt my worries evaporate. This group would not turn vicious. . . . I knew I had nothing to fear. I began to enjoy the whole affair."

The Radcliffe students wanted Polly to be given a chance to answer questions, but the men were ruder, screaming questions, epithets, and obscenities and loudly asking whether she was senile. The assembled reporters had a good view of it all. The *New York Times* described Polly as a "trembling 58-year-old biologist" and wrote, "The gray-haired Mrs. Bunting stood with one arm clenched around her waist, a large brown handbag suspended from it. She squinted in the bright sun and trembled slightly.

"She maintained, despite the taunts, a few of them scatological, that the participation of the students in the panel had not been satisfactory." One of the Radcliffe students, Marjorie Angell, shouted, 'That's not the question. Is Mrs. Bunting's participation satisfactory?'"

After about half an hour, Polly brought things to a close. "We seem to be going around in circles," she said softly and walked into the building. Some of the protestors followed her. "As we go in," one of the students proclaimed, "I think we should tell Mrs. Bunting what we think of her." One student in blue jeans took him at his word. "I think you should be ashamed of yourself," he said to Polly.

Once crammed into Polly's office upstairs, the students continued their tirade. "We demand that there be no punishment for this panel and for the Paine Hall sit-in," Marjorie Angell said, "and we are not going to stop until the university stops throwing people out of their homes and ends R.O.T.C."

Polly sat down at her desk while students crowded around, some holding signs, others hurling questions and charges. The Radcliffe students were becoming increasingly distressed by the acrimony and kept pleading for Polly to be permitted to answer. After about ten minutes, all but three of the Radcliffe students left. They sat on the floor, clutching their green book bags, and talked quietly with Polly for a little while. "The women had been bothered by the incivility of their fellow protestors," Polly commented years later. Once the press left, they really talked, "but by that time the probation issue had lost its charm. The discussion flagged . . . the Radcliffe students wanted to clarify a few points, but they also just wanted it to end. They were quite unhappy about it, and . . . I never heard about Paine Hall discipline again."

The page-one photograph that appeared the following morning in the *New York Times* shows students in the office holding up signs. Polly is in the corner with her chin on her left hand, looking calm. The students don't look too upset either. Afterward she was interviewed by television reporters and said that she didn't think the students really wanted to discuss the issues, they just wanted to take up her time, "which is fine by me." In a sidebar to their main article, the *New York Times* quoted an unidentified Harvard professor as saying, "I wish Harvard had a president who was as much of a man as Mrs. Bunting."

Polly's journal account was unembellished and brief and characteristically devoid of drama. But she put the number of students at about two hundred—in contrast to the seventy-five reported by more objective sources (the *New York Times* and *Harvard Today*) perhaps an indication that they seemed to her more threatening than she was prepared to admit. Still she didn't let the unpleasantness spoil her life. That evening she had dinner with friends, and the following evening went to a performance of the musical *1776*. The following weekend she made special note of enjoying a lovely luncheon. "Cold wind—but great—clams, lobsters, steak etc."

The morning after the confrontation, Polly explained to Erik Erikson over breakfast that she thought the episode hadn't particularly upset her because it was easier for a woman to cope with these situations than for the men at Harvard. She could take them in stride because she wasn't concerned about her reputation or her career. She had never been ambitious for power, and if things went badly it wouldn't change anything. She wasn't worried about her future administrative career the way many of the men were. For them, to have something that public *not* work well would be a blot on their record. Polly reiterated what she had said often before and was to repeat many times later. "My career wasn't that important. I wanted an interesting life."

The takeover of University Hall was the most drastic of the Harvard protests, but it wasn't the last. In a short while students in the Yard holding bullhorns became part of the landscape. "Harvard Square looked like a war zone," remembered Louise Donovan. "So many windows were broken that they were all put up cardboard. No one even tried to repair them because they knew they would just get broken again." There were a series of destructive disturbances at the Center for International Affairs and elsewhere within the University, but there were no more confrontations at Radcliffe. Still, Polly said, she never knew what to expect. "It was indeed an anxious time."

The end of the 1969 academic year marked the end of what Polly called the year of "eruption." As they had the preceding year, Radcliffe students demanded that there be a student speaker at commencement, and the speech she gave was bitter and angry, lashing out at the university for ROTC, the expansion into Cambridge and the taking over of low-cost housing, blaming the university for the students' disillusion and discouragement. When she finished, Polly did not shake her hand.

Polly used that commencement to make a gesture to the students by inviting the Reverend William Sloane Coffin, a hero to many of the radicals and someone high on their list of requested speakers, to give the commencement address. She wasn't surprised that not everyone agreed with her choice, but she took full responsibility, explaining in a letter to a disgruntled parent that she hoped he "could help some of our students formulate the ideas with which they are wrestling." She said that after she had invited him, it occurred to her that a more conservative speaker might well have triggered a more turbulent event, although that was not her reason.

Later in this letter Polly wrote: "I certainly agree with your approach to the improvement of society rather than that of our more militant students who, incidentally, know where I stand. But I also honor Mr. Coffin's sincerity and the way he has backed his words with action over the years. There are so many manipulators influencing the young today—so many whose central concern is power. His idealism and steadfastness of purpose add a welcome contrast to their opportunism. Therefore, although there were parts of Mr. Coffin's speech that bothered me"—(perhaps the sentence about not trusting anyone over thirty, including their parents)—"I'm not sorry, on balance, that he was our speaker, nor surprised that the choice was controversial."[18]

No one knew what was likely to happen when students returned to campus the following fall, so over the summer Pusey wrote Polly to inquire about the safety of her campus. He was concerned, he wrote, about the personnel files, books, and records and asked if any steps could be taken to protect them. Polly sent back an inventory of buildings and their contents, assuring him that "we do have locks on all doors and use them pretty regularly. But it's clear that the Radcliffe buildings and records would certainly be vulnerable to a concerted attack."

Over the summer an important communication went out to all members of the Harvard-Radcliffe community—the statement of "Rights and Responsibilities" that had been drafted by the Committee of Fifteen, spelling out for students what behavior was required and what would and would not be tolerated. Just in case anyone connected with Radcliffe hadn't received it, Polly sent out her own memo, putting Radcliffe students on notice that they were expected to behave and that it was their responsibility to be familiar with the rules and to abide by them.

Polly called the 1969–1970 academic year the "Year of Metamorphosis and Anxiety." It was marked by another occupation of University Hall, this time to protest lack of opportunities for minority employment on Harvard construction projects. Other students occupied the office of the new dean. Building takeovers became so routine that a member of the Harvard news office described himself as the one who had the job of announcing to the press which building it was this time that the students had taken over. But these episodes were expected now—more like the aftershocks of an earthquake rather than the main event.

In October two Radcliffe undergraduates were arrested early one morning for putting up SDS posters in Cambridge and were charged with "idle, disorderly conduct and defacing public property." SDS was trying to become the representatives of the Radcliffe kitchen workers: they labeled themselves the "Worker-Student Alliance" and demanded the end of "male chauvinism" in Radcliffe's kitchens, the elimination of the ninety-cent wage differentials between male chefs and female cooks, extra cooks for special dinners, a second dishwashing machine in East House, plastic-dish machine racks instead of metal ones, and repair of inefficient machines. Polly consulted the kitchen workers and learned that they did not want student interference; they had a union they trusted. Eleven days later Polly issued an official statement announcing that for Radcliffe to negotiate with anyone but the "Building Services Employees International Union ... would be illegal as well as undesirable." She said she had visited the kitchens, observed operations, and talked with the workers there and had found morale to be high. "Although they enjoy knowing students and respect the job students do in the kitchens, the regular staff resents having students act as their self-appointed representatives."[19] That was the end of that.

African-American students began again to agitate for more black personnel in the offices of financial aid and admissions, and now the rhetoric and tone were more adversarial, phrased in terms of "demands" rather than requests. "We feel we deserve an official and immediate explanation," read one letter. When they demanded a meeting with both Polly and the director of admission that very week, they wrote: "It is essential that both of you be at the meeting. An unwillingness of either one of you to act in response to this letter could only indicate a further disregard of the rights of the Black community and your responsibilities to them." In response to a particularly belligerent demand, Polly noted, "This was presented to me at a 6:30 'meeting' of about 40 black men & women in Cabot.... I said that I didnt believe it was in the best interest of any group to be favored above other groups—Someone said that there was 'no use continuing this conversation with President Bunting.'"

Polly took such occasions in stride and responded to each letter, setting up meetings. She gave ground where she could. She accepted the idea of a Minority Student Admissions Committee and always agreed to meet, although she said that "afternoons are better."

It was the bombing of Cambodia and the shootings at Kent State at the end of the 1970 academic year that served to unite the campus. Students, faculty, and administrators came together in their distress and attended a mass meeting to discuss the possibility of a university-wide strike, but this time the students were not attacking the university, but expressing consternation at the expansion of the war and the violence at home. No strike actually took place. Polly noted in her journal the universities that were closing or on strike: Dartmouth, MIT, Princeton, Columbia, Yale. In comparison, Harvard and Radcliffe were calm, but tense. Students called a mass meeting in Radcliffe's gym to vote on a strike. They wanted legislation in the United States Senate requiring the withdrawal of all troops from Cambodia in thirty days and from Southeast Asia in eight months. Polly stayed involved and accessible, attending supper in Whitman dormitory where, she noted in her journal, "People distressed—need specifics." The following day, May 7, students dropped in to her office all afternoon needing to talk. A week later students were still meeting in their houses, giving antiwar speeches.

Things were different, however, from a few years earlier. When an SDS group decided to burn the ROTC building, Shannon Hall, freshmen heard of their plans and beat them to the site, joining campus police in protecting the building.

Nonetheless "that May was a disaster," Polly said years later. "Many students were too upset to work effectively but they were also reluctant to leave their friends or go home. They were in misery." At a May 7 meeting the faculty decided to give students options for finishing their courses: taking exams, completing their papers during the summer, writing extra papers or taking makeup exams the next fall. The idea was to end the semester quickly and send everyone home. As Rachel Ritvo remembered it, "People were beginning to gather and were looking for a way to focus the cause, and I think the decision was, 'Let's disperse this crowd before it finds its voice.'"

The ending had a ragged edge. At the close of the academic year nineteen Radcliffe students were involved in antiwar demonstrations that violated the Resolution on Rights and Responsibilities. Two were given suspended sentences; nine, warnings; charges were dismissed against five; but three were expelled.

In spite of the turmoil most students stayed the course. In a 1970 speech to alumnae, Polly lavished praise on the graduating class that had been "through this whole period of turbulence." She pointed out that seventy-five percent of those who came in September 1966 had graduated on time, and another fifteen percent would graduate the next year, and of those who had graduated, ninety percent did so with honors—a new Radcliffe record. Even during the worst, the 1968–1969 academic year, there was a drop in book circulation in the Radcliffe library of only five percent.[20] "The life of the mind still thrives at Radcliffe,"[21] Polly said.

Looking back on this time years later, Polly gave students credit, not only for the changes they brought about within the university, but also for the moral leadership they provided about the war. She said they were "way ahead" of her in their understanding of Vietnam. She had not been paying attention to it, but after listening to them she joined in several efforts to express opposition to the war. In 1969 she joined seventy-eight other college presidents in signing a petition urging Congress and the president to end the war, a petition not signed either by Pusey of Harvard or Kingman Brewster of Yale. Brewster sent President Nixon his own letter asking for the unconditional withdrawal of American troops. After the bombing of Cambodia, Polly joined more than thirty college presidents in expressing to President Nixon their deep concern and their hope that a meeting might be arranged to discuss the matter. And she was one of the sponsors of an antiwar fund, asking faculty to contribute a day's pay to a fund for peace candidates in the November election. Other sponsors included Polly's old friend Salvador Luria, who had invited her to the Cold Spring Harbor conference and Biology Professor George Wald, who had written to Polly pleading for leniency for his students involved in the Paine Hall sit-in. Nearly twenty years later she said publicly that she had found it "sobering and also exhilarating" to discover as she struggled with the young during these stormy days "that quite often even the more unkempt and inarticulate were reaching for the right questions, questions that most of their elders chose to ignore or overlook."[22]

The year before Polly left Radcliffe, when the worst of the uprisings were past, she spoke at a baccalaureate service of "the emergence of a generation of young people that constitutes a fluid but very powerful social force." There had always been generational affinities, she said, but this particular generation had "a strong horizontal cohesiveness" that was different, and gave them a potential power greater than other "vertical" groups like labor unions and political parties "that have worked for or against change in the past." She had no way of knowing, of course, if it would persist or break apart, "but it has brought profound changes to colleges throughout the nation and those changes that are surviving in this University seem for the most part, to be good ones."[23]

By the fall of 1970 a different spirit was evident. As Polly described it long afterwards, "Many older students had lost confidence in SDS ringleaders. They realized the extent to which they had been manipulated by them. They were still concerned about Vietnam but they were going to be more careful about their behavior. Protests had not done that much good and had put them in positions that they did not look back on with satisfaction. The mood was changing. Incoming freshmen came with quite different perspectives from those of earlier classes. They had been at home with their families when the disruptions at Columbia and elsewhere were being discussed. Many of them had resolved not to get caught up in such activist movements. Students tend always, it seems to me, to be eager to act out what's being thought and said in the world around them, the world they value."[24]

New issues were coming to the fore. "The great student concern that year was related to Harvard's investments and how both colleges voted their proxies.... Students felt that the University should invest with an eye to its social responsibilities."

When African-American students sat in at University Hall to protest apartheid in South Africa, they agreed to leave if the police would promise to protect the hi-fi equipment they had brought in with them. By this time the sit-in was only a symbol. But there were still a few sputterings left. In February 1971 Polly noted in her journal, "SDS planning to stage protest at Currier dinner when Harvard deans come. Authorized Archie Cox to order trespassers off the property and invoke R & R."

When the tumult finally subsided, Radcliffe and Harvard were different in many ways. None of the niceties or restraints of the 1950's had survived. Gracious living had been replaced by convenient living. Sit-down dinners had given way to dinner cafeteria style. The big sign-out books—in which students had written exactly where they were going and when they would be back—were gone. Parietal restrictions gave way to dormitory autonomy. Students had a voice in the college and in the university and served on high-level committees in both institutions. Marijuana was "more prevalent than beer. Someone around was smoking it daily." Both style and substance were vastly and permanently altered. Eventually the university regained its equilibrium. Polly had never lost hers. She emerged, as Derek Bok was to say many years later, "with all her values intact, calm, good humored and steady as a rock."[25]

In September 1970 Currier House opened, relieving some of the most onerous overcrowding. Polly had finally accomplished one of the first tasks she had set for herself when she took up her post ten years earlier. Like Hilles Library, the new house embodied many of Polly's deepest convictions about education. It was a house, like those at Harvard, a residential and academic center for scholars of all ages with the additions she wanted—small kitchens, room for families with children, an embodiment of her belief in a full life.

She had stayed involved in the details of the new house throughout the chaos. While she paid attention to the administrative details, such as the possibility of adding more beds and controlling dining room costs, it was the aesthetic details that interested her even more. She wanted the windows to have a certain shape and to be sure the design of the facade would be interesting. She cared about the furnishings and the colors. There were to be yellow curtains, "really upholstered chairs *not* metal ones," television sets, more counter space in kitchens, cushions on the bench in the living room, and small accoutrements to make students' lives easier: a suitcase room and shampoo bowl on each floor and wooden coat rods outside the dining hall. She hired an official college decorator and landscape designer to make the dormitories more comfortable and the campus more inviting. During the unsettled times, these civilizing influences, she firmly believed, were as essential as ever, if not more so.

Currier House was formally launched with a moving tribute by Paul Mellon to both his sister, who had supplied most of the funds, and his niece, for whom the building was named, as two modest women of principle. In many ways it was the culmination of the work of another modest woman of principle who finally saw the realization of her vision for Radcliffe's campus.

Polly had said on many occasions, that ten years was all she wanted to spend as a college president. But when her tenth anniversary arrived, she was in the middle of one more major struggle and she felt she needed to stay to see it through.

23

The Fuzzy Relationship

When the ferment calmed, the Harvard and Radcliffe governing boards could turn their collective attention once more to an issue which had been raised repeatedly not only since Polly's arrival in Cambridge, but since Radcliffe's founding: the amorphous, evolving, complex relationship between Radcliffe and Harvard. It had been written into Radcliffe's charter back in 1882 that Radcliffe's "funds and property" could be transferred to Harvard when Radcliffe considered such a disposition "wise" and when Harvard would "consent to assume" such a burden or privilege. So the possibility of Radcliffe being subsumed into Harvard had been implicit from the start.

Polly had been thinking about the connection since the beginning of her presidency. How could she not? It would have been like ignoring the elephant in the living room. Even before her inauguration, students who were members of a student committee on Radcliffe-Harvard relations asked if she thought merger lay in Radcliffe's future. She put off answering. And at her inauguration President Pusey said that he had never understood the relationship between Harvard and Radcliffe, but he knew he liked it. Polly thought, "How very, very nice.... He has chosen to keep that relationship fuzzy, and I am not going to ask him to clarify anything, at least not until there is a pressing need."[1]

During Polly's second year, however, Pusey wrote to her asking if she and the Radcliffe trustees would consider a "closer relationship" to Harvard. Pusey, a Midwesterner, had grown up with coeducation. Years later, looking back, he remembered thinking the time had come to discard the "antiquated" arrangement that was "proper in Boston but not anywhere else" and to put Radcliffe where it belonged. He had come to feel that it was "silly" for Radcliffe to have a president of its own when it had no faculty and all its students were being educated in the Harvard Yard.

Polly took Pusey's letter to the Radcliffe trustees, but they weren't ready. They thought it preferable to move incrementally, slowly transferring, "from time to time" whatever administrative functions the two institutions could agree upon, but not Radcliffe's "funds, its real estate, or its corporate organization."

Polly herself dismissed the idea of merging in one of her first annual reports for the 1960–1961 academic year when she quoted former Harvard President James Conant as saying, "Harvard is coeducational in everything but theory," and asked rhetorically if the time had come to revise the theory. She answered with an emphatic "no," saying that women's special needs were overlooked in coeducational institutions and denied in women's colleges and that Radcliffe still had an important role to play in expanding women's opportunities. Using two of her favorite words, she said Radcliffe had the potential for "investigation" and "experimentation," which could be lost if Radcliffe merged "indistinguishably" into Harvard.

In these early years of her presidency she often described Radcliffe as the college and the advocate for all the women at Harvard University—undergraduates, graduate students, postgraduate women of the Institute, wives of graduate students, administrators, staff members—and made a point of welcoming all of them at the start of the academic year. Radcliffe, she said, was "a good vantage point from which to go to Harvard & to which to return."[2] Harvard professors, all of whom were male in those days, were focused on their subject matter and might be unaware of the ways in which women differ; "therefore Radcliffe has a job," and should be noted on the diplomas of the women, just as Harvard's men had the house to which they belonged on their diplomas.[3]

At the same time, Polly worked diligently to end a number of long-standing practices that were discriminatory. During her presidency Harvard finally agreed to award its B.A. to Radcliffe students. Women had been attending classes there since 1943, but it took twenty more years before they received Harvard degrees. This was particularly important for graduate women, finally admitted directly into Harvard's arts and sciences' departments in 1961; the Harvard Ph.D. opened many more doors than the far less prestigious Radcliffe one. And not only prestige, but money was at stake. Once women were Harvard, rather than Radcliffe graduate students, they gained access to far more financial aid. But not all Harvard faculty thought this was a good idea. The chairman of the psychology department expressed his strong preference for the old system, with its separate lists of men and women under which women would be admitted to graduate school by Radcliffe and would have access only to Radcliffe financial aid. Polly responded icily, "One could just trust that the money for the women would run out before there would be too many of them."[4]

She brought Harvard faculty to Radcliffe to solve one of Radcliffe's longtime inadequacies—the advising of freshmen—and convinced Harvard to count advising as part of the teaching load. She established what came to be called "interhouse dining," offering free meals at Radcliffe to Harvard students during the week in exchange for reciprocal meals for Radcliffe students at Harvard on weekends. Once Hilles Library was opened, and so many Harvard students were studying there, she succeeded in finally having removed an exclusion that had rankled generations of Radcliffe students: in 1966 she got Harvard to open its undergraduate library, Lamont, to women.

Then there were the behind-the-scenes administrative mini-mergers that attracted little attention, like combining the two registrars' offices, the two purchasing offices, and somewhat later the two police forces. She ended some practices that were patently ridiculous, like requiring Radcliffe to pay for chemicals for any sections of chemistry courses that happened to meet in Radcliffe buildings. "Mere housekeeping, but not a negligible expense for the College," Polly wrote many years later. "As long as such items were brought up at reasonably tactful moments, justice prevailed. The important thing was not to push for too many the same year, and not to be talked into any that didn't make sense to us at Radcliffe. It was all rather fun."

During her year in Washington, viewing Radcliffe from a distance, Polly began to see the separation of the two colleges as "a silly setup" that interfered with Radcliffe's effectiveness. Radcliffe's lack of money was handicapping its students because of its inferior facilities and inadequate financial aid. Polly ruminated in her journal: "Been going steady quite a while," and wondered about Radcliffe's "dowry" and whether Radcliffe's assets would be sufficient to have it established as "one of Harvard's tubs," Harvard vernacular for each of its discrete schools.

So it was a practical response to a worsening financial situation that initially led Polly to push for closer ties with Harvard. She thought first of what she called "incorporation," bringing Radcliffe into Harvard as a unit, rather like the British colleges within Oxford and Cambridge or Douglass College within Rutgers, a unit committed to women such as those committed to "the best interests of the football players."

Once her AEC appointment was over she did something she had never considered doing before: she interrupted Pusey's summer vacation in Bar Harbor, Maine, telephoning to ask if she could come up and talk with him. Harvard was pretty much run from Maine during the summer, because all the Fellows had their boats there and were, as Pusey put it, "sailing men," who frequently held meetings about university business on one boat or another. Even though Pusey had suggested a closer connection before, Polly felt she needed to clarify matters before "muddying the waters at Radcliffe." Pusey was very cordial, invited her for lunch, and said he would like nothing better than to see Radcliffe incorporated within Harvard. Polly did not know how the trustees would react, since it had been several years since she had raised the issue. She wanted to bring it up at the first meeting following her leave of absence, because she felt obligated to inform them of her luncheon discussion. She hoped they would form a committee to study the question, and resolve it before Radcliffe launched its major capital fund campaign.

As so often happens in delicate negotiations, things did not go exactly according to plan. Although Polly had not mentioned anything to anyone about her conversation with Pusey or her intentions, a couple of trustees had also been thinking about tying Radcliffe more closely to Harvard and made that suggestion in a morning meeting of the finance committee preceding the November 18, 1965, trustee meeting. There had been no collusion, but when Polly brought up incorporation later that day, some trustees wondered whether there was a plot and reacted vehemently against the whole idea. "The coincidence did not help," Polly admitted. But even years later she insisted that she wasn't angry at the unexpected turn of events. It was just one of those "bumps along the way" that can happen as you maneuver an institution toward where you want it to go.

Despite the debacle at the trustees' meeting, she still recommended the establishment of a committee to study what incorporation would involve. What had begun, for Polly, as a desire for greater financial stability for Radcliffe slowly began to take on more significance. She wanted women to have more opportunities, and she began to see that if Radcliffe was a pedestal, Harvard was a far higher one. If Harvard fully accepted Radcliffe as one of its own, if it illustrated by its actions that it valued women's intellectual contributions, that would give a new legitimacy to her crusade.

Ten days after the trustee meeting, she summarized what had happened in a letter to Pusey. She referred to the "number of lively little meetings" that had taken place even after the official one ended, and she had already left Cambridge for a National Science Foundation meeting in Washington. She reiterated her long-standing convictions about the needs of women and the nature of their differences from men, but now she cast them in a slightly new light, emphasizing Harvard's obligation to remedy past inadequacies—a kind of affirmative action for women at Harvard. She said she had concluded "that Radcliffe's special mission will be accomplished when it is incorporated *as a distinctive unit* within Harvard University or, to say it the other way, when Harvard cares enough about the education of women to want to see it carried forward as effectively as possible." She concluded with an uncharacteristically coy little postscript. "I can imagine no step that would have more social and educational impact on women's education in this country than to have *Harvard* believe that women's education is too important to leave to women."[5] To achieve her objective, Polly was willing to do whatever she thought was necessary, even if she had to play the role of the demure female.

Despite their reluctance, the Radcliffe trustees set up a committee to study the question, appointed by the chairman of the board, Mrs. Gilbert. Then a strange thing happened. The new committee held a meeting, and without even inviting Polly to attend let alone make any presentation, its members decided that the time was not right for a closer connection between the two colleges. No proponents of incorporation were on the committee, nor were any called to argue the case.[6] Polly was dumbfounded that she had been excluded, and was never sure how great a role Helen Gilbert had played. According to Polly, Gilbert's feelings on a closer Harvard-Radcliffe connection were "different ways different days. She could be with one group and say it was just the finest thing and had to be, and then she could be with another group and it was a terrible thing." And she did this, Polly thought, without knowing it.

Polly's handwritten response to Gilbert after getting a report of the meeting reflects her frustration. "*Thanks very much:* I had thought the assignment was to decide what the arrangement would or could be if Radcliffe was incorporated within Harvard. . . . I certainly think the Trustees should have a report and I could see the report stating that the committee had met and did not feel the time was right but I'm sorry if the committee (or trustees) decide to drop the matter without either listening to a proponent or clarifying the possibilities."

Years later Polly admitted that she had been frustrated by the turn of events. "I wondered whether to take it as a vote of no confidence and submit my resignation, but decided that that would be over-reacting. . . . A likelier interpretation was that they honestly felt it was such a poor idea that it should be dropped without further consideration. If the key trustees on that Committee were that strongly opposed, it was not the moment to raise the issue."[7]

The moment didn't come again for three years. The catalyst, in the fall of 1968, was the decision of Yale and Princeton to become coed in all ways, including housing. That prompted some moderate, nonradical Harvard and Radcliffe students to decide they would like men and women to live together in Harvard and Radcliffe houses. These were more traditionally minded students who had never liked the violence and disruption, but who still wanted a part in changing their university. Now they had a cause. They went about it soberly, setting up a committee that met over a period of weeks, and doing quite a bit of research both in Cambridge and in other colleges. They came out with a report making the case for coresidence and requesting that it be started with an experimental exchange of about fifty students between three of the Harvard houses and the Radcliffe houses—150 men and 150 women.

It was 1968. Radical students were sitting-in in Paine Hall; African-American students were sitting-in in Fay House; antiwar protests were in full force across the country; rioting students were shutting down universities. So the polite request of moderate students for a change in their housing arrangements was immediately taken very seriously by Polly and the Radcliffe trustees. They were relieved to be presented with a well thought-out proposal by students who were courteous.

When the students, however, sent their proposal to Pusey, he responded that it would be impossible to institute coed housing as long as undergraduates were governed by two separate administrations. If women lived in the Harvard houses, but continued to report to the Radcliffe deans, he said, they would not be full members of the houses. Polly agreed. "One house under two administrations would mean educational chaos."[8] The students responded predictably: then let's have one administration; let's merge the two undergraduate colleges.

Polly immediately saw the possibilities and shifted from pushing incorporation to supporting a complete merger. She speculated in her journal about the best way to proceed. (*"When do we ask??"*) and wondered how best to put together Radcliffe's "dowry." "As long as R has separate corp—women will be dependent on Harvard's generosity —privilege not right. . . . Important for wife to have her own spending money even if its only egg money—" She was still working out in her own mind just how much Radcliffe would have to relinquish. "Could Radcliffe keep property if it didnt keep function?" she asked in her journal. She asked Pusey's advice about the best way to proceed, and he recommended that Radcliffe make the request. For Harvard to initiate merger negotiations would look like "the big guys taking something away."

The students pushing for coresidence were eager for the negotiations to proceed. But Helen Gilbert was distressed that "the cart was driving the horse," that students' pressure for coresidence was propelling Radcliffe toward merger. She wanted to slow things down. The students, on the other hand, wanted to speed things up, and they began to become more aggressive. They had seen in other contexts the effectiveness of demonstrations, and they threatened their own version: staging coed sleep-ins in the Radcliffe dormitories. "The thought of the publicity that would result was very unattractive," Polly said, and had its impact on the trustees' deliberations. Polly convinced them that the time had come to rethink Radcliffe's relationship to Harvard.

She set up a special meeting of the Radcliffe Board on February 22, 1969, and invited Pusey to speak. After full discussion, the trustees, including alumnae trustees, voted without a dissent to recommend that Harvard be asked whether it was willing to consider a new relationship. But now a new factor entered the negotiations. Many of the alumnae became upset enough to send Polly urgent letters warning against obliterating Radcliffe and pleading particularly for the preservation of Radcliffe's name and its "identity," even though no one had yet been able to define exactly what that "identity" was.

Before discussing the matter with Harvard's governing boards, Pusey decided to bring the question to the faculty because they would be asked to assume additional responsibilities in the Radcliffe houses. The faculty discussed the matter briefly on April 8, 1969, and set up an ad hoc committee to report before the end of the academic year. But the very next day, students took over University Hall, and the urgent need to contain the chaos swept everything else aside.

Since the faculty was enmeshed in unraveling the consequences of the University Hall occupation, they did not set up the committee to consider the Radcliffe connection until late summer. Consequently it wasn't until the following January that the faculty endorsed the idea of the merger. This delay produced unforeseen complications. It afforded Radcliffe alumnae the opportunity to rethink the whole question and to realize how much they disliked the idea of their college disappearing. "The symbolism of the name meant more to them than I had imagined," Polly said. In an effort to placate them the Council voted to include the president and vice-president of the Alumnae Association in its meetings when merger was being considered. In the same spirit of cooperation four trustees were invited to join the association's committee on merger. Polly also rounded up some students to attend the alumnae merger committee's meetings.

The discussions began cordially. The alumnae reported that the presence of students, Polly, and Helen Gilbert at their meetings changed them from a succession of dull committee reports to lively discussions. They praised the way the entire college community was working together. But the honeymoon was short-lived.

By September 1969 the Alumnae Association had set up a collection of committees to look into the whole question from many different angles, so that by the time the faculty committee met, even the alumnae trustees who had originally voted for a closer relationship were having second thoughts. And other committees of other constituencies were sprouting: the Harvard faculty and Overseers had several committees, Radcliffe students and trustees each had a few of their own, and finally a small, over-arching committee of members of the Harvard and Radcliffe governing boards was established, which came to be called "the top committee" and included Polly and President Pusey.

The trustees who had voted in favor of merger back in February seemed to be no longer sold on the idea. On April 13, 1970, Polly had lunch with four trustees, including two from the "top" committee, and confided in her journal: "They are worried about my presenting it [merger] too positively. I assured them that I saw no chance this year—did hope the top committee would gather ideas this spring and come in with a plan in the fall which could be acted on next spring." To her journal she made clear just how seriously she took this issue. "If a decision was made to drop the matter I would resign. As long as progress is being made I am willing to stick by since it would be an awkward time to invite anyone else to take over."

Meanwhile the coresidence issue was moving along briskly. Students calmly and deliberately set about transforming their houses. At the start of the second semester in 1970, 150 Radcliffe students moved to the Harvard houses and 150 Harvard men moved to the Quadrangle. There was no money in Radcliffe's strained budget to help them move or to make any changes in facilities, so the entire maneuver was left in the students' hands. Within a week all three hundred students were moved. Polly marveled that it was all achieved "so rapidly, so quietly, really so easily and so successfully." All of the credit, she said, belonged to the students and the care they took to treat one another with sensitivity and respect.[9] They made sure there were two bathrooms on each floor so it wasn't necessary for all floors to have what they called "liberated" bathrooms. Some did, some didn't. If there was even one objection, the bathroom wasn't liberated. In one instance the cleaning woman objected, so the students kept the bathrooms separate. Only parents and older alumnae were seriously uneasy, but while Polly was on the road in search of money, she lost no opportunity to explain what was going on and to assure all the doubters that everything was going well. In each encounter with parents and alumnae she brought up the trio of topics that were of concern: student unrest, coed housing and merger, and discovered more concern with housing than anything else. The vision of men in the dormitory hallways awakened memories of the so-called "sex" scandals of a few years earlier. One alumna from the class of 1907 informed Polly that she was so upset she wouldn't even open her mail from the college.

Polly was impressed with what the students had done. She continued her usual practice of joining students for dinner in the dorms, and they told her the new arrangement was "so natural." For the first time they were socializing in dorms, which were happier places. More of them were staying for meals. They had more of a community. The dormitories had become so much more interesting; they were spending more time there. All the talking led to the only big problem, too much noise.

Polly was particularly amused to hear Radcliffe students say how surprised they were that the men were "so nice." She couldn't understand why that surprised them until she realized that even though they had been attending classes together and going out on dates, they had not known one another that well. The roles men and women were expected to play had gotten in the way of real understanding. When she had dinner one evening in one of the cooperatives, and mentioned the remark about "niceness," she was amused that the young man sitting next to her said, "Mrs. Bunting, when I came to Radcliffe I was surprised to find out how nice I was." "Everyone laughed," Polly said, "but the important thing was that these young people valued 'niceness' and were not ashamed to admit it."[10]

Students on the original committee had argued that coresidence would make dating less of an issue; it would let them get to know one another "in groups and not just in pairs." This was exactly what happened. Someone without a date no longer stood out. Milk and cookies at ten o'clock on Saturday night, when the dorm was locked and all the visiting men sent home, had been a Radcliffe tradition. "When the men came we thought we'd stop that, the men wouldn't be interested. Right away the men said, 'Saturday night and no milk? Why did we come to Radcliffe?' So the milk came back and the cookies—" Rather than consolation for dateless Radcliffe girls, they became the beginning of a party.

Polly was particularly impressed with the Harvard men who chose to participate in that first exchange. "Many of them did not expect to enjoy the semester. They had left plusher and more convenient quarters. They came because there was a job to be done. It hadn't seemed right to many of them that Radcliffe women should live apart and under inferior conditions." By moving to Radcliffe, they hoped to accelerate changes that promised equity for undergraduate women.[11] Despite the more comfortable Harvard accommodations, more Harvard men wanted to come to Radcliffe than Radcliffe women wanted to go to Harvard.[12]

Polly had gone along with the students' desire for coresidence because she saw no dangers in it, but she had also not anticipated any particular gains. She soon became convinced that in terms of the personal development of the students, it was probably the most important change made during her years at Radcliffe because it helped to dissipate stereotypic thinking. Before coresidence many students answered an official Radcliffe questionnaire, "Men do such and such or think so and so." Two years later almost no one thought in those terms. "That shift in perspective," Polly said, "is probably as revolutionary . . . as anything that happened to those young people during that period."[13]

In contrast to the ease with which the coresidence problem was being solved, the merger problem was becoming stickier. Alumnae opposition was gathering momentum. Polly had thought she could build Radcliffe's pride in itself as a part of Harvard, but the alumnae saw things differently. Not being able to define what they meant by "identity" did not stop them from feeling its loss. They were aware of the advantages that would come to Radcliffe with a closer affiliation with Harvard, they just did not think them worth the sacrifices. They did not want to give up their college, where women were valued and didn't have to deal with Harvard's obtuseness and condescension.

Polly was not prepared for the strength of their feelings. She had not anticipated that they would see merger as the loss of their college, which would leave them feeling diminished. Every rational argument, it seemed to her, was on the side of merger. All her life Polly had been a scientist; she believed that if you presented the evidence, argued the case logically, people would behave rationally. It was difficult for her to understand people who didn't. She felt sympathy for the feelings of the alumnae, but she couldn't really understand them.

It was the Boston alumnae who felt most attached to the old Radcliffe and most determined to maintain it. They had been a thorn in Polly's side from the start. They had been antagonistic to the Institute and, when Polly first arrived, had objected to what they saw as her casual style of dress. They had pressured her early in her tenure to formulate a statement about the college's identity. She had told them she felt "about the College the way I felt about my children: I preferred to focus on their character rather than on their image."[14] That response did not endear her to the Bostonians. Now they accused her of maneuvering Radcliffe "toward the inevitability of merger."[15]

She tried to address their fears by keeping them informed through memoranda detailing the latest developments. She always believed in being open and inclusive, but in this instance she was also well aware of the importance of their continued financial support, which depended upon preserving their good will. The Ford Foundation challenge grant had still to be met; money was desperately needed for construction of what became Currier House and for renovation of the old dormitories. Alumnae contributions were crucial to Radcliffe's strength in the negotiations with Harvard. The Radcliffe deficits might well undermine Harvard's willingness to merge.

The Alumnae Association, sparked by the Bostonians, was not to be rushed or diverted. They established committees to examine the issue from every conceivable angle and took the opportunity to speak out against a number of grievances they felt as educated women not only against Harvard but against society in general. They did not seem concerned that their tirades were ranging far from the topic under discussion. Polly had been so successful in communicating her vision of what women needed and were entitled to that now the alumnae were using her causes and in some cases even her own words against her. One report of the alumnae committee on merger admitted as much. "It is a reflection of Mrs. Bunting's leadership that this committee sees Radcliffe's role in broader terms than an undergraduate college." Merger, they argued, would make Radcliffe weak, and only a strong Radcliffe could push effectively for hiring and promoting women faculty; permitting only businesses that did not discriminate against women to recruit on the campus; establishing scholarships for married and older women who could only study part-time. These societal reforms, for which Polly had been fighting for years, were now being recruited in the struggle against the merger.

The alumnae position was also fueled by feelings Polly had seriously underestimated—their intense suspicion of and hostility to Harvard. For many of these women, their undergraduate experience of Harvard's neglect, condescension, and often downright contempt could not be forgotten or forgiven. Whatever else Harvard was, it was the place that had barred them from Lamont and locked them out of the Freshman Union; whose faculty had informed them in a hundred different ways that they were inferior. Their resentment and bitterness had only festered through the years and pored forth now in letters, phone calls, and published diatribes. One Radcliffe trustee actually told President Pusey that Radcliffe women who had grown up in Boston would not even trust their own Harvard-educated fathers to deal justly with Radcliffe.

All this anger came to a head at the end of the tumultuous 1970 academic year, when two former presidents of the Alumnae Association along with the head of the merger committee and alumnae from several previous decades unleashed an angry letter to Radcliffe's governing boards: "We, of the Radcliffe alumnae, look to you to halt the ultimate thrust of merger, lest what remains of Radcliffe disappear through a continuing series of minor mergers and administrative decisions.... This is not an easy step for us to take but we feel that the time has come to take direct action unless we are willing to let Radcliffe be lost by default. And default it will be if Radcliffe continues to be chipped away by the erosion caused by a series of decisions, urged by the president and acquiesced in by all of us. No one of these steps seemed too large at the time, but the total attrition is severe indeed and is not consistent with an independent and viable Radcliffe."

They weren't even prepared to accept the permanence of the changes that had already been made. Radcliffe should be maintained, they said, in case "there be changes of heart in any of the minor mergers which have already taken place.... What undergraduates petition for now may be an anathema to undergraduates five or ten years hence. While change is everywhere in the wind, it is significant to us that no one of our sister colleges is dissolving or going out of existence." And then they turned their acrimony against the president they felt had betrayed their trust. "In fact, we are witnessing the curious, and we believe, unprecedented phenomenon of seeing a president of one of the most prestigious women's colleges in the world seek to dissolve the college to which she was so honorably inducted in 1960."[16]

They also added an extra little threat, stating that no one should take their financial support for granted. It was foolish to assume that Radcliffe alumnae would automatically transfer their loyalty and their contributions to Harvard. Polly knew what that meant. A few months earlier she had noted in her journal what she called a "transient dip" in contributions, but added that she was sure that if the alumnae were "convinced that H now cares—predict the response far greater than anything R can elicit." Polly naively believed that alumnae would realize their grievances were all in the past, would understand that a future with Harvard promised greater benefits, and would abandon those grievances and continue to contribute to the college.

She believed this because she herself didn't hold grudges, didn't permit old wounds to fester. She had discovered how little thought the Harvard Board of Overseers had given to Radcliffe when she outlined for them her vision of a House system, but somehow this incident didn't leave any lasting impression. It was always her temperament to look on the positive side of things and to ignore unpleasantness. What mattered to her about Harvard was the support it had offered to the Institute. Its endorsement of her major project was part of what convinced her that ultimately women students would be better off as part of Harvard, than if, as she put it, they were compelled to continue to use the side door. When the faculty committed itself officially on February 10, 1970, to "assuring full and equal participation of Radcliffe students" in the intellectual and social life of the university, Polly saw this as official remorse for past injustices. From her Douglass days, she had spoken about the damage that women scholars suffered from their loneliness and isolation, their sense of never being perceived by faculty as "being in the same boat." The affirmation now by the Harvard faculty of women's scholarly legitimacy, was from her point of view exactly what she had long been fighting for.

While the alumnae were railing, Polly still had to run the college and cope with the recurring crises created by the Vietnam War. The bombing of Cambodia and the killings at Kent State were causing tumult on campuses. Polly's journal notes are all about the distress of Radcliffe students, not about the distress of the alumnae. She was coping with the threat of another university-wide strike, dealing with the students who were dropping into her office for information and reassurance, and attending deans' meetings where decisions had to be made about exams and academic policies. And as other universities were canceling classes and being shut down, she still had to be on the road foraging for funds. Her journals testify to her sticking to her routine.

Still she managed to find time to hold meetings with the alumnae and respond to their objections. She kept trying to get them to understand how profoundly different the college was from what they remembered. The establishment of coed housing, she explained, was far more than a superficial administrative adjustment. It would profoundly change the connection between future Radcliffe students and the college. Once these students were living at Harvard, she wrote one disgruntled alumna, "It will not be meaningful for a student to say she attends Radcliffe College."[17] And, she was quick to point out, students were pushing not for coed dormitories, but for something more fundamental: coed houses, which "implies full membership in a House under its master and tutors. If this took place, the Radcliffe Deans would have lost their function. There really wouldn't be any valid reason for maintaining the separateness as far as undergraduates are concerned."[18]

The situation struck Polly as ironic. "It seems to me I spent the last 15 years trying to convince men to have more confidence in women and now I'm spending a good deal of my time trying to persuade women to have more confidence in men."[19]

What mattered to her was what had mattered from the beginning—

not the image but the essence—and she feared the opportunity to preserve it was slipping away. The world was changing rapidly; decisions of the other Ivy League universities to admit women on an equal basis with men she believed would change the nature of Radcliffe and the quality of the students drawn to it. "I fear Radcliffe will in fact be but a shadow of what it is now. I worry about having this happen without it being recognized and fear that it will lead to prolonged bitterness on the part of Radcliffe alumnae."[20]

Polly believed merger was inevitable. As one who had always been fascinated by the natural world, this looked to her like another metamorphosis that could possibly be postponed but not prevented. As surely as the tadpole would become the frog or the caterpillar the butterfly, Radcliffe would become part of Harvard.

What the alumnae were saying, of course, was that they refused to accept Polly's basic premise. They did not believe that the changes she was advocating were inevitable. There were forces at work all right, but they thought she was the most powerful of those forces. In a sense, they were right. Polly couldn't acknowledge that compromise might be advisable. There was little to be gained, she said, by what she called "petty negotiations." "If our faith in Harvard's genuine interest in women is not well founded," she said in a speech to the Alumnae Association on June 14, 1969, "negotiations will be of little avail. If our faith is justified, they will be unnecessary."

Finally the alumnae committee came out with its recommendation, and it was indeed a compromise. They favored Polly's original idea of incorporation: Radcliffe College in Harvard University under the Faculty of Arts and Sciences. It was also what the "top" committee finally recommended in December 1970. The new arrangement was set up for a four-year trial period, to be reviewed in 1975. Harvard agreed to accept full responsibility for Radcliffe undergraduates; they would be able to participate fully in the intellectual and social as well as the academic life of the university. Whatever individuals might do or fail to do, Radcliffe women would now be able to go through all the doors and would be recognized as full-fledged participants. Second-class status, at least officially, was a thing of the past.

Under the new agreement, the head of Radcliffe would be a dean who had the rank of other Harvard deans, but whom the trustees could still call "president" if they wished. Polly said often that she found it amusing that at Douglass she had been called the dean even though she had a faculty and some influence over the curriculum and was really a president, whereas at Radcliffe she had neither and was called a president when she was really a dean.

There was to be a unified house system for undergraduates and only one administrative board so that the quandary Polly had faced over how to discipline Radcliffe students involved in protests at Harvard would never plague another Radcliffe president. Radcliffe would retain its physical property and its investments and be responsible for the Institute, for admissions and financial aid for women, and for a variety of lesser functions. All the income from Radcliffe's endowments and the money raised through annual giving would be turned over to Harvard, and Harvard would pay all the bills. The colleges would not merge "corporate identities," but would manage the undergraduate colleges as one unit.

This was one of those compromises that gave something to everyone. The alumnae kept the name Radcliffe College and retained their board of trustees, their real estate, their admissions office and endowment—the institutional elements that were part and parcel of what they saw as the elusive, difficult to define, "identity." Eventually even the alumnae who had most vehemently opposed the merger came to terms with the compromise. Polly was particularly amused by an "alumna who was very down on anything that was going to belittle Radcliffe at all. And then I met her about a year after she'd given me this great talk and she said, 'Guess what—my daughter's been accepted to Harvard.' She could have said it either way but she didn't say accepted to Radcliffe."

The students had the housing arrangement they wanted. By the time Polly left in 1972 all of the dormitories of all of the houses were coresidential and all of the Harvard houses wanted more women than they had. It took many more years for the numbers of men and women to be entirely equal, but things were moving in that direction.

Although Polly didn't get the merger she had hoped for, she got the substantive things she valued, those things which had a direct impact on students' lives. There would be more money for Radcliffe students. As soon as the agreement was signed, Harvard determined that inequities in financial aid should not be tolerated. The first year $100,000 was added for Radcliffe scholarships, and the following year Harvard assumed the full burden. Within two years the women in the Graduate School of Arts and Sciences were getting three times as much as Radcliffe had been able to provide, which enabled many more of them to pursue their studies without interruption. Now men and women shared whatever was. "Radcliffe," Polly said years later, "was no longer an excuse for Harvard to overlook any inequities." From Polly's point of view a merger had taken place—it just wasn't called by that name. The students agreed. They called it "the non-merger merger."

Now it had to be implemented in practical ways. This would be difficult for Radcliffe because under the new agreement Radcliffe would still be obligated to raise its own money, and if it failed there would be a comparable reduction in Harvard's financial support for its programs.

Polly now turned her attention to this myriad of practical details, and it is a testimony to her administrative talent that she was so adept. An apparently endless number of problems and functions had to be dealt with: budgets, food service, buildings, grounds, libraries, career planning, personnel, legal affairs, public relations, loans, health services. It even had to be decided who would pay for choral instructors and piano tunings. It didn't help that administrative procedures had been generally passed down through habit and custom, rather than being formally written down.

Implementation called upon all her skills of negotiation and diplomacy. During one tense meeting, she hit upon an inspired metaphor—the difficulty she had had as a beekeeper in bringing two hives together. It wasn't easy, she told them, since bees station guards at their front doors to keep out other bees. "The traditional procedure has a familiar ring. . . . You open up one hive and put newspaper on it and dribble some nice honey on the paper . . . and then you put the other hive right on top of that paper so there is a layer in between. . . . After about half an hour of eating through the paper, both hives get accustomed to each others' smells. . . . And with a little luck it all works out. . . . I might add that when it comes to honey production, one really strong hive is worth several weak ones any year."[21] "I didn't try to precisely match this up with the situation we had but I think they got the idea," she said many years later. "They got amused and it took the bitterness out of the conversation. And there were lots of remarks all through the coming years about the hives."

Polly, who always looked on the positive side, was struck by how much good will was thrown in by everyone. This revealed itself in small ways as well as large ones. Harvard, when it took over the kitchens, was shocked by the substandard equipment, and so it was replaced. Since Harvard men would now be eating in Radcliffe dining halls, Radcliffe students worried they would no longer be offered the salads they liked. Harvard not only kept the salads at Radcliffe, but also put them in at Harvard.

Ceremonially, too, Radcliffe joined Harvard. The class of 1970 asked to be included in morning Harvard commencement exercises—along with every other constituency of the university—and in 1970, for the first time, Radcliffe students joined their Harvard classmates in the Yard, receiving their diplomas afterward in the Radcliffe Quadrangle.

As Polly had predicted, the move to Harvard houses dissipated students' connections to Radcliffe; and with fewer and fewer Radcliffe students attending the ceremonial opening of each academic year, Polly recommended abolishing Convocation. There was no objection from the Council.

Radcliffe salaries and benefits had always been lower than Harvard's, and one of the advantages that Polly saw in merger was improving the lot of the Radcliffe staff. She had fought from the very beginning to increase Radcliffe salaries, but the financial constraints under which she had operated were too severe. Now at last, Radcliffe salaries would be raised. Ironically this would make no difference to Polly herself. She took virtually no raises during her entire Radcliffe presidency. In 1960 she earned twenty thousand dollars; twelve years later she earned only twenty-five hundred dollars more. Under the new agreement, she was to receive the same five percent raise as everyone else; this would have added $1,125, bringing her "Tentative New Salary" to $23,625. But in the last column of the page where the new salaries were listed Polly penciled in her own salary to stay at $22,500.

Polly insisted that the consolidation agreement contain an ironclad provision guaranteeing comparable jobs at Harvard for all Radcliffe employees, and one of her main concerns was making sure that provision was honored. She always maintained it was.

Polly continued to see Radcliffe as a fine place for young women. In her final speeches and letters to alumnae she spoke of the future of the college in which she had invested so much of herself. Just weeks before her departure, she reiterated her hope that Radcliffe would "continue to play a leading role in opening opportunities for women and assisting them in taking full advantage of their potentialities."[22]

24

A Society Gets the Kind of Excellence It Values

Polly had been looking for the right moment to leave Radcliffe. From observing other institutions, she had long since decided that five years was too short and fifteen years too long to be in charge of a college, "so somewhere around ten would be about right." But in 1970, with all the uncertainty in the negotiations with Harvard, Polly thought it was the wrong time for her to resign. The trustees would not know what sort of person they were looking for, and a new president would be unsure what sort of an institution she was going to run. But once the agreement was signed and sealed, Polly thought the right moment had come. At their meeting on January 28, 1971, she told the trustees she planned to resign in eighteen months, as of June 30, 1972. That would give them enough time to look for her successor and would give her time to help Radcliffe metamorphose.

She was, however, no lame duck. She remained engaged in Radcliffe's fortunes right until the end. During her last months she was able to celebrate Harvard's new commitment to women's education; the almost unanimous faculty vote of approval for the recommendations of the new Committee on the Status of Women, their support for having more women on the Harvard faculty, and their acceptance for the first time of her proposal for part-time appointments with full faculty privileges in all professorial ranks.

She continued her work off the campus too, serving as the cochair of the Values, Ethics and Culture Task Force for the White House Conference on Youth, picking up four more honorary degrees (bringing the total number to twenty-nine) and giving some major speeches in which she again sounded her familiar themes but also warned about some disturbing trends. A shrinking economy, she cautioned, might well make some of the new opportunities won by the women's liberation movement into pyrrhic victories. The expansion of opportunities could not continue indefinitely, and she feared that the contractions might, once again, leave women scrambling for crumbs.

She warned against discouraging young women by exaggerating the barriers confronting them. Polly had always accentuated the positive, sometimes to the point of underestimating negative realities, but she was aware that she, too, had been guilty of stressing the obstacles too often and the rewards too seldom. Constantly harping on the prevalence of male chauvinist remarks and practices, she said, could discourage young women. "Endless complaining is not likely to produce tomorrow's leaders."[1]

She was even more concerned about the emergence of new stereotypes that women were foisting on one another. She did not approve of turning the opportunities won for women against those who chose to be homemakers and volunteers. Polly had always believed that helping others was a good life, whether those others were one's students or one's family. Her mother and aunt had been community volunteers all their lives; her sister Winifred had involved herself totally in caring for her family. Polly believed they had made honorable choices that should continue to be honored. What she saw happening, and deplored, was the development of a definition of women's supporting roles as nothing but trivial chores—"physical assistance in running the household, feeding and chauffeuring the children, or licking campaign envelopes," whereas she believed that women of "extraordinary ability, wide interests, and deep concerns" could make their homes "a source of strength and delight not only to their families but to a wide group of friends."[2] She expressed these views in a speech at Pine Manor Junior College, titled "Freedom to Chose One's Own Life Style." "Those who criticize the woman who doesn't seek a career of her own generally conceive her role in the family and the community far too narrowly—and so in many cases does she,"[3] she said. Polly always maintained that it mattered far less what one did than how one did it. It was no accident that she chose to deliver this major speech at a junior college. Ivy League administrators were not generally known for their respect for women's junior colleges.

These statements might well have been Polly's tribute to her dear friend and Vassar roommate, Leal, who died in June 1971, after a five-year battle with cancer. In spite of her Hopkins Ph.D., Leal had lived a traditional life, staying home to raise five children and not going to work as a high school science teacher until they were grown. She had been the kind of mother Polly had urged others to be, majoring at Vassar in child studies, using her training to become the mother other mothers turned to for advice and wisdom.

During this last Radcliffe year, Polly delivered several speeches that were both a summing-up and a looking ahead, recapitulating not only her own major achievements of the preceding decade, but also the progress women had made. These speeches were carefully typed, unlike earlier ones in which she spoke almost extemporaneously, from scrawled notes or file cards with phrases jotted on them. These were statements of her Radcliffe legacy and what she thought still needed to be done. She frequently quoted John Gardner's remark that she said had first made her see the barriers standing in the way of women: "A society gets the kind of excellence it values."

She made that point effectively in a speech she titled "From Serratia to Women's Lib and a Bit Beyond," which she delivered to the American Society for Microbiology, on May 5, 1971. It was her first scientific audience in a long time, and she took particular pleasure in being invited to address them. She emphasized the ways in which the bacteriologists' methods could be used effectively in constructing social experiments, insisting as she had before, that developing an enriched environment could produce significant results even outside the laboratory and lamenting that such environments had not been developed "to grow our women scholars and scientists. Perhaps they are rare and delicate variants—but then again, the soil could be teeming with them and we ignorant."

She continued to criticize educational institutions for failing in their obligation to create the environments in which women could thrive. It was still the racetrack, where what mattered too often was "the speed with which the course is completed."[4] She was still waiting for the gardens, or at least for the separate ladders to become "great jungle gyms which permit people to move sideways when they can't or don't wish to continue to climb upwards."[5] There were still too few women role models, too great an attachment to rigid schedules and entrenched practices that did not mesh with the reality of women's lives.

She hammered away at the prejudices that still remained. She wanted each woman, each human being, to be judged as an individual, not according to preconceived assumptions about groups. "It is the endless debates about whether women are or are not inherently as talented or productive as men that seem to me so boring and irrelevant," she said. "Most men are not as able as some men, but that doesn't disqualify them as a group. Only as we succeed in providing optimal environments for both men and women will we be able to judge their innate capabilities and limitations."[6]

Just a few months before her departure, Polly set up a conference at Radcliffe, officially sponsored by the Institute, called "Women:

Resource for a Changing World," which was to examine new research and plot future directions in the work for women. Close to four hundred people, mostly women, attended—academics, Institute fellows, Radcliffe students and alumnae, professors, people from the community, and representatives from a variety of newspapers and magazines. There were even seventeen men, among them Derek Bok, the new Harvard president, and Erik Erikson.

Polly delivered a speech at the conclusion of the two-day event. She was preparing to leave Cambridge and was thinking about the society beyond the Harvard-Radcliffe enclave. Her longstanding democratic commitments were coming to the fore. In recalling the progress for women over the past decade, she began with the Institute—the place she began almost all of her speeches during this last year of her presidency. It was the achievement that meant the most to her, that demonstrated her commitment to lifelong learning. But while not ignoring her pride in it, she acknowledged that it dealt with only what she called "one small corner of the problem, the special needs of able and motivated women, including those who are devoted to their families and to the life of the mind. There are a multitude of other groups of people, younger and older, whose educational needs are not being met." She urged other colleges, universities, libraries, and cultural offices to pay attention to the other "multitude," to offer them services and facilities. The Institute, she said, was "truly innovative, or subversive if you prefer," because it admitted women from the community who had work they wanted to do. Colleges and universities should do the same, she said. They should "become centers of learning" for adults who are not looking for degrees but for an environment conducive to the pursuit of knowledge and artistic expression. She also urged them to pay attention to the needs of women on their faculties and staffs or "attached to them through marriage."

After the first joint Harvard-Radcliffe commencement, Polly spoke about a student who had participated in the hunger strike four years earlier because she wanted to make her mark on Radcliffe. "She said she loved the place and didn't like to think she might spend four years here without having left a trace. I know the feeling." But Polly didn't have to worry. She left Radcliffe a far more humane institution.

Polly changed Harvard as well. On her watch Harvard opened Lamont and its business school to women, abandoned its policy of denying funds to graduate women studying part-time, admitted women directly into graduate departments, established a standing committee on women and included the Institute dean as a member, created an Equal Opportunity Officer in the Faculty of Arts and Sciences and appointed a woman to fill the slot, and finally gave Radcliffe undergraduates its ultimate imprimatur—a Harvard diploma. Because of Polly Bunting's efforts, the Arts and Sciences faculty finally recognized their responsibility for the women they had been teaching and agreed that women students should participate fully and freely in the life of the university. Some members of the Harvard faculty still slid back into bad old habits, but, Polly noted in a speech, students told her gleefully that whenever a professor made a male chauvinist remark, "most of the class hisses."

As much as she had changed Radcliffe, it had not changed her. Old friends coming to visit in the president's house found her as she had been in Bethany, dressed in shorts and sneakers—"no presidential attire for her," one of them said.

Unsurprisingly Polly insisted that her leave-taking from Radcliffe be neither protracted nor elaborate. She specified that there be one present and one event, which took place at the Cronkhite Center. But the trustees had some ideas of their own. They threw her a fancy dinner at what she called "a very flossy place," the Vale in Waltham. At a prescribed moment in the proceedings, the glass doors opened and a large cow was led into the dining room. (The trustees had arranged for her son John to come to the restaurant with a truck to transport the cow to the Bunting farm in New Boston.) Polly accepted the beast graciously and pronounced it a very beautiful animal. But never one to be sentimental, she said later that she and her family had gotten more than six hundred pounds of very fine beef from it.

Part IV
Endings

25

Enough of Women

Polly had thought she would retire to her farm in New Boston, New Hampshire, grow her vegetables, keep her gardens and her bees, and read. But once her impending resignation became known, her phone began ringing. Educational institutions of all sizes and shapes, from small liberal arts colleges in the East to huge universities in the Midwest, invited her to fill different administrative positions. She turned them all down. She did not feel like running anything. "I remember one gentleman from the Middle West saying, 'But we have 60,000 students.' He thought that was going to be an inducement and he was quite wrong."[1]

She did accept positions on a number of boards of the sort she had refused before for lack of time. She had made only two exceptions during her Radcliffe years, in instances where she believed the combination of her interests and her training could make her useful and offer her some satisfaction. One was the Kaiser Foundation Health Plan and Kaiser Foundation Hospitals, where her microbiology background was relevant. Kaiser was also on the West Coast, and her three paid flights a year afforded her the opportunity of doing some climbing and hiking with Mary, Reiner, and their two daughters, who were living in Seattle.

The other exception was the Population Council, the creation of John D. Rockefeller III. She had joined that organization in 1965 because she had been interested in its issues for a long time, keeping track in her journals of population trends and their likely impact. Even more important from her point of view, the Rockefeller family had been generous in supporting the Institute and Laurance Rockefeller's backing had been critical to its success. She felt an obligation to return a favor.

It was this motive, more than anything else, that determined the board positions she accepted in her waning Radcliffe months. She went with the companies that had supported the project that meant the most to her: the Radcliffe Institute. She also realized that she needed some income.

She wanted to contribute to the medical school costs of Bill's wife, Lonna, to whom she felt close. Lonna, who had been a member of the crew of the sailing ship Bill had joined when he took his leave of absence during his sophomore year, was an only child whose father had died in World War II. She was at loose ends after the voyage, didn't want to go back home to Kansas, didn't think she could manage college, and was an undiagnosed narcoleptic. She hadn't been to a doctor and believed that she fell asleep, even in the midst of conversations, because she didn't have enough will power to stay awake. After the year at the AEC, Polly took Lonna under her wing. She found a specialist who explained to Lonna that narcolepsy was a disease and prescribed medication. She invited Lonna to move into the president's house, where Lonna lived until she and Bill were married. Lonna was interested in biology, got a job in a laboratory, and with Polly's support, guidance, and encouragement decided she was ready to give college a try. She picked Wellesley, did well there, and after graduation decided to go to medical school. Polly entrusted her with Henry's microscope, the one he had bought with the money he earned while working nights in the University of Wisconsin observatory. (The Bunting children heaved a collective sigh of relief when Henry's microscope found its way into Lonna's hands; it made it easier for them to admit that none of them wanted a career in science.)

In addition to Lonna's tuition, Polly wanted to contribute to Gwy's care. Her mother was coping with dementia and would soon have to go into a nursing home. Winifred and Gardner were looking after her, but Polly wanted to contribute, and she was aware of the skimpiness of her savings. She had been president of an impecunious college and had steadfastly kept her own salary in line with the low salaries of her staff, so now, at sixty-two years of age, she felt she needed to have some money coming in.

She decided to join three corporate boards. The Sperry & Hutchinson Company had been a supporter of the Institute for five years and was broadening beyond the green stamps for which they were known into household furnishings. Another Institute supporter was Arthur D. Little, a Cambridge-based consultant for private and government agencies that did research on weapon effectiveness. Polly said she had been assured the company "was not doing anything with offensive military weapons" and declared that she would not join if they were. She also joined the New England Electric System.

On three of these boards—Kaiser, Sperry & Hutchinson, and Arthur D. Little—Polly was the only woman. That didn't trouble her. She was accustomed to working with men and had more important matters to think about at meetings. But she did try to keep an eye on what they were doing for women in their organizations and in any of their programs. "It was an interesting moment to become available," she said years later. "The pressures of women's liberation were having an effect on corporations across the country and many of them were anxious to get a woman on the board . . . their token woman."[2] Even so, the corporate culture hadn't quite caught up with the trend. As late as October 1975 Polly received a letter from a Kaiser staff member informing her of arrangements for the next month's meeting. It noted that "the wives of Directors are not explicitly invited."

Polly planned to retire and focus on these boards when she received a telephone call that intrigued her. It came from William Bowen, who was just assuming the presidency of Princeton. He asked if she would consider joining his administration to work with him on a variety of issues. Princeton was well known to Polly because she had known Robert Goheen, the outgoing president, when she was at Douglass and he "really stuck his neck way out" to gain admission for a Douglass student to one of the Princeton graduate schools. (The Douglass graduate was the first woman ever to be admitted; her acceptance letter began, "Dear Sir.") Princeton had awarded Polly an honorary degree in 1961— the only woman among eleven men. And when Princeton began to seriously consider admitting women undergraduates, they invited Polly as well as a number of other women educators to spend an afternoon with their senior administrators discussing the advantages and problems of coeducation. At the time, Princeton had only three female faculty members and the idea of admitting female undergraduates made its alumni suspicious at best and downright antagonistic at worst.

When Bowen called, the first few classes of women undergraduates were on campus and struggling, not least against the hostility of the male undergraduates. The university was struggling too. It had been all-male, a virtual monastery, and suddenly women were there, "and we were trying to think of everything that could make the environment more welcoming," remembered Neil Rudenstine, later president of Harvard, who at the time was Princeton's dean. Bowen, who was only thirty-seven years old, thought that a woman of Polly's experience, wisdom, and good sense, "who was at home in the world," would be very helpful to the few women, both students and faculty members.

Polly, however, was more attracted by the other questions Bowen told her he was interested in addressing. What should Princeton be doing in the field of continuing education? Should it get into medicine and the medical sciences? What about a law school? How should Princeton strengthen its program in the life sciences, Polly's field?

The idea of turning her attention, once again, to serious educational issues, unfettered by obligations to raise money, shrink deficits, and cope with crises was highly appealing. She decided to "give it a whirl." She had only a few conditions. Because of the board positions she had already accepted, she said she could work only part-time; she wanted the fall off to enjoy, for the first time in many years, the New England mountains in October; and her title could have nothing to do with women. "I'd had enough of women," she said. "I wanted to get out in the real world." They settled on "assistant to the president for special projects."

It was to be what she called a "free-wheeling job," and last for only three years, until she turned sixty-five. In those days no one in the academic world stayed on past that magic date. In accepting, she wrote Bowen that she welcomed the chance to think about "some of the educational questions that trouble and intrigue us," and she felt confident joining a university that was "moving forward strongly and sensibly."

She spent some time during her final Radcliffe spring going down to Princeton for various meetings and dinners. She turned down a seat on the General Motors board, which would have been very lucrative, because it met on the same day as the Princeton faculty and she thought it would undermine her effectiveness if she were unable to attend Princeton faculty meetings.

In July she moved out of the Radcliffe president's house at 76 Brattle Street. Bill took the beehive from the apiary on the porch roof and carried it, very carefully, down the steps and into the car. John managed to tip the huge dining room table off its base and walk it up the plank into the moving truck. It took a U-Haul truck and three full VWs to finish the job. But barely a week later she was mowing the lawn in New Boston before heading to Northport for some time with the family at her beloved spot.

She spent time during the fall attending conferences on public health, advising a girls' boarding school on what they should be doing to start students toward management jobs, attending board meetings, and serving on a Health, Education and Welfare committee on the rights and responsibilities of women in HEW programs.

She still had time left to enjoy the mountains. Monadnock, Kearsage, Uncanoonuc, all made their way into her journals, which were filled once again with the kind of observations she had made during less busy days in the past: "excellent views," "worth returning on a clear day," "a fine little mt." She kept track of all the birds: "robins & varied thrushes," "lots of redpulls," "starlings a great sight," "family of white crowned sparrow eating seeds," "a very talkative family of red-bill nuthatches;" the animals and vegetables she met, and the changing seasons:

"last of the corn, first of the tomatoes," "a light frost—got the tops of the tomato plants but not the lower branches," "chipmunk busy in maple tree—storing away seeds."

By November she was on the job at Princeton. She moved into a cozy campus apartment and a small second-floor office in Nassau Hall, Princeton's main administration building. Bowen took "special pains" to see that her office was in the same part of Nassau Hall as his own because he wanted to have ready access to her. She still kept up her frenetic pace, going to board meetings, to panels, to conferences, and most weekends, to visit her ailing mother.

The university that she found was not only overwhelmingly male, it was also very traditional, invested in doing things the way they had always been done. The year before Polly's arrival, when the wife of the provost asked to complete her bachelor's degree on a part-time basis, finishing her last two years in four because she had three small children, she confronted antipathy. "It just wasn't done," Lucy Hackney remembered. "The attitude was, 'We're not only going to have women, we're going to have these older women wanting us to readjust our curriculum for them.'" The administration eventually reluctantly relented. And slowly change began to undermine Princeton's traditional ways. By the end of Polly's second year, ten older students were enrolled as degree candidates, three on a part-time basis, and seven women were part-time graduate students.

Polly began by focusing on the questions Bowen had asked her to address: first of all, the advisability of establishing professional schools at Princeton. Unlike other major universities, Princeton had none. Polly disposed quickly of a medical school: "awfully expensive and there were enough of them on the east coast." She took a little longer to decide a law school was not necessary either, at least not right away.

Another concern of Bowen's was strengthening the life sciences at Princeton. The biology department invited Polly to become a lecturer, so she attended departmental meetings and worked with them on the program that came to be called molecular biology. Even though she had not been actively engaged in research for some time, she could assess what was being done.

As a kind of minister without a portfolio, she worked on many different fronts, not only academic, but also political. The biggest political problem for universities was Title IX, which had just been passed, and didn't apply only to athletics but to any programs with federal funding. The wording—that "no program shall discriminate"—had yet to be limited or defined. "Nobody knew what it meant," said Tom Wright, then Princeton's general counsel and later vice-president. "There were questions about scholarships and prizes. We thought we would have to get wills and trusts broken and spend lots of time and money in court." Polly untangled the language, and determined that "the fundamental principle would be honored if there were no discriminatory impact. She wonderfully cut to the core," Wright said, "and didn't allow herself to get bogged down." Polly and he lobbied in Washington and were able to have Polly's principles written into the national Title IX regulations, where they still stand.

Her main responsibility was developing a program of continuing education—a congenial assignment—because she had become increasingly interested in the reciprocal relationship between universities and their communities. It was a brand new idea at Princeton. As she had done at Douglass, Polly convinced them that there were many people in their community, most but not all of them women, who for a variety of reasons had missed the opportunity when they were young to have the kind of education they needed. They wanted to return to college, to brush up, to change fields, or to pick up where they had left off and finish their degrees.

By this time Polly was well aware how nervous faculty could become when they feared something might endanger academic standards. She assuaged their anxieties by pointing out to them that these continuing education students would get no credit—only grades, transcripts, and a certificate acknowledging the completion of the course. In February 1974, her second year, the faculty approved the program as a three-year experiment with a limit of one hundred students per semester.

Then some faculty members began to get nervous and wanted guidelines set up before candidates applied. That was exactly the kind of rigidity Polly opposed. She didn't want rules in place before anyone knew who the applicants were going to be. She saw that she needed to get things moving in a hurry, but she had no budget for staff or publicity. So she turned, once again, to the Rockefellers, and said, "We've got an interesting little problem on timing that's quite important down here." And they came through with the $28,000 needed to launch the program. By the end of its first year, forty-five courses in twenty-eight departments had at least one continuing education student.

One of the first students applied both to the program and to be Polly's secretary. As a single mother in her late thirties, Loy Carrington needed a paying job as well as more education. She told Polly frankly that she had never been a secretary before and remembers Polly saying, "Well, if you think you can do it—" And Polly put up with the consequences of her decision, tolerating delays and inefficiency, giving Carrington "a little more time to look things up." As Carrington explained, "She would say, 'just send a letter and tell them I can't come,' and then I would go through this book to find letters I could copy. And I always emptied my own wastebasket." Carrington got a Princeton B.A. a few years later.

The continuing education program had exactly the impact Polly had expected and hoped for. It helped the students, but it also helped Princeton's women. "It added to our mix some of the seniority and experience of life that the younger women—be they faculty or staff or students—simply didn't have," said Bowen. "And the fact that older women were interested enough in their education to want to take the kinds of courses in the liberal arts that Princeton offered, that said something to everyone, men and women alike, about the importance of that kind of education and how much at least these continuing education students valued it." Polly had seen this phenomenon before.

The continuing education program she created at Princeton was different from those at other colleges. It made all the university's regular classes, undergraduate as well as graduate, available to any qualified person. Most other universities used Harvard's system; they established a segregated group of courses, taught usually in the evenings and by specially hired part-time faculty. In Polly's view this was a watered-down version of the liberal arts. Her system not only offered students more choices, it fit in with her economical way of administering, making use of what was already in place. It was not only, in her opinion, a better way of operating, it was cheaper.

It was the same principle she applied when discouraging the Princeton administration from creating separate offices for women. Many colleges still had a dean of women and a director of women's athletics "and on and on and on," said Bowen. "But she was just steadfastly opposed to all of that. She thought it would diminish women by treating them as if they were outside the mainstream. And she thought it would also deprive the men of the benefits of coeducation by making it less easy for interaction to occur. And finally she thought it was just a waste of money and resources." Princeton did not set up any such offices.

Although Polly said she'd had "enough of women," she couldn't completely escape their concerns and didn't really want to. She served on a Women's Rights Task Force for Brendan T. Byrne, the successful Democratic candidate for governor. She spoke at Radcliffe clubs and at Douglass on one of her favorite themes, the importance for women of part-time work. She attended conferences about birth control, sexuality, and ways femininity was defined and emphasized at different periods of time. She was particularly impressed by the idea, expressed by one speaker, that women define themselves through their sickness. She copied the description of "nervous diseases" into her notebook.

On campus she attended seminars at which Princeton women faculty spoke about their careers. She also attended meetings of the official women's faculty group. She was the only significantly older, significantly more experienced woman around. "She really filled a void," said Nancy Weiss Malkiel, one of the nine women professors; six more had been hired since 1969. "We were inventing as we went along, so Polly was an extremely important resource for us." She helped them get a grant from the Clark Foundation to bring fourteen young women scholars to campus to give lectures—a strategy to help universities identify promising female scholars.

She also gave support to the young women administrators, and almost all of them were very young. Polly gave them practical advice and helped them identify the men on campus who were most likely to be interested in women's concerns. She stepped in when one of them needed a better secretary and made sure one was hired. She also influenced them through her own style of doing things. At a meeting at which the main topic of discussion was the relationship between a female faculty member and a male undergraduate, the men all agreed it was scandalous and had to be stopped. The lone, young woman administrator remembered a tactic Polly had taught her; look at the clock, wait ten minutes, and hope that one of the men figures it out first. When none of them did, she waded in with a reminder that if the administration took a position regarding this woman, they would also have to intervene with the male faculty members who were sexually involved with undergraduates. Years later she still remembered the stunned silence around the table.

The few older women students who had fought for and finally earned the privilege of studying part-time welcomed Polly's encouragement. "It never occurred to her I couldn't manage it all," said Lucy Hackney, the young mother of three returning to finish her B.A. "Just having her presence there" was reassuring. "She was one of the few people in a high position who could be an advocate for women at the university." Polly managed, as one of her male colleagues put it, to "provide counsel and support without starting the revolution."

Steadily and carefully she alerted faculty and administrators to the stereotypic traps in their thinking. She warned them not to assume that all the women were going to go into the arts and humanities; some, she hoped many, might venture into the sciences. And some might want to play sports. "She thought it would be very important," said Rudenstine, "to have strong women's athletics, so we had terrific teams and it kind of made what was always thought of as a particularly male domain less of a male domain."

Polly was still finding vestiges of the climate of unexpectation and worked to counteract them. When she sat in on discussions with the biology department about candidates who had applied for graduate school, she began to realize how often letters of recommendation for women lacked the paragraph about what the writer expected the individual to contribute in the future. "They might describe the candidate's academic record in glowing terms and praise her personal attributes," Polly said, "but because, as I interpreted the phenomenon, the writer did not have high expectations of any woman's potential as a scientist, he, or sometimes she, omitted that critical paragraph. As a result, the letters about women sounded unenthusiastic compared with most of those about their male competitors."[3] It was a phenomenon she had not spotted before. Once she pointed it out, faculty members began noticing it too, and some of them confessed to Polly that they had caught themselves making the same mistake.

She observed the difference in faculty attitudes toward scientifically top-notch candidates who had prickly, even difficult personalities. If the candidate was a man, the faculty would put up with him, but not if the candidate was a woman. "If one did not believe that a woman could make an outstanding contribution, then why put up with her if she seemed rather uncooperative." Once Polly pointed this out to faculty, she was delighted to observe how quickly some of the most influential caught on.

In meeting after meeting she would pose the question: "How do you think a woman would react to this?" remembered Will Reed, then Princeton's personnel director. "She was never fiery and 'OK this is what you have to do.' She was reasoned and skillful. She was such a lady but with such a powerful mind and with such a reputation that it's like the old ad, when she spoke, people listened." Her presence convinced everyone that President Bowen was serious about changing the Princeton culture. "He could have brought in someone who was a radical," said Reed, "and was going to scare everybody. But instead he brought in somebody who was so reasonable and of such substance that she won the day over and over again."

She put one administrator on the spot when they were formulating an antidiscrimination statement for the university. She wanted to simply state: "There will be no discrimination on the basis of race or gender." Sheldon Hackney, then the provost, admitted that he wanted "some weasel words" in case situations came up in the future in which it might be appropriate for some discrimination to take place. Polly said, "Name them." "The only one I could think of was locker room attendant," Hackney said. She found a way of working that into the statement.

Mostly, Polly operated quietly, but when necessary, she didn't shrink from speaking out. She attended a monthly lunch meeting with heads of departments, which was "sort of show and tell of what you were doing for women," according to Reed. "And the dean of the School of Engineering stood up and was extremely proud that he had just hired—had stolen from some place—a woman professor of engineering. At the time it was very hard to find women in that field. And he went on and on about her academic credentials and he ended it by saying, 'And besides that, she's good-looking.' Polly stood up and said, 'Don't ever do that again. That is unacceptable.' It was the most direct I'd ever heard her. That was all she said. But I never heard anything like that said again."

She didn't automatically take the woman's part. When a woman administrator sued because she insisted she was entitled to a promotion, Polly sided with her male boss because she believed he was in the right. "She was a friend to me," he said. "It was the first time I had ever been through this, and she was seasoned, experienced, wise."

That was, finally, what Bowen had really hired her for. "She was meant to work with faculty and administrators and to help them," he said. "And she did, powerfully. And had she never done any special project, she would have been worth twice whatever it was that we paid her just because of her presence and her wisdom."

She had what Rudenstine called "the run of the place." But she was careful not to usurp anyone's authority. When, soon after her arrival, she was invited to "represent the university" at a Western Electric meeting, she refused, saying that it would be inappropriate for her to be presented that way. She was an assistant only, not a spokesman.

Princeton was the final chapter in Polly's career in academic administration. In some ways she had come full circle, back to New Jersey, back to the concerns that marked the beginning of her administrative career—opening opportunities, establishing links to the surrounding community, exploring the ramifications of the climate of unexpectation. For the rest of her days she would continue to think about the purposes of education and ways to enrich the lives of women. But she would never again be in a position as visible or powerful as those she had enjoyed. And that was fine with her. When she left Princeton at the end of the 1975 academic year, at the age of sixty-five, she said, "I think I was a little tireder than I realized."

26

I Don't Look Back Much

Now Polly really settled down in her 1810 farmhouse in New Boston. She was back in the kind of country she loved, with fields and farms in one direction and woods in the other, where she could spend whole days in blue jeans, close enough to the White Mountains to get to them easily for skiing and hiking where she could even go skinny-dipping, which she did occasionally along with her daughter-in-law. It offered quiet peace. She bought another twenty acres of woodland to add to the twenty-five she already had.

Although it had been her retreat for fifteen years, she hadn't done much to fix up the house except to put in an oil-burning furnace, a few hot-air ducts, and a new roof. Now that it was to be her year-round home she decided to add insulation, a picture window in the back and a porch on the side, and to modernize the bathroom and kitchen. She had already established ample perennial beds and gardens of corn, potatoes, asparagus, and other vegetables, which gave both fun and food for visiting children and grandchildren in the summer, and from the freezer, for herself all winter. When she weeded her garden at sunup, she still did it topless, with Band-Aids over her nipples; but since a town road was close, she kept her shirt close as well. The gardens gave her the satisfaction she needed of something outdoors to take care of, but required so little attention that she still had the freedom to come and go to all the meetings and conferences she continued to attend. She had brought her beehives along, but when she was away during the 1977 winter, heavy snow drifted over them suffocating all the bees. She tried the next year to round up some new hives, but most beekeepers had suffered as she had. Besides, the hives, weighing sixty pounds or more, were becoming too heavy for her to handle alone.

Grandchildren came. She played croquet with them, taught them to drive a tractor, to pick beans in the garden, to trap a skunk. She showed them how different stalks of corn responded to changes in water and sunlight.

Her boards still took up considerable time, and appointments as a Vassar alumnae trustee, a director of TIAA-CREF, the financial institution handling investments for academics, and the Woods Hole Oceanographic Institution were added to her list. Although she had never been a member of any official feminist organization, many women recognized her as an elder stateswoman of the women's movement and she was much in demand as a speaker, not just for her reminiscences about the past, but also for her predictions about the future. Soon, however, she started refusing all invitations for formal speech-making. Although she had been making all sorts of speeches for more than twenty years, she "dreaded" standing up in front of audiences and talking, and she felt she wasn't very good at it. Now, without the pressure and responsibility of an official position, she insisted on participating only in discussions with small groups or giving informal talks, saying she enjoyed "exploring a provocative topic with a group of interested individuals," but would not tolerate being the main attraction. When Rider College in New Jersey listed her as the "Distinguished Visiting Lecturer," she rebelled. All she thought she had agreed to do was give a few introductory remarks to get a discussion started. When the Louisville Junior League tried to turn what was to be an informal discussion about "evolving patterns of women's lives" into a grand event with much advance publicity, she balked. "What can you do at this point to reassure me?" she wrote to the organizer of the event. She made it clear they would either have to revise their arrangements or do without her participation. She tolerated no fanfare or advance publicity and no taping or broadcasting. Television "terrified" her. She prepared no written texts for her informal talks. She spoke from handwritten notes on four-by-five cards or scraps of paper, with corrections scrawled in the margin, making it virtually impossible to know what she actually said.

The only exception she made resulted from a confluence of causes which were all of the utmost importance to her. She gave a speech at a symposium on "Women & the Arts" held in Detroit, to honor Radcliffe's centennial and to benefit both the arts fellowships of the Radcliffe Institute and a Detroit innovation, a combination museum and arts center for African-American children. This was exactly the kind of local initiative for a local community which she believed was most effective in "promoting constructive social change."

She accepted invitations from those with whom she still felt an affinity: young students, Radcliffe alumnae, or Vassar classmates. She joined a panel on the "Changing Status of Women in Science" on Radcliffe Junior Parents Day, March 13, 1976, when invited by a Radcliffe junior biochemistry major. She addressed high school girls at St. Paul's School, reaching into her own history for stories of her struggles when she was about their age. She revealed how wounded she had been as a child by "adult laughter," and why she had resolved to keep a journal. She told them about wrestling with her identity in her "thinking tree." She described her excitement in high school when, for the first time, she encountered real science. She told them about the lobsterman in Maine who nodded toward a distinguished Harvard professor and remarked to Bill, "He knows so much but he don't realize nothin'." What she wanted to leave them with, she said, were a few of the things she had "realized" along the way. But this speech was an exception. Despite many opportunities to relive her past, she preferred to look ahead. "I don't look back much," she said. "I take satisfaction from what is going well."

She maintained her connection to educational institutions that she had attended or worked at. She went to reunions at Packer Collegiate and Vassar, to meetings of Vassar clubs in New England, to ceremonial events at Douglass, to seminars and brown bag lunches at the Institute, to lectures at Radcliffe's Schlesinger Library. She kept tabs on Princeton's continuing education program, meeting with the new director from time to time; she served on a committee to take a look at Harvard's School of Public Health.

She offered her insights and her expertise to schools and colleges, particularly when asked to do so by friends. At the invitation of Adele Simmons, a Radcliffe graduate who had been a Princeton administrator and was now the president of Hampshire College, Polly participated in a two-day symposium on Hampshire's present and future. She collaborated on drafting a report on Barnard for its newly inaugurated president and her old Bethany friend and Radcliffe employee, Jacquelyn Mattfeld. This report afforded her an opportunity to look at another women's college contemplating a merger with another large university—in this instance, Columbia. She did not recommend the kind of non-merger merger she had worked so hard to effect at Radcliffe, but instead suggested something similar to what Radcliffe eventually became: "a kind of cross between a women's center, a foundation for the advancement of women's education, and an institute for research and pilot projects related to their education and productivity." Such a foundation, she wrote, would not dissipate its fortunes or energies in administration, but could instead be responsive to new ideas and needs. She also saw this organization as a source of financial support for Barnard alumnae, recycling her old Radcliffe idea of "Operation Backstop," a fund to provide backing to alumnae at critical points in their careers, providing tangible proof that the college believed in its "product." Even though she rarely second-guessed herself, some of her comments suggest she might have been having second thoughts about guiding Radcliffe into Harvard's orbit. "The trend at other universities with women's colleges," she wrote, "has been one of gradual absorption of the college, an awkward process at best that invariably leaves many alumnae and some students with an unpleasant sense of personal loss."[1]

It wasn't only about education that she was asked to comment. She was recognized as someone who had much to say about the future of American society. During the bicentennial year, a time of national soul-searching, she was invited to testify before a Senate committee examining long-range planning. She was part of a three-day symposium on the future and reiterated her conviction about the importance of "approaching social and environmental problems in an experimental manner" rather than "pushing blindly toward precise, predetermined solutions. Too often we have settled for an alchemist's solution, seeking magic keys to sudden transmutations rather than developing the basic information and testable theories that could enable us to move forward in a dependable fashion. In setting goals we must seek understanding rather than gold."[2]

She had always been concerned about social justice, and spoke out more often now about the gaps in American society, pressing elite institutions to "assist non-traditional students whenever possible & however." At Princeton she spoke about the "inadequate start that so many children from disadvantaged homes receive" and urged the university to pay more attention to the moral development of students, taking steps to heighten their sensitivity and concern for the less fortunate. Educational institutions with resources and prestige, she said, should make sure that faculty had the capabilities necessary to clarify ethical issues, and she encouraged them to keep such considerations in mind when making tenure decisions. Continuing education courses, she suggested, offered another opportunity for elevating the moral consciousness of students by affording undergraduates the opportunity to discuss moral issues with older people who had life experiences.

She served on a committee to give an award in the name of a Pennsylvania judge, William Hastie, who had fought for an end to discrimination in housing in the 1940's. In addition to awarding the prize to Patricia Harris, the United States Secretary of Housing and Urban Development, Polly attended panels on aspects of housing segregation and urban decline.

These years had their share of sadness. On September 2, 1978, the youngest of her siblings, her much-loved brother David, died. He was married to a former student of Polly's from Bennington. Polly had introduced them, or as she recounted, "David came up to Bennington to see me and then he saw *her*." He was eight years younger than Polly, a frequent visitor to the Bethany farm, in attendance at her various triumphs. But barely eight days after his death, when Polly was being interviewed for her Oral Memoir and was asked about her siblings, she gave the dates of their births, saying that David had arrived five years after Winifred. She did not mention that he had died only one week earlier. At times Polly even refused to acknowledge life's pain. At this moment, as in so many others, she soldiered on. On the date of David's death, her small pocket notebook has her mother's initials penciled in, and a few days later, the name of her sister-in-law, Laura. Nothing more.

She gave only one indication in all this time that retirement might be weighing on her. At a conference in Philadelphia at which she was a member of a panel discussing continuing education, she sat in on a session called "Rewarding Retirement Living" and took notes on coping with loss, anxiety, forgetfulness, and the fantasy of a second career. Most of the time, however, as she told an interviewer, she was happy with her life. "Each phase of life," she said, "has its special pleasures. One of mine now is the freedom to come and go as I choose. I can land at Logan on a late flight and drive home on a cold winter night without worrying anyone. No one knows that I'm doing it. That's a new luxury."[3]

This luxury, as it turned out, was to be short-lived. Just a few months later, Polly's life took a whole new turn and she enthusiastically surrendered this freedom.

Dr. Clement Smith, an eminent pediatrician and retired member of the Harvard Medical School faculty, had been a friend of Polly's since her arrival in Cambridge. He and his wife had been Radcliffe benefactors. In one of Polly's earliest Radcliffe journals is a note of a contribution from them of $150,000. Mrs. Smith had been a Radcliffe trustee and a member of the search committee that hired Polly. She became terminally ill with cancer during Polly's first year as president. When she could no longer leave her house, Polly made a point of visiting her often to tell her about the latest developments at the college and to make her feel she still had insights that could be helpful. She died in 1960, and once Hilles Library was built, Clement Smith arranged for a plaque to his wife to be mounted in its courtyard. As a wealthy widower, he was, according to one of his daughters, "a popular, single, available, much-courted man with lots of options open to him."

Polly and Clem Smith moved in the same Cambridge social circles and shared many interests, in addition to Radcliffe: medical science, literature, education, and the countryside. He had been a pioneer in the study of neonatology, saying that he cared for the tiniest children as they passed through what he called "the valley of the shadow of birth." He had published a book in 1945, *Physiology of the Newborn Infant*. He knew English and American poetry, from Chaucer through Frost, and Polly said he used quotations wonderfully "to enrich daily life." He had seriously considered becoming an English professor, but decided instead on medicine. He was nine years older than Polly, and she found him to be "a very well educated, complex, interesting person." Described by his daughter as "very much a 19th century guy," he was almost never seen without a tie.

After his wife's death, his path often crossed Polly's. "And every once in awhile we'd go out to supper or on a Thursday night when his maid was out I'd go up and we'd have soup and a sandwich and a nice chat by the fireplace. It was all very relaxed. He was interested in Radcliffe and I was, and he was a good person to talk some things over with and get a different perspective. And so we got to know each other quite well."

Then, after about eighteen years of such dinners, she became aware of deeper feelings. She told her daughter-in-law, Ann, that one weekend she had felt funny and finally she realized it was love. They decided to marry.

They went about the delicate task of informing their families. When his daughters had asked him in earlier days about re-marrying, Clem had always said, "But I was so totally married to your mother." Now he called each of them early one morning to tell them of the decision he had made.

Polly told Chuck the news when one of her Vassar trustee meetings conveniently coincided with a business trip of his. They arranged to meet at a large public reception where she let him know she wanted to talk with him privately about something important. She told him she had been spending a lot of time with Clem Smith, that they had become quite fond of one another, and she wanted to be sure it would be all right with him if they got married. "As she asked it," Chuck said years later, "I wasn't totally sure that she knew what my response would be. Maybe she did—maybe it was just a really nice gesture. I think she used the word 'permission.'" He gave it.

Polly then went out to Long Island to tell her brothers and sister. Without a hint that she had any special reason, she asked Winifred to assemble the family for dinner because she would like to see them. They were all sitting around the living room when Polly's brother-in-law, Harold Warner, said, "Polly, have you heard the story about the two young girls having cinnamon toast and tea at the Copley Plaza? They were discussing marriage. And one of them said, 'How about that rich old Mr. Jones?' And the other said, 'Oh, my dear, he's too old to be eligible.' The other said, 'My dear, he's too eligible to be old.'" Then Polly said, "Well, I've got something to say. I'm getting married, and is he ever eligible."

"And they were just absolutely stunned," said Polly. She had, after all, been single for twenty-five years and she was sixty-eight. Harold Warner had been just about to open a bottle of wine. He put it down, went to the cellar, and brought up a much more expensive bottle. Polly always remembered that gesture. Gardner was the most incredulous. He kept asking, "You mean, you are going to get married?" Eventually they all got used to it, but it took Gardner awhile. "He just hadn't thought of me doing something like that."

Polly hadn't really thought of it herself, she admitted, "until it sort of happened." "It never occurred to me that someday I'd be married to him. And it suddenly looked like a good idea." As she thought back on that evening in Northport with her family, she chuckled and said, "So that was that."

They were married on May 19, 1979, in Clem Smith's elegant Cambridge home at 37 Fayerweather Street, a beautiful, formal house with a greenhouse in back full of flowers and a fully stocked wine cellar. The dean of the Harvard Divinity school, Krister Stendahl, a Lutheran minister, performed the ceremony. For the rest of her life Polly hyphenated her name, Bunting-Smith, and kept a small photograph of Clem on her dresser, opposite the one of Henry Bunting. When asked by an interviewer what she did after Princeton, Polly said, "I married Clem Smith—that's what I did."

What startled Polly's family even more than the marriage was her transformation. "It was an amazing change," said her son-in-law, Reiner Decher. Clem became her center.

"Everything was for Clem," remembered Polly's granddaughter, Laura Decher. "She was no longer thinking about Polly and Polly's career, she was thinking about Clem and his needs and his heart and his breakfast and how he liked his eggs and whether the table was set just right for him. And I remember she couldn't pick us up somewhere because she had to take the lawn mower to get fixed for Clem." And the wood had to be stacked a certain way for the fireplaces, because Clem considered stacking wood an art form. It took some doing for Polly to allow anyone to stack the wood, because Clem was so particular about how it was done. "I had always thought of her as a scientist not as my grandmother," said Laura. "She was a caring person but she wasn't a grandma who made us cookies every Christmas. So it was a big revelation when Polly got married."

"She did dote on Clem; no doubt about it," said Chuck. "I saw it as a return to the kind of life she had with Henry—a wonderful return for her. She had lived alone for so long." Polly wrote to an old friend that life was "quite wonderful."

Where nothing else had changed her, this marriage did. Until now, friends had found the person they visited in the president's house on Brattle Street to be no different from the Bethany farmer: informal, in blue jeans, grocery shopping in shorts and sneakers, keeping bees on the roof, eating supper in the kitchen. But when they came to Fayerweather Street that was not the case. Here she was "the elegant lady of the house, complete with maid and a buzzer under the rug of the dining room table with which she could signal the maid to bring the next course."[4] She was open, even eager, to let people know that this was a passionate, physical, sexual relationship, even confiding to a friend that Clem had used royalties from a book to pay for a double bed, something he had never had before. They were so physically affectionate with one another in public that some family members were embarrassed and disapproving, saying, "Can you believe the way those two act?" Shortly after their wedding, Polly wrote to her young Bethany friend, Susan Bonner, "I'd always thought that marriages between older folks were a good thing, leading to less lonely, more comfortable lives. I had no idea it could be so exciting, even so passionate."

She told some family members who wanted to come to Cambridge soon after the wedding that they were welcome for the weekend, but then they had to leave because, after all, she was on her honeymoon. "That struck me as being more girlish, more emotional, more demonstrative than I had ever known her to be before," remembered Susan Bonner.

The families melded together surprisingly well. Clem and Polly kept their finances separate, removing that possible source of tension. Her granddaughters loved him. "He was the most grandfatherly figure I had in my life," said Meika, Mary's younger daughter. Laura stayed with them whenever she was in the East; the Fayerweather house was the home for the holidays. "They were the family I brought my boyfriends to meet." Harold Warner and Clem shared a love for Robert Frost, a bond that was established at their first meeting, when Harold set up something of an obstacle course. "What was that poem—that line," he asked, pretending to be searching for a line he knew by heart, "'it is with an April day'"—and Clem took the bait—"Robert Frost, Two Tramps in Mud Time." He had passed the test.

Clem's family was equally fond of Polly. His daughters had always been grateful for Polly's attentions to their mother when she was dying of cancer. Clem's grandchildren loved her too. They called her Granpolly. She went to Grandmother's Day at their school and often invited them on weekend afternoons for pizza and a swim.

In addition to three daughters, Clem Smith also had one son, Reynolds, who was autistic. When Polly and Clem took him out for dinner on one occasion, the food took a long time to come. Becoming impatient, Reynolds took off into the kitchen, the doors swinging closed behind him, before his frantic father could struggle out of his chair to stop him. Polly, who was not particularly concerned about proper restaurant behavior, restrained Clem, saying, "Let's just see what develops." In a few minutes Reynolds came out of the kitchen, and about thirty seconds later the food appeared. Polly had shown that, at least in some instances, Reynolds could take care of himself. "That moment was a real change in our family," remembered Hillary Smith, one of Clem's daughters.

Polly and Clem's life together was extremely happy. They divided their time between the Cambridge house and Clem's farm house in Peacham, Vermont. He enjoyed hearing about her Bethany days in the basement and on the farm, and when old friends turned up, he relished hearing anything they could remember about that time in Polly's life. He greatly enjoyed working around the Peacham place, and it gave Polly another outdoor place to plant and to tend. She planted flowers—blue and white delphiniums against the porch, white iris around the pond, orange and yellow daylilies everywhere. They spent a lot of time reading aloud to one another and passed books on to their children. He introduced Polly to a quieter, more contemplative life, hours spent reading and talking. She attended more concerts—the Boston Symphony, Harvard-Radcliffe orchestra, harpsichord concerts of seventeenth- and eighteenth-century music—and art exhibits at Harvard's Fogg Museum and the Boston Museum of Fine Arts—Eakins, Ruisdale.

They traveled, which Polly had not done much of before, except for trips with the Atomic Energy Commission and the Population Council, and a childhood trip to England with her Aunt Ruth. Clem enjoyed it, "knew all the ropes," Polly said. They went to Ireland, where his family had come from, and then up through Norway and Sweden and Finland on another trip. They always spent a few days in Holland, where Clem had friends with whom he had done research after the war into the effects of malnutrition on babies.

Increasingly she and Clem attended ceremonial occasions. To celebrate the 350th anniversary of the founding of Boston, *Time* magazine invited those who had been on their cover with Boston connections to attend a black-tie dinner at the Harvard Club. Polly and Clem went. There were celebrations of the twentieth anniversary of the President's Commission on the Status of Women, the thirtieth anniversary of the Population Council, and the bicentennial of the Harvard Medical School. She attended events that celebrated women's achievements: inaugurations of women as college presidents, as members of the New York Planning Commission, or dinners honoring individual women she had known and worked with. She still kept tabs on Radcliffe, still went to Radcliffe Club meetings, seminars, and lectures at the Institute and the Schlesinger Library, and Radcliffe dance performances, where she was listed as one of the people who had made a "vital contribution" to the program.

She took an interest in a couple of new causes—nuclear arms control and reproductive choice—going to meetings and sometimes writing letters on their behalf. When the American Academy of Arts and Sciences held a two-day centennial symposium on Darwin, she attended and took copious notes.

Very occasionally she agreed to say a few words in public. She gave a sketchy round-up of the 1950's and 1960's at a meeting recounting the history of the American Council on Education's Commission on Women. And in this speech she struck what came to be her major theme at this point in her life, the importance of women looking beyond their own movement toward other causes and the needs of others, "joining forces with as many others as possible to provide fair shares of work for all individuals and peoples—particularly the young, more especially the disadvantaged young."

Clem's interests and his career took her to medical conferences on pediatric diseases, lectures at Children's Hospital and the Harvard Medical School. She was at his side for the ceremony in 1985 when the medical school created the Clement A. Smith Chair of Pediatrics in recognition of his career as a distinguished pediatrician.

There were inevitable sorrows. In April 1981 Polly's mother, Gwy, died at the age of ninety-four. And then, four years later, on February 22, 1985, came the terrible news that Bill's young wife, Lonna, now a pediatrician, had died in an automobile accident. On her way from a friend's house to the farm in Maine that Bill had bought while she was in medical school, she fell asleep at the wheel. When the police brought in her purse after the accident, Bill saw that she had run out of her narcolepsy medicine. He said he had always known, in some part of himself, that one day that would happen. Many of the families Lonna had cared for built, in her memory, a wooden labyrinth of ladders and bars for children to play on. Even years later, whenever Polly visited Bill in Maine, she said people who recognized her would tell her what a wonderful doctor Lonna had been.

As Clem aged, their universe began slowly to contract, becoming more a world of gardens, bird-watching, and family and less one of formal dinners and academic events. Polly gave up positions on a number of boards. Her journals recorded small, daily happenings—the boys who left a patch of lawn for her to mow because they thought it too close for comfort to a hornet's nest; an afternoon spent making shortcake "from scratch," which, nonetheless, did not turn out well; double solitaire with Clem; observations of the beaver making a dam and the birds who frequented their birdbath. The names of their children and grandchildren occurred more and more frequently: when they came for dinner, when she and Clem drove to their homes for visits, when they telephoned. Her grandson was homesick at camp; her sister, Winifred, was recovering well enough after surgery to begin cooking dinner again; John arrived at the same time as the new television set. "The excitement today is having Meika come—on NW—4.23." "Nice supper with blue plates for Meika." The disappointment when Laura's plans changed, indicated by the triple underlining under *not* coming. Polly kept daily track of the weather—the heat, the thunderstorms, the cloudy days. She conducted an elaborate experiment with her grandsons, tracking the temperature of the water in the pond and comparing it with the temperature of the air and the stream. She noted when she planted, when she spread the lime, how the tulips were doing and when she transplanted "the scrappy forsythia." "Unbelievably & very sadly—I cut the wrong minitrunk of a bush with dead branches—and one live one—that hung over bird bath." She briefly noted Gardner's call to say that Aunt Grace had died at the age of ninety-six, and then, as was her style, moved right on; "Tulips splendid—and grape hyacinth, which have spread nicely. And the narcissus along the driveway hold their own remarkably well." She noted, without explanation, that she did so little reading these days.

Clem's health began to fail, but he did what he could: worked on his wood pile and trimmed the yews by the front steps. And on Polly's seventy-seventh birthday, he composed a poem in her honor, an "extraordinarily well written, thoughtful & generous poem," she wrote in her journal. He tried as hard as he could to do what he had always done, writing Christmas letters, keeping in touch with people who mattered to him, even drafting a letter of congratulations in July to a friend who was going to turn one hundred in October. They still occasionally ventured out: to a Planned Parenthood lunch to hear about programs and facilities for poor young women and to an MIT seminar on the origins of cancer.

Polly still managed an occasional excursion on her own. She attended a seminar at Radcliffe on the prospects and progress of women in Fortune 500 companies. She served as a guinea pig for a doctor at Harvard conducting tests on the mental abilities of older people. She participated in a Douglass conference on women's colleges, and gave something close to a speech, urging colleges to examine whether they were doing all that they should, and celebrating the fact that women's colleges seemed to be thriving as never before.[5]

When she was away, one of Clem's daughters stayed with him. He had become, one of them said, "a pretty confused elderly gentleman," forgetting what it was he had started out to look for before he could find it. He would write checks, the same check, a number of different times. He threw out the flower bulbs before they could be transplanted. He often said, "When you get older everything takes longer; but don't worry, you'll have less to do."

Polly was occupied more and more with his care. During the summer of 1987 she cleared paths for him at Peacham to make it easier for him to take strolls and was "rewarded' when he was able to venture out one afternoon to look at the dam an enterprising beaver had made in their stream. Her journals contained terse statements reflecting her concern with his well being: "Clem OK but now alternating Amphagel with Maalox because of diarrhea. Some discomfort after supper." When they celebrated his birthday by attending a movie based on a Chekhov story, it proved to be too difficult for him to follow. Polly did what she could to bolster him. She showed his daughters some screens he had repaired, saying, "Look what your father did today." "She poured out endless warmth and approval," remembered Hillary Smith, "and used her considerable organizational skill to reorder his life, to make him feel safe." He knew what she was doing and expressed his gratitude to her and to his daughters. But on September 14, 1987, she "woke up to wonder—more seriously—whether the time had come to move from 37 to either an apartment or 'a place.' Investigate possibilities."

They decided to move into a retirement community in Hanover, New Hampshire, that was in the planning stage. Called Kendal, it was to be run by Quakers and was near Dartmouth, with all its promises of intellectual stimulation. Hanover itself was a familiar and comfortable environment, a New England college town with lots of red brick and white wood. The nearest post office was in the back of a hardware store. They thought they would spend the winters at Kendal, where someone else would shovel the snow from the walks, and their summers in Peacham, where they could enjoy the flowers, the stream, and the pond. It amused Polly that their children praised them for being so "responsible."

Before Kendal was completed, however, Clem Smith awoke one morning in their Cambridge home and let Polly know that things were not quite right with him. He felt strange and unwell. She climbed back into bed and held him until he died, in her arms. "He was ready to die," said Chuck's wife, Ann, who had spoken to him just two weeks before, when he was struggling to finish his Christmas letters." He was clearly ready to die. He didn't like the lapse in his functioning." He was eighty-seven. For all of Polly's refusal even to acknowledge life's sorrows, she didn't shrink from the reality of death. She didn't absent herself at the moment; she didn't avoid confronting its enormity or its finality. Death was a part of life, to be faced and dealt with. She did that, yet again, and moved on.

She decided to keep to their plan, moving into Kendal as soon as it was open, in July 1991, just as she turned eighty-one. Her children let her know she would be welcome with them, but she didn't have friends or contemporaries where they were, while her sister-in-law, Laura, David's widow, and one of her college roommates, Eliza Janeway, were going to Kendal. It made more sense to begin a new chapter.

Now in her eighties, scoliosis was bending Polly's back and the pain was forcing her, for the first time ever, to take a host of medications. It was becoming harder for her to maintain the gardens in New Boston, so she decided the time had come to sell the house and land. Meika kept her company there for four months while she packed up, watching the birds, talking about horses—a shared passion—going to a nearby town to hear the orchestra. When Reiner took a sabbatical at MIT, Polly offered him a quiet weekend haven and a place to write. So in her final New Boston fall—as it turned out, an exceptionally beautiful fall—she had the company of her family as she prepared to relinquish her garden and a place she loved. She was somewhat melancholy but, nonetheless, had spirited conversations with Reiner, particularly at breakfast as they listened to National Public Radio. They did a lot of reminiscing about times they had spent there before. "It was a beautiful fall," he said, "this fall of Polly's life."

In April 1992 the New Boston sale was final. Polly gave some of the marshlands she had acquired in her retirement to the town in order to protect them. She hoped the town would put a picnic table at the foot of a particularly big tree at the end of a "nice path," so that families could take picnics there. "And maybe some day that will happen," she said.

It made it easier for her that Chuck and Ann bought the Peacham place from Clem's estate. Her children knew how important it was for her to have a country place in her life, something she had always had for them while they were growing up. Now they had a chance to do the same for her. And Peacham maintained her connection to Clem's family and her life with him, although she went less and less frequently, perhaps because it was now Ann and Chuck's or because it was becoming increasingly difficult for her to navigate on the paths.

Now her two-bedroom apartment in Kendal was home. She filled it with what mattered to her: many books—shelves of poetry, from seventeenth-century metaphysicals to twentieth-century iconoclasts—history, fiction, biographies of Jefferson and Truman, Anne Sexton, and Franklin and Eleanor Roosevelt. "Somebody generally tells me about one, or gives me one, then if I like it I think of other people to share it with." There were braided rugs, comfortable chairs, a wooden rocker, a lovely old quilt on her bed. Plants were everywhere—on top of bookcases, in corners, on her balcony. She carefully watered them each day. It was the next best thing to having a garden. She tried a bird feeder, but only pigeons came, so she decided not to go on with that. The refrigerator was too full of food because she said she couldn't believe she wasn't a family. She never used the dishwasher—silly for just one person—and instead stored dishes in it. On the walls were Japanese prints that had belonged to her parents and one of a Scottish mountain she had made a point of visiting when she and Clem were in Scotland. There were paintings of Bill's—one of the New Boston house "with a snowstorm just brewing," another of bears that she had found once rolled up in his closet, and a photograph of her parents' Mary Cassatt, the picture of the mother and child. It had become too valuable, so after careful thought she had decided that since one tends not to look too closely or too often at a picture that has been on the wall for a long time, it would do more good to sell it and give the money to her grandchildren for their college tuitions. It was enough to have the photograph as a reminder.

Polly didn't fuss over her surroundings. She was amused by the woman who had painted a mural on one of her apartment's walls and then had a party to unveil it. Polly didn't go in for such serious decorating. There were a few reminders of her past celebrity, but almost hidden away. In the second bathroom and an out-of-the way corner of her bedroom were the photographs with the American flags in the corner: Polly at the AEC, at the National Science Foundation during a visit from President Nixon, and at the National Advisory Committee on Health Manpower, a seat away from President Johnson.

The apartment was smaller than any of her previous homes. Her nephew, Sandy Ingraham, who often visited her, thought that even though she wouldn't admit it, she had to be unhappy in such a small, institutional place. But she assured him that it was interesting to have dinner with a different person every day. She knew why she was there, why she had chosen it. Unlike her former roommate or her sister-in-law, who spoke poignantly about their old homes in Weston and Lyme, Polly wrote in a letter to Henry's last doctor, William Winternitz, "Life here at Kendal will suit me very well these last years. It is an astonishly [sic] interesting community." Her spelling had never improved.

If she needed confirmation that she had made the right decision, she got it not long after her arrival when she tripped on a stair and broke her knee. Kendal was well equipped to take care of her, and the crutches provided had an unexpected and welcome side effect: they proved to be exactly the right treatment for her scoliosis. Walking on crutches straightened her back and freed her from the pain, enabling her to stop all her pain medication. It was such effective treatment that even after her knee healed, she still did laps on crutches around her apartment and urged her doctors to prescribe crutches for others with scoliosis. Nonetheless, she could not avoid the awareness of her increasing physical frailty, noting objectively, as if she were chronicling the condition of someone else, that it hurt her back to carry her plants in from the balcony. But she was still getting around and was able to meet Meika and Mary in Grand Junction, Colorado, and go on to the Black Canyon at Gunnison.

Joining Kendal, Polly said, was like going to college—being thrown together with a group of people you hadn't chosen, becoming part of a new community. You could reinvent yourself. Her Vassar roommate actually did change her name from Betty to Eliza, something she had wanted to do for a long time. All the residents had to wear name tags with only their first names. They were told they were starting a new experience and needed to forget the people they had been. That was fine with Polly. She didn't want to come in as the former president of Radcliffe. "I'd like to just be a person," she said. Many embellished their name tags with needlepoint or calligraphy or fancy chains. Polly's was unadorned, but she kept saying she was going to ask Mary—always good with her hands—to fix it up a little. Residents made a point of greeting one another in elevators, in hallways, at meals, calling one another by name. "It's a way of practicing keeping your memory," Polly said.

There were opportunities, which Polly shunned, to be involved in the administration of the place, serving on landscaping or other committees. "I don't want to take my time with that stuff," she said. "I have been waiting for years for time to read." She preferred individual gestures. When one of her neighbors mentioned that walking with her walker took so long and was boring, Polly bought her a Walkman.

The residents looked out for one another in many ways. Everyone had a buddy to call or be called by no later than nine every morning. Polly and Eliza called one another. Some pushed the wheelchairs from the full-care section to enable those in the worst shape to attend the events in the large public room called "The Gathering Room." Some worked in the woodworking shop using tools they had brought from shops they had had in their own homes. They worked to repair the furniture they off-handedly described as being as old and decrepit as they were themselves. They wanted it to be in good enough shape to leave to someone or to sell in order to help out those who had outlived their money and could no longer pay the monthly fees. The shortness of the future was understood.

In many ways Kendal was a good fit for Polly. It was not oppressively institutional. There were some beautiful Asian screens in some walkways that had been given by a resident who had been to China and Japan. The dining room was light and airy with a cheerful flowered carpet. At meals, if you had no one to eat with, you could just join a table. Unlike other retirement complexes that Polly had heard about, at Kendal people didn't dress up. On the main bulletin board were notices of plays, poetry, and short story readings at Dartmouth. The telephone number of the White House comment line was also listed along with encouragement to call with protests. The library, with nearly four thousand books, was open twenty-four hours a day. Politicians running for office stopped by to give speeches. Experts from Dartmouth delivered lectures. Singing groups from nearby towns came to perform. A retired Juilliard faculty member and highly respected pianist, Beveridge Webster, was a resident and gave concerts most Saturday nights.

Even more important for Polly, the complex of tan vinyl-sided buildings was surrounded by acres of woods, some of which were owned by Kendal, making it possible for her to stay connected to the natural world she loved. When she first arrived, she explored the woods thoroughly. As the years wore on, she still went there, although on shorter walks, and finally with a cane, which she reluctantly admitted was "a nuisance." She set her small dining table right by the window in her apartment, where she could see the Vermont hills. She complained only about the building across the courtyard, because it interfered with her view of sunsets and she disapproved of the way too many trees had been planted too close together in the courtyard below. She could see that some of them were going to have to be removed before too long.

Most important of all, Kendal was close to her family. Clem Smith's daughters lived close by. Mary was still living in Seattle, but Polly's three sons all lived in New England, close enough to visit her often. Chuck was the chancellor of the state colleges of Vermont, and he and Ann lived in Shelburne. Bill lived on his Maine farm, and John, who had become a fire fighter, lived with his wife, Meredith, in New Boston, near where Polly's house used to be. Polly said John had had "a little bit of a hard time" deciding to be a fire fighter. But she told him, "if that's what you want to do, go do it. But do it well." It mattered far less, she always said, what people did than how they did it. She told many of her visitors how satisfied she felt that all her children were living the lives they had chosen.

Kendal's proximity to Dartmouth had attracted other intellectuals, and Polly found a number of congenial acquaintances. Two other former college presidents and one of Polly's successors as dean of Douglass were residents. The former chairman of the New York Stock Exchange was there, along with a host of writers. Soon after her arrival, she wrote a friend about an exhibit of at least fifty books written by residents. She also found some past acquaintances and established new connections. She was surprised to find the son of Vassar's old president, Henry Noble MacCracken, the little boy she had taken birdwatching more than sixty years before. Another bird enthusiast was also a resident. He had been in the Washington office of a national bird society when word arrived that the chimney swifts Polly and Henry had banded in Bethany had been found in their winter nesting place. He told her they "jumped up and down in the office" at the confirmation of the birds' migration patterns. "That was a wonderful link," Polly said.

The most fortunate and most important friendship of all was with Harold Greenwald, a chemist from New Jersey, whose hobby was woodworking. He was a remarkable person, but not a very healthy one, afflicted with a back deformity that had required repeated operations through the years. He had gone to college in a full cast. "Can you imagine that?" Polly said. "It must have been horrible. He managed to keep his equanimity and go right along and everybody loved him everywhere he went." He relied on canes for walking, but he could drive, and Polly and he went off on excursions together. When they visited Bill in Maine and were checking in to a bed-and-breakfast, Harold became tongue-tied, but Polly piped up—"one room, one bed."

His stoicism, courage, and good humor appealed to her. Like her, he always tried to make things better. When he saw that one of the women who had only one hand couldn't applaud at concerts, he made her a hand clapper. Seeing that a lot of people had trouble opening and closing doors, he made door stops with long handles, so they didn't have to bend down and could be in a wheelchair and still prop the door open. He made a device for women who couldn't pull the upper latches in their windows because they were too high, "a nice little thing you could slip into the hole and just pull," explained Polly, which gave the old women more of a feeling of independence. "He just observed what was going on," said Polly. They had dinners together most evenings. His friendship made Polly's adjustment easier.

At the end of 1992 Polly suffered another terrible loss, the death of her brother Gardner at the age of eighty from heart failure. He was the sibling closest to her in age and someone she had been close to all of her life. His death affected her profoundly.

Soon after, Harold was hospitalized and expected to die. Polly was temporarily thrown off balance. Her children found her frightened and disheartened. Harold rallied that time and survived, but about a year later, in January 1994, his health deteriorated precipitously. He had to have transfusions. When they became more and more frequent, he decided that was no way to live. He put himself into Kendal's hospital wing and stopped all the medication.

Polly told Eliza that she might not be around the next morning for their nine o'clock "buddy" call because she would be staying with Harold in the hospital. And she was with him through the night, into the next morning and the next afternoon, until he died. She called Eliza in the middle of the afternoon to tell her it was over. Once again, when it came to facing death, Polly was right there, without tears. Hillary Smith came up the next day to express her sympathy, and Polly let her get out two sentences before she said, "Yes, but think of all the good times we had."

Polly had never had a good memory. She even wrote a thank-you letter to Susan Bonner years earlier admitting that she could not remember what present she was thanking her for. "Age hasn't helped an old problem," she wrote. "I do go in for lists but don't always use them." During her administrative years she had made a point of keeping track in her journals of names and details about people she was meeting or asking for money. But now, more and more was slipping away. She made light of it as long as she could. The joke in old age, she said, "is to find your glasses before you forget what you are looking for." She said, while working on a report for Radcliffe in 1993, "it is very hard to write well when you cannot remember what you said in the last paragraph." She kept a small notebook of all her "written communications"—legal as well as personal—checks sent and statements received from financial institutions, reminders of books ordered and sent, thank yous for visits and lunches as well as postcards and "good letters" to friends and family. Sometimes she even noted telephone calls she had made and what she had said. Occasionally she still inserted more personal notes; "7/22/92 Bill did get some hay in but ⅔ of crop is standing in water."

She wrote herself notes. ("Be sure to call Eliza by nine,") and left them by her telephone. As hard as she could, she tried to keep track of the details of her life. She checked the money in her purse before she went out, wrote down everything she bought, and tallied it up at the end of the day. She was acutely aware of what was happening, telling an interviewer that her memory was really "going to pieces. I've gone over some kind of hump that one goes over," and she made an arc with her hand like a mountain peak. "I find you sort of sink, and then you level off for a while and then you go down another thing." To Ann, she was franker. "I'm just unraveling," she said.

She accepted an invitation from the Population Council in June 1992, but for the most part she stopped going to official, formal events, even turning down commencements at Harvard and Douglass. She removed her name from lists. She asked to be deleted from the mailing list of the Democratic National Committee, asked the NSF to stop sending big reports, just the biweekly newsletter. To one organization she wrote in August 1992, "I recognize my limitations." She accepted an invitation to meet with new Institute fellows, but then changed her mind. She declined to attend Vassar's Environmental Sciences Forum and cancelled *Natural History* magazine. She lost her AARP card, her Fidelity card, her Social Security card and wrote requesting replacements. She asked Winifred what the date was of their mother's death. As her memory was failing, she still felt her attachment to her family. When Winifred was ill, Polly sent her a letter, saying she was prepared to come to Long Island at any time if she could help. At the end of 1994 she wrote in her notebook that she had sent a letter to her sister-in-law and was keeping a copy. Then the next day she wrote, "10/17/94—Wonder if I did keep a copy—just one more example of my disappearing short term memory."

Nonetheless, she remained engaged politically. She wrote letters to senators about the clean water act, to the president about nuclear testing, even to the Emir of Bahrain and the president of Colombia, pleading for amnesty for political prisoners.

By the end of 1994, she decided consciously to begin weeding things out, determining to leave "a less cluttered apartment before I'm moved to the hospital wing—which is not imminent but at 84 one never knows."

She said Alzheimer's first. She had seen it before, in Henry's father, in her mother, then in Clem. She knew the signs. She resisted moving out of her apartment. She continued to drive, assuming, as she said, that as long as no one was honking at her she was still all right. But then she returned from a visit to some friends in early 1995, went to sleep in her apartment, and awoke the next morning thinking, "I know I have been here before, but I don't know where I am." That was the turning point. She decided not to take any more excursions alone. In the summer of 1996 she spent a week with Bill in Maine; he photographed her next to his oxen. He drove her home and thought all was well, but that evening she telephoned him in some confusion, asking if he knew where she might have been and who the nice man was who had brought her home. By 1996 she was getting lost at Kendal.

She didn't give up. When the new dean of Douglass, Barbara Shailor, asked to come to Kendal to talk with her because she was trying to meet with all of the former deans, Polly agreed to see her. It was difficult for Polly to hold up her end of the conversation—it was hard to remember what she had just said—but she did her best.

Her decline was painful for her children to witness, but Mary found the best words. "Maybe we can just think that she used so much mental energy that she just used it up. Most of us don't do that."

It was fitting that her last public appearance was at the thirty-fifth anniversary of the Radcliffe Institute, May 16, 1997. She was already very ill with gallstones and had to leave before the ceremonies were over. As Mary, Chuck, and Ann drove her back to Kendal, Mary urged Polly to go into the assisted care section—at least at night—in case she needed help. It was what Polly had asked of her own mother more than thirty years earlier. When she was at the AEC, she had written Gwy, urging her to get the help she needed, not to think about how much it cost, but only how relieved her children would be to know she was being taken care of. Perhaps her old advice lingered in the back of her mind. After Mary's appeal, "Polly got very clear," Mary said, "like her old self and said, 'Well, I guess if it will make my children worry about me less, I'll go.'"

Almost until the very end, she remained herself. When she fell and broke her hip, Chuck came rushing down and asked her urgently, "Which hip is it?" to which she had the apt response, "Does it matter?" And after a lengthy conference with her doctor, she responded to his, "See you soon, Polly," with "I hope not too soon."

It was fitting too that her last excursion was with two of her children to Peacham. It was a beautiful, somewhat chilly June Saturday, and Mary thought they should go outside and have a picnic. It was Polly who said they should have it at Peacham. Ann and Chuck and their son, Matt, met them there. They bundled Polly up and sat on the porch and had their picnic. The daffodils were blooming where Clem's ashes were buried. "We kept saying, 'Mother this was such a great idea.' We had a wonderful day." "A magical, magical afternoon," said Matt "saying good-bye." When Polly got in the car to go back to Kendal, Matt put his hand up against the window and Polly touched her hand to the other side of the glass, her fingers matching his. He started to cry, "and she sort of turned around and smiled and sort of let us know it was OK." She did not cry.

The six months from June 1997 until the following January were all downhill. Polly's children closed her apartment and moved her into a room in the assisted living section of Kendal. They furnished it with her favorite prints and furniture. She lost more and more ability to communicate. When Chuck arrived on Sunday, January 17, she was in great difficulty. The Kendal staff told Mary, Chuck, and John that although Polly could no longer speak, she could probably still hear the voices of the people she loved most. They spoke to her lovingly, assuring her they were all well. Her grandson Adam wrote a poem in tribute to "her great ability and strength to be open to life, to be open to anything." Chuck held the phone next to her ear while Adam read, "I love you Polly, Good luck on your journey." Mary, Chuck, and John were at her bedside, but Bill was stuck in Maine. There had been a fierce ice storm and his farm was without power. He couldn't leave because he had to keep a generator going so that his animals could have water. Mary, Chuck, and John kept talking to Polly, telling her what Bill was doing for his animals, assuring her he would come as soon as the power came back on. They urged her to stay with them a bit longer; told her that, if she could just hold on, Bill would be there. Late Tuesday the power came back. As soon as he could, Bill started the drive south to Kendal. He got there at about five on Wednesday afternoon. He came straight to Polly's bedside, spent about ten minutes talking to her quietly. And then Polly Bunting died. She had waited for Bill. "One last heroic struggle," said Chuck.

She died, said Mary, "before she stopped recognizing her children and grandchildren. This was her final gift to all of us." It was Wednesday, January 21, 1998. She was eighty-seven.

Polly's death was marked by the *New York Times* and the *Boston Globe* with half-page obituaries; *Time* magazine noted her death as did newspapers up and down the East Coast.

There were three memorial services for her: formal ones at Douglass and in Harvard's Memorial Church, and one for family and friends in Kendal's Gathering Room. Chairs were lined up on two sides of the room, facing one another, in the form of a Quaker meeting, which was what it was. It was the sort of cold, winter New England day Polly loved, with lots of bright white snow and a cloudless blue sky. At the entrance to the Gathering Room were two large easels with pictures of Polly—holding an infant Mary, pumping up an air mattress with her foot while reading a book, and in old age, sitting on the floor rolling a ball to a small child. Much laughter rolled across the room as one after another, people rose with reminiscences, testimonies to her courage, her modesty, her flexibility—such as calmly carving up and serving a roast in the Radcliffe president's house, to an assembled group of dignitaries unaware that the dog of one of the guests had already enjoyed a good part of it. Beveridge Webster, whose playing Polly had enjoyed so many Saturday evenings, played a Chopin nocturne. The service concluded with Francois Couperin's short piece, "The Nightingale in Love," for piano and flute—Henry's instrument—a way of including him one last time. Chuck said that in his mind he could still hear the clear tones of Henry's flute as they wafted through the air in the evenings in their Bethany home.

The next day Polly's family interred her ashes at Peacham, near Clem Smith's where the daffodils bloom.

27

An Interesting Life

Polly Bunting's life spanned the twentieth century and is emblematic of its changes, if not of its turbulence. She saw much of her childhood world of ordered domesticity come to an end and played some part in ending it, as she demanded and then celebrated more opportunities for women. She understood before most people that women's lives had an inherently different pattern from those of men, and she worked to turn the ingrained habits of our society and the rigid schedules of institutions toward more flexibility so that women would not be constrained nor their lives defined by one short span of childbearing and rearing. Life could be—must be—a combination of family and study and work, not all at once, but sequentially. She saw life in its entirety, understanding how long it is, how complex, and how essential that human beings realize themselves over the full span of their years.

At the same time she never doubted that families were paramount. At first glance, it may appear contradictory that such a determined feminist should have so deeply respected traditional female roles. But she herself found no contradiction. She accepted that women bore the primary responsibilities for keeping the home and raising the children, and that those responsibilities deserved to be respected. She said openly that had Henry not died, leaving her with four young children to support, she never would have ventured so far from home. She would have continued her scientific research and happily lived out her life on her Bethany hilltop. She honored and valued her many roles as wife, mother, daughter, grandmother, mother-in-law, aunt, sister, friend. She was both a part of and apart from her world.

Her concept of the "climate of unexpectation" defined her professional life, but she was never willing even to consider that her own scientific career might have suffered from it. It wasn't until she saw the stunting impact it was having on other women that she "awakened," recognizing a problem that had to be solved, defining it before anyone else. She wasn't looking for a crusade. She wasn't planning on leading a movement. She just knew it was wrong for a democracy to deny opportunities to half the population and that once women were afforded their rightful place, everyone would benefit: the women themselves but ultimately the society, which would finally have the efforts of everyone.

Profoundly democratic, she believed that denying opportunity to anyone, particularly educational opportunity, was to deprive them of the most significant promise of our democracy. No individual should be cheated out of that promise. Each and every person, regardless of sex, age, or circumstances, had the right to develop and contribute, and to "shove into the stream of life."

The concept of evolution had fired her imagination when she was a child and continued to fascinate her throughout her life. It became her metaphor for her belief that the ingrained capacities of human beings had been honed over the millennia for a purpose. Modern society needed the contributions of all, but even more important, individuals needed to work at tasks that ignited their enthusiasm. She knew from her own experience that anything less than the full employment of one's capabilities made life insipid, "like water when one is not thirsty." For her children, her students, her colleagues, her friends, the message was always the same: find what interests you and do it.

She became a great educational leader without preparation, courses, or training in the ways of academic governance, because she was committed to clear and worthy goals. Her parents, she said, had been into "doing good." So was she. She followed her instincts, drew on her experience, identified and then swept aside the obstacles in the way of the students under her care. Her commitment to simple principles—opportunity, fairness, equality—animated her actions, giving her administrations a driving focus and clarity of purpose.

She summed up her pragmatic, experimental approach: "I think one thing you learn in administration is not to worry about the things you can't do. You do what you can—the thing that seems most important that you can do at this place, at this time, for whoever is there. And if you were in a different sort of a setup you'd do something else." "One does what one can where one is."

Polly always had her vision of the life she wanted to lead and a sense of the person she was. She never turned away from the insight she had in her thinking tree: that she, herself, could determine what kind of a girl she would be, that she could determine her own destiny. She had a center that always held, even at the end, even in the face of Alzheimer's.

To others it might appear as if a stroke of good fortune plucked Polly Bunting from obscurity and gave her an opportunity to achieve national prominence. But national prominence was never what she wanted. Fate compelled her to abandon the quiet, rural life she had chosen and always preferred.

In the final analysis, Polly Bunting achieved what she wanted most. Never a climber of ladders, she never aspired to fame or fortune. Eminence neither attracted nor intrigued her. From the very first to the very last, what she wanted was "an interesting life." She had one.

Afterword

In my many conversations with Polly Bunting during the course of my research, she urged me often to interject myself and my own experiences into the telling of her story. I kept insisting that the hallmarks of a respectable biographer are detachment and objectivity and that such an intrusion would be inappropriate. This, after all, was to be the record of her achievements and accomplishments.

But now that her story is told, I find that I would like to add a personal note. When I first began work on this project, I went to the library to find out if Polly were still alive, if anyone had yet written her biography, and then to find out what material about her was available. I turned first to the *New York Times* index and came upon the 1961 *New York Times Sunday Magazine* article in which Polly had written so eloquently about "the climate of unexpectation." I had been squinting at the microfilm for several minutes before I realized that tears were streaming down my face. All those shelved dreams, lost opportunities, sacrificed ambitions that characterized my generation of women had not been our fault after all. There really had been societal forces arrayed against us. Some of this awareness had occurred to me before, of course, but never with such clarity and such force. Like most women of my generation, I had accepted the unexpectation of my time.

Polly worked to free us and the generations of women who came later from the stultifying assumption that domesticity was our only choice, the only kind of life we were entitled to. There were certainly more flamboyant feminists, more charismatic speakers, flashier personalities. But none had her clarity of vision, her depth of perception, and the almost evangelical fervor with which she fought for her cause.

She never sought recognition and never expected gratitude. But now I ask for them on her behalf. I hope that young women of today who hold the world in their hands, and hold it whole, will come to recognize the debt they owe her. I hope they will see how her words helped to shape the revolution that ultimately freed them to aspire.

I hope they will understand the ways in which she helped to change the environment in which they grew, the ways in which her language framed a new consciousness. I hope they will celebrate her accomplishments with respect and—yes—be grateful.

Appendix: Speeches

The Modern Scientific Revolution
Introductory Remarks at Alumnae College, Douglass College,
June 3, 1959

Alumnae College is a new venture in education for Douglass. It is planned to give both faculty and graduates an opportunity to gain and share a better understanding of an important phase of the intellectual life of our time and its significance for society.

The rate of flow of scientific discovery has affected all of us. Its acceleration will present each of us with new problems and new opportunities. During these two days of personal discovery we shall explore not only the nature and impact of contemporary scientific output, but also science's logic and its ideals. Scientists have shared their hardware freely, but they have often been reluctant to share their vision. Science's tolerant but critical spirit, its free-enterprise carried on under an unwritten but binding code, its self-government and its universality are the product and the promise of liberal scholarship and humane civilization. These also have implications of great significance to society.

Within the last few years some scientists, diverting their eyes from the enticing vistas opening ahead in their own special fields long enough to catch the gleam of excitement in other areas of research, have begun to sense the phenomenal variety and scope, and depth, and pace of discovery that is now in progress. They have come to speak of a scientific revolution or, sometimes, a scientific explosion; for although the study of science today is continuous with that of the past, its acceleration is new and presents new dimensions and complexities to scientists themselves and to the society in which they work, the society that has become global because of science.

An important aspect of the scientific revolution is the confidence that many scientists feel in their ability to break the barriers lying ahead in their own fields, and the belief that with new knowledge will come new major concepts of great beauty and usefulness. Established truths of today will, of course, be found to be conditional, but the finding will bring greater truths.

I suppose it would be academically proper at this moment for me to attempt to define science, but I shall not do so. Science is like love or the color blue; we all have a pretty good idea about the general concept, but who can set its boundaries? Hobbes said long ago, "Science is of that nature that none can understand it to be, but such as in good measure has attayned it." Even though it may be misleading to attempt precise definition, one can gain insight from descriptions of science in which those with valid experiences record their experiences and reflections. Science is a response to curiosity, an area of study, an endeavor. One distinguished scientist at the Symposium on Basic Science held last month in New York—when pushed for a definition—said "If you can find out when you're wrong, then it's science." Another described it as "a philosophy of ignorance." Certainly it is characterized more by the way it tests the validity of its concepts than by the way it arrives at them. The kind of report the scientist writes is very different from that of the artist, but the creative act in both cases has aesthetic components.

This morning Mr. McGar and Mrs. Ellis will speak to you on the progress being made in physics and biochemistry, and I shall give a few illustrations from biology, but first I should like to tell a story of local origin that is one of my favorite illustrations of the scientific revolution. It seems that Dean Martin of the Rutgers College of Agriculture had reason to speak to a member of his faculty about his final exams which used many of the same questions year after year. "It really is quite all right," the professor explained, "research is progressing so rapidly in our laboratories that although the questions may be the same, the answers each year must be different."

There is little question in my mind but that the reason I decided to plunge into microbiology rather than some other science was because the living cell presented an area of ignorance that seemed to me particularly annoying and intriguing. The notion that a tiny bagful of unorganized freely interacting materials could reproduce itself every half-hour, indefinitely, complete with untold carbohydrates, fats, proteins, purines, pyrimidines, enzymes, co-enzymes, and genetic mechanisms, seemed too incredible to let alone. Furthermore, there were obviously thousands and thousands of different kinds of microorganisms, each with its characteristic kind of behavior. Nothing seemed quite so necessary as trying to find out something more about how all of this was accomplished.

Today our concept of the cell has changed drastically. We know that it is a highly organized microcosm with a complex structure that we can begin to reveal with the electronmicroscope and to analyze by methods borrowed from chemistry, physics, genetics, cybernetics, and anywhere else. There is a long way to go, but we have reached a level of understanding of a basic structure that is intricate enough to be a helpful model and we are rapidly accumulating data relating specific types of reactions to specific submicroscopic structures. Thus, for example, protein synthesis is known to be associated with certain small dark particles or microsomes found in the endoplasmic membrane within the cell, whereas cholesterol synthesis which also takes place at the membrane does not involve the microsomes. Furthermore, the tremendous molecules that are being teased out of cells and mapped by a variety of techniques have properties that could conceivably enable them to serve as templates for the replications and reactions known to take place.

There are many other beautiful examples of new insight—the gene responsible for sickle cell anaemia in man brings about its effects by altering a particular amino at just one location in the 300 unit molecule of haemoglobin. Genetic particles from certain bacteria can be labelled with radioactive phosphorus, extracted from the parent cell, and introduced into other cells whose progeny will then inherit the specific characteristic (e.g. streptomycin resistance) conveyed by that transforming principle. Furthermore, we are beginning to understand how the gene produces its effect so that it becomes possible to modify gene action even when one cannot alter or exchange the genes.

These are just a few examples. By similar methods and with similar confidence biologists of assorted kinds are working in cancer and psychology and geology and astronomy. New relationships are being established on every front. It seems incredible that a creature with man's limited senses and crude manual skills should be able to discover so much. The more he learns the more insignificant becomes his role, but the more magnificent his universe and the more astonishing his insight and power. Thus, it is precisely now as we comprehend that our earth is probably one of millions of similar planets on which life undoubtedly exists that we also begin to understand how to arrange conditions to permit living material to create itself in our laboratories.

Knowledge has always meant power and new knowledge has always meant change. The implications of the new knowledge that science is producing opens up new choices throughout society. The implications for education are inescapable. Education can no longer be planned just for youth, but must be a continuous part of adult life since, as Oppenheimer said some months ago to the press, "Most of what we know today was not in any book when most of us were in school." The fear is, of course, that our institutions and our individual citizens will not be equal to their new responsibilities. I should like to close these introductory remarks with a quotation from a paper on the need for new knowledge that Oppenheimer presented three weeks ago. He said: "I believe most simply in the nobility of this great effort to understand nature and what we can of ourselves, that is science. I hope, less simply, that it may be a brave and worthy chapter of man's history to cope, with a full awareness of the frailty of his institutions, of his society, and of himself, with the new problems and new choices that this knowledge has opened. For if we do not treasure the great inheritance on which all our work and life are based, and understand the radical novelty and the gravity of the situation in which we find ourselves, there will be few of our children to ask again of the need for new knowledge."

Women's Education for New Horizons
The University Women's Forum, Philadelphia, February 4, 1961

If at the close of these remarks you conclude that I have been talking about matters of which I am quite ignorant, and that I have been concerned primarily with how one proceeds in the face of ignorance, you will be entirely justified. I have no special knowledge of the new horizons we share, consider myself a novice in the field of education, and certainly claim no insight when it comes to women. But I *have* been interested for a considerable time in relationships with things I do not know, and at the moment I am particularly intrigued by problems of cultural innovation in unexplored territories. The unknown is, of course, a special concern of scientists—as it is of artists, scholars, priests, and indeed each human individual. I sometimes think that it is one's ever present relationships with the unknown that provide the continuity one finds even in a woman's changing life. Whether a student or a homemaker, a scientist or a parent, a citizen or just a college administrator, there is always that surrounding dark circle of ignorance into which one peers.

Little by little, research approaches and techniques have been developed and our penetration of the no-man's-land where new knowledge and understanding is sought has been broadened and accelerated. We have come to appreciate how extraordinarily difficult it is to recognize that which is not known, and how important it is to fashion the specific question that can permit experimental verification. Thus, it was not easy to imagine the possibility that milk need not sour or meat putrefy but once such a question was formulated it could be approached experimentally, and the answer illuminated much larger but otherwise unmanageable questions, such as spontaneous generation. Today we need the useful handles to a host of difficult concepts, such as the possibility that men can live at peace, or that all individuals, of any age, could spend some of their time and talent in appropriate creative enterprises.

There are other things about dealing with the unknown that we have learned. We have learned obvious common-sense things that follow from the fact that the answer we do not know today must always in some measure be unexpected and that therefore one must be ever tolerant of other approaches, ever alert to the unexpected finding, ever ready to see the possibility in the unconventional concept. Above all one must have that faith in the basic harmony of nature that insists on testing theory by observation and not vice versa. When his engineers explained the limitations of the gasoline motor, and that it could never go more than 38 miles per hour, Kettering is reported to have snorted, "Let us ask the engine, not tell it." Surely these same approaches and criteria must be our guides as we seek greater understanding of human potentialities.

Recently I have been doing a little reading about women. Many current statements and some statistics are available but claims are often contradictory and one does not always feel assured that Kettering's advice has been applied. Rather, in many cases, it seems that theories have been used to select data; that women may have been told what they can do rather than asked. "As if," in the words of Thomas Wentworth Higginson, "the Lord did not know how to create a woman."

Now it so happens that as I have been doing this reading about women—their habits and their inherent natures—I have also been using the Metropolitan Museum's calendar for 1960 entitled "A Cloisters Bestiary." One could not help noting some striking similarities in approach, precision and objectivity between certain pronouncements about women and the medieval accounts of the natural history of the beasts. The Bestiary does contain a few cautious, well-authenticated observations, such as "The duck spends almost all his life in swimming. There are many varieties of ducks, some of which feed more than others on marsh grass." Or, "The griffin is seen in these parts but rarely." But most of the selections impart much more intimate and interesting information. "A sick bear that has eaten the poisonous fruits of the mandrake knows that it can cure itself by eating ants"—difficult to disprove—almost as difficult as to disprove that "women, whether they conceal it from themselves or not, prefer not to excel intellectually." Or, "There is a plant called dittany which also is helpful to the stag, for when he has eaten it he is immune to the arrows of the hunters"—a most attractive hypothesis. Like the concept of Atlas holding up the world, it solves real difficulties. Or again, "The meat of the cock is said to be excellent medicine if eaten with a mixture of liquid gold." Again, difficult to check. However, some of the statements would have been rather easier to verify. "Many horses live to be seventy years of age. Males generally have a longer life than the females. Their virility is removed by clipping their manes." Remember, these were not the tales of the ignorant but the writings of learned men, for only the learned could write.

If the Metropolitan is interested in a calendar for 1962 (entitled "The Modern Womanry") and it would offer an opportunity to present reproductions of some magnificent art, I should be glad to supply the quotations. It might begin with the advice of Dr. Edward Clark to Matthew Vassar a hundred years ago: "You cannot feed a woman's brain without starving her body. Open the doors of your college to women and you will accomplish the ruin of the commonwealth. Disease will become without exception. Girls will lose their physical stature and your boys their mental stature." And after an array of more contemporary selections I think I might conclude with the answer given by Maria Mitchell at the Congress of Women in this city in 1873: "I wish something of the physicist's readiness to try experiments would come into our moral reform work. We are all afraid of new experiments, as if the law of growth through failure were not similar in moral, mental, and material work. There is not a worker in the physical science who has not ruined lenses and wasted chemicals. He would scarcely care to have you look over his broken vases and still less would he be willing that you should grope among his absurd hypotheses. But he knows perfectly well that he has grown with the effort, that his true theory, if he has found one, has started up from the graves of a score of enterprises." This is really my text today: our attitude toward ignorance, even ignorance of ourselves.

Let me take a moment to describe to you a yardstick that may be convenient and enlightening in estimating the maturity of individuals and groups in their relationship to the unknown. It is a kind of attitude-toward-ignorance test involving a simple observation of emotional reaction in the face of unpredicted findings. The scale ranges from joy through gloom to apathy. Let me illustrate. At a recent seminar Dr. Sonneborn described a very beautiful series of observations and experiments that, step by step, made it quite clear that a particular type of inheritance of structures in paramoecium could not be explained on the basis of gene action or even cytoplasmic inheritance. Smiles broke out in the audience, joyful glances were exchanged, and as he finally and with poorly suppressed glee described a crucial experiment that had given results quite the very opposite from his own predictions there was almost a cheer.

This kind of emotional reaction to adequately demonstrated but quite unexpected findings, this confidence that observation *will* bring understanding is not always found. I remember a recent, informal discussion among members of one of the less experienced sciences. Here also there was confrontation with accepted new data that contradicted theory but the reaction was one of gloom and defeat, as if the train had gone off the tracks instead of just switched from a siding. Such a reaction would give a rather low reading by the attitude-toward-ignorance test but at least there was reaction and no evasion. Sometimes the reading is zero—indicating utter confusion or unconcern as to what *is* theory and what fact. For example, you may remember that there was a recent report that certain virologists had at last been able to demonstrate to their satisfaction that a virus could under controlled conditions cause the common cold. Yet it has long been common to hear even well educated persons explain with great confidence and amazing detail how they acquired their own particular diseases. I fear that the factors controlling women's potentialities are at least as complicated as those involved in catching cold.

It is a curious thing that, with all their education, emancipation, and longevity, American women have remained so uninvolved, at least on many intellectual, social and political frontiers. Their high ability has been amply demonstrated in our schools and colleges, but this has seemed to carry little commitment on their part, or interest on anyone else's in their later high achievement. Rather we all seem content to let them serve as intellectual pace setters, useful during training but not expected to run in any important races.

However, now that this country has at last awakened to the necessity of developing its total intellectual resources it is looking with new interest at the potentialities of women, and at once it is apparent that although doors of opportunity may have been opened, little thought has been given to how they should be designed or located and little concern as to whether they are used.

The obvious thing about women, as distinct from men, is that they are apt to have children and, in our society, generally wish to devote considerable time and attention to their care. Therefore it follows that the pattern of their lives during early adult years is distinctly different from that of men and that useful educational programs, and vocational and service opportunities, must be designed with these facts in mind.

Very real complications arise when we consider the possibility of involving women in advanced intellectual efforts, because of the rate at which knowledge is expanding, as well as the fact that competence soon slips away from those who cease to use their skills. If women are to participate effectively in the advancement and interpretation of knowledge, it is essential that we make it possible for them to keep in touch with their fields and even progress in their studies during the years when their primary responsibilities are in the home.

It is not difficult to see some of the steps that higher education needs to take. Able women as well as men must plan to prepare themselves for the contributions they can make in the second half of their lives. Ordinarily for women there will be interruptions and geographic dislocations which will present problems in programming their advanced education, but surely the logistics can be solved if we are interested.

Studying in appropriate doses mixes wonderfully well with homemaking. Lectures and discussions are the perfect antidotes to the mental stagnation that threatens any adult isolated in the modern home. The longer hours of study can be fitted around the household's schedule. In any event, one's husband and soon one's children will be opening their briefcases in the evening. One can join them. And when one does so freely, for the satisfaction one finds in learning and the prospects of usefulness one sees ahead, is one not establishing through example the values one is most eager to encourage in one's children? How better can one motivate them to carry on the increasingly demanding schooling that we believe so crucial to their later well-being?

Clearly, educational institutions must make it possible and attractive for women to carry on their education in whatever doses they can manage conveniently during the years when their primary concerns are in the home. Moreover, because married women are not free to travel far, appropriate opportunities must be developed in every community. It seems odd that we have made so little effort. In many cases even colleges for women have closed the doors to part-time students. It is difficult to see how we can expect to convince young women that education is important in undergirding the home and community as long as we seem to lose interest in any who marry early.

If we offered fellowships to brilliant young married women to continue part-time study and the fellowships went begging there might be justification for our remarks about women's lack of ambition, but more often we have ruled against any such form of financial aid. We have not seemed to question an arrangement that lets brilliant and highly trained young women devote their time to routine jobs in order to put husbands through medical schools. We have preferred that the talented minds we cultivated so assiduously for twenty years go stale—or as one young husband put it recently, "go sour" during the next ten. Sometimes I think it would be more realistic to say "dropped out" where we now speak of "drop-outs."

It is equally important, of course, to make available part-time vocational opportunities with attractive financial rewards in teaching, business, government and a host of other areas if we are serious in wishing to use the wealth of untapped resources that able women offer. However, my assignment today is confined to their education; I trust that Mrs. Leopold will speak to these points.

I come back to the observation that amazingly little effort has been made to design higher education so that it will provide realistic opportunities for many women. Instead of experimenting, we seem to have accepted limitations on theoretical grounds, and when data do appear contrary to common expectation they often command little attention or are greeted with dismay. What is it that we are so reluctant to risk?

There is, of course, the distinct possibility that all or at least most women may be inherently unsuited for certain kinds of achievement, such as higher mathematics or musical composition. So are most men. It would be interesting to know. But until many women have had the encouragement and the opportunity to try, it is most difficult to assess their capacity, particularly their capacity for genius. It is an odd thing that in a world in which variety of traits and of experiences are both so abundant, and genius so rare, it is so easily assumed that the proper combination of traits is all that is needed to produce genius.

Another and quite different cause for hesitation in opening educational opportunities to married women is concern for the next generation. Here it is particularly important to consider "new horizons" and the possibility that we may give undue weight to practices that once were functional and valuable but are now merely vestigial. It is true that over long years there has evolved a family unit in which women have primary responsibility for the care of the children. (Of course, not too long ago men were far more apt to be at home also.) But it must be remembered that the woman then was an important part of a vital economic unit and had demanding responsibilities with respect to the preparation and preservation of food; spinning, weaving, and the making of clothes; care of the sick; and a host of other activities quite apart from the children, who, quite early, took their places and made their contributions. This is fundamentally different from the situation in the electrified modern home, with its smaller family and limited scope, in which so often the woman stays solely to minister to the children's needs. It may well be that far more imaginative relationships between family and community must be developed in order to recapture those attributes that were important within the family unit in days gone by.

Many other reasons for fearing to risk the higher education of women can be suspected. I shall mention only one more and that is the fear of competition in the labor market at home. It is during depressions that for obvious reasons the fences of nepotism are built. It is quite possible that fear of competition on the home front is greater than fear that we shall lose the cold war through inadequacy of total resources. This fear cannot be ignored but it should be recognized as part of a much larger problem—a problem that seems always to be lost by the timid and solved, if at all, by the bold. (Legislation against bricklaying machines in the end only encourages the use of other building materials.) Somehow—and education will be important—we must find ways to distribute and use and thus maintain the worth not only of the products of labor but also its personnel.

There is one frontier that unlike all others opens ever more invitingly the further and harder it is explored. This is the frontier of new understanding, and in spite of all the difficulties that new knowledge brings, in the long run and on balance it opens new possibilities for those who follow. "We seek knowledge," as Oppenheimer says, "because it is useful and because the search is ennobling." Many women at this moment in society, just because they are not the traditional breadwinners, need not compete in the marketplace but have the precious freedom to pursue the by-ways, ingeniously, thoroughly, without need to publish prematurely. They have the opportunity to evolve a way of life, combining useful and necessary routine labor, affectionate personal ministrations, the pursuit or the application of new understanding for the benefit of all. This is the new horizon that I see. The road lies ahead—it will offer better traveling in so far as we pave it with educational opportunity.

Radcliffe Inauguration Speech
May 19, 1960

This is of course a tremendously proud and happy moment for me. However, even at the happiest of weddings there may be a tear. I am sure that there are others here as well as myself who remember with some nostalgia the wealth of possibilities predicted just a year ago when some of the provocative minds in the nation joyously contributed to the Harvard *Crimson* cartoons depicting the assorted characteristics and generally unintegrated personality of Radcliffe's next president. I share with all of you the touch of inevitable shadow as those glorious possibilities become a delimited reality.

Perhaps I also share, particularly with the Radcliffe Trustees, some impish satisfaction that the cartoonists did *not* precisely call the shots.

They did not portray a white-coated figure shoving aside microscope and test-tube cultures to examine the culture on a woman's campus, a myopic biologist diverted from the study of heredity and variation in microorganisms to stumble upon that astonishing mechanism of human evolution, our modern, creative, multistructured institutions of ever-higher education.

The cartoonists did suggest the possibility of a kind of Univac, or a Snoopy Dog, or any of a variety of rather ambivalent two-legged creatures, including a Harvard undergraduate, but they failed entirely, I believe, even to hint a mother hen, let alone a deviant bird that may have had too much fun on the range to worry about early nest building, but certainly did not feel frustrated later when cooped up with the chicks.

Yet it is as a geneticist with nest building experience that I choose today to consider the role of institutions of higher education in human evolution, with some clues provided by an analysis of the predicament in which women find themselves today.

Living organisms hand on their heritage and preserve their capacity for variation by many mechanisms; cytoplasmic, chromosomal, instinctive, instructive, sexual, political, depending on one's point of view. Man has now added an entirely new and different kind of mechanism, the open-ended institutions of higher education that combine the functions of research, instruction and public service revealing wonderfully creative potentialities. These have had many origins. Some were established to prepare young men for the ministry, and others to occupy young women until matrimony; some grew out of public or private schools and some developed within industries or hospitals or research institutes. But no matter what the origin or early history or label, if they flourished they have inevitably tended to assume liberal, vocational, research and service aspects. They have tended to become universities, for these are the climax forests of our culture; balanced, controlled from within, a way of life. They establish a climate of participation in important creation in which individuals play successive roles with common purpose. It is to maintain this essential climate that it is important that many teachers be also scholars, with concern for society. And although it is less well recognized, it is equally important that many students aspire to scholarship and service. The university relates the inquisitive student to the research front, the foundations of knowledge and the history of mankind to the needs of society.

Undoubtedly the present high regard for education is due in no small part to the impressive advances made in science. However, we seem to have mistaken the part for the whole. We identify a Scientific Revolution or Scientific Explosion, whose magnitude surprises no one more than the scientists themselves, and many have come to think of science as different and even opposed to humanistic studies whereas in reality it is, I think, simply the area of study in which it has proven easiest to gain skill and therefore confidence in liberal attitudes. The scientist has learned to put his faith in the ability of man to formulate definitive questions and arrive at partial answers, to use theories as suggestions rather than conclusions, to build on knowledge of the past without relying on authority, to consider every conceivable approach relevant and to question all beliefs including his own. However, these characteristics are not unique to science. They are, as many scientists have pointed out, a description of the liberal point of view that is just as promising in other fields, including even the arts and religion, only in such areas it seems much harder to distinguish findings from theories and establish one's criteria. Curiosity, if trusted, can undoubtedly prove fruitful in other fields and it is not the only instinct that has been built into our natures by evolutionary processes; there is also the sense of beauty and the quality of concern. If we but trusted them, what new horizons might be achieved!

We do not need to be reminded today of the serious difficulties that have come with the scientific revolution. Advances in knowledge have always brought problems but the problems now posed are of a new order. They are the problems of abundance that force selection and control. We have produce without markets, power without purpose, birth without death, knowledge without understanding. The very appetites that fitted us to survive in a world of scarcity become our despair. It is not enough to know; we must act.

Once again and at a new level man must choose where previously he had only to accept. And this time, scarcely a hundred years after he had first become aware of the phenomenon, the direction of human evolution itself has become a matter of conscious control, something to be guided by the mind of man. Still without knowledge of the ultimate design we must again choose the hypothesis that our will is free, we must take responsibility. Therefore our dilemma—for choices are difficult when one is not sure what one wants.

Furthermore, the strength of a democracy depends on having as many choices as possible made at the level of the individual citizen, for democracy is based on faith and respect for the individual's potentialities. The kinds of choices that must now be made require therefore widespread agreement as to the direction in which society must move and general understanding of the methods by which progress seems best assured. Let us consider in some detail an example that not only illustrates the problems but may provide clues to the nature of the solutions.

Women have of course been deeply affected by the changes wrought by the application of scientific knowledge. Their special function in society, as dictated by the presence of that second X chromosome, and those more general potentialities that they share with men, as a result of the elaborate mechanism for random distribution of the other 47 chromosomes, are both involved.

Modern technology has rendered obsolete many aspects of the *accessory* tasks that once complemented women's special function in the home, the tasks of feeding, clothing, nursing and educating the family. The home that was once a complicated productive, relatively permanent economic unit into which the children fitted, is now a shifting base in which activities largely revolve around their lives.

Small wonder that there are such desperate efforts to magnify and dignify women's special role. Her status is involved. (I am told that the psychiatrists have come to speak of "the status baby.") Older societies made laws to prevent women from practicing medicine or attending learned institutions. Today the laws are repealed but American women seem somewhat like a dog I knew, who long after the front fence had been removed, ran down the road to the place where the gate used to be, before turning into the yard.

Let us examine more closely the woman's special function, the contribution she is uniquely able to make to the next generation. There are of course the genes that she transmits, but here in spite of very promising advances in our knowledge the individual's choices are few. The baby starts at scratch and carries on with inherent abilities that are not appreciably different from those possessed by primitive man.

Our civilization is built on what the infant learns and the demands are heavy but with the accelerating expansion of knowledge the amount of useful information that any one person, let alone a mother, can pass along to another is limited. Often what one knows is more of a hindrance than what one does not know. The child in the crib today will see possibilities tomorrow that will be beyond today's wisest professors or its graduating seniors. Even our medical schools have stopped thinking that they can teach the doctor everything he needs to know. In terms of transmission of specific information the mother's function is limited.

There is, however, a third and highly important kind of attribute that the mother is preeminently qualified and inescapably responsible for passing on and that is attitude. For if it is the random distribution of chromosomes that is largely responsible for problems such as those of our admissions offices, it is the differences in motivation that prevent accurate prediction in either direction. Thus, the uneducated woman who values learning may contribute far more certainly than the Ph.D. who shows no continued satisfaction in the acquisition or use of knowledge. Attitudes are not transmitted by diplomas; they depend far more on example than advice.

Motivation toward education is only one of many worthy attitudes but it is an important one, for increasingly in a world in which the rate of discovery is accelerating, the wealth of an individual or a family or society must be measured in terms of trained talents. It is of the utmost importance to the welfare of all that the child acquire attitudes and skills that will promote learning.

Therefore, if my thesis is correct, and there are some findings to support it, the woman's success in her special role may to an appreciable extent depend on the satisfaction she can find from full development and use of her more general potentialities.

I shall purposely neglect in this discussion the many other ways in which through the use of modern knowledge the mother can provide the optimum cultural conditions for the child. Here again, once one has decided upon one's goal, the ways and means are relatively easy.

So also I shall neglect the difficulties that beset the woman in our society who seeks to combine her multiple roles. Length of life opens new possibilities but these can be realized only when plans are well laid and doors kept open. Women will continue to wish to pattern their lives differently from men but with a little ingenuity on the part of the women and a little flexibility on the part of society, including educational institutions, the logistics can be accomplished. Differences in pattern need not dictate differences in purpose.

That the practical aspects can be solved is well illustrated by what happened in Russia when there was a drastic shortage of manpower and brain power. For a few decades the relative scarcity of persons in the middle years in this country may, as Dr. Adams has said, create such a demand, but those of us who remember the depression do not see paid employment as a basic solution. When jobs are scarce they will not be distributed two to one family and none to another.

The problem of maintaining status in the face of technological unemployment is not unique to women. It is the problem of almost any individual whose traditional job is threatened or minimized because in our society, outside of universities and other research-oriented communities, the individual is valued in terms of specific occupations rather than potential contributions. As scientific and technological advances are made, education must evolve and extend within reach of all ages so that those who may be occupationally displaced at one point can find their way to new frontiers.

Nothing is more indicative of our total bewilderment than the position that has been quite generally but quite unconsciously adopted with respect to women in America. For the conclusion has been, I fear, that it really doesn't matter what they do and that it isn't important that they be excellent at anything. Our lack of concern about whether the able high school girl gets into the accelerated physics course—when apparatus is short, or into college—if there are more boys than money in the family, or how she plans to use her talent and training in later life, are illustrations of our point of view. I think we do not even care that she be excellent in homemaking, for if we did would not our faculties seriously debate the adequacy of present curricula for her needs and would not our best efforts be turned toward research upon this question? True, we all have theories but do we have valid findings? Or is it possible that we dodge this question too because its investigation demands decisions that we fear to face? Do we know what we want in the enlightened child? The mature citizen?

No wonder that most of the highly talented youth in this country who fail to go on to college are girls. No wonder that those who do go so often drop out at the flick of the ring. They have never really been in. They have not aspired to scholarship or service. This is not the dream of democracy; this is Brave New World. It is not so much a question of anti-feminism as of anti-intellectualism. If we truly valued the full development of each person's potentialities, and felt women to be handicapped, would not our approach be compensatory rather than negligent?

Perhaps our modern creative institutions of high education will prove valuable as models, as well as instruments, for they are communities planned for dynamic development and they have hitched their wagons to the stars. We do not know where the next breakthroughs will come, but we do know that, if they can work freely, bright minds, with training, will make them. We are learning also that unexpected strengths are contributed by a variety of kinds of minds and backgrounds working together, in each area, with common purpose. Society's total aim must be far broader than that of any university but I believe the model can, and will, prove useful.

It is within this framework that women as individuals, and women's colleges as institutions, have their special opportunity to contribute. The very fact that what they do is not considered so important gives them freedom to be creative. Someone has said that women's education had to be as bad as men's before it could get better. Perhaps that time has come. If so, it will be by facing courageously, with all our talents and all our skills, those questions that need to be answered to discover the criteria and the techniques for the good life.

It is a hopeful thing that the American public wants almost all of its children to go to college (even if it doesn't want to foot the bill), and that there are now more students over eighteen enrolled in formal education than under eighteen in our bursting schools. We were slow to discover the tidal wave, even when it was seated in our elementary schools. The wave of increased desire for education is *annually* unanticipated. Its magnitude threatens to dwarf as well as confound the tidal wave. It may be a threat in the sense that it makes difficult demands but it is the clearest evidence I know that our democracy is alive and alert. The tragedy is that it had to erupt from below, rather than be planned from above.

It is not that every college need enlarge in size or program but that each should understand that it will be unimportant, as the New England academies became unimportant, if it considers its function apart from the total effort. Rather, it is in relation to the entire phenomena that each institution finds its particular value. We shall need far more diversity than we have now, for the advances at the growing edge of knowledge bring a multitude of different changes in different lives. Each of us has his own research front, each of us needs appropriate techniques and liberal attitudes, each of us must understand the nature of the choices to be made.

I do not need to tell this audience that I believe that Radcliffe has a very special part to play, that cultural change is a flying wedge directed most readily from the front, that what happens here can be of profound significance.

During this past year I have had many wonderful letters of congratulations but my favorite is still the one from Ada Comstock Notestein. I quote: "It was relatively easy to know what needed doing when I came to Radcliffe. It is not so easy today." I do not think it will be easy but with Radcliffe's inherent strength and your continued help we shall do our best. As one among you, with deep concern and high hopes, I pledge what I have, that through this college, life on earth may be a little more as it is in heaven.

The University's Responsibility in Educating Women For Leadership
Southern Methodist University, January 28, 1966

Madam Chairman, President Tate, Fellow Members of the Conference:

Among the many reasons that I am happy to have accepted President Tate's invitation to this fine conference is the fact that my topic has proved so much more interesting to me than I at first anticipated. I have discovered that the points I particularly wish to emphasize this morning are rather different from those I would have selected had I accepted the same invitation even a year ago. And the differences bear directly on your theme. I shall come to them in due time.

My approach is colored, of course, by personal experiences of many kinds: a life-long interest in biological investigations, especially those concerned with mechanisms of evolution; thirty years in and around universities; a decade, almost, of debating with myself and others about women's special needs in our society; last year in Washington working with the Atomic Energy Commission and thinking about The Great Society; very recent conversations with college students, to name a few. Of these I suspect that the first and the last, my gleanings from biological evolution and from contemporary students, have been particularly influential in determining my present views.

It is hard to remember that in spite of occasional insights such as those of Aristotle who, commenting on the arrangement of cutting and grinding teeth in man and other species, wrote "things that happened as if they were made for something seem to have been preserved"—in spite of such glimpses, there was no real awareness of biological evolution until the middle of the last century. Today the basic concept permeates and directs our thinking about phenomena as diverse as the origin of stars or the future of human society. Yet our knowledge of the precise mechanisms involved even in relatively simple biological systems is rudimentary. I have been working in the laboratory for thirty years with pedigreed strains and carefully controlled conditions to understand mechanisms of color variation in a bacterium known as *Serratia marcescens* and I still am not certain whether its elaborately controlled variability is advantageous or merely incidental, let alone how it operates. I try to keep *Serratia* in mind when tempted to make pronouncements about such things as leadership or the motivation of women or the responsibilities of universities.

The beautiful mechanisms of genetic control and response that have been evolved over the ages and that are now being revealed to us were not imagined by our most brilliant scientists just a few years ago. Along with the truly surprising discovery that a simple four letter alphabet is sufficient for cells of vastly different kinds to control their individual growth and development and to transmit their genetic heritage to the next generation, comes a growing realization of the variety of complex regulatory mechanisms involving so-called operons, inducers, repressors, etc., etc. that exist in each cell. These intricate systems, and the ability to reproduce them complete in perhaps twenty minutes, have been developed by brainless bacteria, given time. Our own cells are undoubtedly even more elaborately devised without our being at all conscious of the details of their structure or function. Therefore, again, any generalizations about topics such as the one you have assigned to me must be viewed as hypotheses of the crudest kind. This does not mean that they may not be useful, useful and desperately needed.

For the fact is that although we are woefully ignorant of the mechanisms responsible for human evolution we are now called on to direct its course. The forces science has set in motion, not only physical forces such as atomic energy but also forces manifested at biological, psychological and sociological levels, forces related for example to the increasing density and inter-relatedness of human populations, mean that man must assume responsibilities of a new order, and promptly. We cannot avoid decisions on a multitude of fronts that may affect life on this planet forever. Planning even on a small scale such as for one's family or one's community, one's business, one's profession or one's university needs to be done in the light of wisely conceived and widely shared guides and controls. We are no longer free-living creatures for whom the "wages of sin is death" to the individual or the clan; rather we are parts of a world-wide organic complex in which each individual's actions are inescapably linked to the welfare of others, and leaders, or their absence, may affect perceptibly the course of human evolution.

It is not, of course, the first time that increased capability has opened new possibilities and new responsibilities. But the scale on which we must perforce operate in consciously attempting to guide human development; the speed with which many critical decisions force themselves on us; our lack of knowledge and understanding, especially about ourselves; and the stakes involved seem unprecedented. Yet we gain nothing by not daring. What I have just begun to appreciate is the courage with which many young women are indeed planning to prepare themselves for later serious involvement. But I'll get to that anon.

A few observations now about leadership. We shall need a great many kinds. Not only will we need leaders in a host of different fields, like politics and social work and journalism, medicine and education and urban development, but in each field we shall need many kinds of skills and many combinations of skills. Thus there must be lawyers who know a great deal about chemistry and others who know about South America and still others who know Chinese and perhaps one or two who know all three. Similarly in medicine and in our schools and above all as volunteers opening up the new fields that will some day be professions, and in politics which must be concerned with every aspect of society.

Clearly those responsible for the guidance and selection of students in our educational systems are going to need great wisdom. It is not at all certain, for example, that only students with early aptitude in mathematics will prove productive scientists or that only scientists need mathematics. Yet this criterion alone may play a far more decisive part in determining educational opportunities in our so-called free enterprise system than in many overt dictatorships. There is real danger that concepts too narrow in several dimensions are determining educational opportunities, especially those of women. To produce stars in any discipline, not just in baseball, requires starting with a broad base and building a solid pyramid of talent. We don't know nearly enough yet about either selection or training, not to mention the needs of the future, to rely on any other approach, certainly not in educating women for social and political leadership.

One further observation about leadership. We have an unfortunate tendency to play up the rarer kinds and overlook the importance of quality in familiar fields. Name ten mothers whose findings on child growth and development have had notable impact on thinking or practice. Leadership here has not been valued. Why hadn't one of them, or a group, written Gesell's book years ago? How many of today's college students will prepare as carefully for their responsibilities in their homes as for their final examinations? How many will see their experiences with their own children as an integral part of a program leading later to wider service perhaps in managing a day care center, or in teaching and research.

Education for leadership in a society characterized by rapid and accelerating learning and innovation means that effective education must be current as well as advanced. This is the nub of the problem facing women and the universities concerned with their preparation for social and political or any other kind of leadership. The woman who drops out of any specialized field for long will have a lot of catching up to do if she wants to get back in. Some years ago I realized that most of what I teach in my freshman seminar on microbial genetics was not known to anyone when I took my Ph.D. The great majority of American women with college degrees, some 70 per cent of them, hold paying jobs between the ages of 45 and 65 but they do not have the training or the experience that would qualify them for the positions of leadership that they could fill if they had been able to keep in touch during the years when their primary responsibilities were at home.

There are, as I said earlier, many kinds of leadership needed in our society. The intelligent secretary or wife who asks the right question at the tactful moment, the maverick whose extreme position helps others to formulate their own, the persistent fighter whose cause happens to be unpopular but who keeps it alive through a dark period, the original mind that sees a possibility that has been bypassed remind us that opportunities are open even to those whose formal education may not be so very advanced or current. But if women are to move into positions of leadership in recognized fields they will need to be well informed in these fields. We may have laid a broad base in educating women in this country but we have not built the pyramids.

As I see it, universities must always keep three kinds of education in mind. First they must provide freedom and backing for those of identified ability and high motivation to move as their talent takes them. Few if any investments are as rewarding to a society, or as ennobling. Second, they must grow experts for socially important fields. This takes vision and persuasiveness, real leadership within our universities. And third, they must seek to develop the potentialities of people in all segments of society. This is implicit in the concept of democracy with its promise of open opportunity for all individuals according to their abilities and interests. The handicapped provide our special challenges.

The importance of backing identified talent does not need to be defended in this great university, but I would like to touch for a moment on my second point, the need to develop experts for socially important fields. The key here, I believe, is to give far more time and attention in formal classes and outside of the classroom to what is not yet known and has not yet been done to ameliorate or enhance the human condition. We are so busy trying to convey what is known and has been done that we neglect the very thing that young people most need in order to orient their lives constructively: insight as to where they can best use their talents. Of what use are the results of a personal inventory if one is not aware of the needs of society. In a dictatorship individuals can be tested and assigned. In a primitive society the child sees valued tasks that need doing. There is not the same need for an identity crisis, difficult personal decision, the search for a calling. More attention in the classroom to the problems of society could mean many fewer problems within the university. It could also mean, I believe, more effective education and more imaginative scholarship. Participation in discovery is the key to fine teaching as well as to research. The problems that youth is seeking to formulate today will perforce be those that most concern society tomorrow. It is not only in physics that fresh insights and experience working together can accelerate the advance of knowledge. It was to an embarrassing extent students rather than faculty who sparked our recent concern for civil rights but the impact on research in many fields has been profound, as well as the impact on student motivation for education.

The third educational responsibility that I cited was the need to develop the potentialities of people, including leadership in all segments of society. The encouraging thing about last summer's White House Conference on Education, in my opinion, was the way in which representatives from widely different kinds of institutions, schools, junior colleges, private liberal arts colleges, vocational schools and public universities thought in terms of the country's total needs. Yet almost nothing was said about the special problems of women. Let me take a moment now to tell you how I, rather belatedly, became concerned with the educational complications facing the larger half of our population.

The whole question of equality between the sexes with respect to abilities has always left me cold. It still does. The possibility of sorting out genetic and environmental factors for a valid assessment in our present state of ignorance seems unrealistic. It is also irrelevant to the problems of the individual or of society. Clearly there is a tremendous range of overlapping abilities in each half of the population and wherever one's own score may place one, one's personal problem is to live a satisfying life and society's problem is to give one all possible assistance. The sad fact is that as yet our institutions of higher education have made so little effort even to do the research necessary to discover how to develop leadership, let alone leadership among women or any other disadvantaged groups.

It was a few statistics that sparked my interest in the special problems faced by women. I grew up believing, gratefully, that the doors of educational opportunity in this country were wide open. No special impediments hampered my efforts to learn and when I was ready to begin serious investigation of bacterial inheritance and variation, which was considered a most unpromising field in the 1930's, the fact that I was not worried about recognition or the need to support a family freed me to pursue the research that interested me most. Nor, as a matter of record, did I feel frustrated when I left the laboratory for six years to start a family. Later, thanks to Yale's enlightened policies and grants from the Atomic Energy Commission and the American Tuberculosis Association, I carried on research on a part-time basis. In each phase I was doing what I most wanted to do. I thought that other women were also. I might question their taste but not their right, or their freedom, to decide the course of their lives.

The statistic that jarred me was the finding during the postsputnik period of national soul-searching that of those high school students who scored in the top 10 per cent by ability tests and did not go on to college, more than 95 per cent were girls. It wasn't so much the waste of a national resource that bothered me as the satisfactions that I believed these girls were missing in life. How had they happened to decide against college?

My clue came with the realization that the government wished to suppress the statistic. As I've said elsewhere, I was reminded of the difficulty scientists had in Wisconsin in publishing results showing that oleomargarine was nutritionally equivalent, or perhaps superior, to butter. It seemed that those concerned with scientific manpower felt that if it was known that nearly all of the able boys were going to college it would breed complacency. In other words, there was no belief in this country that women would make significant use of scientific education. Was there any expectation that women would contribute effectively along any advanced frontier? If not, was this climate of unexpectation an important factor in their career decisions, their whole motivation for education? Was there a basic fallacy from which peer wisdom had protected boys, whereas girls had remained vulnerable? In other words, was planning for later use an important ingredient in educational motivation? I began to wonder and watch.

It quickly became apparent to me that there was a real difference in the way most adults talked to little girls and little boys about their futures and in the expectations of their teachers in school and college. The early interests of little boys were encouraged in quite a different way from those of little girls. Even if their interests might change later the boys had gained a sense of support which their sisters had not enjoyed. Could this have come at a critical time in their development? The effect was reinforced by the prevalent attitudes of teachers in our schools and colleges. As a working hypothesis I postulated that in America in the late 1950's there was a climate of unexpectation as to the use women would make of their talents and education that dissuaded girls from preparing for significant intellectual involvement.

The hypothesis was soon supported by many other observations. Girls did as well or better than boys in our schools but their studies did not seem to them to be relevant to their later plans. They worked for grades or approval, not for understanding or later service—certainly not for leadership. Why should they argue a point with their teachers? Why not drop out as soon as a reasonable proposal of marriage came along? Radcliffe records indicate that involved students who happen to get married generally continue their education. Marriage is a symptom not a cause of educational failure.

Support for the hypothesis could also be found in the lack of concern of educational institutions, including women's colleges, in providing opportunities for married women with families to continue on a part-time basis. Even they showed little interest in women's potential contribution. No wonder college women were confused. Their processing was valued but not the product.

It was to explore the possibility of changing this climate of expectation that the Radcliffe Institute was started in 1960. Radcliffe offered encouragement, facilities and even financial assistance to married women in the Boston area who were qualified and who wished to carry forward promising scholarly or creative projects on a parttime basis. In practice we have never confined assistance entirely to women living in the immediate area or to those with major family responsibilities but for reasons that I will discuss later, this was the principal objective. The impact was almost immediate. It was like dropping a crystal into a super-saturated solution. "You don't know it but I'm really in your Institute. Since reading about it I've started . . ." women reported from all over the country. One young mother wrote, "I may never get a chance to go on to college but it's nice to know that it's all right to want to." Evidently it was possible to affect the climate. In addition we are finding out a great deal about the background of the women who were ready when we opened the doors, about the problems that they and others encountered, about what happens when encouragement and assistance is provided to young mothers, and about the effects of our concern for advanced educational opportunity on the plans of younger students.

It was startling to discover how little our institutions of higher education knew or had thought about optimum conditions for the education of women. But our so-called liberal colleges have always believed in training, except for their own instructors; research, except on curriculum and educational methods; advanced education, but only for the individual who learns fast and can work full time. I began to realize to what an extent education has used "speed of learning" as its most important yardstick. It does give a crude measure of ability and motivation. And at a time when the life span was short and few could be spared from manual labor there was a good deal to be said for this criterion. Fortunately some protection derived from the use of other measures by the aristocracy. A Darwin could, even if he did not excel in college, spend most of his life at home writing, stay in touch with active thinking in his field, and take his time about bringing his ideas to fruition. So also could a woman novelist. But men and women whose family responsibilities prohibit full-time professional education are ordinarily ruled out by rigidities in scheduling and lack of financial assistance. Since they would be delayed in obtaining their degrees it has not been deemed worthwhile to provide for them. Anyway, since most of them were women, why bother?

If on the other hand one measures success in terms of total contribution over a lifetime and if one realizes that the thirty-five year old mother of school children still has more than half her life ahead, then the importance of the educational opportunities open to her on a part-time basis between twenty-five and thirty-five becomes highly significant. American universities have not begun to face their responsibilities here, particularly in professional education. This is now the critical bottleneck.

For today I find that young women assume, as they have for a long time, that they will wish to marry and start their families in their twenties; but now they also assume that later they will wish to be deeply involved in tasks that will demand not only high ability but also long and arduous preparation. In the past the fact that their full involvement was long years ahead tended to discourage them from aiming high; now they see that it frees them to set their sights high indeed. They have time. They can alternate formal study with work experience. As one of them said to me recently, "The pattern of a woman's life may be a handicap in the rat race for position, but for what I want to do it may prove an advantage." She is heading for urban development. Her present plans call for a major in economics in college, followed by law school. "I can read sociology and things like that later when I'm home with the children, while I'm getting experience in volunteer work and local politics." She is preparing for leadership.

Perhaps the most interesting aspect of this new breakthrough in women's education is the fact that these ambitious young women are planning for contribution rather than competition. "We're each going to fix something," said a junior last week. Perhaps something more important than Betty Friedan, or any of us, suspected was being won during the 1940's and 50's when college women chose not to get Ph.D.s. Little children learn to say "yes" and then practice saying "no" before they have the power of choice. Perhaps solid choice must evolve in much the same manner. The young women with whom I have been talking are planning with a new serenity. No longer is there any doubt about the relevance of college work to later life. Furthermore, they see the freedom they have as women. One Radcliffe sophomore who is going into hospital surgery put it this way: "As a woman I don't need to worry too much about money. Either I get married, in which case I won't need to earn that much, or I don't, in which case I won't either. I can do exactly what I really want to do." She's right—if our medical schools and hospitals will meet her half way.

Let me cite one more example, this time the story of a woman in mid-career. Jean had her M.D. when she got in touch with the Radcliffe Institute. She also had two very little children. Her problem was to get an internship in pediatrics without spending her nights in the hospital. We approached the Children's Hospital in Boston and offered to pay for essential expenses such as baby-sitters if the hospital would provide "an intern-like experience" on a part-time basis, as an experiment. It was some months later that I discovered that the hospital's idea of half time was nine to five six days a week. Jean admitted that it was not what she would choose for the children but pointed out that at the end of two years she would have had one of the best internships that anyone had ever had at children's hospital. Talk about motivation!

Today Jean is the doctor for sixteen schools in the Nashoba Valley some forty miles from Boston. A surprising number of her school children have never before been seen by a doctor. She has set up a novel program with the residents of the Children's Hospital that brings specialists in nose and throat, for example, or allergies, out to her local clinic on monthly visits. Now she is looking for a part-time social worker and a part-time lawyer to add to her team. She is experimenting with the kind of service that is now so desperately needed in this country. I doubt that any young male M.D. of comparable talent and training would have provided just this leadership. Jean, like the undergraduates I have mentioned, is interested in contribution, contribution at a very high level. She is now 33 and her third child is 3½. Had she not received assistance at a critical time she might now be classified as a medical drop-out. This year a tenth of Radcliffe's senior class is hoping to enter medicine. Will medical education be ready to meet their needs?

Obviously the advanced education of young mothers, like that of their children, needs to be available near-by. Every urban center must provide realistic opportunities in medicine, law, social work, education and other professions and disciplines. If one believes in education for the able; if one believes in meeting the needs of society, then it is triply important for our universities to provide, and provide well, for the highly motivated young women now coming to the fore in our schools and colleges. How well motivated are our universities?

These women will need flexibly scheduled opportunities but that's what computers are good for. They will also need money, even when they are studying part-time. We have more than 600 women working for Ph.D. degrees at Harvard. We have an excellent chance to study their needs and also the needs of the wives of graduate students, many of them able college graduates who would like to take advantage of their proximity to continue their studies but are not financially able to do so. "My husband gets $400 per dependent but that won't pay for anyone else to baby-sit except me." These young women are tied to our universities but fenced out. Who lacks motivation?

Providing realistic educational opportunities isn't the whole responsibility of the University in educating women for leadership but it will help. There is also research and guidance, no doubt. But the importance of providing a visible educational path to the top is not to be underestimated. At present the college graduate, if married, sees only a thicket. She knows a few have wiggled through but there is no clear path. And her motivation is pure. She has it made—in other ways. She's ready to go. And the leaders of the future in politics—in volunteer work—are going to need advanced education to understand the world in which they work. The basic decision for institutions as well as for individuals is whether to bother, whether to let opportunity slide by—or to try to take hold and do something. Universities in this country have found it convenient to prejudge women's potential contribution for leadership. What I ask is that they experiment.

From Serratia to Women's Lib and a Bit Beyond
New Brunswick Lecture
American Society for Microbiology
Minneapolis, May 5, 1971

Why I was invited to give the New Brunswick Lecture, why I accepted the invitation and why you came to hear it are mysteries into which I shall not probe. Perhaps we all felt the need of a change.

Whatever our motives, it is a pleasure for me to be with you. I wish that more of my time could be spent listening to your new findings rather than reflecting on my own disparate experiences, but I didn't make the rules—not this time.

At first, I could think of only one urgent message to give you. Would it be possible for this great Society, sensitive to the financial burdens of institutions of higher education and the work loads of instructors, to make one basic decision—to rule that from now on the word "inoculate" be spelled with two n's?" Think of the saving in red pencils and faculty time!

More—or perhaps less—seriously, it took very little reflection to convince me that anything I could tell you about Serratia could be merely of historical interest—unless perchance word of some forgotten line of unfinished research happened to excite the imagination of a young investigator who was still casting about for a promising lead.

And surely anything I could tell this enlightened group about women's liberation would be gratuitous—although possibly familiarity with some of the findings of the Radcliffe Institute would strengthen your influence in academic, industrial and civic councils.

What I can do, and would like to do, is try to express my indebtedness to science in general and microbiology in particular for the adventures and satisfactions they gave me when I was actively engaged and the excellent preparation they afforded for later work in quite different fields.

Before tackling my main theme, I should like to take a few minutes to tell you how I happened to get involved first in microbiology and then in women's liberation (although I recognize that more militant advocates may dispute my claim). In both instances, the process was somewhat atypical but revealing, the former involvement throwing light on the latter and vice versa.

As far as I can remember or piece together from early diaries and letters, I grew up thinking that women *had* been liberated. Perhaps I thought it had happened in 1919 with women's suffrage. In any event, being a woman wasn't anything I had to worry about, although I had a healthy curiosity about what kind of woman I would become. Like my brothers, I certainly expected to be engaged in interesting work and presumed that, in due time, I would also marry and have children.

It did seem that surprisingly few women chose exciting occupations but that was their choice and not to be questioned. Women were, if anything, freer than men for they weren't expected to support families. Career success was less important. They could do what they wished—or so I thought. I majored in physics in college, but at no time saw myself becoming a physicist. It was in junior year, prompted, I don't doubt, by Paul de Kruif's *Microbe Hunters,* that I elected a course in bacteriology taught by Anne Benton (now Riebeth), of this city, and found the problems with which I wished to tangle. I wonder how many others of my generation were led into microbiology by Paul de Kruif—and who is writing for the enlightenment of today's adult nonscientists and voters and the inspiration of future scientists? It will not be by complaining about the anti-intellectual and strongly anti-scientific climate that surrounds youth today that we affect it, but by sharing the excitement of discovery and the deep satisfactions that come with greater understanding of natural phenomena.

It was not because bacteriology offered relatively good opportunities to women, which it did, that I was drawn into the field, but because the mix of what was known and what wasn't known about microbes themselves was so appealing. The myriad of different forms of life, the intricacies of immunology, but above all the inadequacies of our concepts of the bacterial cell were what attracted me. "Simple colloidal systems reproducing by simple fission" the textbooks said, but there were thousands of these systems, each made of complex organic molecules, each exhibiting astonishingly sophisticated metabolic systems, and each capable of reproducing its own kind, often at fantastic rates. It was not for a temporary job or to satisfy career ambitions or to produce socially useful knowledge that I went to graduate school, although these would be welcome by-products. Rather, here was a ridiculous and intriguing state of ignorance, to which I felt I might make a contribution. The so-called search for identity is, of course, the search for a meaningful life. Everyone really wants to be able to devote himself or herself to work that he or she enjoys, feels to be worthwhile, and can do. In this spirit, today's socially concerned activists turn to medicine and law. For all too many, science is suspect on all three counts. Even if one has scientific aptitudes, there is a question about associating oneself with the self-seeking, ambitious intrigues of academia, not to mention serious doubts about the ways in which one's findings may be used. These doubts were not a problem in 1930.

My interest in the status of women came very much later—not until after Sputnik, when I was the Dean of Douglass College and served concurrently on the American Council on Education's Commission on the Education of Women and on a National Science Foundation Committee on Scientific Personnel.

Congress was slightly hysterical. The future of the country was thought to depend on science. I recall a bill before the House to withhold mid-morning milk from school children who had not done well that day in arithmetic. The problem then was how best to use the funds which Congress voted, how to do the least harm. Many scientists, including those at NSF, were worried about the over-reaction, but I believe we were not sufficiently troubled by the long-range effects of coupling science so closely in the popular mind with national defense.

It was a single statistic that first sparked my interest in women as such. It seemed important as we checked over the flow of talent into science to know, along with many other inquiries, how many able high school graduates did not continue to college. Foundation staff analyses of data from three sources indicated that of all high school graduates scoring in the top ten per cent by ability tests, at least 97 per cent and perhaps 99 per cent of those who did *not* go on to college were female. This statistic surprised me. I expected girls to be in the majority, but not by such a margin. How sad, I thought. What a waste. Who were they? What had stopped them?

But what really alerted me to the possibility that women *hadn't* yet been liberated was the fact that the statistic was suppressed. (I was reminded of how difficult it had been for a Wisconsin colleague to publish research on the nutritional equivalency of oleomargarine and butter.) I never received an explanation of the suppression of the statistic on college entrance, but my best guess was, and is, that the Foundation staff believed that if America knew that all the bright boys were going to college, no one would think there was a problem in the schools. It was then that I first sensed that in this country we did not expect women to contribute anything really important to science or—I soon realized—to any intellectual frontier.

The presence of women in higher education was a gesture to democracy, not its expression. It was a luxury we happened to be able to afford, but women were marginal. Bright, admittedly, but not important. Suddenly I perceived those free career choices in quite a different light. A "climate of unexpectation" had conditioned women's decisions. Here was a situation as complex, as un-understood and possibly as important as the genetics of Serratia. It gave me a new interest in women's education. Since I was by then in college administration, my approach was that of an activist. Past training led me to set up a laboratory (the Radcliffe Institute) to study the problem.

So much for the events that attracted me to microbiology and women's liberation.

I doubt there is any discipline at this point in time that provides a better understanding of the interplay of genetic and environmental factors on growth and behavior than microbiology. In working with microbes, one quickly gets an intimate feeling for growth curves, population pressures, selectivity, genetic stability and variation, symbiotic relationships, the triggering of inductive mechanisms and a host of other phenomena that cannot help but open one's mind to possibilities in education which one might otherwise fail to consider. Above all, one learns to live with ignorance. If it is so difficult to find out why pigmented variants of Serratia survive better than those lacking pigment under certain conditions, if one's best guesses prove wrong so often when one can test them, one becomes cautious about educational hypotheses which cannot yet be put to the test.

To take one simple example: To distinguish or compare two related organisms, the microbiologist first cultures them in a series of differential media under otherwise identical conditions and observes the appearance and behavior of the resulting populations. This, however, is too often the last thing that the educator is encouraged or permitted to do. Rather, people argue for generations about the relative capabilities of blacks and whites or boys and girls without ever attempting to grow them under the same conditions. If they really believe that significant differences exist, and it would seem to me surprising if they do not, then why not settle that question, determine their nature and degree and turn to the more important question, which is, "Given the differences, if any, what, if anything, should be done differently for the average woman or for the woman with special talents and interests?" The fact that society has chosen *not* to offer the same opportunities or give the encouragement to both sexes (or to members of different races) suggests something far more sinister, a deep fear of the results.

My own studies of color variation in Serratia began with some very elementary observations. It is difficult in 1971 to realize how foolish it was considered in the 1930's to choose to study microbial genetics. Requests for grants were turned down with unusual alacrity. One's friends did their best to dissuade one from stepping into what they considered a hopeless morass. I doubt that I could have afforded to do so had I considered myself the family breadwinner. Limited as I was to the New Haven area, I could not have done so without the backing of Professor Leo Rettger of Yale, who paid me $600 a year to transfer his acidophilus cultures and gave me full access to his laboratory—in effect, gave me a postdoctoral fellowship that permitted me to use my previous training as an independent investigator, the privilege that so few married women enjoy.

Some mechanisms, some series or coincidence of events, I reasoned, must be responsible for the striking changes in pigmentation that certain strains exhibit on standardized media, but so little was known about the rates at which specific variants arose or the effects of environmental factors on rates of variations, that the nature of the events was obscure. In fact, it soon became apparent that specific color types could be distinguished by the appearance of the colonies they produced on a suitable minimal agar medium and that each color type gave rise to one or more variants in a regular and reproducible manner. It was a good system with which to observe the effects of environmental factors, including mutagenic agents; work on biosynthetic pathways of the pigment prodigiosin and detect unstable color-phase variations which were quite different in character from the stable mutants first described. If anyone is looking for a likely problem which should now be manageable, see me later about some of the questions suggested by the culturally induced phase variants we have encountered.

It might amuse you that when I first reported on color variations in Serratia in 1938-39, the editors of the Proceedings and of the Journal of Bacteriology insisted that the word mutant not be used since it might imply a genetic change, which seemed to them most unlikely.

Of course, they were quite correct. One must be very careful. Environmental effects can be subtle and appearances deceptive. Let me illustrate with a true story involving Harvard and Radcliffe students. During my first five years at Radcliffe, I taught a freshman seminar on microbial genetics in which six to eight students pursued as many related independent projects, all involving Serratia. The number of applicants was always much too large and I tried a variety of arbitrary devices to ease the decision process. One year, I decided that I would not take any student who hadn't done well on College Boards in chemistry. Unfortunately, to my chagrin, all of the male applicants had taken

Board exams in chemistry and nearly all of them had done very well. However, only one out of the 16 women who had applied had chosen to take a Board examination in chemistry. Why the sex difference? Was it genetic? They were all bright students who planned to major in the sciences. A look at the women's folders revealed that all of them as well as all of the men had taken chemistry in school and had done well in it. Why hadn't they taken the exams? When I interviewed them in the course of making my selection for the seminar, I discovered that in each case someone—a teacher, a parent, a friend—had advised them that since boys do better on CEEB chemistry exams than girls, they should avoid that subject. How utterly ridiculous! A difference of a few points in the national averages of thousands of boys and girls had influenced the specific choices of 15 out of 16 young women, each from a different school, whose own scores would undoubtedly have placed them far out at the high end of the curve. Here indeed was a subtle environmental effect—one that happened to be identified. How many others that are never detected nevertheless affect the educational, and career decisions of countless individuals?

Working with color-variants of Serratia—as with other bacterial species—heightens one's awareness of the power and subtlety of relatively minor genetic and environmental differences in determining the survival of specific types in mixed populations. As yet, I know no definitive work clarifying the role of the pigment prodigiosin, but I cannot believe that so many strains of Serratia would have developed such elaborate mechanisms to insure reversible color variations were it not true that under certain conditions it is advantageous to make or accumulate the pigment and under other circumstances quite disadvantageous. But that nice little problem is also for someone else to resolve.

I am grateful for the appreciation I have gained from bacteria of the complexities involved in trying to sort out genetic and environmental effects in growing cultures.

Another example of differential behavior in an apparently homogeneous educational environment is the situation in which male and female graduate students find themselves during that traumatic first year when so many are so discouraged. Actually, their situations are very different. If a man drops out, what are his alternatives? All too often only another graduate or professional school. So he sticks. A woman, however, has many options—and her family never did think it a good idea, nor her boy friend. Thus, external social forces tend to hold the young man in the track, but draw the young woman away. To make their situations more comparable requires counter-forces, some of which can be supplied by encouraging faculty and staff. All too often, however, academic advisers do not believe that the loss of a young female scholar is of any real significance. "She is bright, but not important." The difference in the ways in which faculty members, often quite unwittingly, treat their male and female students probably introduces the most telling environmental difference of all. But, of course, I'm speaking primarily of your colleagues in the humanities and social sciences and physical sciences.

And then one thinks of the use microbiologists make of enrichment cultures. Prepare the right medium, throw in a little soil and—presto!—one can have a population of yeasts or cellulose fermenters or auxotrophs or whatever. Perhaps open enrollment is not such a bad idea after all, although there might be advantages in starting it a bit before age eighteen. If we're clever enough at concocting the right educational programs, we'll probably be able to grow some extraordinarily able individuals—men and women who would otherwise have had no chance to develop. If many are to find satisfying careers in our chaotic, ever-changing society, we must not build so many separate ladders, but, rather, great jungle gyms which permit people to move sideways when they can't or don't wish to continue to climb upwards.

John Gardner once wrote that a society gets the kind of excellence it values. He was talking about enrichment cultures and his remarks apply not only to the society as a whole, but to its various sectors. In our American culture, women have not been expected to contribute intellectually. Many enter teaching but the career lines have not looked open to professorships in prestigious universities or to top positions in other demanding professions. Particularly they have not looked open to married women. And precious little has been done about it. Even the women's colleges have made few provisions to enable young married instructors to keep up their research during the critical decade after they received their doctorates. Had they held full-time appointments, they would have been expected to spend at least one fourth of their time on research. But as part-time instructors, they are seldom given a chance, every third or fourth year, to catch up and be productive. And the AAUW still, I believe, insists that all of its fellowships be used full time. We haven't done much to develop the enrichment cultures that will grow our women scholars and scientists. Perhaps they are rare and delicate variants—but then again, the soil could be teeming with them and we ignorant.

Given my preparation as a microbiologist, it was not surprising that my approach to the problems of able women was experimental. What were the limiting factors? If these were corrected, would there be a significant response?

In 1960 almost as many females as males entered college, but with very different aspirations. Relatively few, however, undertook postgraduate studies. My analysis had indicated that the drop out before or at the B.A. level was not due so much to inadequacies in curricula or even to poor guidance as to attitudes about women's roles that were widely held by men and women in our society. Could the attitudes be altered at least in one locality? Could the hypothesis be tested?

The Radcliffe Institute was established in 1960, thanks to generous gifts from a few foundations, corporations and individuals, as a laboratory in which to discover and provide the kinds of assistance that able and motivated women need to work more effectively in their chosen professions—particularly married women, since they constitute the great majority and have the most difficulty. It seemed to me that until girls in high school, and boys too, could see the career lines open to the top for married women, many would hesitate to commit themselves.

Our approach was so obvious that it has always been difficult for me to think of it as an innovation. That the announcement of the opening of the Radcliffe Institute made the front page of the New York Times and resulted in a deluge of letters underlined the fact that almost no effort had been made in this country to further the careers of professional women. We began by inviting women in the Boston area who had serious scholarly or creative projects on which they wished to work to apply for assistance. We wanted to find out what they needed, to supply it, if possible, and to observe the results. Very simple, but it hadn't been done. If nothing else, we hoped our offer would demonstrate that we valued what bright, educated women might contribute in their chosen fields. We hoped we might begin to change the climate of unexpectation.

The program for independent study proved to be highly instructive and gratifyingly productive. Other programs have followed, each designed to meet the needs of a group of able women who for one reason or another had been prevented from moving ahead. Their ages have varied from the mid-twenties to the mid-seventies, the majority being in their thirties. Many have been women with Ph.D. degrees and little children, who needed a chance to continue their research in order to establish themselves as independent scholars or investigators. Some have been medical women who because of family responsibilities were unable to get residencies until we made arrangements for them to work on part-time schedules and paid for their baby-sitters. Hospitals that didn't hesitate to import non-English speaking interns had been rigid about not hiring part-time women graduates of top medical schools. Talk about waste! A few were young poets and artists who never went to college or mature women from disadvantaged backgrounds who, with access to appropriate seminars at the Institute, could be helped into careers in environmental design or child care. Under a Merrill Foundation grant, we have given fellowships to part-time women students in graduate and professional schools in Southern New England. Tuition is high in these schools but fellowships for part-time students have been rare. The high motivation and stick-to-it-ivness of this group, and their good records indicate how foolish it has been to categorically disqualify them from financial assistance.

It has been interesting to observe the sequence of questions asked over the years by the public. When we first announced the program of independent study perhaps the commonest question was, "Do such women exist?" The applications quickly settled that one. "What will they do after a year or two at the Institute?" was another early question. We know now that virtually all continue in their chosen fields. Nearly half of our fellowship holders are now in college teaching—many in main line positions, thanks to the book they wrote at the Institute. For a large number—the painters, poets, lawyers and doctors—academic careers are ordinarily not appropriate, but they also attest eloquently to the importance of Institute recognition and assistance. "What is the effect on husbands and children?" This question cannot be answered quite so easily. The Institute staff is working on these and other related questions. It is clear that in many cases where full-time work would put an unfortunate strain on the family, part-time professional work can be carried forward by the mother without detectable ill effects and in some cases with distinctly beneficial results, but this is a complex question. We need a great deal more information before we can generalize or prescribe. Lately, I am happy to report, most of the questions have been requests for information from people who are interested in opening opportunities to women. "To what extent is the Institute exportable?" I have been asked most recently.

What we have been finding are a few nutrients or growth factors —an educational vitamin in some cases, or an osmotic balance, so to speak—that hadn't been appreciated. In the sciences and other demanding professions, for example, it is difficult to come back if you've dropped out for long. Far better, in most cases, for a woman to continue her study or work on a part-time schedule while the children are young, but this calls for flexibility on the part of institutions, which means on the part of the people in them. There are plenty of cases where there is no institutional policy against part-time work, for example, but where departments refuse to consider women who apply to study on a part-time basis.

We know, too, that intellectual and creative productivity for women as for men depends very much on contacts with stimulating minds in the same and in related fields. I have had faculty husbands comment, "If she were really motivated, she should be able to finish the book at home," to which I respond by asking how much of his work gets done at home—when the children are around—and why, when he has the stimulation of associates and students, does he think it important to attend professional meetings?

This is not the time to report in detail on our findings at the Institute. Lack of money for baby-sitters, isolation, lack of recognition and encouragement, difficulty in continuing study or in finding jobs in a new location can be limiting factors for professional women. The glaring gaps in women's education are at the top and they are all too apparent to the young. The remedies *are* exportable, not necessarily as a package. The waste of talent and early education can be greatly reduced by modest but properly timed and properly conceived assistance.

Unfortunately, a great deal of nonsense about sex is shouted on both sides, although Radcliffe students tell me gleefully that now, whenever a professor makes a male chauvinist remark, most of the class hisses. It is the endless debates about whether women are or are not inherently as talented or productive as men that seem to me so boring and irrelevant. Most men are not as able as some men but that doesn't disqualify them as a group. Only as we succeed in providing optimal environments for both men and women will we be able to judge their innate capabilities and limitations. The important thing is to try to provide the best possible educational and vocational opportunities for each individual, which, of course, is what America is all about. Unfortunately, we were slow to recognize the complexities. We thought it would be sufficient to open educational opportunities to all, unaware of the extent to which that would favor those who already had almost everything going for them. Our naivete led to the ever widening gaps that now characterize our society. We didn't design for the different needs of different groups. Women were among those who lost out.

When I say "lost out" I am thinking primarily of their own well-being. For I start with the basic assumption that, for good evolutionary reasons, healthy people's personal satisfactions depend on their being able to use a fair share of their capabilities in ways that seem worthwhile to them. For women of intelligence, this means using their intellects. It's basic, and for the same evolutionary reasons, it could be fatal for a group of people—a nation—to ignore the potential intellectual contribution of any sizeable segment.

From a wider perspective, how ridiculous it is to argue about male and female roles when there are so many more important issues at stake. Not only opportunities for women but opportunities for science, for scholarship, for decent living depend on finding solutions for critical social and environmental problems that affect us all. The logarithmic expansion of educational and other activities cannot continue. Competition for limited resources and the accumulation of waste products threaten us all. Unless we can introduce new nutrients and/or achieve a balanced steady-state, women's liberation will be an empty victory—like my short-lived success in persuading government agencies to permit traineeships to be used for part-time students, only to have the Bureau of the Budget virtually eliminate traineeship programs.

But these larger problems will not be solved, in my opinion, without the application of scientific knowledge and experimental methods. We don't know enough to advocate sweeping reforms or universal solutions. We do need better machinery to release individual and small group initiatives.

One worthwhile step, which I have been advocating whenever I've had the chance, is the establishment of a National Service Foundation with funds to make grants to individuals, associations, universities, corporations, towns or cities that have promising ideas for social innovations and well-conceived plans for carrying them out. This also is a research front, but as yet too little attention has been given to the development of definitive experiments, the accurate reporting of what has been tried or the evaluation and publication of results. The establishment of a National Service Foundation with an expert staff and public accountability would provide the machinery we need to move ahead sensibly. Only as new ideas proved their validity and experience had been developed in implementing them would they ordinarily be recommended as national programs. Among the great benefits of this experimental approach would be the possibility of providing public funds to the private sector, opening new jobs under skilled management in service fields, but with accountability and full opportunity for the public to benefit from all findings.

This has been a very rambling discourse but I hope it has conveyed to you my appreciation of the privilege of having worked among you. I believe I speak for many other drop-outs in expressing a personal debt to good science education and an awareness of some of the rather subtle ways in which the feelings one gains for biological phenomena at the microbial level can be useful in working with higher forms.

Women: Resource for a Changing World
An Invitational Conference at the Radcliffe Institute,
Radcliffe College, April 18, 1972

If you will indulge me, and how can you do otherwise, I should like to speculate briefly on a few of our findings at the Radcliffe Institute and their implications for the future; not their implications for the future of the Institute, which will be for others to chart, but their implications for women and for higher education. In doing so, I count on many of the formal and informal remarks made by conference speakers and participants to give my statements added texture and meaning.

The Radcliffe Institute was conceived as a laboratory with a mission and also as a center of continuing education. We wanted a laboratory in order to find better ways of helping women do the things they wished to do and we wanted a center of continuing education to maintain programs that the laboratory found promising.

It was my belief in 1960 that the central problem in women's education stemmed from confusion about its goals. Although largely unrecognized then, it was generally assumed that women could not be expected to contribute significantly to intellectual advances in any rigorous field of study or action. One educated women for the greater pleasure and support they could provide as wives and mothers, as school teachers and research associates, but not for what they might acccomplish intellectually in their own right. The further they advanced in their studies, the less support they received. Families and institutions that cared strenuously about whether a bright applicant was admitted as a freshman took little interest in whether she completed her doctorate or got a good medical residency. No wonder women undergraduates were confused.

Higher education itself has been confused about its goals, preaching the virtues of liberal education at the undergraduate level but insisting that graduate programs be open only to those whose motivation is vocational and paying scant attention to either the liberal or the vocational needs of its graduates.

It all worked rather well for undergraduate men as long as strong cultural forces shaped their goals. They knew that their careers were of paramount importance. They needed to be told to broaden their interests in college and they didn't take the advice too seriously. The women, on the other hand, although subject to the opposite cultural forces, were given the same advice and did take it seriously but not themselves. Lacking viable models, they desperately needed to be encouraged to focus and make commitments to long-range vocational and intellectual goals but this happened all too seldom, especially in coeducational institutions dominated by male faculty members.

Able young women need to believe that what they do with their good minds is important, for personal satisfaction depends in large measure on using one's capabilities in ways that one believes to be worthwhile. What could we do to help at Radcliffe, I asked myself in 1960. There was little evidence that exhortation would be effective and, in any event, others were far better qualified than I to argue the case. If, however, Radcliffe College were to demonstrate its concern by aiding those women who wished to pursue advanced studies or research, might that not make an impression? What if we went all the way and helped at least a few highly motivated married women with families to fulfill their career aspirations? How wasteful it really was, not to do so. But how to proceed? We didn't know. A laboratory seemed the logical answer. Hopefully, its very establishment would convey our concern and whatever we learned would be instructive to others.

The concept was presented to the Radcliffe Trustees in the spring of 1960 and they endorsed it enthusiastically, provided that funds could be found. An alumna, Mabel Daniels, made the first gift of $5,000; a parent, Agnes Meyer, gave the idea reality with a gift of $50,000; and the Carnegie Corporation and Rockefeller Brothers each contributed six- figure gifts. Sperry and Hutchinson Foundation offered to support the Institute's staff research over a five-year period and other foundations, corporations and individuals made generous contributions. Without the support of the Radcliffe Trustees and those who provided financial backing, we would not be here this evening and I would have no findings to report or implications to discuss.

The public announcement of the Radcliffe Institute for Independent Study, as it was then called, was made in November, 1960. We wrote, "The time has come to enter into a wholly new exploratory venture beyond orthodox education in the conviction that a way can be found to stem the drift away from the life of the mind among educated women." And today we must think also of an increasing number of able young men intellectually adrift, unable to find satisfying commitments.

The attention that the press gave to the original announcement of the opening of the Institute was evidence of its novelty and of its controversial nature. The publicity complicated our lives but it helped the cause. Applications poured in weeks before Constance Smith could leave her post as professor of political science at Douglass College and become the Institute's first director and dean. And with the applications came letters from women all over the world who thanked us for releasing them to pursue careers about which they had previously felt guilty. Better confirmation of the original hypothesis that prevailing attitudes were at fault could not have been found.

The Program of Independent Study was the first experiment set up by the Institute. Connie Smith called it our seedbed because it became the source of so many of our ideas. She was right. With very little structure but borrowing freely from concepts of academic freedom that had proven important for the careers of talented men, we invited women who had specific scholarly or creative projects of high promise to become members of the Institute. Independent Study is only one of the programs administered by the Institute but most of the findings I wish to share with you this evening have been drawn from it and from the closely related fellowship programs for women in medicine and women in part-time graduate study to which it gave rise. Not that Independent Study is inherently more important than the research or the guidance or the Radcliffe Seminars or other Institute activities, but I believe that it is less well understood, has proved itself, and is exportable.

In announcing the Program for Independent Study, we offered women "time that is free of personal pressures and obligations; a place to work; all the facilities of a great University from libraries to laboratories, from museums to computers; the companionship and guidance of renowned authorities in a hundred fields; and the financial means to take advantage of all of this without abandoning her domestic responsibilities." Most importantly, we said, "it will offer her a way to renew her commitment to her area of specialized knowledge." I can't say that we have delivered everything we promised or that we visualized everything that we had to offer. At least we didn't box ourselves in.

The context in which the offer was made implied that we were concerned primarily with finding ways to help married women with children who wished to resume or continue advanced studies but we have never limited our fellowships to women of any age, preparation, marital state or discipline. We have asked that applicants have well conceived projects on which they wish to work but there are no contracts, no deadlines, no institutional pressures. It is truly the free university and for the women we have accepted, this is enough.

You know the general outline of the story and Alice Smith has just completed a report, soon to be published, which will give you the details. Let me only say here that Independent Study works wonderfully well for mature, able, motivated women and that it is relatively inexpensive. It costs us less to support the average Fellow for two years than it costs to educate an undergraduate for one. We know now that for many women with children the opportunity to continue their professional contacts and intellectual involvement on schedules compatible with the needs of their families can make a critical difference to their careers and their lives. Virtually all Institute Fellows, some 300, have continued in their chosen fields with growing effectiveness and personal satisfaction and their families seem to have thrived. Their testimony shines through the turbulence and cacophony of shrill feminine and student complaint. We must have done something right but only if other institutions follow suit can many women benefit.

Although this is not the occasion to go into details about the Program for Independent Study or its products, I would like to point out two respects in which the Institute's emphasis was distinctive. We offered a supporting rather than a competitive structure and we faced openly and squarely the problems of married women and their families. I should like to comment briefly on both.

Educational programs for the most part are designed as race tracks and may the best man win. The free enterprise system, currently called meritocracy, displays the same monopolistic tendencies in education that it does in industry. Those who have almost everything going for them move rapidly ahead but great gaps develop and little attention is given to the needs or the potentialities of those who, for whatever reason, fall behind. If the promise of democracy is to be fulfilled, a very different approach is needed. Not race tracks but gardens. The Radcliffe Institute offers its members a place to grow, each according to her own design. It provides in so far as possible, the nutrients and the atmosphere that scholars and artists require and the resulting cross-disciplinary community provides extraordinary stimulation and support as the testimony of its members makes abundantly clear. Both their liberal and their vocational interests are advanced. I am convinced that they should never be viewed as alternatives, that either pursued seriously involves elements of the other and that this should be recognized at all age levels. Creating educational gardens for those who do not thrive on race tracks will not be easy. Without assigning limits to anyone, we must plan in terms of people's real needs and potentialities. At the Institute we have been dealing with only one small corner of the problem, the special needs of able and motivated women, including those who are devoted to their families and to the life of the mind. There are a multitude of other groups of people, younger and older, whose educational needs are not being met. Planning in these humane terms will require unusual imagination, sophistication and integrity.

It is my thesis tonight that the kind of problem that we have been tackling at the Radcliffe Institute is symptomatic of fundamental strains in an advanced society that is no longer expanding but is seeking to attain stability yet remain open, alive and interesting to its individual citizens. Chimpanzees often find puzzles more rewarding than bananas. The issue in an advanced, stable society is to provide scope for active intellects. Bright women were among the early casualties of a competition fought to secure or preserve the privilege of using one's capabilities, a competition not foreseen by our forefathers but one that threatens their vision of a democratic society. This competition has become a prime source of corruption and the driving force behind many kinds of discrimination and categorical deprivation. Only by much more imaginative and comprehensive planning in which our universities must take a leading role can these issues be resolved. These are some of the implications of the Institute's efforts.

The Radcliffe Institute placed the married woman on center stage because it valued women's contributions in their homes as well as through their outside careers. Also, we believed that until better solutions are found to the problems they encounter in developing their careers, younger women will continue to face cruel career decisions and single women will continue to experience discrimination. In 1960, I remind you, some of the most prestigious women's colleges had rules against admitting married women, or admitted them only if they agreed to work at the full-time rate. They had adopted the same nepotism rules as men's colleges and showed little interest in working out procedures that would have been helpful to the scholarly growth of young married mothers on their faculties. It seemed that they were concerned with the training of girls, not the education of women. Certainly married women and their families were not a major concern.

As for Institute findings to date about career patterns for married women, let me make just a few observations, drawn from our fellowship programs for graduate and professional women as well as from Independent Study. First, I know of no data that would rule out any of the various patterns of work that women with children have chosen or been forced to choose. We need to expand the options and to continue to study the outcomes, hopeful that eventually we shall be better qualified to recommend appropriate choices to specific women. It is clear the re-entry after prolonged absence from work can be difficult, especially in fast-moving scientific fields, and that the opportunity to continue one's involvement on a flexible schedule, an option that has been all too rare in demanding disciplines, can make a vital difference in the career development of a woman, or a man, who does not feel free to work the conventional hours in the conventional places. If, instead of prejudging the results, we can give professional women the option of altering their rate of work rather than their goal it will be an important liberation, and we shall have the data required to make sensible individual and institutional decisions.

A related observation I should like to share has to do with the problems many women have in finding opportunities to do productive work of their own. This is where the Program for Independent Study has been so valuable. It gives the qualified woman who is otherwise cut off from such a possibility the chance to do her own thing. She may be a housewife in the suburbs, a young college teacher whose classes and children leave inadequate time for research, or a social worker or business woman with a perspective to express. The resulting evidence of her productivity reaffirms her faith in herself and gets her that next job too. It is because this step is so critical that I urge educational institutions everywhere to open their doors at least a crack for the potential scholar or artist or activist who is qualified and can profit from the opportunity. I also urge them to take a sharper look at the developmental needs of women on their faculties and staffs or attached to them through marriage.

In addition to giving us some ideas about women, the Program for Independent Study has provided insights about higher education. What was truly innovative, or subversive if you prefer, about the Program was the notion of admitting people from the community for the purpose of pursuing their own research interests. Colleges and universities have rarely offered such opportunities to men, let alone women. I am proposing tonight that they do so, that to at least a small degree they become centers of learning for adults who are not looking for degrees but for an environment conducive to the pursuit of knowledge and artistic expression. It should be done selectively; experimentally if you wish; without stipends if necessary, but also without charges, I would hope; and with honor and all the additional hospitality and support that is possible. Such a program would help relations between town and gown and add some very interesting people to the university community. An admissions committee would probably be advisable but there could be many sponsors, departments, or living units, for example, as well as centers such as the Institute. In fact there can be distinct advantages in promoting a close association between Fellows and working units of the university, as we have observed this year when one Institute Fellow has been made a lecturer in social anthropology and another a resident in Currier House.

I am often asked whether the Radcliffe Institute should be replicated in other universities. My answer is cautious—that many of its functions should certainly be adopted but not necessarily the Institute as such with its fellowship, guidance, research, seminar and other programs, at least not unless the financial underpinnings can be assured. It would be wonderful if a major university in every large city would set up such havens of scholarship and research open to those citizens, men as well as women, best qualified to make use of it. We were right, I think, given the experimental nature of what we were doing, to proceed without endowment or other assurance of continuing support, but with all its success, the Radcliffe Institute's future is precarious. The number of women who have sought its assistance is very large, the number who have offered financial support is beginning to grow but is still very small. I am certain that any similar institution would have customers and would meet real needs. I would advise its founders to start with an endowment of $5,000,000, a modest sum as such things go today but one that would assure the center the independence that it will need to maintain its strength and flexibility.

But colleges and universities and other centers of learning including libraries could offer their own versions of Independent Study. They could offer recognition, a place to work, moral and hopefully financial support, access to facilities not otherwise available, and association with other stimulating minds. Not all such havens would meet the needs of every worthy candidate but I do not doubt that there is a great variety of persons with projects that they could, with a little backing, pursue very profitably, enriching their lives, setting convincing examples to the young, changing the national climate of intellectual understanding and expectation. Colleges hope that their graduating seniors have found the life of the mind so rewarding that learning will have become an ever-liberating part of their lives, but their actions have not matched their words and are therefore suspect. They have done little to assist even the most able living in their immediate neighborhoods to pursue their intellectual interests.

Other Institute programs such as those providing financial assistance to part-time graduate and professional women are being adapted and adopted by a few universities, hospitals and other institutions; we hope the movement will spread. Flexibly scheduled and adequately supported opportunities for study and work do not yet begin to meet the demand. Programs similar to the Radcliffe Seminars, which predated the Institute and have flourished with it, should certainly be more generally available than they are. Much remains to be done.

Let me conclude with my favorite quotation from John Gardner, a quotation that triggered my thinking about women's education. He said, "A society gets the kind of excellence it values." His law was illustrated dramatically last January when three Olympic gold medal winners came from the little town of North Brook, Illinois, that truly valued speed skating and valued it for girls as well as for boys. The group of Cambridge citizens that, with the backing of President Eliot and leading members of the Faculty of Arts and Sciences, founded what was to become Radcliffe College, valued women and the intellectual life sufficiently to make it possible for women to study under Harvard professors. Among the benefits, they explained, would be the superior preparation that such women would give to future Harvard men whom they taught in the schools. In establishing the Radcliffe Institute, Radcliffe College demonstrated its confidence in the intellectual and creative contributions that educated women were capable of making themselves in whatever fields they chose to work. The initial experiments seem to have had merit. Among the benefits will be the superior preparation that undergraduate and graduate men and women as well as school children will receive in the future. Even more important has been the effect that the effort itself has had on women's views of their own capabilities.

This conference has pointed to advances that have been made and to the far larger tasks that remain to be accomplished before women can flower as they should and participate freely in the intellectual life and work of their times. I trust that Radcliffe College through the Radcliffe Institute will continue to play a leading role in opening opportunities for women and assisting them in taking full advantage of their potentialities.

Endnotes

During the course of the research for this book, I exchanged many letters with Polly Bunting, spoke often on the telephone, and conducted a number of interviews. The first interview was on December 18, 1992, at what was then the Bunting Institute in Cambridge, Massachusetts. Subsequently I stayed with Polly in her apartment at Kendal in Hanover, New Hampshire, over the Memorial Day weekend in 1993 and from December 5 through 10, 1994. Many of the quotations from Polly included in this book are taken from those letters and conversations.

Chapter 1 The World Is Such a Good Place
1. Elliot Willensky, *When Brooklyn Was the World: 1920–1957* (New York: Harmony Books, 1986), 52.
2. Ibid., 25.

Chapter 2 A Funny Little Girl
1. Oral Memoir, interviews with Jeanette Bailey Cheek, sponsored by the Arthur and Elizabeth Schlesinger Library on the History of Women in America, Radcliffe College, in cooperation with Columbia University Oral History Research Office, 1978, 36.
2. Ibid., 6, 7.
3. Letter from MIB to John W. Jenkins in response to a questionnaire for the University of Wisconsin History Project, Dec. 10, 1984, 1.
4. Oral Memoir, 37.
5. Description of Packer's facilities and program from the Packer Collegiate Institute, the Seventy-fourth Annual Catalogue, 1927.
6. Grace Glueck and Paul Gardner, *Brooklyn: People and Places, Past and Present* (New York: Harry N. Abrams, Inc., Publishers, 1991), photograph, 133.
7. *Packer Magazine* (Spring 1995), reprint from *Packer Alumna* (1889), 39.
8. Oral Memoir, 17.

Chapter 3 The Life of a Grind

1. Barbara Miller Solomon, *In the Company of Educated Women: A History of Women and Higher Education in America* (New Haven and London: Yale University Press, 1985), 56–57.

2. Caroline Bird, *The Invisible Scar* (New York: David McKay Co., Inc., 1966), 294.

3. Mary McCarthy, *On the Contrary: Articles of Belief, 1946–1961* (New York: Noonday Press, 1946), 198.

4. Henry Noble MacCracken, *What Vassar Means* (New York: Kalkhoff Press, Inc., 1911), 4.

5. Elizabeth A. Daniels, *Bridges to the World: Henry Noble MacCracken and Vassar College* (Clinton Corners, N.Y.: College Avenue Press, 1994), 7.

6. Wisconsin History Project letter.

7. Oral Memoir, 19.

8. "Implications of the Modern Scientific Revolution," MIB speech to Douglass Alumnae College, June 3–5, 1959.

9. Hans Zinsser was a noted bacteriologist who wrote a definitive textbook.

Chapter 4 All Things Seem Visible

1. Wisconsin History Project letter, 3.

2. Ibid., 5, 7.

3. Ibid., 5.

4. Ibid., 8.

Chapter 5 Niches as Well as Nests

1. "Education and Evolution," MIB speech for The Centennial Convocation at Vassar College, Oct. 12, 1961.

2. Oral Memoir, 25.

3. Ibid., 27.

4. Ibid., 26.

Chapter 6 A Garden Not a Racetrack

1. Oral Memoir, 16.

2. Margaret W. Rossiter, *Women Scientists in America: Struggles and Strategies to 1940* (Baltimore and London: Johns Hopkins University Press, 1982), 167.

3. Wisconsin History Project letter, 5.

Chapter 7 A Busy Life

1. Oral Memoir, 16.

2. Ibid., 37.

3. Evelyn Witkin, Barbara McClintock Professor Emerita at Rutgers, who was working for Luria at the time, Jan. 16, 1997, interview.

4. Oral Memoir, 39.

Chapter 8 The Best Years of All

1. From a biographical sketch written by MIB for Radcliffe College in 1965.

Chapter 9 Heaven on Earth

1. Oral Memoir, 50.

2. Ibid., 49.

3. Ibid., 50.

Chapter 10 A Sightseer in a New Land

1. MIB remarks for Annual Women's College Conference at Douglass College, Mar. 7, 1981.

2. George P. Schmidt, *Douglass College: A History* (New Brunswick, N.J.: Rutgers University Press, 1968), 88.

Chapter 12 A Neophyte at the Deaning Business

1. "Higher Education—How Much for How Many?" MIB speech to Phi Beta Kappa, May 7, 1956.

2. Annual Report of Douglass College for the Academic Year 1956–1957, 4.

3. Ibid., 3.

4. Schmidt, 212.

5. Oral Memoir, 82.

6. Letter from MIB to the chairs of the Curriculum Committee and Educational Policies Committee, Oct. 26, 1955.

7. Oral Memoir, 54.

8. Letter from MIB to Provost Mason Gross, Dec. 3, 1956.

Chapter 13 Mother, Scientist, Educator

1. Sophomore Convocation speech at Douglass College, Oct. 2, 1956.

2. Speech to Douglass student leaders, Sept. 16, 1956.

3. Oral Memoir, 57

4. Letter from MIB to Rutgers Assistant PR Director, Sept. 18, 1958.

5. William B. Perry, Jr., *Patterns of Development in Thought and Values of Students in a Liberal Arts College*, noted in MIB journal.

6. David Halberstam, *The Fifties* (New York: Villard Books, 1993), 589.

7. Ibid., 590.

8. Ibid., 590.

9. Ibid., 589.

10. Margaret A. Judson, *Breaking the Barrier: A Professional Autobiography by a Woman Educator and Historian Before the Women's Movement*

(New Brunswick: Rutgers University Press, 1984), 120.
   11. Schmidt, 210; and Aug. 28, 1959, Annual Report.
   12. Oral Memoir, 57.
   13. Ibid., 59.

Chapter 14 The Tidal Wave
   1. "New Patterns in the Education of Women," MIB speech to Old Guard Summit, Oct. 22, 1957.
   2. "Higher Education—How Much for How Many?"
   3. *Douglass Alumnae* Magazine, Winter 1957–58, 4.
   4. Oral Memoir, 60–61.
   5. Douglass College Annual Report to the President, July 1958.
   6. "Higher Education—How Much for How Many?"
   7. MIB Douglass Convocation Speech, Sept. 15, 1955.
   8. Letter from MIB to Frederic W. Smith about the new dining hall, Apr. 9, 1959.
   9. Department chairmen meeting minutes, Jan. 17, 1957.
   10. Recommendations concerning future development and policies presented to Board of Governors as requested at meeting of Mar. 11 and Apr. 4, 1957.
   11. MIB memo or speech to students on the new schedule. Underlined at the top is *Points to be Covered*. No date.
   12. Ibid.

Chapter 15 The Awakening
   1. "New Patterns in the Education of Women."
   2. Oral Memoir, 65.
   3. Halberstam, 625.
   4. National Science Foundation 8th Annual Report for Fiscal Year ended June 30, 1958, copy of a presidential address to Congress, Jan. 23, 1958.
   5. MIB speech to Annual Women's College Conference at Douglass College, Mar. 7, 1981.
   6. This long quotation is a compilation of comments made by MIB at the Annual Women's College Conference at Douglass, in her Oral Memoir beginning on page 65, and in interviews with me.
   7. Oral Memoir, 132.
   8. Ibid., 132.
   9. "Education and Evolution."
   10. "From Serratia to Women's Lib and a Bit Beyond," MIB speech to the American Society for Microbiology, Minneapolis, Minnesota, May 5, 1971.
   11. Annual Women's College Conference at Douglass, Mar. 7, 1981.

12. "Women: Resource for a Changing World," MIB speech at Radcliffe College Conference, Apr. 18, 1972.

13. Letter from MIB to Douglass Trustee Mrs. John Moxon, Aug. 6, 1957.

14. MIB letter to Rutgers President Lewis Webster Jones, May 8, 1957.

15. Prepared question-and-answer sheet, Jan. 9, 1958.

Chapter 16 A Bit of Rebellion

1. Letter from MIB to George Holsten, Rutgers Assistant Public Relations Director, Aug. 20, 1958.

2. *Boston Daily Globe,* June 9, 1959.

3. Douglass Women's College Conference, Mar. 7, 1981.

Chapter 17 A Kind of Pedestal

1. Helen Homans Gilbert Oral Memoir, interviews with Jane Knowles, Radcliffe Archivist, 38.

2. Radcliffe College Board of Trustees minutes, June 13, 1960, 2.

3. *Milwaukee Journal,* Oct. 11, 1960, 5.

Chapter 18 The Messy Experiment

1. Radcliffe Institute for Independent Study, Nov. 1960, 4.

2. Oral Memoir, 110.

3. Helen Gilbert Oral Memoir, 38.

4. David E. Lilienthal, *The Journals: Volume V, The Harvest Years: 1960* (New York: Harper & Row, 1971), 133.

5. Ibid., 243.

6. Oral Memoir, 97.

7. Institute Executive Committee minutes, Jan. 5, 1961, 3.

8. Memo to MIB from Rene Bryant, Dec. 2, 1960.

9. Mary I. Bunting, "The Radcliffe Institute for Independent Study," *Educational Record, American Council on Education,* vol. 42, no. 4 (Oct. 1961), 281.

10. Barbara Swan, *Radcliffe Quarterly* issue on Institute's 25th Anniversary, June 1986, 17.

11. MIB's eulogy for Constance Smith, who died in Nov. 1970.

12. Oral Memoir, 120.

13. Alice Kimball Smith, *Radcliffe Institute Report,* 1960 to 1971, 3.

14. *Educational Record,* 281.

15. Diane Wood Middlebrook, *Anne Sexton: A Biography* (Boston: Houghton Mifflin Company, 1991), 152.

16. *Radcliffe Quarterly,* Mar. 1991, 4.

17. Middlebrook, 152.

18. Oral Memoir, 115.

19. Alice Kimball Smith's report, 31. For an early and incomplete list, see July 1965 progress report, 16–19. Also see November 11, 1971, report of Advisory Committee, 6–7.

20. Alice Kimball Smith report.

21. "Women: Resource for a Changing World."

22. Oral Memoir, 92.

23. "Women: Resource for a Changing World."

Chapter 19 A Geneticist With Nest-Building Experience

1. *New Yorker,* May 21, 1960, 34–35. The other two presidents were Thomas Corwin Mendenhall of Smith College, a close friend of the Buntings who had delivered the eulogy at Henry's funeral, who was referred to as Mr. Mendenhall. The other was Calvin Hastings Plimpton, M.D., the new president of Amherst, who was referred to as Dr. Plimpton.

2. Letter from MIB to Stephen Benedict, Rockefeller Brothers Fund, Dec. 14, 1965.

3. Oral Memoir, 139.

4. *New York Times,* Nov. 2, 1963, 27.

5. Oral Memoir, 144.

6. Ibid., 148.

Chapter 20 It's Hard to Say "No" to the President

1. From statement naming Robert Hollingsworth general manager of the AEC, August 11, 1964 (Historian at Department of Energy).

2. Introduction by D. Clark to monthly Government Information Officers luncheon, Feb. 26, 1965.

Chapter 21 We Believe in Education for Women

1. Council Minutes, Jan. 23, 1967, 3.

2. Ibid., Apr. 3, 1967, 5.

3. MIB letter to Mrs. W. Houston Kenyon, Jr., about the book *The Right to Be People.* Jan. 27, 1967.

4. MIB speech to Alumnae Council, Nov. 15, 1966.

5. MIB 1966 article in "Science and Psychoanalysis."

6. "The University's Responsibility in Educating Women for Leadership," MIB speech at Southern Methodist University, Jan. 28, 1966.

7. Jill Ker Conway, *True North* (New York: Alfred A. Knopf, 1994), 58–59.

Chapter 22 Radcliffe Sticks to Its Knitting

1. Description of this incident is taken from *In Retrospect: The Tragedy*

Endnotes 363

and Lessons of Vietnam by Robert S. McNamara with Brian VanDemark (New York: Times Books, Random House, 1995).
2. Oral Memoir, 276.
3. Ibid., 199.
4. *Radcliffe Quarterly*, vol. 53, no. 1 (Mar. 1969), 26.
5. MIB letter to alumnae, Dec. 12, 1968.
6. Harvard *Crimson* editorial, Dec. 13, 1968.
7. Letter from Robert Finch, Mar. 22, 1969.
8. Many of the details of the University Hall takeover are taken from a description of the event in John T. Bethell, ed., "Harvard Today: Report of April 1969 Events," *Harvard Alumni Bulletin* (Spring 1969), and Roger Rosenblatt, *Coming Apart: A Memoir of the Harvard Wars of 1969* (Boston: Little Brown and Co., 1997); as well as from interviews with many of the protesters.
9. "Harvard Today."
10. Oral Memoir, 203.
11. MIB letter to Mrs. Alan R. Morse, May 21, 1969.
12. MIB letter to Cyrus Pangborn, July 18, 1969.
13. MIB letter to Mrs. Edward C. P. Thomas, June 30, 1969.
14. MIB alumnae luncheon speech, June 15, 1968.
15. Oral Memoir, 192.
16. Statement of the President and Fellows of Harvard College, Apr. 18, 1969.
17. Number from account in "Harvard Today."
18. MIB letter to Mrs. Anthony Skotnicki, July 18, 1969.
19. Radcliffe press release, Nov. 18, 1969.
20. MIB notes for 1968–69 annual report.
21. MIB alumnae luncheon speech, June 13, 1970.
22. Statement in dinner program for the organization "Catalyst," Mar. 7, 1978.
23. MIB Speech at Harvard-Radcliffe baccalaureate, June 15, 1971.
24. Oral Memoir, 210.
25. Eulogy at MIB's memorial service at Memorial Church, Cambridge, Mass., Apr. 25, 1998.

Chapter 23 The Fuzzy Relationship
1. Oral Memoir, 226.
2. MIB speech to parents' meeting, Sept. 18, 1966.
3. Letter from MIB to Robert I. Hunneman, Dec. 21, 1961.
4. Letter from MIB to Edwin B. Newman, Nov. 2, 1961.
5. Letter from MIB to Nathan Pusey, Nov. 29, 1965.
6. Letter from Thaddeus Beal to Helen Gilbert, Feb. 7, 1966.

7. Oral Memoir, 232
8. MIB speech to Alumnae Association annual luncheon, June 14, 1969; reprint, *Radcliffe Quarterly* (Aug. 1969), 2.
9. MIB speech at Harvard-Radcliffe Baccalaureate, June 15, 1971.
10. Oral Memoir, 221.
11. MIB commencement address to class of 1970.
12. Annual report of residence office for 1970–71 academic year.
13. Oral Memoir, 221.
14. Ibid., 229.
15. Alice Skinner memo to the Committee on Harvard-Radcliffe Relationships, Oct. 28, 1970.
16. June 10, 1970, statement to governing boards of Radcliffe College from Miriam Greene Hurley '31, past president of the Alumnae Association, former trustee, former national chairman of the Ten Year Plan for Radcliffe. Also signed by another former president of the Alumnae Association, the head of the Alumnae Committee on Merger and the editor of the *Radcliffe Quarterly*, two graduates of the 1930's and two from the 1940's.
17. Letter from MIB to Mrs. Arthur H. Bush, Jr., Apr. 2, 1969.
18. Letter from MIB to Mrs. Paul Raushenbush, Aug. 18, 1969.
19. Letter from MIB to Mrs. William Jagoda, July 30, 1970.
20. Letter from MIB to Radcliffe trustee, Mrs. Donovan, Mar. 10, 1970.
21. Meeting of Harvard and Radcliffe staff members, July 12, 1971.
22. "Women: Resource for a Changing World."

Chapter 24 A Society Gets the Kind of Excellence It Values
1. "Education: A Nurturant If Not a Determinant of Professional Success," MIB speech to New York Academy of Sciences, May 12, 1972.
2. MIB speech at Harvard-Radcliffe Baccalaureate, June 15, 1971.
3. Handwritten notes for speech at Pine Manor, June 12, 1971.
4. "Education: A Nurturant If Not A Determinant of Professional Success."
5. "From Serratia to Women's Lib and a Bit Beyond."
6. Ibid.

Chapter 25 Enough of Women
1. Oral Memoir, 266.
2. Ibid., 261.
3. Ibid., 273.

Chapter 26 I Don't Look Back Much
1. Mary Ingraham Bunting, George Weathersby, and John D. Mil-

lett, Report to President of Barnard College—Jacquelyn Mattfeld, Sept. 1976, 33.

2. Testimony before the Senate Committee on Government Operations, Sept. 1976.

3. Oral Memoir, 279.

4. Letter from Margaret Albrink to Elaine Yaffe, Apr. 5, 1998.

5. Annual Women's College Conference at Douglass College, Mar. 7, 1981.

Bibliography

Allardice, Corbin, and Edward Trapnell. *The Atomic Energy Commission.* New York: Praeger Publishers, 1974.

Antler, Joyce. *Marriage And/Or Career: Lucy Sprague Mitchell and the Dilemma of Educated Women.* Cambridge: Mary Ingraham Bunting Institute of Radcliffe College, 1978.

Bird, Caroline. *The Invisible Scar.* New York: David McKay Co., Inc., 1966.

Brownmiller, Susan. *In Our Time: Memoir of a Revolution.* New York: Dial Press, 1999.

Conway, Jill Ker. *True North.* New York: Alfred A. Knopf, 1994.

Cremin, Lawrence A. *The Transformation of the School: Progressivism in American Education, 1876–1957.* New York: Vintage Books, 1964.

Daniels, Elizabeth A. *Bridges to the World: Henry Noble MacCracken and Vassar College.* Clinton Corners, N.Y.: College Avenue Press, 1994.

Deckard, Barbara Sinclair. *The Women's Movement: Political, Socioeconomic and Psychological Issues.* New York: Harper and Row Publishers, 1983.

de Kruif, Paul. *Microbe Hunters.* New York: Harcourt, Brace and Co., 1926.

Eble, Kenneth E. *The Profane Comedy: American Higher Education in the Sixties.* New York: Macmillan Co., 1962.

Eisenmann, Linda. *Weathering "A Climate of Unexpectation": Academic Women at the Bunting Institute, 1960–1990.* Cambridge: A Paper Prepared for the Annual Meeting of the American Educational Research Association, 1992.

———. *Weathering "A Climate of Unexpectation": Gender Equity and the Radcliffe Institute, 1960–1995.* Academe, July–August 1995.

Gitlin, Todd. *The Sixties: Years of Hope, Days of Rage.* New York: Bantam Books, 1987.

Halberstam, David. *The Fifties.* New York: Villard Books, 1993.

Heilbrun, Carolyn G. *Writing a Woman's Life.* New York and London: W. W. Norton & Co., 1988.

Hewlett, Richard G., and Oscar E. Anderson. *A History of the United*

States Atomic Energy Commission: Volume I: "The New World" 1939–1946. University Park, Pa.: Pennsylvania State University Press.

Hymowitz, Carol, and Michaele Weissman. *A History of Women in America.* New York: Bantam Books, 1978.

Judson, Margaret A. *Breaking the Barrier: A Professional Autobiography by a Woman Educator and Historian Before the Women's Movement.* New Brunswick: Rutgers University Press, 1984.

Kass-Simon, G., and Patricia Farnes, eds. *Women of Science: Righting the Record.* Bloomington and Indianapolis: Indiana University Press, 1990.

Keller, Evelyn Fox. *A Feeling for the Organism: The Life and Work of Barbara McClintock.* San Francisco: Freeman, 1983.

———. *Reflections on Gender and Science.* New Haven and London: Yale University Press, 1985.

Keylin, Arleen, and Laurie Barnett, eds. *The Sixties as Reported by the New York Times.* New York: Arno Press, 1980.

Kunstler, William M. *The Hall-Mills Murder Case: The Minister and the Choir Singer.* New Brunswick: Rutgers University Press, 1964.

Lewis, Sinclair. *Ann Vickers.* Lincoln and London: University of Nebraska Press, 1932.

Lilienthal, David E. *Journals: Volume II, The Atomic Energy Years, 1945–1950; and Volume V, The Harvest Years, 1959–1963.* New York: Harper & Row, 1971.

McCarthy, Mary. *On the Contrary: Articles of Belief, 1946–1961.* New York: Noonday Press, 1946.

MacCracken, Henry Noble. *What Vassar Means.* New York: Kalkhoff Press, Inc., 1914.

———. *The Hickory Limb.* New York: Charles Scribner's Sons, 1950.

McNamara, Robert S., and Brian VanDemark. *In Retrospect: The Tragedy and Lessons of Vietnam.* New York: Times Books, Random House, 1995.

Marwick, Arthur. *The Sixties: Cultural Revolution in Britain, France, Italy, and the United States, 1958–1974.* New York: Oxford University Press, 1998.

Maynard, Joyce. *Looking Back: A Chronicle of Growing Up Old in the Sixties.* Garden City, N.Y.: Doubleday & Co., Inc., 1973.

Middlebrook, Diane Wood. *Anne Sexton: A Biography.* Boston: A Peter Davison Book, Houghton Mifflin Co., 1991.

O'Hern, Elizabeth Moot. *Profiles of Pioneer Women Scientists.* Washington, D.C.: Acropolis Books, Ltd., 1985.

Rosenblatt, Roger. *Coming Apart: A Memoir of the Harvard Wars of 1969.* New York: Little, Brown and Co., 1997

Rossiter, Margaret W. *Women Scientists in America: Struggles and Strategies to 1940.* Baltimore and London: Johns Hopkins University Press, 1982.

———. *Women Scientists in America Before Affirmative Action: 1940–1972.* Baltimore and London: Johns Hopkins University Press, 1995.

Rudolph, Frederick. *The American College and University: A History.* New York: Vintage Books, 1962.

Schmidt, George P. *Douglass College: A History.* New Brunswick: Rutgers University Press, 1968.

Solomon, Barbara Miller. *In the Company of Educated Women: A History of Women and Higher Education in America.* New Haven and London: Yale University Press, 1985.

Taylor, James Monroe. *Before Vassar Opened.* Cambridge: Houghton Mifflin Co., Riverside Press, 1914.

Ware, Susan. *Holding Their Own: American Women in the 1930s.* Boston: Twayne Publishers, 1982.

Willensky, Elliot. *When Brooklyn Was the World: 1920–1957.* New York: Harmony Books, 1986.

Women's Lives Through Time: Educated American Women of the Twentieth Century. San Francisco: Jossey-Bass Publishers, 1993.

Yost, Edna. *Women of Modern Science.* New York: Dodd, Mead & Co., 1959.

Zuckerman, Harriet, Jonathan R. Cole, and John T. Bruer, eds. *The Outer Circle: Women in the Scientific Community.* New York and London: W. W. Norton & Co., 1991.

Index

Abramovitz, Max, 205
Adams, Arthur, 146
Adams, John, 138, 166
Advisory Committee of National Science Foundation, 147
American Academy of Arts and Sciences, 290
American Association of Retired Persons (AARP), 299
American Association of University Women, 151–52
American Civil Liberties Union (ACLU), 217
American Council on Education, 146, 158, 159, 290
American Cyanimid, 135
American Men of Science, 66
American Society of Biological Chemists, 46
American Society for Microbiology, 48
American Tuberculosis Association, 123
Amherst College, 199
Amity Star, 96–97
Angell, Marjorie, 239
Ann Vickers (Lewis), 40
Arrowsmith (Lewis), 40
Atomic Energy Commission, 123, 198–207, 289, 294, 300
Auden, W. H., 136
Austen, Jane, 181
Autobiography (Franklin), 83
Averitt, William G., 128

Barnard College, 174, 283
Batts, Deborah, 214
Baumann, Carl, 46, 49
Beer, Katherine, 214
Beloit College, 213
Belser, Bill, 105
Bennington College, 49, 52–55, 57, 80, 106, 127, 150, 284–85
Benton, Anne, 34, 48, 49, 55
Berkeley, University of California at, 208
Bethany, Conn.: description of, 67–68; moving in, 68–70; natural beauty of, 71; Henry becomes town doctor in, 71–72; 75, 79, 88, 90, 92–93, 100, 113, 117–18; 119, 129, 139, 189, 268, 283, 288, 289, 297, 302, 303
Bibring, Grete, 194
Bingham, Mary Caperton, 168
Biochemical Journal, 49
Bok, Derek, 246, 267
Bolman, Sue, 165, 166, 217
Bonner, Susan, 67, 288, 298
Boston alumnae, 177–78, 256–59
Boston Children's Hospital, 182, 290
Boston Globe, 301
Boston University, 213
Bowen, William, 273, 274, 277, 279
Bowers, Dr. John, 182
Bozyan, H. Frank, 103
Brewster, Kingman, 244
Brooklyn, 4–5, 11, 75, 166
Brooklyn Academy of Music, 15
Brooklyn Botanic Gardens, 18

Brooklyn Bridge, 9
Brooklyn Council for Social Planning, 11
Brooklyn Hospital, 7
Brown University, 206
Browne and Nichols (prep school), 169
Bruce, Ailsa Mellon, 222, 246
Bryn Mawr College, 150, 189
Buck, Frank, 15
Buck, Paul, 160, 166
Bundy, McGeorge, 192
Bundy, Mary, 174
Bunting, Adam (grandson), 301
Bunting, Ann (daughter-in-law), 286, 293–94, 297, 299, 300–301
Bunting, Dr. Carlotta Sweat (Henry's mother), 45, 96
Bunting, Charles ("Chuck") (son): 12–13; birth of, 82; 84, 91–92, 96, 99, 102, 103, 114, 119, 169, 199, 225, 286, 288, 293–94, 297, 300–301, 302
Bunting, Dr. Charles Henry (Henry's father), 45, 96, 103
Bunting, Elizabeth (sister-in-law), 45–46, 52, 101
Bunting, Henry (first husband): family background of, 44–46, 49; marries Polly, 57, 60, 62, 64, 67, 80; his life in the TB sanatorium, 82–83, 84, 87–89 (passim); death of, 101; memorial service of, 103; 113, 149, 272, 287, 288, 295, 297, 302, 303
Bunting Institute. *See* Radcliffe Institute for Independent Study
Bunting, John (son), 94, 105, 118, 120, 166, 169, 195, 199, 202, 213, 268, 274, 291, 297, 301
Bunting, Lonna (daughter-in-law), 272, 290–91
Bunting, Mary Ingraham ("Polly"): birth and childhood of, 3–13; adolescence of, 14–21; and college, 25–35; first interest in bacteriology, 31–32; and Cornell summer, 35; and graduate school at University of Wisconsin, 37–46; presented paper at meeting of Society of American Bacteriologists, 43–44; teaches at Bennington, 53–55; marries Henry, 57; teaches at Goucher, 59–60; publishes papers on *serratia marcescens*, 66; settles in Bethany, 67; establishes farm, 70; and birth of Mary, 75; tries to balance research with motherhood and working the farm, 76–80, 84–86, 91–92; and birth of Chuck, 82; and birth of Bill, 87; gives paper at Cold Spring Harbor, 89–90; teaches at Wellesley, 91, 92; lives in the basement, 92–93, 95; and birth of John, 94; on committee to establish regional high school, 98–100; Henry's death, 104; offered deanship at Douglass, 106–07; relations with Douglass students, 115, 122, 124, 126, 128; administrative and curricular innovations of, 122–29; experimental courses of, 128; fund-raising for new buildings, 139–41; urges closer connection to Rutgers, 141–45; joins NSF committee, 146–47; recognizes "the climate of unexpectation," 148–49; launches experimental Program in Mathematics, 151–52; and part-time program for older women, 153–57; accepts Radcliffe presidency, 162; establishes the Radcliffe Institute for Independent Study, 171–86; views on women's roles, marriage, 178; views on the Institute years later, 185–86; transforming life of Radcliffe undergraduates, 187–97, 213–15; works for AEC, 198–207; deals with various student protests, 217–31; and University Hall takeover, 231–35; and Fay House

protest, 238–40; signs petition opposing Vietnam War, 244; favors merging with Harvard, 247–61; implementing "the non-merger merger," 262–63; salary of, 263; resigns Radcliffe presidency, 264; reforms at Princeton, 275–80, 285; marries Clement Smith, 287; and his death, 293; moves to Kendal, 293; friendship with Harold Greenwald, 297–98; last public appearance of, 300; death of, 301; summary of her life and achievement, 303–05
Bunting, Mary (daughter). See Decher, Mary
Bunting, Matthew (grandson), 300–301
Bunting, Meredith (daughter-in-law), 213, 297
Bunting, William Henry ("Bill") (son), birth of, 87; 91–92, 102–04 (passim), 113–14, 117–18, 119, 169, 191, 199, 206–07, 210, 225, 272, 274, 290–91, 294, 297, 299–301 (passim)
Bunting Program (at Douglass), 156–57
Byrne, Brendan T., 277

Cabot, Thomas, 237
Cabot Hall, 221
Cage, John, 136
Cambridge School, The, 202
Cambridge University, 249
Carnegie Corporation, The, 175
Carnegie Endowment for International Peace, 128
Carrington, Loy, 276–77
Carter, Hodding, 136
Cassatt, Mary, 5, 294
CCNY, 11
Center for Opportunity for Education, 227
Charles E. Merrill Trust, 182
Chaucer, 286

Chevalier, Maurice, 30
Clark, Dr. Edward, 25
Christoffel, Katherine Kaufer, 233–34
Chicago, University of, 47
Civil Rights Act, 208
Clark Foundation, 278
"climate of unexpectation," 148–49, 210, 279, 280
Cloisters, The, 7
Coates, Nora, 61
Coffin, William Sloane, 241
Cold Spring Harbor, 89, 244
Collins, Grace, 37
Columbia University, 233, 243, 245, 283
Commission on the Education of Women, 146, 159
Committee of Fifteen, 236, 242
Comstock, Ada L., 162
Conant, James, 248
Copland, Aaron, 136
Cornell University, 36–37, 151
Corwin, Margaret Trumbull, 114–15, 125, 167
Couperin, Francois, "The Nightingale in Love," 302
Cox, Archibald, 245
Crary, Mary (cousin), 8
Crary, Miner (cousin), 56–57
Crary, Steven (cousin), 206
Crick, Francis, 89
Crimson (Harvard newspaper), 218, 230
Cronkhite Center, 268
Currier House, 222, 245, 246

Daniels Hall, 205, 212
Dartmouth College, 243, 292, 296, 297
Darwin, Charles, 6, 290
Daughters of the American Revolution, 39
Davis, Bette, 133
Decher, Laura (granddaughter), 287–88, 291
Decher, Mary (daughter): birth of, 75; 80, 82–84 (passim), 87, 90,

91–92, 99, 101, 103, 106, 114, 117–20 (passim), 169, 199; marries, 206, 223, 225, 271, 295, 297, 300–302 (passim)
Decher, Meika (granddaughter), 288, 291, 293, 295
Decher, Reiner (son-in-law), 206, 271, 287, 293
Delbruck, Max, 66
Democratic National Committee, 299
Dodds, Alice, 238
Donovan, Louise, 176, 216, 237, 240–41
Donovan, Richard, 203, 207
Dorfman, Elsa, 180
Douglass, Mabel Smith, 111–12, 113
Douglass College: 106; history of, 111–13; formal style vs. Polly's informality, 113–16; 117, 122, 123, 124; faculty concerns of, 125–26, 127; chapel attendance at, 126; experimental courses at, 127–28, 129; World Poetry course, 137; student concerns, 130–33, 135–36; expansion of the campus, 138–41, 145; closer relations with Rutgers, 141–45, 146; Program in Mathematics, 151–52; part-time program for older woman, 151–57; 158–63 (passim), 165, 171, 183, 188, 192, 194, 195, 219, 235, 249, 259, 273, 276, 277, 283, 292, 299–301 (passim)
Dow Chemical Corporation, 219–22
Dwight Memorial Chapel, 103

Eakins, Thomas, 289
Edmundson, Yvette, 55
Einstein, Albert, 31
Eliot House, 233
Elliott, Kathleen, 209, 220
Erikson, Erik, 240, 267

Faraday, Michael, 34
Fay House, 216, 226, 227, 233, 238
Fielder, James T., 111
Finch, Robert, 231
Fine, Elizabeth. *See* Bunting, Elizabeth
Fine, John (nephew), 83

Flower Hospital of New York, 182
Fogg Museum, 289
Ford, Franklin, 230, 234
Ford Foundation, 151, 205, 217, 222, 257
4-H clubs, 97–98, 200
Frank, Barney, 217
Franklin, Benjamin, *Autobiography*, 83
Fred, Edwin, 42, 43
French King Bridge, 56
Fromm, Erich, 136
Frost, Robert, 136, 286, 288

Gardner, John, 148, 175
General Motors, 274
Gilbert, Helen Homans, 165, 166, 173, 200, 206, 237, 251–53 (passim)
Gilbert and Sullivan, 68, 206
Gilman, Arthur, 164
Ginsberg, Allen, 136
Gleason, McLanahan, Merritt, and Ingraham (father's law firm), 9
Glimp, Fred, 233, 234
Goethals, Mary, 220
Goheen, Robert, 273
Goucher College, 57–58, 67, 127, 150
Gourley, Ronald, 224
Graham, Katharine, 174
Graham, Martha, 136
Greene, Harry, 80
Greenwald, Harold, 297–98
Gross, Mason, 189

Hackney, Lucy, 275, 278
Hackney, Sheldon, 279
Hall-Mills murder case, 118
Hampden, Walter, 39
Hampshire College, 283
Handel's *Messiah*, 39
Harris, Patricia, 284
Harvard Board of Overseers, 189, 192, 254, 258–59
Harvard Club of New York, 169, 208, 290
Harvard Today, 240
Harvard University: 47, 56, 89; discourages women from working

for advanced degrees, 134, 160, 168; 161, 164, 166–69 (passim); Radcliffe students intimidated by, 188; 190, 192, 196, 198, 205, 208–10 (passim); practically no women on faculty of, 211; popularity of Hilles Library with male students of, 212; 213, 214; student protests at, 216–46; and the non-merger merger, 247–63; how Polly changed, 267–68; 273, 277, 283, 284, 290, 292, 299, 301
Hastie, William, 284
Haverford College, 42
Hechinger, Fred, 176
Heilman, Gerhard, *The Origin of Birds*, 15–16
Heine, Mrs. M. Caswell, 143
Hellman, Lillian, 175
Heuer, Ann, 123
HEW (Department of Health, Education, and Welfare), 274
Hilles, Susan, 197
Hilles Library, 211–12, 218, 246, 249
Hillhouse High School, New Haven, 99
Hoffman, Stanley, 232
Holmes, Burton, 15
Holmes, Kathryn Voelker, 214
Holyoke Center, 237
Homer, 83
Houghton Mifflin, 176
Hutchins, Mary Lee ("Leal"), 28, 58, 149, 191, 265
Hutchinson, G. Evelyn, 93

Indiana, University of, 89
Ingraham, Barbara (sister-in-law), 82
Ingraham, David (brother), 4, 9–10, 30, 39, 59, 89, 284–85, 293
Ingraham, Edward (uncle), 4, 7–8, 15
Ingraham, Gardner (brother), 4, 29, 37, 59, 82, 103, 272, 287, 291, 298
Ingraham, Grace (aunt), 7, 291
Ingraham, Henry Andrews (father), 3, 8–10, 51, 82, 104, 206, 304

Ingraham, Henry Charles Murphy (paternal grandfather), 6, 86–87
Ingraham, Laura (sister-in-law), 80, 293
Ingraham, Mark (uncle), 7, 36
Ingraham, Mary Shotwell ("Gwy")(mother): goes to Vassar, 6, 8; happy marriage of, 10; formality of, 10–11, 40; civic duties of, 11, 12, 14, 16; disapproves of Polly's clothes, 29, 40–41, 73; 45, 51, 73, 82, 149, 169, 202, 206, 272; death of, 290; 300, 304
Ingraham, Ruth (aunt), 7, 289
Ingraham, Sandy (nephew), 294–95
Ingraham, Winifred. *See* Warner, Winifred
Ingraham, Winifred Andrews (paternal grandmother), 6–7, 118

Jacobs, Diane, 213
Jane Coffin Childs Memorial Fund for Medical Research, 63
Janeway, Charles, 182
Janeway, Eliza, 28, 93, 103, 182, 293, 295, 298, 299
Jefferson, Thomas, 138, 294
Johns Hopkins University, 45, 57, 58, 62, 265, 266
Johnson, Lady Bird, 205, 207
Johnson, Lyndon Baines, 198, 199, 200, 202, 205, 207, 208, 294
Jones, Barbara, 54, 106
Jones, Lewis Webster, 106, 111, 154–55, 159, 189
Jordan, Wilbur K., 166, 168
Joseph, Toni, 203
Journal of Bacteriology, 43–44, 46, 65
Journal of Biological Chemistry, 46
Judson, Margaret, 134–35
Julliard School, 296

Kaiser Foundation, 271, 272–73
Kashket, Eva, 213–14
Kendal (retirement home), 292–301
Kennedy, John F., 189, 198

Kent State University, 243, 259
Kerby-Miller, Wilma, 200
Kiwanis clubs, 140
Kline, Lee, 50–51
Kunstler, William, 118

Lacy, Anne, 67
Ladd, Florence, 186
LaGuardia, Fiorello, 11
Lamont Library, 167, 249
League of Women Voters, 140
Lewis, Sinclair, *Ann Vickers*, 40; *Arrowsmith*, 40
Lieberman, Donna, 217
Lieberman, Judy, 217
Life, 133
Lilienthal, David, 173, 198
Link, Karl, 41
Lions clubs, 140
Little, Arthur D., 272
Los Alamos, 203
Louisville Junior League, 282
Lovett, Rev. Sidney, 103
Luria, Salvador, 66, 89, 244

McBride, Katharine, 160, 189
McCamy, Julia, 54
McCormick, Katheryne, 156
McCormick, Richard, 122, 142, 158
MacCracken, Cody, 30, 297
MacCracken, Henry Noble, 30, 49, 297
McDonald, Lindsay, 224
McNamara, Robert, 216–17, 220–21
Macy Foundation, 182
Malkiel, Nancy Weiss, 278
Mallinckrodt Laboratory, 219, 220
Marshall, Thurgood, 136
Massachusetts Institute of Technology, 89, 206, 243, 292, 293
Mattfeld, Jacquelyn, 72, 283
Mayo Clinic, 102
Mead, Margaret, 136
Meitner, Lise, 146
Mellon, Paul, 246

Mendenhall, Thomas, 103, 189
Messer, Ellen, 237
Messiah (Handel), 39
Meyer, Agnes, 174
Meyer, Carlin, 234
Michigan, University of, 134–35
Minnesota, University of, 157
Morgan, Thomas Hunt, 8
Morrell Act, 147
Monro, John, 195

NAACP, 136
Nash, Ogden, 136
Nassau Hall, 275
National Academy of Sciences, 159
National Advisory Committee on Health Manpower, 294
National Advisory Council for the Peace Corps, 198
National Association of Deans of Women, 152
National Conference of Christians and Jews, 11
National Defense Education Act, 147
National Public Radio, 293
National Science Foundation, 146–47, 158, 159, 171, 186, 250, 294, 299
Natural History, 299
Neal, Reginald, 163
"Needed: Prestige for Mothers" (Spitz), 93–94.
Neilson, James, 113
New Boston, N.H., 196, 222, 237, 268, 271, 274, 281, 293
New Brunswick, N.J., 106, 118, 119, 120, 169
New Brunswick United Fund, 159
New England Electric System, 272
New Jersey College for Women, 111
New Jersey Department of Education, 139
New Jersey Federation of Women's Clubs, 143
New York City Board of Higher Education, 11

Index 377

New York Council for Adult Education, 11
New York Planning Commission, 290
New York Stock Exchange, 136, 297
New York Times, 16, 175–76, 200, 238–40 (passim), 301
Newby, Edna, 123–24, 155
Newsweek, 176
"Nightingale in Love, The" (Couperin), 302
Nixon, Richard, 244, 294
Nobel Prize, 66, 89, 150
Northport, Long Island, 3, 8, 14, 18, 19, 55, 57, 71, 91, 94, 274, 287
Nuclear Test Ban Treaty, 199

Olsen, Tillie, 180
Origin of Birds, The (Heilman), 15–16
Ormandy, Eugene, 60
Outlines of Science, The (Wells), 8
Oxford University, 249

Packer Collegiate Institute, 20–21, 283
Paine Hall, 230, 238, 244, 252
Palfrey, John, 201
Parry, Marian, 186
Peace Corps, 205
Peacham, Vt., 289, 292–94, 302
Pearl Harbor, 80
Peck Pond, Bethany, 98
Piel, Gerard, 201
Pine Manor Junior College, 265
Pingry (prep school), 119, 169
Planned Parenthood, 291–92
Population Council, 289, 290, 299
President's Commission on the Status of Women, 290
Princeton University, 243, 251, 273–80, 283, 284
Program in Mathematics, 151–52
PTA, 68, 97, 140
Public Health Nursing Association, 72
Pulitzer Prize, 185
Pusey, Nathan, 192, 229, 232–37 (passim), 241, 247, 249–50, 252–54 (passim)

Quakers, 10, 12, 65, 176, 292, 301–02
Quincy House, 217

Radcliffe Alumnae Association, 253–54, 256–59
Radcliffe Board of Trustees, 164, 165–66, 171, 189, 222, 247, 250–51
Radcliffe College: 48; appoints Polly to presidency, 160–62; history of, 164–65; neglect of students, 166–68; academic pressure of, 167; 168–79 (passim), 181–85 (passim); transformation of campus and student life of, 187–97; and Helen Gilbert, acting president during Polly's leave of absence, 200; 206; Women's Movement having its effect on, 208–10, but not entirely, 210–11; effect of new buildings at, 211–12; 213–15 (passim); involvement in student protests, 216–46; the non-merger merger, 247–63; 264–68, 271, 274, 277, 282, 284, 290, 292, 295, 298, 302
Radcliffe Council, 164, 200, 218–19, 233
Radcliffe Institute for Independent Study, 171–86, 271, 281, 282, 300
Radcliffe Judicial Board, 236
Radcliffe Policy Committee, 219
Radcliffe Ten Year Plan, 173
Radcliffe Union of Students, 225–26
Ramey, James, 201
Rappaport, Carol, 214
Rawlings, Marjorie Kinnan, *The Yearling*, 60
Reader's Digest, 176
Reed, Will, 279, 280
Rettger, Leo, 63
Reynals, Mary Louise Duran, 120
Rider College, 282
Ritvo, Rachel, 225, 232, 244
Rockefeller, John D., III, 271, 276
Rockefeller, Laurance, 175, 271, 276
Rockefeller Brothers Fund, 175

Rockefeller Institute, 44, 49
Rockefeller University, 214
Roger Sherman Beauty Parlor, 85
Roosevelt, Eleanor, 136, 294
Roosevelt, Franklin D., 294
Rotary clubs, 140
ROTC, 229, 239, 243
Rudenstine, Neil, 273, 279, 280
Ruisdael, Jacob, 289
Rutgers Prep, 119
Rutgers University: 91, 106, 111; assumes no financial responsibility for Douglass, 112; 115, 122, 125, 126; antinepotism rule, 135; 139, 142, 143, 151, 159, 189, 249

Saint Paul's School, 283
Saltonstall, Leverett, 201
Sandburg, Carl, 39
Sarah Lawrence College, 157
Schapiro, Naomi, 238
Schlesinger Library, 283, 290
Schmidt, George, 131
Seaborg, Glenn, 201, 204, 205
Segovia, Andrés, 136
Sexton, Anne, 180, 181, 185, 294
Shailor, Barbara, 300
Shakespeare, 83
Shehadi, Fadlou, 125, 141, 142, 156
Shotwell, Alice Gardner ("Nana") (maternal grandmother), 6, 18, 19, 75
Shotwell, Henry Titus (maternal grandfather), 5, 18, 19
Shotwell, Willets (uncle), 5
Shutkin, Dr. Ned, 102
Sierwierski, Marie, 135
Simmons, Adele, 283
Smith, Clement (second husband), 285–93, 294, 296, 301, 302
Smith, Constance, 179, 181, 185
Smith, Hillary, 289, 292, 298
Smith, Reynolds, 289
Smith College, 159–60, 199
Society of American Bacteriologists, 43, 79

Society for the Collegiate Instruction of Women, 164
Sophia Club. *See* Bunting Program
Sperry and Hutchinson Company, 272
Spitz, Rene, "Needed: Prestige for Mothers," 93–94
State Federation of Women's Clubs, 112, 159
Steenbock, Harry, 46, 49, 50
Students for a Democratic Society (SDS), 228, 229, 231, 235, 236, 242–45 (passim)
Swan, Barbara, 180
Swink, John L., 162

Tackman, Arthur, 204–05
Tape, Gerald, 201, 203
Tatum, Edward, 38
Tchaikovsky's Sixth Symphony, 69
Teller, Edward, 147
Tennessee Valley Authority, 173
Thomas, Norman, 193
TIAA-CREF, 282
Time, 176, 289–90, 301
Title IX, 275
Tomas, Pat, 214
Trayes, Marjorie, 127, 132, 145, 158–59
Treffers, Pete, 99, 105
Truman, Harry, 11, 294

United Nations Conference on Peaceful Uses of Atomic Energy, 203
United Service Organizations (USO), 124
U.S. Chamber of Commerce, 209
U.S. Public Health Service, 123
University Hall, 230; student takeover, 231–35; 237, 240, 242, 245, 253

Vale in Waltham, 268
Vassar College, 6, 11, 25–35, 48, 49, 54, 67, 149, 265, 282, 283, 295, 299
Vermont, University of, 118, 169, 199
Von Stade, F. Skiddy, 225

Wald, George, 244
Walker, Sandra, 233
Warner, Harold (brother-in-law), 6–7, 18, 286–87, 288
Warner, Winifred (sister), 4, 7, 82, 104, 105, 265, 272, 285, 286, 291, 299
Washington, D.C., 202–07, 249
Washington, University of, 206
Watson, James, 89
Weber, Thomas, 155, 158
Webster, Beveridge, 296, 302
Webster, Leslie, 44
Weld Hall, 233
Wellesley College, 48, 53, 91, 93, 96, 179, 272
Wells, H. G., *The Outlines of Science*, 8
Welty, Eudora, 193
Wesleyan College, 6, 8, 11
White House Conference on Youth, 264
WHRB (Harvard student radio station), 232, 234
Widener Library, 177, 180
Wilson, Robert E., 198
Wilson, Woodrow, 111–12
Winternitz, Dr. Milton, 70, 101
Winternitz, Dr. William, 101–03, 295
Wisconsin, University of, 36, 37–43, 104, 138, 272
Witkin, Evelyn, 91

Women in academia, 65, 133–35, 152, 184, 210
Women's education, 25, 134, 152, 153–54, 194
Women in science, 64, 135, 150, 204, 211
Women's suffrage, 3
Women working, 94, 133, 134, 184, 189, 209–10
Wood, Barry, 58, 191
Wood, Grant, 39
Wood, Leal. *See* Hutchins, Mary Lee
Woods Hole Oceanographic Institution, 282
Woolf, Virginia, 171
World War II, 80–81, 88
Wright, Frank Lloyd, 39
Wright, Tom, 275

Yale University: 44, 47, 48; offers Polly research grant, 63; reduces Henry's stipend, 64; 67, 68; offers Henry permanent job, 70; 71, 72, 99; Henry's memorial service in campus chapel of, 103; has no full-time job available for a woman, 105, 149; 106, 114, 120, 134, 243, 251
Yearling, The (Rawlings), 60
YWCA, 7, 11, 140

Zaica, Frank, 68
Zinsser, Hans, 33

✟✟✟✟✟✟✟✟✟✟✟✟✟✟✟✟✟✟✟✟✟✟✟✟✟✟✟✟
This book was composed in Adobe's Brioso Pro by
the Nangle Type Shop in Meriden, Connecticut.
Brioso was designed by Robert Slimbach, of
Adobe Systems, who endeavored to
capture the "liveliness" implied
by the typeface's name.

DEC 2005

Northport - E. Northport Public Library
151 Laurel Avenue
Northport, N. Y. 11768
261-6930